CORPORATE LIQUIDITY

A GUIDE TO
MANAGING WORKING CAPITAL

CORPORATE LIQUIDITY
A GUIDE TO
MANAGING WORKING CAPITAL

Kenneth L. Parkinson
Managing Director
Treasury Information Services

Jarl G. Kallberg
Associate Professor of Finance
Stern School of Business
New York University

BUSINESS ONE IRWIN
Homewood, IL 60430

© RICHARD D. IRWIN, INC., 1993

Senior editor:	Amy Hollands
Project editor:	Rebecca Dodson
Production manager:	Bob Lange
Art coordinator:	Heather Burbridge
Printer:	Book Press, Inc.

Library of Congress Cataloging-in-Publication Data
Parkinson, Kenneth L.
   Corporate liquidity : a guide to managing working capital /
Kenneth L. Parkinson, Jarl G. Kallberg.
     p.   cm.
   Includes bibliographical references.
   ISBN 1-55623-864-9
   1. Cash management. 2. Liquidity (Economics) 3. Corporations-
-Finance. I. Kallberg, Jarl B. II. Title.
   HG4028.C45P37 1993
658. 15′244—dc20   93–21755
Printed in the United States of America

1 2 3 4 5 6 7 8 9 0 BP 0 9 8 7 6 5 4 3

To Joyce, Jeff, Jenn and Sue
KLP

To Peggy, Erik, Thomas and Kerry
JGK

Preface

Managing corporate liquidity has become a major challenge to corporate financial managers in companies of all sizes and locations. The original focus on managing cash increased and decreased in importance as interest rates changed and as basic procedures and techniques developed. Today, a financial manager cannot afford to be too restricted in managing the company's liquidity.

We have participated in corporate financial management in addition to teaching and researching it. We know that corporate financial managers need assistance in carrying out the responsibilities of their jobs. That is the primary reason we have written this book. It is intended for the corporate financial manager who must ensure that his or her firm's liquidity is safe and sound.

The subject matter of this book is more comprehensive than others available. This is because we have adopted a broad viewpoint in considering the short-term liquidity of the firm. It is also because the approaches to corporate finance are changing. They are being shaped by significant changes in the leverage that companies maintain (or are saddled with), shifts in regulation and financial stability of the major financial institutions in the U.S., advances in technology that have given the financial manager tools that were unimaginable a generation ago, and the availability of massive amounts of information that must be deciphered continually.

We have included a number of features in this book for the busy manager. For instance, Chapter 3 reviews the basics of cash management. This can be used as a refresher for those relatively new to the area or those coming back to it. Active treasury managers can skip this chapter. We have also separated activities and processes from strategies and decision making. This is evident in the breakdown of treasury management topics and in our treatment of borrowing and investment instruments separate from the strategic aspects of these activities. In addition, we have included many checklists that can be used right away in tackling a major problem or in reviewing a major activity. Finally, we have added a special section in every chapter — Management Review Items. The purpose of these items is twofold: They serve as a quick review of the main points in the chapter, and they offer quick ideas for implementing the strategies discussed in the chapter. We have drawn on our own hands-on experiences to provide these insights, in effect giving the reader some consulting advice, chapter-by-chapter, throughout the book. We have also included a detailed index to make it as easy as possible to find a spcific topic quickly.

Readers will benefit from our book because of the comprehensive treatment of corporate liquidity. We have touched all the bases in providing what we think is a unique tool for today's corporate financial manager. We have updated all major regulatory and institutional issues where appropriate. We also explain the more intricate topics affecting corporate liquidity and have included broader coverage of the evolving topics, such as EDI, innovative investment and borrowing tools, financial distress, new approaches to credit management and inventory management, and an integrated treatment of global finance. The bibliography contains some additional assistance for those looking for more help.

Kenneth L. Parkinson
Jarl G. Kallberg

ACKNOWLEDGMENTS

We would like to acknowledge our great debt to our many students from NYU's Stern School of Business and at other venues. We'd especially like to acknowledge the sharp eyes of Alice Lee and Evan Mitnick. All our students have greatly assisted in this project by working through earlier drafts of the book and by their keen interest in the subject. We would also like to acknowledge the assistance of our colleagues at NYU's finance department, especially Edwin Elton, Martin Gruber, William Hark, Kose John, Tony Saunders, and Greg Udell. In addition, we'd like to acknowledge the help we received from several treasury professionals, including Pat Scanlon from Continental Bank, Joe Proto from Cashflex, Jack Meckler from Littlewood Shain, and George Rush from Phoenix-Hecht.

A special thanks goes to Joyce Ochs, who typeset this book. Her additional comments and support while the book was being completed were invaluable.

Finally, the staff at Irwin has worked hard to take this project to its completion, especially Amy Hollands.

TABLE OF CONTENTS

CHAPTER 1

INTRODUCTION AND OVERVIEW

This book is about how companies manage liquidity. Their liquid *reserves* range from the tangible — cash, accounts receivable and inventory — to the less tangible, such as commitments for credit. This book also addresses how liquidity should be measured. Again, this measurement has many dimensions, from the evaluation of the performance of different asset classes to the assessment of a company's failure potential.

This book emphasizes how all of the discrete components of a firm's overall liquidity fit together within the current corporate finance environment. These components include working capital management, short-term corporate finance, and treasury management. Throughout the book the concepts will be illustrated with an analysis of actual examples from corporate practice.

This is not a book about theory, although more or less formal frameworks for analysis are developed throughout, and analytical tools are presented when they have shown their practical value. Neither is it a book about accounting. While accounting measurements play an important role in many sections of this book, the primary focus is on corporate decision-making.

Briefly stated, this book tries to interpret corporate liquidity issues in the modern context of the company and its environment.

These issues are greatly influenced by a number of key factors:

- **Technology**: The pervasiveness of the computer, especially the personal computer (PC), has allowed for a far more complete analysis and development of the data bases that allow a financial manager to make decisions based on timely and accurate information. One of the most important technological advances is **electronic data interchange** — the evolving ability of business entities to exchange business documents (purchase orders, invoices, payment instructions, etc.) in a standardized form. This innovation has had broad impact across inventory, credit and cash management.

- **Changes in the banking environment**: The huge shifts in worldwide banking have radically altered the corporate-banking relationship. This greatly influences corporate borrowing and use of non-credit services, such as cash management, as banks cut back on non-profitable operations and generally downsize. Another aspect of this is the spillover to corporate decisions from the Federal Reserve's attempts to control bank risk, which, in turn, affects how companies can move money.

- **Risk**: Greater levels of company risk, in part due to the overleveraging of the 1980's and the coincidental economic malaise that opened the 1990's, have placed greater emphasis on the company's cash flow management and on how companies assess the creditworthiness of their debtors and their banks. This has also led to the development of many forms of credit enhancement — tools that enable a deal to be made by shifting the risk to a party more prepared to bear it.

- **Globalization**: The growing linkages and radical changes in the world economy influence corporate borrowing and investment and the overall business environment.

- **Financial innovation**: The 1980's produced an overwhelming diversity of financial tools for investment, borrowing and risk management. This has been pared down somewhat, but an incredible diversity is still available to the corporate financial manager.

This chapter presents an overview and some general perspectives that will subsequently be developed throughout the book. Its major sections are:

- **History**: discusses a brief history of treasury management, highlighting major events and developments

- **Corporate organization**: deals with how the functional areas of the company are organized to handle the functions analyzed in this book

- **Environment**: describes the major influences on the corporate liquidity function and includes a brief perspective of the historical developments that have shaped the current corporate setting

- **Ethics**: discusses some of the ethical issues that are part of the corporate short-term finance function

- **Integrating short-term finance functions**: outlines some of the concepts that are used throughout the rest of the book

HISTORY

To understand better how the focus on managing corporate liquidity has evolved, it is useful to review briefly the evolution of the cash/treasury management function. The active period of development began in the early 1970's, although there were a few highlights prior to that time.

Prior to 1970

The first major development in treasury management was the corporate lockbox, generally attributed to the RCA Corporation in the late 1940's. For the next 20 years, however, little in the way of innovation occurred. There was little focus on the *mechanics* of cash management as most concerns were focused on credit. With low, stable interest rates, companies had little choice in terms of investments. Cash on the balance sheet was regarded as the true sign of liquidity.

A few companies had "discovered" the benefits of remote disbursing, but, since very few banks offered any special non-credit services, cash or treasury management was largely accomplished through "finesse," that is, on an *ad hoc* basis at best. Companies dealt with many banks because there were few bank holding companies and states that permitted widespread branching. In addition, the means to concentrate funds were still under development. Most companies handled payments and receipts in a decentralized fashion. The treasury function was usually a part of the controller's department.

Float Games of the 1970's

The 1970's saw cash management develop big time. As interest rates were cut loose, they rose and fell with unheard of volatility. Corporations and their bankers discovered that managing cash and other short-term assets and liabilities was beneficial to their bottom lines. Many banks began to develop and offer non-credit services that permitted corporations to increase returns from their previously idle cash balances. On the one hand, many banks offered the remote disbursement "float game" to many companies looking to extend their disbursement float, while others offered efficient lockbox collection points to accelerate the collection of check payments. Major movements also began in electronic banking, with the development of sophisticated wire transfer systems — Fedwire and the automated clearing house (ACH) network.

Bank compensation became more explicit, as banks began to distribute account analysis statements to their corporate customers monthly, but was still primarily in the form of collected balances. Credit was still the predominant reason for maintaining bank relations,especially after the Penn Central default sent the commercial paper market reeling. The market did recover fully in the last half of the decade, but for a few years companies were heavily dependent on their banks for short-term financing (and during a time of tight credit). The credit squeeze eased as the commercial paper market rebounded and as foreign banks began offering credit facilities at cut rates.

The 1980's: PCs Appear on the Scene

The rapid developments in cash/treasury management of the 1970's slowed in the 1980's as companies attempted to take control of their cash management systems. With the proliferation of the personal computer, information management became a major challenge for the corporate treasury manager. Banks helped by providing more and more information in PC-compatible formats, and by marketing treasury work station products to process the data. Most companies, however, turned to do-it-yourself approaches and sought only balance and transaction information from the banks.

Bank compensation began moving from all balances to a mixture of explicit fees as bank service charges showed steady and rapid growth throughout the decade. Bank charges became "big ticket" items for most major corporations and growing profit centers for cash management banks.

The instability in the money markets and interest rates of the previous decade showed its effects in the incredible variety of investment and borrowing alternatives available to the corporation. Money market funds began investing heavily in the commercial paper market, expanding its size significantly. Commercial banks even began invading the turf of investment banks aggressively.

The Federal Reserve and Congress issued a number of new regulations that affected banks and, in turn, their corporate customers. These regulations began to reduce float in the banking system, tighten controls over bank overdraft positions during the business day, and establish acceptable capital reserves for banks. Mergers and acquisitions began to change the nature of commercial banking as well as the size of corporations and their treasury functions. Leveraged buyouts ravaged many corporate balance sheets and added substantial pressures to the income statement.

The 1990's: Technology and Regulation Continue

As the 1990's begin to unfold, corporate treasury managers are becoming more computer literate as rapid advances in PCs and related systems technology permit greater efficiencies and productivity gains. Banks have attempted to overcome their profitability problems of the late 1980's and early 1990's by focusing on non-credit services. The cash management *industry* has grown to approximately $5.5 billion in annual sales of corporate cash management services. Growth in electronic services through the ACH has been paced by developments in electronic data interchange (EDI). The benefits of cash management techniques have been refined further, so the threshold for establishing sound cash management practices, in terms of company size, has continued to drop. Interest rates have begun the decade at record low levels and a steadiness reminiscent of pre-1970. The corporate treasury function has been expanded in scope, focusing on the company's broader working capital and related liquidity needs, rather than staying fixed on the narrower view of cash management.

CORPORATE ORGANIZATION

The management of corporate liquidity involves (at least in a larger company) a number of different functional areas. This is a major reason that an integrated approach to corporate liquidity is important. The functional areas covered in this book include:

- **Corporate cash management**: This encompasses the ways in which corporations manage cash flows, bank relations, and treasury information.
- **Credit management**: This analyzes standards for granting credit and monitoring accounts receivable.
- **Debt and investment management**: This involves controlling the company's short-term borrowing and investment.
- **Inventory management**: This describes how companies determine their investment in inventory.

The Functional Organization

Figure 1-1 illustrates a functional treasury organization for a typical large corporation. Although organizations may differ from company to company, the essential treasury functions are represented in the figure.

These areas may not all be included in the typical treasury organization of a company but may report to another operating area of finance, such as accounting. The different functional areas reporting directly include pension and retirement fund administration, long-term or special financing and investments, cash management, and international treasury. One or more of these functional areas may

Figure 1-1
Functional Treasury Organization

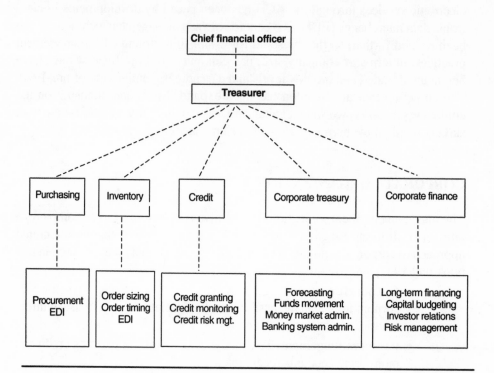

be combined, depending on many of the factors discussed below. Our discussion
will focus on the treasury management area specifically. The treasury management function usually has as its basic activities:

- Forecasting
- Funds movement
- Money market administration
- Banking system administration

Depending on the individual corporation, these activities may be combined.

Forecasting involves coordinating and consolidating short-term projections
of cash needs and surpluses from the major users and providers of cash throughout
the organization. It usually also includes preparing or obtaining independent
estimates of future interest rates or other critical factors. The analysis of the
variance between actual results and prior estimates is also an important task for

this area in order to pinpoint forecasting problems or those factors that have exerted major influence on the precision of the forecast. The standard output provided by forecasting is often used as a guide by the other areas of treasury management, one that assists in the daily planning for treasury management activities.

Funds movement is the nerve center of treasury management, entailing the daily cash position maintenance for the corporation, monitoring and controlling key operating bank accounts, and regulating the flow of funds to, from, and within the corporation. This area interacts with the corporation's banking network as well as with the local operating units and other financial areas as appropriate. It may also be involved with the international units by processing funds transfers to and from overseas points. Its activities are influenced by other areas of treasury management in that it utilizes the cash forecasts to anticipate or plan for major cash flows, provides funds for or requests funds from money market administration (depending on the net cash position), uses the banking network established by banking system administration, and maintains the target balances for compensation purposes set by banking system administration.

Money market administration functions as the provider of short-term funds when needed or the investor of short-term excesses when available. In the past, this function was considered the primary and perhaps only role of corporate treasury management, especially at the central staff location. Today, of course, the entire scope of treasury management has been expanded much further. In many corporations the money market activity may not be of sufficient size to require a separate staff and, consequently, may be incorporated into the funds movement activity. In other companies, however, this function is very important and is a separate activity that must interact and coordinate with the daily cash position management for the company.

Banking system administration provides the liaison between the corporation and its banks for administrative and analytical purposes. General levels of bank compensation, whether paid by fees or balances or for credit or non-credit services, are established here and translated into target balance levels for each bank. It is safe to assume that some level of target balance will remain for each bank even if compensation for services is on a fee basis. This is particularly true for operating banks where maintenance of zero balances is usually extremely difficult if not impossible. This area also conducts special treasury management studies that involve the review, evaluation, or modification of existing banking arrangements or daily treasury management practices. Such studies can be performed by in-house staff, by the use of outside consultants, or by a combination of the two. By establishing this function as a separate area, the corporation can obtain objective and more timely analyses of its treasury management

Figure 1-2
Responsibilities of the Treasury Manager

Company Sales under $500 Million	*Company Sales over $500 Million*
Cash Management	Cash Management
Bank Relations	Bank Relations
Short-term Investing	Short-term Investing
Short-term Borrowing	Long-term Borrowing
Long-term Borrowing	Short-term Borrowing
Accounts Payable	International Cash Management
Accounts Receivable	Investor Relations
Investor Relations	
Credit Policy	
International Cash Management	
Insurance and Risk Management	

Source: *Journal of Cash Management*

function. This may not be possible if assigned to other operating areas that cannot devote sufficient time or independent perspective to reviewing ongoing practices or services. It can also serve as a practical and effective entry point into the corporate treasury function for newer staff members to learn the fundamental aspects of the corporate system.

Figure 1-2 gives the key responsibilities for treasury managers from companies with annual sales of under $500 million and those with sales above that figure. The responsibilities are listed in order of their mention by compensation survey respondents, with activities noted by at least 30% of the treasury managers listed. It is interesting to note that treasury managers in smaller corporations report more responsibilities than their counterparts in larger corporations. In very large firms and much smaller ones, the responsibilities are specialized and generalized (respectively) even more.

All these functions and their relative structure within the corporate treasury organization are by no means ironclad. In any given situation, any one function may take on a larger, more significant role, thereby determining the appropriate organization. On the other hand, one or more of these functions may be combined under the same treasury area and will be treated on a concurrent or part-time basis. The individual functions are not any less important whatever the individual corporate situation. The functions have to be completed efficiently for sound treasury management practices to be maintained.

ENVIRONMENT

Effective management of the liquid resources of a company entails recognizing the inherent environmental and organizational factors that make one company's "correct" decisions different from another's. The environmental factors affecting liquidity can be distinguished as internal vs. external.

Internal Factors

There are a number of internal factors that influence liquidity decisions:
- Company size
- Degree of centralization
- Globalization
- Accounting

Company Size

Company size, in terms of sales and the extent of operations, provides the order of magnitude for many areas of short-term corporate finance. While it may be arguable that smaller corporations have the same problems as larger companies but on a lesser scale, larger corporations are usually able to cost justify changes in practice because of the size of their funds flow and resultant savings through possible improvements. Larger companies also tend to deal with far more suppliers, more banks, require more substantial and more diversified credit facilities, and have numerous operating locations. Such situations create the need for an active, specialized corporate finance function, whereas smaller companies may not possess such concerns, dealing with a relative handful of banks and having few operating locations as a rule. Financial managers will often find more common interests with their counterparts from companies of similar size than in ones of much smaller size within their same industry.

This does not imply that the business characteristics or mix of the company is not a major factor. For instance, cash-intensive businesses generate large amounts of funds and usually have large short-term excesses. This requires more cash mobilization and short-term investment activity. For example, companies whose business encompasses a great deal of retail sales will have different treasury management and credit problems and concerns than companies whose major businesses comprise manufacturing and distribution.

Furthermore, the number of product lines or the presence of a wide variety of types of products can create different problems because of individual characteristics or recurring seasonal peaks and valleys. This diversity can create more complexity in the inventory and credit functions.

Degree of Centralization

The centralization or decentralization of the company's operations will probably have a similar effect on the finance function as well. It is usually the case in such instances for central staff to be looked on as the provider of the "bare essentials," which have not typically included treasury, credit, and inventory management. However, many large corporations have discovered that without some degree of centralized treasury, credit, and inventory management their corporate financial activities will not be extremely effective for the total corporation.

Globalization

The global scope of the company's operations also influences its working capital activities. The necessary movement of funds to and from overseas points, whether to the company's subsidiary locations or from export customers, affects overall treasury management operations. The need to make credit assessments on foreign customers and the need to deal with foreign exchange exposure all complicate the short-term corporate finance function. Most companies have not yet addressed the same issues of organization, reporting, and so on, for international as they have for domestic (U.S.) financial management. To date, most companies have concentrated only on the foreign exchange and exposure management aspects. This status seems to be slowly changing as the scope of corporate treasury management is broadening and the role of credit, treasury, and inventory is becoming wider in geographic terms.

Accounting

The final internal influence is the accounting/audit function. Accounting may often play a leading role in establishing documentation standards between the corporation and its banks, as well as usually performing the reconciliation function for all transactions affecting the cash account on the company's books. Historically, accounting's figure for cash was the only one considered or even monitored on any kind of periodic basis, and much of the treasury management function was contained within this area. Sometimes the accounting function can unwittingly influence the treasury management greatly.

Differences between Accounting and Treasury Cash Flow Information

The objective of accounting cash flow information is to provide a historical measurement of assets, liabilities, equity and profitability. On the other hand, the objective of treasury cash flow information is to determine the available or necessary collected cash *on hand* as of the current day or a specific day in the future. The collected cash balance represents available funds that can be used by the company. Therefore, it excludes such items as deposits and outstanding checks that have not cleared through the banking system. For this reason, the timing of cash flow information is more dynamic than accounting information.

The accrual basis is not used for treasury cash flow information. This is the primary reason why accounting systems yield significant timing differences from cash flow information. The major differences are:

- Cash receipts are recognized by treasury when the funds deposited in the bank become available to the company (not when the sale is booked).
- Cash receipts are relevant to treasury regardless of their source. That is, a sale of an asset is as important as a product sale in terms of cash flow management.
- Cash disbursements are not recognized by treasury until the check clears against the bank account (not when it is produced). All cash payments are important in managing cash flows, just like receipts.
- Depreciation and other non-cash items are less significant to treasury, especially for the purposes of managing cash flows.

External Factors

This book will develop the key external factors that drive the company's liquidity decisions. These include:

- Internationalization
- The banking system
- The regulatory setting

Internationalization

While many of the principles and techniques discussed in this book have originated and been developed in a U.S. context, this does not restrict the application of cash management fundamentals to other countries. Although there may be differences in the payment methods, banking systems, and sources of financial information in other countries, the basic concepts are universal. As is the case with other financial disciplines, the basic concepts must be tailored to suit the particular environment or the individual requirements of any one country. The inclusion of foreign exchange considerations simultaneously affords the company greater risks and opportunities.

The Banking System

The recent shocks to domestic and international banking have had a major influence on corporations. Some of the most important include:

- **Reduction in availability of credit products**: Banks have been less able or willing to finance less creditworthy companies. As their credit ratings have dropped, the value of their credit enhancement products (such as letters of credit) have diminished in value. Banks have also been focusing more heavily on fee-based sources of revenue, further reducing the availability of credit services.

- **Impact of downsizing**: As regulations increasingly squeeze banks into smaller sizes relative to their global competitors and into consolidation in the U.S., banks are curtailing or outsourcing marginally profitable services. This has left corporations with fewer choices in many cases and will likely continue in the future. It is also possible that cross-border mergers among banks will have a limiting effect on the competitive choice many treasury managers have taken for granted for many years.

The Legal and Regulatory Setting

One of the more complex areas of short-term corporate finance is the interface with the regulators. Corporations need to keep abreast of the rapid changes in regulation in banking, bankruptcy law, credit granting law, tax law, etc. Some important examples include:

- **Payment systems regulation**: Although targeted at bank risk, recent moves by the Federal Reserve to control risk in the domestic payments systems have also influenced the ways that companies can move funds.

- **Changes to the Uniform Commercial Code**: Changes in the underlying law for commercial transactions will affect the assumption of liability for electronic funds transfers and check clearing. Corporations need to stay up-to-date on such developments so they can be prepared before a problem occurs.

- **Bankruptcy law**: The rapid evolution in the interpretation of the Bankruptcy Code has affected corporate finance in many ways. It has seen the development of bankruptcy as a strategy to avoid litigation and to create an opportunity to recontract. It has seen the erosion of contractual priorities of debtors.

ETHICS

Ethical and legal issues play a central role in much of liquidity management. Many of the decisions taken in the interests of corporate liquidity have far-reaching effects on the corporation and on the individuals and companies that deal with the corporation. For example, how a company pays its suppliers and employees can have ethical implications, especially if disbursement-delaying techniques are used, such as physically altering checks or using remote banks that increase the float to depositors of check payments. When a company selects those individuals or companies to which it will grant credit it is subject to a wide range of laws that cover discriminatory practice. There are also ethical issues involved in bank-corporate relations decisions. In the wake of the E.F. Hutton scandal (described below) and changes in the Uniform Commercial Code governing bank liability, many companies have re-examined their bank agreements in order to ensure that they offer proper protection to both parties.

A pair of recent events involving questionable ethics are important to present in some detail: E.F. Hutton, which was a case of its abuse of the banking system for a period from 1980 to 1982 and the allegations of unethical selling practices at Dun & Bradstreet's Credit Services Division.

E.F. Hutton

On May 2, 1985, E.F. Hutton & Company pleaded guilty to 1900 counts of mail fraud arising from the mailing of checks to its banks and 100 counts of wire fraud stemming from the wiring of funds to cover overdraft positions. Hutton agreed to pay a fine of $2 million, plus $750,000 for the cost of the government investigation. The company also established a reserve of $8 million for restitution to the damaged banks.

These charges arose from the company's handling of its cash concentration system. (The cash management concepts introduced here are analyzed in later chapters.) This system was intended to move funds from about 300 field banks where local offices deposit funds. These funds were then upstreamed into two major concentration accounts in New York and Los Angeles.

The government did not challenge the legality of Hutton's cash concentration system. Nor did it allege that drawing on uncollected balances was *per se* illegal. It charged that Hutton had misused the float through two practices:

- **Excessive drawdowns**: This is the practice of writing excessively large checks against deposits before the checks creating those deposits had cleared, in effect, creating interest-free loans.

- **Multiple transfers**: This refers to passing checks through several banks en route to the final concentration banks. Again this permitted Hutton to benefit from inefficiencies in the check clearing system.

It appears that the main fallout from this affair has been two-fold. First, banks and corporations have become much more conscious of formalizing agreements regarding any non-routine transactions. Secondly, it appears that most observers believe that the real import of the fraud ruling is that while taking advantage of inefficiencies in the check clearing system may not be illegal, it is probably illegal to create transactions with no business purpose other than to exploit these inefficiencies.

It should be noted that these practices could not happen as easily in the present context. The check clearing system of today does not have many of the inefficiencies that Hutton exploited. In addition, the highly decentralized structure of Hutton greatly contributed to the expansion of the scheme.

Dun & Bradstreet

Dun & Bradstreet's Credit Services Division is the major supplier of business credit information in the U.S. Its market share is approximately 90%; the remaining market share belonging to TRW. In January, 1989, this division came under severe criticism for illegal selling practices.

The allegations were that D&B salespersons had deceived customers about the amount of credit information they had purchased. The difficulty comes from two peculiarities in the way D&B, prior to 1990, charged for credit information. First, D&B customers had to purchase a certain number of "units," paying in advance. (Which proves that D&B understands credit very well.) As the customer used the various D&B products over the year, it would be charged a certain number of units for each. If a customer used more than it had contracted for, it was charged a substantially higher rate. At the end of the contract year, apparently a number of salespersons deceived customers into believing they had purchased far more products than they actually had, hoping thereby to induce the customer to increase the number of units it ordered for the next calendar year. This increase would result in bonus income to the salesperson.

Figure 1-3
Cash Flow Timeline

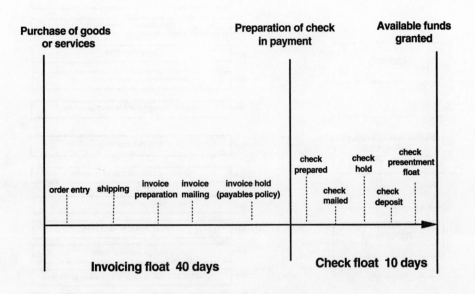

While the scope of this practice was limited, it did result in sweeping management and product changes. The major change was a much clearer and more easily accessed report on year-to-date usage. Again, these changes and the resulting publicity basically ensure that this could not happen again.

Both of these cases illustrate some general principles that these two companies did not follow. One of the most basic is the need for clearly defined corporate policies in areas where there is potential for corporate personnel to engage in self-serving activities.

INTEGRATING SHORT-TERM FINANCE FUNCTIONS

Before launching into the remainder of this book, it is useful to emphasize the nature of the relationships between the individual functions. An important way to visualize this is the cash flow timeline (Figure 1-3).

Figure 1-4
Working Capital Problems and Solutions

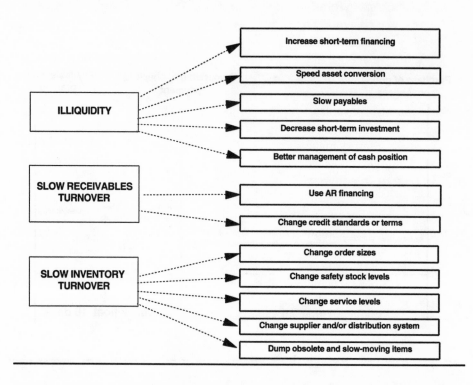

is schematic allows the financial manager to visualize the interactions between the various functions. These linkages also point out a key difficulty: performance evaluation. The degree of interaction and potential conflicts make an overall view crucial to effective management. In addition, it is interesting to note that most corporate treasury managers have spent most of their efforts on the right-hand side (check float) of this time line, which, in example shown, is only one-fourth the size of the left-hand side (invoicing float). Treasury managers in smaller companies have been more successful in getting involved in more than the check float side, probably because they wear many financial hats, not just treasury's. On the other hand, treasury managers in large companies have not been as successful. One development may help change this — electronic data interchange. This change in purchasing and related paying activities is bringing all the members of the cash flow timeline "team."

Diagnostics

Figure 1-4 attempts to foreshadow some of the major topics that will be outlined in the remaining chapters. The emphasis will be on developing solutions to and on detecting problems with illiquidity or poor asset performance.

Illiquidity can pose major problems for the company and to the financial manager whose job it is to solve them. This is where an efficient, fine-tuned cash flow management system becomes valuable because it allows the treasury manager to control payables, tighten the company's cash position, and draw down already-in-place financial reserves. With appropriate warning signals built into the system, the treasury manager can alert management to potential problems and provide alternative routes for resolving them.

Slow receivable turnover can be detected early on by using effective credit management techniques. Monitoring credit performance and evaluating alternative credit approaches can pay benefits in slow times. In addition, understanding the quality of the company's receivables is important in identifying receivable financing alternatives.

The effects of **slow inventory turnover** can be mitigated by using efficient inventory management techniques. Implementing up-to-date techniques can alert the financial manager in time to make necessary changes to order sizes, safety stock levels, or to dump obsolete and slow-moving items.

MANAGEMENT REVIEW ITEMS

➡ Keep a list of all the treasury functions, matching them up with job descriptions and a formal organization chart. Specifically, note who is in charge of forecasting, funds movement, money market administration, and banking system administration. If you are managing these functions, plan a staff rotation, so each of your staff members can become cross-trained in the company's major treasury management activities.

➡ Keep a *functional* organization chart for the company's financial functions. This will come in handy in making changes or in describing how the company's financial management is handled.

➡ Categorize your financial function by degree of centralization or decentralization, looking for economies of scale or benefits from central treasury management functions, such as short-term debt and investing or foreign exchange.

➡ Maintain a regulatory checklist (e.g., Federal Reserve regulations pending and UCC updates) to discuss with your bankers or other treasury managers.

➡ Periodically review how payments and receipts are handled at each deposit and disbursement point. If necessary, work with your internal or external auditors to identify potential control problems. Look for such things as unauthorized movements of funds, unauthorized instructions to banks, and weak security in your treasury information systems.

➡ Look for unethical cash management "procedures" in your own collection and disbursement systems as well as those of your customers and suppliers. Review any possible questionable situations quickly with the appropriate people.

➡ Try to lay out an average time line for major customer payments. Get help from other participants in the timeline. Look for possible improvements in all areas.

➡ Use Figure 1-4 to develop a checklist for planning how to handle illiquidity, slow receivables turnover, and slow inventory turnover. Use the checklist to structure periodic (e.g., quarterly) treasury planning sessions.

CHAPTER 2

PAYMENT SYSTEMS AND REGULATIONS

This chapter addresses the institutional and regulatory framework for corporate liquidity management. It primarily focuses on the domestic (U.S.) payments systems. These include the paper-based systems (essentially checks) and electronic systems (both large- and small-dollar). Understanding the mechanics of these payment systems is impossible without considering the regulatory framework in which they operate.

There are five major payment mechanisms in the U.S. The one with the most item volume is the paper-based check payment system. The remaining four systems are electronic ones, one of which is intended to handle small-dollar payments (the automated clearing house). The other three handle large-dollar payments within the U.S. and throughout the world.

All four electronic systems have shown steady growth in recent years at a faster rate than the paper-based system. Although the electronic systems may be growing more rapidly than checks, the use of checks continues to grow, and check volume far exceeds the total volume of electronic transfers in all systems combined. When considering why more paper transactions are not being replaced by electronic transfers it is important to remember that the paper-based check system is very efficient and profitable for banks.

This chapter will cover the following topics:

- **Paper-based systems**: This section describes the mechanics of check clearing and analyzes some other check-like transfer mechanisms.
- **Electronic systems**: This section describes the two major branches of electronic payment mechanisms: the ACH, Fedwire, S.W.I.F.T., and CHIPS, designed for the settlement of major corporate and bank transactions. Although this distinction is useful but imprecise, many

relatively large dollar corporate and bank transactions are moved through the ACH.

- **Bank and payments system regulation:** The final section deals with the key aspects of regulation aimed to control bank risk and to mitigate risk in funds transfer systems.

PAPER-BASED PAYMENT SYSTEMS

In the U.S., Canada, and relatively few other countries, the check is still the most common method of making noncash payments. The volume of checks written in the U.S. continues to grow, although at a much smaller rate in recent years. To put things in perspective, the absolute growth in checks still exceeds the absolute growth (in numbers of items) of electronic payments.

Clearing Methods

One of the major services provided by commercial banks to their corporate customers is check clearing. Checks in the U.S. must be physically transported back to be presented to the bank on which they are drawn, and the commercial banks, in conjunction with the Federal Reserve, provide the mechanism for this **presentment** process. **Magnetic ink character recognition (MICR)** is used to read and identify checks. The use of MICR was a significant technological breakthrough in commercial banking and makes possible the rapid clearing of checks in the U.S. The line at the bottom of the check where all the pertinent data appear and on which the deposit bank encodes the dollar amount of the check is called the **MICR line**.

Checks, which are bundled together in **cash letters** to be transported, can clear in a variety of ways:

- **On-us:** This is the simplest case where the bank on which the check is drawn is also the bank of (first) deposit. These checks are generally considered immediately available to the corporate depositor.
- **Local check swapping or clearing house:** This occurs when two nearby banks that receive many checks drawn on each other meet on a regular, prearranged basis to exchange the checks, usually once early in the morning on each business day. This can be just a bilateral agreement or several banks can be involved in a more formal procedure. It eliminates the unpredictable, inefficient procedures that would otherwise have to be used.

- **Federal Reserve clearing**: The Federal Reserve (Fed) is the leading clearer of checks, processing checks throughout the country that are deposited with it by its member banks at the Fed district, branch, or remote processing centers.
- **Direct sends**: This works like local check swapping except that the two banks are not in the same city. This practice is mostly carried out by aggressive banks that offer extensive cash management services.

Federal Reserve Clearing

Checks are delivered to the Fed by commercial banks that are members of the Federal Reserve and other Federal Reserve locations. There are 12 district banks, 25 branches, and 47 **regional check processing centers (RCPCs)**.

Since checks must be presented (i.e., physically returned) to the bank on which they are drawn, the Fed maintains an elaborate system to move checks around the country. Checks are delivered to district and branch locations, where the items are read (magnetically) and sorted for physical delivery through the Federal Reserve system back to the banks on which they are drawn. The Fed grants **availability** to the depositing bank of 0, 1, or 2 days. A 3-day availability is possible if the deadline for 2-day deposits is missed.

Alternatives to Fed Clearing

Although the Federal Reserve is not the only means available to clear checks, it is often the easiest alternative and thus used as the fallback. Other choices are usually more expensive and have to be cost justified by substantial savings in reduced collection float gained by the bank over and above the Fed's granted availability. Local clearing houses are an exception as they are usually inexpensive alternatives to the Fed.

The decision on which of these methods should be used is made by the clearing bank, taking into consideration the time the check is received, the dollar size of the check, the location of the drawee bank (the bank on which the check is drawn), whether the clearing bank has a correspondent bank relationship with that bank or with another in the vicinity, and the overall (average daily) volume (number of items, or checks) that the bank has from the location of the drawee bank. The corporation has no real direct influence over which method is used.

In 1992, two new competitors to the Federal Reserve were established:

- The National Clearing House, which has eight bank members and is owned by Chexs (a joint venture of Huntington Bancshares Inc., Littlewood, Shain & Co., and U.S. Check)

- Payment System Network, which was established by eleven large banks and J.D. Carreker & Associates as a part of the Electronic Check Clearing House Organization and will begin operations in 1993

The former organization announced plans to compete with the Federal Reserve for the approximate six billion the Fed clears annually (this represents approximately 35% of all interbank items). The latter will compete with current direct send programs. Both programs ostensibly will offer cost savings over comparable Federal Reserve services.

Other Paper Instruments

There are two other paper-based payment mechanisms that are important:

- **Payable through draft (PTD):** This instrument is handled essentially like a check except that the check issuer has a 24-hour period in which it can exercise its option to refuse to honor the instrument. Its major application is for insurance companies, which issue PTDs for such transactions as claim reimbursement, the extra time is used to verify the legitimacy of the claim. Note that with checks, a company can issue a **stop order** in order to refuse payment. However, this is only used in exceptional cases and is expensive since it involves a significant amount of bank processing effort.
- **Depository transfer check (DTC):** This is a signatureless check used for moving funds from one of a company's accounts to another. Its main purpose is to move funds from deposit banks into a concentration bank when an ACH debit transfer is not used.

Availability Schedules

One of the key concepts in bank compensation is the **bank availability schedule**. Actually, there are many availability schedules, and a treasury manager should know the basics of a schedule to be able to negotiate or understand what is obtained from the bank. Banks grant **availability** to their corporate customers on deposited checks. Availability defines the timing of the use of funds and may be different from the bank's actual collection of the funds. Although the availability of funds should theoretically match presentment (i.e., the depositor gets to use the funds in the same amount of time it takes the depositing bank to clear the check back to the drawee bank), this is not always the case. The depositing bank, in a sense, guesses how long it will take to clear a check, on average, back to a specific bank. If it uses a direct send or local clearing house swap, the estimated time is probably quite accurate. If, however, it uses the Fed or a correspondent bank, the time may be more uncertain.

In any case, a bank usually provides an availability schedule to its corporate customer. This shows the availability, expressed in business days, and the deadline time by deposit end point, or drawee location. The availability schedule may only apply to types of deposits, such as lockbox or checks already encoded by the company. Other items, such as checks deposited at a local branch, might be subject to a different schedule.

Banks usually monitor their performance in meeting deposit deadlines. They also are usually able to determine whether corporate deposits meet prearranged deadlines and can provide reports showing corporate customers how their checks are clearing (i.e., what availability is being granted, deposit by deposit) on request or by conducting a special study.

Check Truncation

In recent years, there have been a number of experiments to test the concept of **check truncation,** or the electronic clearing of checks, instead of the physical movement of checks. A cooperative group of commercial banks formed the Electronic Check Clearing House Organization (ECCHO) in 1990 to clear checks drawn on each other without transporting the checks back to the drawee location. The Fed has also been involved in similar tests. Corporate treasury managers should expect further advances in this area.

Check truncation is attractive to banks and the Federal Reserve because it has the potential to reduce the time and expense involved in physically transporting checks back to their drawee location for posting and clearing. For corporations, check truncation offers lower expense — but possibly at the cost of reduced disbursement float.

ELECTRONIC PAYMENT SYSTEMS

Electronic payments are usually thought of in two groups: those with primarily a consumer or small-dollar orientation — the ACH system — and those intended for large-dollar corporate applications: Fedwire, CHIPS, and S.W.I.F.T.

Automated Clearing House (ACH)

The ACH exchanges electronic funds transfer instructions between banks. Most ACHs are run by the Fed, which means that most ACHs are a local Fed office or

---

Box 2-1
Typical Corporate ACH Applications

Direct deposit of payroll

Pre-authorized debits (payments) - taxes, insurance premiums, mortgage payments

Pre-authorized credits (deposits) - annuities, travel advances

Pension retirement fund payments - Social Security payments, company plans

Stock dividend payments

Vendor (corporate trade) payments - company and government

Deposit concentration (electronic depository transfer checks)

Funding disbursement accounts - controlled disbursing

---

branch. However, their oversight and membership comes from banks and other financial institutions in the geographic area served by the ACH.

In 1992, there were 32 local ACH associations and 9 bank associations, which are operated by the largest ACH banks in the country. The National Automated Clearing House Association (NACHA) is the national association that makes the rules that apply across all associations, deals with the Federal Reserve on a national level, and serves as a forum for national ACH policy development.

The ACH system began in the early 1970's but failed to gain much volume until the federal government began to use the ACH for its payments. The first nationwide ACH application was the United States Air Force payroll in 1976. The federal and state governments continue to play a very important role in the ACH; in 1989, the federal government represented 37% of the volume and had represented the majority of all payments until 1986.

There are several ACH applications typically used by corporations. These have shown noticeable growth in recent years and are becoming more common-place among corporations. Perhaps the most well known application is direct deposit of payroll. This is discussed in more detail in Chapter 3.

Prior to live transactions being handled through the ACH, a **prenotification transaction (prenote)** or entry is executed. Prenotes are intended to determine whether the receiving bank account is able to handle ACH transactions. Some companies and their banks have found that prenotes are not always handled properly by the receiving bank, and, consequently, when live transactions are made, errors occur. Some companies have tried transmitting small dollar amounts to ensure that the receiving bank has to handle the transaction properly, but this may not always be practical. As more banks increase their ACH activity, it is thought that the prenote problem will disappear.

The most important corporate applications of the ACH are shown in Box 2-1. Many have become standard for large and medium-sized corporations. The major area of growth is the use of the ACH in conjunction with EDI.

Fedwire

Wire transfers are often used by companies to fund disbursement and payroll accounts at banks other than the company's concentration bank or banks. The treasury manager initiates most routine transfers through a personal computer or other terminal. Non-routine transfers are usually made by calling the bank. A company may also use wire transfers to concentrate funds from its regional banks. These transfers may be completed by calling the regional bank, through standing instructions with the regional bank (e.g., the bank is instructed to wire out all funds that come in today tomorrow, or the bank may be instructed to wire out all collected balances each day) or by issuing a drawdown instruction to the concentration bank, either via terminal or telephone.

Fedwire is the bank-to-bank payment system operated by the Fed for its member banks. The reserve accounts that banks maintain with their local Federal Reserve Bank are used to receive or disburse funds. Larger banks usually have on-line access to Fedwire and can, therefore, receive regular notification electronically concerning funds movements. Smaller banks have to depend on their local Fed for telephone confirmations concerning finds transfers and receipts, and this can create delays in corporations being able to use their funds on a timely basis. Payments are guaranteed by the Fed as soon as they are made; that is, the funds are immediately available (good funds) to the bank receiving them. This is called **payments finality** and is an important component of the regulation of bank risk.

Clearing House Interbank Payment System (CHIPS)

CHIPS is a payment settlement system operated by the New York Clearing House Association. It was established in 1970 to replace paper settlement of international transactions between U.S. and foreign banks. It has 144 banks as members, They use CHIPS to settle their accounts at the 12 major New York City clearing banks and the Fed. During the day, each of the CHIPS member banks has credits and debits recorded against it. At the close of the day, each member settles its net

FIGURE 2-1
Types of S.W.I.F.T. Messages

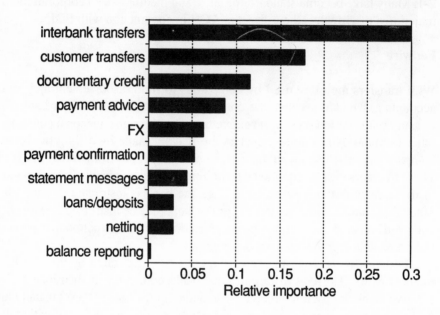

position (positive or negative) by a Fedwire transfer. CHIPS announced payment finality, similar to Fedwire, in 1990. This has assured more safety and certainty over the CHIPS system. CHIPS is used to settle most major foreign exchange transactions, and its current daily volume exceeds $600 billion.

S.W.I.F.T.

S.W.I.F.T. is the acronym for the Society for Worldwide Interbank Financial Telecommunications. It was incorporated in Belgium in 1973 with 239 banks from 15 countries participating. In 1992, S.W.I.F.T. includes more than 2200 banks in 55 countries as members. It is important to note that S.W.I.F.T. is not *per se* a settlement system. It is an international communications network for the exchange of bank information. The eventual settlement of transfers resulting from S.W.I.F.T. messages is through CHIPS, the UK equivalent of CHIPS (CHAPS), or through correspondent accounts. Unlike Fedwire, which is open from 9 A.M.

to 5 P.M. (EST), S.W.I.F.T. is open 24 hours a day, seven days a week. Figure 2-1 shows the relative importance of the major S.W.I.F.T. messages. The data are from the recent survey of S.W.I.F.T. banks by Aggarwal and Baker (1991).

Extinct Electronic Systems

One of the most controversial areas of payments systems is the dual and conflicting role of the Fed: regulator and competitor. (See Tucker (1991) for further discussion.) This has been manifested in the demise of two alternatives to Fedwire: CHESS and BankWire. BankWire was created by a group of major U.S. banks in the 1950's to provide bank communication and funds transfers (Cashwire). It ceased operation in March 1986. A similar fate was earlier dealt CHESS, Clearing House Electronic Payment System, which was established by the major Chicago banks.

BANK AND PAYMENT SYSTEMS REGULATION

This section deals with those aspects of bank and payment systems regulation that are most relevant to corporations. These issues mainly involve bank safety and payment systems efficiency.

Bank Regulation

The U.S. has a dual system of bank chartering. Banks can be either federally or state chartered. State jurisdiction is more common. This dual nature creates some important differences in bank regulations.

Federal laws prohibit banks from branching across state lines (**McFadden Act**). States regulate whether and/or how many branches a bank can have. States also determine whether out-of-state banks can buy in-state banks or establish branches in the state. This differs greatly from state to state. As federal authorities have allowed healthy banks to cross state boundaries to assume failed ones, this restriction is *de facto* breaking down.

Another controversial area of bank regulation deals with the separation between commercial and investment banking (the **Glass-Steagall Act**). This Act was created in 1933 after the decimation of the banking industry at the beginning of the Depression. Since then the effectiveness of this Act has gradually eroded. Commercial banks have gradually entered further into investment banking although thus far only the largest money center banks have had significant inroads.

The third major aspect of banking regulation is the **Depository Institutions Deregulation and Monetary Control Act** of 1980 (**DIDMCA, or Monetary Control Act,** for short). It radically changed the nature of U.S. banking by requiring all depository institutions to maintain reserve accounts with the Fed, effectively placing them all under greater Fed control and allowing them access to Fed services. It also established a long-run cost recovery objective for the Fed. This meant that over the long run, Fed services *in aggregate* must break even. This was subsequently amended:

> *This internal objective of cost recovery for each service line was subsequently modified to provide that revenues for each service line must cover all operating costs, float costs and certain imputed costs, such as the cost of interest on short- and long-term debt, as well as make some contribution to the pre-tax return on equity.*

Board of Governors of the Federal Reserve, *policy statement, 1990*

This cost recovery objective has had sweeping impact across banking and cash management. For instance, it meant a radical reduction in Fed subsidies of check clearing and other bank services.

Federal Agencies

Adding to the complexity of banking regulation in the U.S. is the diversity of federal and state agencies involved with regulating banks. In addition to the central role played by the Federal Reserve, a number of other agencies are important.

- The **Federal Deposit Insurance Corporation (FDIC)** gets involved in cases of bank failure or anticipated failures. Depositors are insured up to $100,000. Note that this applies to each *depositor*. This means that if a company keeps several accounts in its name, the cumulative total is only insured up to $100,000. This may apply to consolidated accounts among wholly owned subsidiaries as well. One of the contemporary debates has raged around the traditional structure of deposit insurance, which has been a fixed percentage, irrespective of risk considerations. While rates nearly tripled from 1988 to 1991, from .00083 to .0023, this has failed to stop the depletion of the insurance fund's reserves. Rates are expected to increase, even with the risk-based assessment plan announced by the FDIC in 1992.

- The **Office of the Comptroller of the Currency (OCC)** grants federal banking charters and conducts regular bank examinations of federally chartered banks.
- The **Securities and Exchange Commission** plays a less direct role in its oversight of public securities markets. This is most significant in the supervision of bank holding companies. Bank holding companies consist of a group of banks and/or other financial institutions. This organizational form permits the holding company to engage in certain activities that are not permitted commercial banks.

Major Federal Reserve Regulations

These regulations are established, modified, and enforced by the Federal Reserve Board in Washington. The Fed routinely calls for comment on proposed regulations or changes to existing regulations. Trade associations, such as the American Bankers Association or the Association of Reserve City Bankers, and corporate associations as well as large corporations, such as American Express or Merrill Lynch, monitor Fed developments and comment formally as required. From the corporate viewpoint, the major regulations deal with controlling payment system risk and bank safety.

Daylight Overdrafts
One of the most important aspects of payments system regulation is the control of daylight overdrafts. In 1991, the daily average of daylight overdrafts was $75 billion. Daylight overdrafts affect how banks can access the Fedwire system to transfer funds, thereby potentially affecting how easy (or hard) it may be for corporations to move funds. The Fed has established limits — **daylight overdraft caps** — for bank overdraft positions based on a bank's financial stability. A bank that reaches or exceeds its limit is unable to transfer funds out of the bank until its net position changes so that it again is under its limit. This can prevent customers of the bank (e.g., corporations) from moving their funds out of the bank. While there have been few instances of substantial delay in funds movement, corporate treasury managers should be aware of the possibility of delay. The Fed is also expected to implement a system to charge for daylight overdrafts. In its original proposal, the Fed suggested a rate of 25 basis points (one basis point = 0.1 %). In 1992, the Fed announced a phased approach to charging for daylight overdrafts. The first phase, which calls for a charge of 10 basis points on the average minute-by-minute overdraft will be implemented in April 1993. The charge will be increased in two additional yearly phases.

Box 2-2
EFAA Availability Rules

Category	Release Date*
Cash or electronic payments	Next day
Government checks	Next day
Local checks	Two days
Nonlocal checks	Five days

*The number of business days after deposit

Banks are unsure as to whether or how they will pass their daylight overdraft charges on to their corporate (or other) customers. The chargeback is complicated by the fact that some or much of the daylight overdraft can be caused by the bank itself, not its customers.

Other Regulations

Same-day presentment could affect how banks (and the Fed) clear checks back to each other by establishing a later deadline than at present, thereby preventing banks from notifying their corporate customers in time to fund their disbursement accounts on the same day. The Fed has proposed requiring all banks to accept cash letters up to 8:00 A.M. daily. It further specified that paying banks could not charge a fee for honoring this presentment and settlement must be in same-day funds. It is not expected to have much effect on bank special controlled disbursement services because it should not delay notifying their customers on a timely basis.

Regulation Q prohibits banks from paying corporations interest on their checking accounts (demand deposit accounts). Many corporate treasury managers believe that it would be beneficial to earn interest on their accounts and that it would allow them to simplify their banking systems.

Regulation CC is the regulation the Fed established to implement the Expedited Funds Availability Act in 1988. This act defined check availability times, altered payable-through-draft processing requirements, and updated check return processing procedures.

The **High Dollar Group Sort (HDGS) program** was initiated by the Fed in 1984. It is intended to expedite the handling of large checks (high dollar items) by the Fed. This program has had a significant impact on corporate disbursing since it permits the Fed to make a second presentment daily on any bank branch up to 12:00 noon. The Fed does make the MICR information for the HDGS items available to the bank prior to physical delivery.

The **Expedited Funds Availability Act (EFAA)** of 1987 was designed to provide further assistance to failing banks and to control nonbank banks. One part of the EFAA addressed retail and small business deposits, in particular, rules on how consumers are granted availability. The rules that came into effect on September 1, 1990 are shown in Box 2-2.

While the major impact of EFAA was on retail payments, it affected corporations in three major ways:

- Payable through and payable at drafts were subject to the same rules as checks, which significantly changes a firm's handling procedures.
- It changed rules on check endorsements.
- It expedited the handling of return items.

MANAGEMENT REVIEW ITEMS

➡ You can assume your bank is an active collector if it has an aggressive (i.e., widespread) direct send program. This usually means that it will be a better *collector* of funds. It may not be as effective for disbursements.

➡ Your bank (or banks) should be able to provide a report showing actual availability received for items deposited over time. In addition to assuring that the availability promised is the one being routinely attained, you should look for inefficient procedures, such as deposits that miss clearing cut-off times and the effects of *mixed* deposits. These are deposits of cash and checks, as well as checks with wide sending points. Sometimes, banks will assign a single availability for a deposit, treating all items as though they were drawn on the farthest point.

➡ Determine whether you require actual return of checks after they clear. For some high volume, repetitive items, such as payrolls, stock dividends, and employee reimbursement checks, you may not need to save and store the canceled checks. Some banks that offer check truncation services may offer reduced prices for truncated checking accounts.

➡ When considering a bank for ACH services that require prenotes, such as direct deposit of payroll, you should ask for and talk to other corporate users that have similar volumes and that have undergone prenotes with the bank under consideration.

➡ You should attempt to move as many wire transfers as possible to off-peak times, such as mid-morning or after the mid-day crunch, to avoid delays.

➡ To monitor your exposure should any of your banks fail, keep a monthly report of average ledger balances at all your banks or maintain a list of those with ledger balances in excess of the $100,000 FDIC limit.

CHAPTER 3

REVIEWING CASH MANAGEMENT BASICS

Traditionally, managing cash flows meant handling paper-based remittances from customers and making check payments to company suppliers, creditors, employees, and shareholders. Today, this definition is expanded to include electronic payments to and from the company. This chapter provides a review of the fundamental techniques companies use to handle collections, disbursements, concentration, and cash position management.

The corporate cash manager must manage the flows to, from, and within the company. The most decentralized company can realize benefit by establishing a central cash pool to receive inflows and regulate outflows. Cash flows in from many sources, such as the collection of accounts receivable remittances from customers, short-term borrowings from banks or other external sources, subsidiary dividends or intracompany loan repayments, proceeds from long-term financial transactions or equity issues, and the liquidation of marketable securities. Cash flows out of the central pool to pay for operating and manufacturing expenses, purchases or additions to long-term assets, employee payroll, taxes, debt and interest, dividends to corporate shareholders, and the purchase of marketable securities.

Cash management involves the structuring, managing, and streamlining of the flows to the central pool. The economic benefits of a central cash management are diluted greatly if the function is splintered into decentralized operating units. However, the tools and techniques discussed below still apply.

The major sections of this chapter are:

- Collections
- Concentration
- Disbursements
- Cash position management

COLLECTIONS

Cash gathering entails the collection of customer remittances and the movement of these receipts to a primary corporate concentration bank. The mobilization and concentration of funds creates an available cash pool for satisfying the cash requirements of the company, such as funding corporate disbursements and local payrolls or investing in short-term instruments. Cash management systems that are more centralized have fewer such concentration points.

The major objective in handling cash receipts efficiently is to reduce or eliminate delays in processing customer payments and entering them into the check clearing system. Customer payments can be deposited by a company employee at a local (field) bank, or a company can use a bank lockbox service. A deposit by a company employee may be the result of checks being received at a company's office location. This is particularly true for smaller companies. The deposit may also be the result of an internal company processing unit, which is very similar in concept to a bank lockbox department. Company processing centers are usually established in cases of high-volume, low-value payments, quite similar to bank retail lockbox applications discussed later in this chapter.

A lockbox can also be used to receive mail from company locations. Some companies do this in order to have all remittances deposited through the same bank or group of banks and to avoid company personnel handling remittances. However, this remailing creates unnecessary mail float and increased bank processing charges. There are several criteria that determine which collection method is used. The deposit track depends on the dollar size, volume, and location of the depositing unit.

Industry-specific Collection Characteristics

Collection methods are influenced by the firm's industry. Examples include:

- **Retail**: Characterized by a large volume of local, non-mail collections, often over weekends or at night. Local banks are typically used for collections. This can make concentration of funds difficult.
- **Supermarkets**: Characterized by heavy currency deposits, usually heaviest over weekends. In such cases, this is truly *cash* management, and the banking needs are more physical in nature (e.g., coin and currency deliveries and pick-ups).
- **Insurance**: Insurance companies have been in the vanguard of electronic collections, especially for regular premium payments. They are heavy users of the automated clearing house network. Many insurance

companies also have established internal company processing centers for their nonautomated payments.

- **Manufacturing**: These companies tend to have much larger transaction sizes, making them ideal users of basic bank cash management services, especially wholesale lockboxes and controlled disbursements.
- **Utilities**: These companies often have enough volume to justify internal company processing centers. Also, they may receive payments from third-party collectors, such as financial institutions, in a variety of formats and media.

Lockboxes

Historically, corporate cash management systems were built around local deposits. This method is still common in many small companies, but it is rare in larger corporations. The use of bank lockbox services has proliferated so much that the corporate lockbox networks of most large companies have become quite sophisticated and are a fundamental part of the company's cash management system.

Using a lockbox accelerates collections faster than local deposits by reducing the mail and local office processing time as well as reducing the time required to clear the checks. Customers are instructed to send their payments to a specific location (collection point) that has been strategically selected, usually by conducting a collection study of the company's regular remittances or by cost considerations. For consumer customers, many companies provide return envelopes to facilitate payment. These are rarely used for corporate customers, however, because most corporations generate their own envelopes and payment details. At each collection point, a corporation establishes a post office box that is accessed by a local bank. Most post office boxes are *phantom boxes*. The U.S. Postal Service does not fine sort the mail to the individual boxes but just sorts all boxes for each particular bank together. The bank then does the fine sorting. A unique zip code, favored by many regional and a few money center banks, has the same effect.

There are several types of lockboxes, as shown in Figure 3-1. Each type is discussed in the following sections.

Figure 3-1
Types of Lockboxes

Lockbox Type	Characteristics		
	Checks	Volume	Sensitive to:
Wholesale	High $	Low	Float
Retail	Low $	High	Costs
Automated	Varies	High(usually	Costs
Mixed media	Varies	Varies	Processing

Wholesale Lockboxes

Wholesale lockboxes are characterized by relatively low volume levels but higher value per item. A typical wholesale lockbox might include 500 checks per month with an average value of $5000 per check. The main objectives in establishing this type of lockbox are optimizing the mail time for receiving customer checks and reducing the time required to clear these checks and provide the company with good funds. Float improvement usually far outweighs bank charges, and, accordingly, location and availability are more important factors.

Envelopes, payment details such as invoice copies or statements, and copies of all checks are sent by the bank to the company to permit further processing of the receipts. Many bank wholesale lockbox services are heavily manually intensive and, consequently, banks charge more for these services, often breaking down their charges by the number of extra tasks required by the corporate customer. Wholesale lockboxes are usually located at Fed City points (37 major cities in the U.S. where the Fed has district or branch offices). Companies tend to arrange a network of wholesale lockboxes at strategic, regional points, depending on the geographic spread of the customer base.

Retail Lockbox

The primary purpose of the **retail lockbox** is the efficient processing of high-volume, low-dollar checks, in many cases replacing in-house processing of the items. Examples of retail lockboxes are credit card payments, mail order business payments or utility bill payments. Typical volumes for retail lockboxes can exceed 100,000 items per month; typical average item size can be as low as $5-$10.

Bank charges for retail lockbox services are usually quite important, since companies often establish only one such arrangement. Given the smaller dollar size of each item, float considerations are of lesser concern. Many banks do not offer this type of lockbox on a manual processing basis as the labor costs can be prohibitive. Usually any enclosed details and only check copies from "exception" items; that is, those items that cannot be routinely processed by the bank according to the company's standard instructions (otherwise considered as "clean" items) are returned to the company. Increasingly, retail lockboxes are being transformed to automated lockboxes by incorporating a machine-readable turnaround document in the billing procedures or by instituting machine capture (even if by manual entry) at the bank.

Automated Lockbox

The **automated lockbox** offers acceleration in the receivables processing as relevant customer remittance data such as customer number, invoice number(s) and dollar amount can be captured in machine readable form at the bank and transmitted electronically to the company ready to be processed further by the company's computerized data processing systems. Bank charges for this type of service will vary, depending on whether machine readable documents are utilized or whether manual key entry of receipt data is required. Many banks do not offer this service because the investment in sophisticated scanning equipment or in many manual key operators is quite substantial and requires significant transaction volume to be economically feasible.

Although automating lockbox services has been more the case for retail lockbox services, many banks have done so for wholesale lockbox services as well in order to reduce escalating manual labor costs, dependence on the scarce supply of skilled personnel, and to utilize the advantages of newer technologies, such as sophisticated image processing systems.

Mixed Media Lockbox

The latest type of lockbox service is a **mixed media lockbox** (see Figure 3-2). It combines paper-based and electronic remittances and reports the consolidated information to the corporate treasury manager. By means of a table look-up — based on information contained on the MICR line on customer checks and information contained in the electronic transaction — the banks can provide customer information to the treasury manager.

Figure 3-2
Multi-Media Lockbox

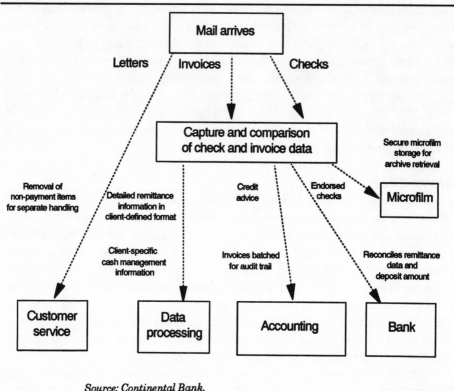

Source: Continental Bank.

Establishing a Lockbox

In establishing a lockbox arrangement a company must be certain that processing instructions are acceptable, formalized, and understood between it and the lockbox processing staff of its bank so that processing errors are minimized.

Often, it is essential for the treasury manager and accounts receivable personnel to visit the prospective lockbox bank in order to review procedures and assure that service requirements and procedures are completely understood. This is especially true in the case of a new bank or when special procedures are involved.

Box 3-1
Types of Lockbox Networks

Processing centers
Mail intercepts
Alliance
Joint ventures/non-bank vendors

Lockbox Networks

Lockbox networks offer corporate customers the option of multiple collection points while dealing with one bank or bank holding company. The types of lockbox networks are shown in Box 3-1.

The most common type of network is the **processing center**. Processing centers are all part of the same organization (usually a bank holding company) and have actual operating centers in a number of locations. One type of processing center is a multiple lockbox service offered by banks with one or more major cities in their banking area. For example, banks in Texas offer combined lockboxes in Houston and Dallas with just one bank account needed. Multi-state bank holding companies (e.g., in the Southwest and the Northwest) also offer a similar type of network throughout their banking network. Another type of network features local processing centers in which out-of-state banks pick up and process checks in local areas, just like local banks. However, they then must ship them to their headquarters or deposit them with a local bank. This can be attractive in that it would not involve dealing with another bank. Similarly, some banks provide courier pickups at numerous mailing locations with the mail being delivered to the bank's central processing center. Again, this allows the company to pick up items around the country while dealing with just one bank.

Other banks offer **mail intercept** networks. In this type of network, a bank arranges with local (major) post offices to segregate mail for pick-up by a messenger or courier. The mail is then shipped to the bank's central lockbox facilities for further processing.

Another type is the **alliance**. This is a consortium of independent banks that have formed a cooperative effort to offer lockbox collection points throughout the country. A corporation only has to deal with one bank in the alliance, not the full group. This allows broader collection by experienced lockbox banks without additional administrative effort by the corporation, such as maintaining individual bank relationships. There are possible problems with this approach if the bank systems are incompatible.

Joint ventures between a bank and non-bank and non-bank networks have been offered occasionally. They are similar to alliances with the exception that only one processor is used. These types have been offered for retail lockboxes with some success. They have had little success for wholesale lockboxes, although several banks have successfully outsourced their wholesale lockbox services to third party, non-bank vendors.

Lockbox networks may not be useful for every company. They seem attractive to smaller or mid-sized companies and larger companies with small or temporary volumes in a special location. They are something to be considered when evaluating or establishing a lockbox collection system where stand-alone, multiple lockbox points cannot be cost justified or as a minor enhancement to a single lockbox arrangement.

In-house Processing Centers

In special instances, a company may choose to collect and process remittances at its own processing center. Compared to using a lockbox system, a company processing center offers a greater degree of control. The processing is geared to the company's needs rather than to a general standard of an outside supplier, which means it is often easier to make changes in the system. There is usually less employee turnover at the company, resulting in fewer errors and faster updating of payor account information. Depending on the volume, company processing centers may be considerably cheaper than banks. A company processing center ensures future processing capability, whereas third parties may eliminate the service with little or no warning.

The major disadvantages of company processing centers are increased costs and collection float. The company has to dedicate personnel and equipment to the processing center. Check volume must be large to have a cost-efficient operation, as this represents a large capital investment. There could be a greater time lag between processing the items and depositing the checks than with a lockbox. Company processing center mail pickup times may be less frequent than those of lockbox banks and may not match mail arrival times at the post office. Company processing centers are likely to be located where the company has operations, not necessarily at a point to minimize float.

Outsourcing

In recent years, a number of banks have contracted with third parties (i.e., non-bank vendors) to handle the lockbox services they offer to corporate customers. This was first done for retail lockboxes, where the third party company could

---

Box 3-2
Electronic Receipt Formats

CCD: **Cash Concentration and Disbursement** entries are used for transactions involving businesses when it is only necessary to transmit the payment amount.

CCD+: **Cash Concentration and Disbursement Plus** is a modification to the CCD. It includes an additional record (and only one per transaction) to show additional remittance information. This format is used by the federal government for payments in its **Vendor Express** program.

CTP: **Corporate Trade Payment** entries are used for corporate payments when more than one additional addenda records are required. The CTP format, which calls for fixed-length records, can accommodate up to 4,990 addendum records in a single payment amount. Unlike the previous transaction format, receiving financial institutions (RFIs) are not required to accept this format.

CTX: **Corporate Trade Exchange** entries are similar to CTPs in that they accommodate up to 4,990 multiple addenda records. The CTX format was introduced as an improvement on the CTP format, so that files could be created with variable-length records. This format also conforms to the American National Standard (ANSI) X12.4 format, which is important for consistency in EDI payments.

---

provide a commodity-type service and, by offering the service to enough banks or other financial institutions (e.g., insurance companies), the company could enjoy economies of scale that their individual clients could not realize. This move to outside services has now spread to wholesale lockboxes as well.

Corporate Trade Payments

These electronic transmissions of payment and related invoice data are made through the banking system and/or the ACH. This type of payment offers the benefit of moving invoice information efficiently, as well as many of the same advantages and disadvantages of pre-authorized payments for moving funds. As more companies adopt EDI systems, the electronic transfer of funds should increase significantly.

Electronic receipts can come in a variety of transaction formats (see Box 3-2). Because the movement to convert payments to an electronic medium has often been initiated by the *paying* company rather than the *receiving* company, there hasn't been a consistency in which formats are used for the payments. The multiple number of formats has posed problems for some companies, especially smaller ones, as they have become involved in receiving electronic payments. As more banks become EDI capable, this problem should ease.

Net Settlement Systems

In several industries (e.g., airlines) where there are a large number of reciprocal payments among the major companies in the industry, the payments are netted out between companies on a predetermined date. Only the net amounts are actually transferred. This greatly reduces the number of transactions between the companies in the system. It was thought that tighter controls resulting from the Federal Reserve's payment risk reduction program would create more opportunities like this, but so far this has not been the case.

Consumer Payments

Funds can be received electronically through **point-of-sale** (POS) terminals (e.g., in department stores) or when a customer uses a debit card (e.g., at a supermarket or service station). The funds are transferred electronically from a customer's account into the company's account. This type of collection system has shown modest growth in recent years.

CONCENTRATION

Companies concentrate funds deposited at their collection banks so that the funds can be used effectively. How the funds are concentrated depends on the number of collection points and dollar amounts. The number of collection points, in turn, is determined by the extent of field banking vs. lockbox collections.

With field banking, a local bank receives cash or checks over the counter from a sales office or from other cash collection points of the firm. Although the systems can vary, most field banking systems have similar features:

- **Large number of banks**: Many geographically dispersed companies have hundreds of field banks. These banks are generally chosen for convenience, not for operational sophistication.
- **Use of small banks**: These banks often lack the sophistication of lockbox banks.

- **Small daily deposits**: These are small, especially when compared to daily deposits in lockbox banks.
- **Poor daily deposit and balance information**: Because the banks tend to be smaller, often a monthly statement is the only form of data available from the bank.
- **Limited use of bank services**: Field banks frequently provide only coin and currency, deposit, and transfer services and are rarely used for credit lines and other services.
- **Local deposits**: Deposits generally consist of cash or locally drawn checks. Currency is usually given immediate availability while local checks may take one business day to clear unless they are on-us items, which should receive immediate availability. In small banks, the distinction is seldom made between ledger and available balances.

On the other hand, lockbox systems usually entail concentrating from a small number of collection points to one or a few concentration points. For example, few corporations have systems of more than ten lockbox banks. The trend in recent years has been toward fewer lockbox banks for any given company. Lockbox banks are generally larger, more sophisticated banks with advanced information gathering and reporting capabilities. Daily balance and deposit reporting and detailed monthly account analyses are standard. Deposits tend to be much larger than typical field bank deposits. Lockbox banks are frequently used for credit lines and other specialized services. Hence, lockbox banks sometimes require large balances (or combinations of fees and balances). With checks, a significant portion of the daily deposit has delayed availability (generally one or two business days from date of deposit).

Recent developments in EDI and related electronic payment methods may reduce the need for field banking and/or lockbox systems. With electronic payments, a company's bank can be located anywhere because the remittance data do not have to be transported physically to a bank or to the company's offices. While still in the beginning stages, electronic payments offer substantial processing cost savings for most companies.

Once checks have been received and deposited at a company's bank, there are two basic methods used by corporations to achieve the concentration of funds — wire transfers and depository transfer checks (DTCs).

The choice of a concentration system depends on many factors, as cited earlier. Once chosen and established, it becomes routine and automatic, a regular procedure or aspect of the overall corporate cash management system. A company does not normally switch concentration systems often, since the disruption to routine, standard operating systems, and procedures is apt to cause more

Figure 3-3
Wire Concentration of Funds

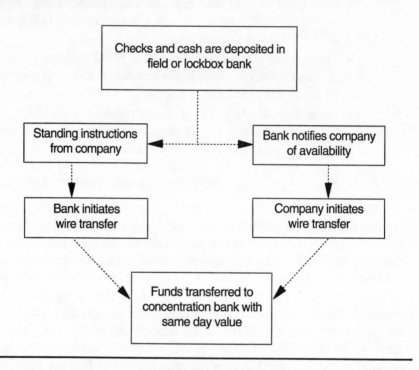

problems and resultant loss of funds than could be gained otherwise. The choice of DTC or wire transfer is not optional for each deposit on any given day. This should not be overlooked in the establishment of a funds concentration system. Wire transfers can be effectively used as a backup in emergency situations, such as when errors occur in the transmission of deposit information and funds would be left at the depositing location for another day or more. However, if such situations should occur very frequently, there may be serious problems with the structure of the concentration system or the performance of the depositing points in reporting accurately and on a timely basis.

Wire Transfers

Wire transfers (see Figure 3-3) are the logical alternative for concentrating large amounts. Either the field manager or headquarters staff may request the deposit bank to wire cash into the concentration bank. In some cases, the field or lockbox bank has standing instructions to transfer down to a specified level on a periodic basis. Headquarters could also send transfer instructions to the concentration bank to advise the deposit bank to wire in the funds (a **wire drawdown**). Deposit information can flow to headquarters through written deposit reports, third-party vendors, phone calls or data transmissions. Wires provide immediate availability and reduced excess balances at deposit banks. The primary disadvantage of this method is that it is the most expensive transfer mechanism, often costing upwards of $15-$20 per transfer.

Wire transfers offer advantages in special cases where large amounts of funds clear the same day and would otherwise be unavailable to the corporation until the next business day. Although these funds could be used for compensation purposes, many corporations may want to use the funds centrally, especially if the amount of funds exceeds the level required for compensation or if the corporation wishes to pay for bank services on a fee basis. Many banks can report such same-day clearances in time for the good funds to be moved to the company's concentration point that day. Obviously, if the depositing point also happens to be a major concentration point, the funds can be easily moved and used the same day.

Note that the decision to transfer should be based on the return gained by the transfer. That is, the company should more on the funds (or, conversely borrow less) than the all-in cost of the wire.

Depository Transfer Checks (Paper and Electronic)

There are several types of **depository transfer checks (DTCs)**.

Mail depository transfer checks are one of the oldest ways to concentrate funds for a low processing cost. The field manager makes a deposit into the field bank and at the same time prepares a DTC drawn on that bank, usually in the amount of the deposit, which is mailed to the concentration bank. The concentration bank grants one- or two-day availability and clears the DTC back to the deposit bank. Note that this alternative is applicable only to field management systems and is only used for very small deposits. It requires no deposit information gathering facility; the DTC is essentially the deposit report. It also has low administrative and transfer costs. On the other hand, mail, processing, and availability time delays mean that balances accumulate in the deposit account. In addition, there is no centralized control of transfers and less control over field managers.

Alternatives to mail DTCs all have one thing in common—they depend on local initiation but central creation of the DTC. The point where the DTC is

Figure 3-4
DTC Concentration of Funds

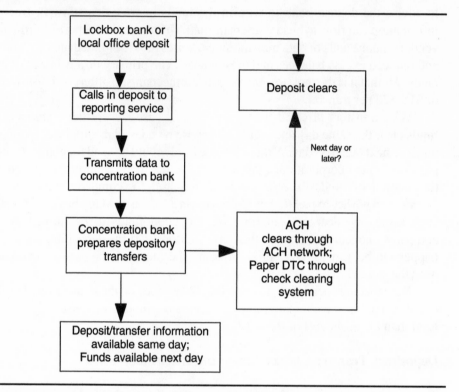

created separates one type from another. These alternatives are faster because there is no mail float. They offer centralized control of the amount and timing of transfer and provide some direction over field managers. They are relatively inexpensive (compared to wire transfers) and create lower excess balances than mailed DTCs. Conversely, they do not offer immediately available funds. They are more expensive than mailed DTCs and require a system to gather and to transmit deposit information.

Centrally initiated DTCs (see Figure 3-4) offer more efficient handling of field deposits or lockbox concentration. With this approach, the local manager makes a deposit at a local bank and notifies the concentration bank of the deposit. For lockbox deposits, the lockbox bank notifies the concentration bank. The concentration bank prepares the DTC, deposits it into the company's account, grants availability and clears the check back to the deposit bank. There are several ways the field unit or lockbox bank can send deposit information to the concentration bank:

- **Third-party vendor**: Several firms specialize in gathering deposit information from field units. Deposit data may be transmitted to both the concentration bank (for DTC preparation) and company headquarters (to follow-up on non-reporting units). In some cases, deposit data are sent to headquarters first for decisions on DTC amounts. This information is then phoned into the concentration bank for DTC preparation and deposit.
- **Through headquarters**: In some companies, managers call headquarters directly or transmit the deposit data to a headquarters computer via a remote terminal. Deposit data are then relayed to the concentration bank by headquarters.
- **Direct**: Some banks are able to receive deposit reports directly from field units or lockbox banks. DTCs are prepared from these reports.

An **electronic DTC (EDTC)** or **electronic depository transfer** is an ACH transaction used for concentration. The process of transmitting deposit information to the concentration bank is identical to that for DTCs. Instead of producing a DTC, however, the bank produces an ACH debit record and sends it into the ACH system, usually with next-day availability. Electronic depository transfers offer all the benefits of paper DTCs, plus later processing cut-offs. It also provides lower expenses than paper DTCs and simplified reconciliation and transfer systems. It has become the method of choice among most companies, especially larger ones or those with widespread geographic locations since most banks are now members of a local ACH association.

Since electronic depository transfers and paper DTCs can be used to concentrate funds on the next business day, they are easily the more cost-effective method. Their all-in costs usually range around ten percent of the wire transfer cost. Also, since most wire transfer systems either transfer out funds one day after deposit or only transfer funds when an economical balance is attained, they offer no real financial advantages.

Concentrating Weekend Deposits

For many retail companies, especially supermarkets or stores that handle large amounts of currency, concentrating funds that are deposited on the weekend is a special problem. To avoid building up excess balances, a company can use a wire transfer or anticipate the deposits by initiating an **anticipatory DTC** on Friday. The former alternative is costly while the latter is risky.

Anticipatory DTCs can be paper or, more likely, electronic depository transfers. They work in the same manner as described above. The difference is that a central manager initiates the transfers before the deposits are actually made so that the transfers clear on the same day the deposits are made. By studying the levels of deposits of currency and immediately available checks over time, a cash manager can estimate how much is likely to be deposited on any given weekend and can transmit instructions to the company's concentration bank to create transfers to move the funds from the deposit bank to the concentration bank. Usually, only a percentage (e.g., 75% of the expected level) of the anticipated deposits are moved.

An alternative is using the **weekend ACH** service offered by banks. This service provides the ability to concentrate cash with an ACH tape deposited Sunday evening. This may be significant for companies that have large weekend deposits. A weekend ACH transfer solves the problem at little cost and allows deposit information to be collected on Friday and Saturday and possibly part of Sunday, thereby reducing the risk of overdraft. Information gathering even on weekends is fairly inexpensive if a third-party vendor is used.

DISBURSEMENTS

Handling cash disbursements is one of the treasury manager's most important activities because it has offered a valuable financial benefit to the company. In most cases, the actual disbursements are handled by the accounts payable staff, which is usually a part of the company's accounting function. The treasury manager's involvement is with the funding of disbursement accounts. By using effective funding techniques, the treasury manager can extend disbursement float. In fact, when most treasury professionals speak of the *float game*, they are primarily talking about maximizing the use of disbursement float.

The corporate treasury manager's role in managing the funding of the disbursement accounts is very important in establishing an efficient cash management system. If left to local managers, disbursement funding will often become uncontrolled and generate significant excess operating balances at the banks used for disbursing. These balances are normally far in excess of any required levels and may represent substantial unused funds to the corporation. Companies often develop hybrid disbursement systems in which check-writing and account reconciliation are performed at the local level, but the disbursement banks are chosen, payees are assigned to banks, and disbursement accounts are funded centrally. This attempts to combine the advantages of both central control and funding with decentralized processing.

Figure 3-5
Staggered or delayed funding

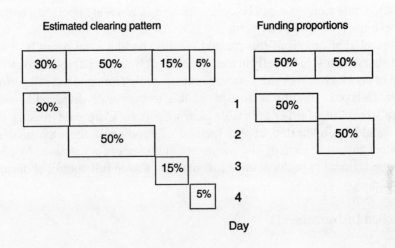

Estimated clearing pattern   Funding proportions

Disbursement Techniques

There are several basic techniques for controlling or using disbursement float. The three major techniques — **staggered funding, controlled disbursing**, and **zero balance accounts** — all involve timing the disbursement funding to minimize excess balances in the disbursement accounts. Each technique has its own distinct characteristics and application to the corporate cash management system. In addition, the three may exist simultaneously in any corporation, re-flecting different levels of cash management expertise or different operating circumstances.

Staggered or Delayed Funding

The simplest means of funding disbursement accounts is **staggered** or **delayed funding** (Figure 3-5). Originally, it was one of the original funding methods since perceptive corporate treasury managers noticed that they did not have to fund their disbursements on the day the checks were mailed. Staggering the funding by spreading the total deposit over several business days instead of transferring it on the day the checks were mailed allowed companies longer use of their funds. The approach uses a formula for transferring funds to the disbursement account (based on historical clearing patterns). To the extent that clearing patterns are predictable, this technique can be quite effective in reducing operating balances and is extremely simple to implement.

Typical applications of this method include funding local payrolls or other local disbursements. Especially in the case of weekly salary payroll accounts, the pattern of check clearance does not vary substantially from one payroll period to another. Delayed funding is also applicable to corporate dividend accounts, which also exhibit a fairly predictable clearing pattern. Corporate treasury managers should be interested in this method of funding if they are unable to implement any other form of disbursement funding or are constrained by corporate organizational or political impediments from taking full control of disbursement funding.

Controlled Disbursements

Although staggered funding offers some benefits, it is a fairly crude technique and is ineffective if the clearing patterns are not very predictable, which is often the case for major disbursement accounts. **Controlled disbursing** (shown in Figure 3-6) is such a technique. Originally, this type of funding was only available at banks with remote branches or those that were located in a remote section of the country. Consequently, this technique was first termed **remote disbursing**. As such, it was not enthusiastically embraced by most major corporations, which did not want to pay major disbursements from a geographical point with which they had no connection or wished to avoid the disreputable image of taking unfair advantage of the check processing system. However, most corporations were not really interested in absurdly elongated disbursement float, but they were interested in *controlling* that float. This was evidenced in the popular acceptance of controlled disbursing when the latter method was offered by major money center banks. Now it has become the individual bank cash management service most used by corporations and is offered by all major cash management banks.

The basic technique is simple; disbursement accounts are not funded until the day checks are presented against the account. The controlled disbursement account is located in a specific branch such that the clearance can be funded on the same day. The disbursement bank must receive its final cash letter of the day from the local Fed early in the morning so the checks can be sorted and the company notified of its funding requirement. Alternatively, if the bank does not physically receive the checks, it must be able to receive a computer transmission

Figure 3-6
Controlled Disbursements

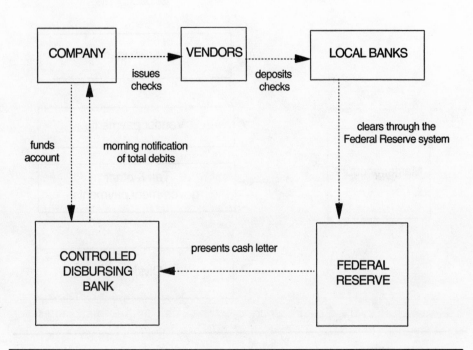

from the local Fed listing checks (or totals) to be presented. Same-day funding of presentments received after the initial presentment should be kept at a minimum. These presentments may arise from direct sends (cash letters from correspondent banks), from on-us checks received over the counter or from the second presentment by the Federal Reserve as part of its High Dollar Group Sort program. Note that the vast majority of controlled disbursement points are High Dollar Group Sort points.

Most banks currently offering controlled disbursement services can provide the majority of clearing information by late morning (usually no later than 11:00 A.M.) so that the corporation can still access the short-term credit markets. The second notification usually is made around or shortly after noon. If there is a problem with late presentments of disbursement clearings (the second notification), companies and their banks often work out a funding formula that is based on historical clearings (for the second notification). This type of funding can be

Figure 3-7
Zero Balance Account Arrangements

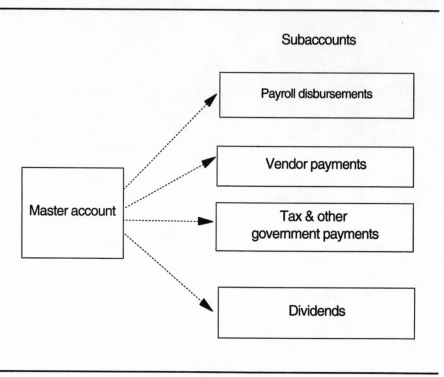

implemented for any number of corporate accounts, all of which can be funded with one transfer of funds.

Zero Balance Accounts

One of the major developments in corporate cash management has been the **zero balance account**. By using this technique, the corporate treasury manager has been able to lace together many diverse accounts at the same bank and establish an automatic control of funds flow to and from these accounts and a central concentration account. A typical zero balance account arrangement is shown in Figure 3-7. Although not shown in the illustration, accounts can be zero balanced either way; that is, deposit accounts can automatically upstream funds and disbursement accounts can be funded automatically. The main advantages of such arrangements are the elimination of excess balances in the operating accounts, the elimination of misguided transfers among various operating accounts, and the reduction of local bank balance monitoring efforts. Zero balance arrangements are effective tools in consolidating cash management activities at a specific bank. They alter the target balance levels in that they transfer all activity to one central account. This, however, is not an unpleasant situation for most treasury managers as they tend to target by bank rather than by individual account.

Payable Through Drafts

In the early days of cash management many companies used **payable through drafts** to improve disbursement control and disbursement float. Such drafts are similar to checks but are payable by the individual company, not its bank. The drafts clear back to an issuing bank that, in turn, presents them to the issuing company for review and approval before any payments are completed. The review period is typically 24 hours. Drafts are not actually checks, but Federal Reserve Regulation CC has set specific guidelines and restrictions on payable through drafts with the effect that they are essentially handled just like checks. As a result, they offer little in the way of disbursement float improvement.

There are, of course, situations in which payable through drafts can be utilized as effective tools. In instances where local issuance of payments are involved, they can offer effective control over the dispensation of corporate funds. Local insurance agents or salesmen may be the issuers of such items, and a system of review and control may be necessary. In any case, drafts should not be used for normal cash disbursements. These items should rightfully be treated as collection items by the depositing bank with the lack of credit to the receiving customer until the item clears back to the issuing party and is approved. Thus, the receiving party has not really received payment until the actual review period has expired. This may affect the regular collection process and cause credit problems for the issuer if drafts are used.

Multiple Drawee Checks

Multiple drawee checks (or **payable if desired checks**) are checks that will be honored by a bank other than the issuing bank. Both bank names appear on these checks, which are primarily used for payroll in states that require employees to be paid by checks drawn in that state (e.g., California and Florida), although the issuing bank's information appears on the MICR line.

Establishing a Disbursement System

Setting up a disbursement system follows the same procedures used in setting up a collection system. First, possible disbursement banks are identified. This group typically includes banks already providing the company with substantial business, although this is not always the case. New banks that offer better use of disbursement float may also be considered.

Next, vendors and suppliers are grouped, usually by their location (or the location where they ask to be paid). Based on either a rough estimate of the number of checks and the amount to be disbursed over a typical paying period (e.g., a month) or a detailed disbursement study, it is possible to estimate the float from each payee group and potential disbursement bank. Then, based on the cost savings and other qualitative factors, such as the existing relationship with the potential banks and the effect of changing disbursement banks on vendor relationships, the final step is to select the disbursement system with the highest net benefit.

Relationships with vendors and suppliers may be harmed if the increase in float is obtained at their expense, that is, by increasing their collection float. Also, it should be noted that vendors and suppliers may not sit idly by and maintain the same collection location. Just as the paying company studies its disbursement and collection locations, so do its vendors. If the disbursement change is too drastic, the vendor may tighten its collection float, which reduces the anticipated benefits of the disbursement changes.

Note that these discussions have assumed that maximizing disbursement float is only pursued for payables accounts, not payroll accounts. Most companies believe that it is not appropriate to gain disbursement float at the expense of its employees.

Electronic Disbursements

Companies have been increasing their use of electronic means of making payments. As mentioned previously, there are several formats used for making such payments. The typical formats for include the formats shown for electronic receipts (see Box 3-2) as well as the **Prearranged Payment and Deposit (PPD** and **PPD+)** formats, which are used for direct deposit of payroll. The PPD+ format includes one addendum record.

Direct Deposit of Payroll

Payroll was one of the earliest examples of staggered funding. It is also an area where electronic disbursement through direct deposit has been well established.

While it is an advantage to minimize the number of payroll accounts, most companies like to offer their employees the benefit of local check cashing. An alternative to creating numerous local accounts is to use an electronic direct deposit of payroll service.

For companies with diverse employee locations, payrolls have been a tough operating problem. Drawing paychecks on local banks has been the alternative used most often, and the treasury manager or local financial manager transfers funds to these accounts by payday or on a staggered funding scheme. With a great number of these accounts, this process is inefficient at best and usually creates substantial excess balances in these small local banks. Some companies have consolidated their payrolls into one major bank to keep the excess funds in one central place and utilize other forms of disbursement funding. However, local paycheck cashing privileges must be arranged, and they usually require compensating balances or the equivalent. As an alternative, some companies have used multiple drawee checks (described above) for eliminating excess local balances created by local payroll accounts.

Direct deposit of payroll offers an electronic alternative to either of these. The payroll system run generates data that are transmitted through the ACH network to the individual employee's bank account. Obviously, the employee's bank must be a member of an ACH somewhere, but the end points are tested thoroughly prior to any real transmissions. This service is attractive to the company with many widespread paying locations, with employees who travel frequently, or with a need to transfer payrolls to local employees quickly at relatively low cost. The company gives up the disbursement float generated by the paper-based paychecks, but this may be unproductive for the company in any case if it remains in local payroll accounts.

Freight Payments

Freight payments represent a large percentage of disbursements for most manufacturing companies. Banks and third-party vendors offer freight payment services that, in addition to effecting payment for the company, provide data bases that assist in determining efficient distribution methods. Freight payment plans, historically an intensive paper-based system, have become more automated as more companies adopt EDI systems.

ACH Debits

Many corporate treasury managers long resisted granting any outside party (vendors, et al.) access to debit their disbursement account automatically with an **ACH debit**. What electronic paying was done was made by means of an ACH credit initiated by the paying company. In recent years, however, this has changed. Although many EDI/EFT experts often extolled the advantages of ACH debits, it was a movement by state governments (initially, Indiana) that required electronic payment of state taxes that accelerated the acceptance of ACH debits. It should be noted that many companies do not allow automatic debit to their main accounts, but have set up separate disbursement accounts for automatic ACH debits. It is expected that ACH debit growth will be strong for some time.

Bank Account Reconciliation

A bank service related to disbursements is **account reconciliation**. This service is offered by most banks and is useful for accounts with relatively high volumes of check disbursing activity such as payroll or disbursement accounts. It is also used when the company does not have sufficient staff to perform the function in-house. Banks offer a range of reconciliation services, ranging from full to partial.

The basic process for full reconciliation is very simple. The company sends a record of its checks drawn to the bank, and the bank matches them with the checks that have cleared. Much of this data-matching is done by computer. The company usually receives a listing of all checks paid and those issued but not yet cleared. These reports are typically used by the accounting function.

Partial reconciliations represent variations in the full service. Companies may be interested in these partial reconciliations when they have their own in-house routines and only need check clearance data from the bank. Some banks do offer the reconciliation software as a product. This allows companies to do their own reconciliations, usually on a personal computer.

Some banks can calculate the average clearance time for a company's checks in the reconciling process. This can be useful in establishing funding patterns or in providing cash estimates. However, the computation depends on accuracy of the issue date submitted by the company to the bank. If this field is not accurate, the resulting clearance times will be invalid.

Many banks are offering a newer service that ties reconciliation to disbursement clearing. With this service, the company provides a file (on tape, diskette, or by transmission) of its check disbursements to the bank. The bank verifies clearing checks against this file and rejects any items that do not appear on the file. One of the primary objectives of this service is to alleviate the risks of check fraud.

Figure 3-8
Cash Position Management

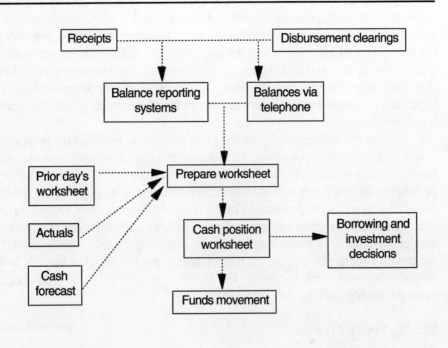

CASH POSITION MANAGEMENT

Cash position management is the focal point of cash flow management; it represents the core function of the company's funding activities. Cash position management determines whether internal sources are available to fund the company's cash requirements. In most companies, the cash position must be determined daily by accumulating the inflows and outflows throughout the company's banking and cash management systems. This typically takes the form of a worksheet, although sometimes this sheet may resemble the back of an envelope.

The essential aspects of cash position management are shown in Figure 3-8. The preparation of the worksheet is shown as the central focus for the activity, with the prior day's sheet being recycled to start the new day's sheet. The link between the prior one and the actual results is a reconciling procedure; that is, the treasury manager must review actual results with the worksheet to determine that everything that was supposed to occur did. The information from the company's banking network is entered on the new worksheet, as is the current day's cash estimate. The cash position can then be computed, and transactions can be initiated to fill deficits or invest excesses. Fund transfers are also triggered by the computation, and appropriate actions are taken. This activity, however mundane it may appear, is a vital and extremely time-sensitive one. Actions must be taken in a short period of time, and the cash position management procedures must be organized in a logical and efficient manner to function smoothly in this dynamic, hectic environment.

Another reason for managing the cash position is to minimize borrowings and/or to maximize investments. Here again, the use of internal funds to avoid having to borrow externally is important to the company's profitability. Similarly, mobilizing excess funds and investing them for as long as possible are positive financial actions for the company. Timing is everything, however. Obtaining cash management information too late in the day or after a key investment or borrowing decision has been made is as bad as not obtaining the information at all. For the treasury manager, this means that obtaining the information as early in the business day as possible (or, better yet, as much before the business day begins) eases the timing crunch.

Making Funds Transfers

Although it could be considered as a part of both cash gathering and disbursing, funds transfers can be considered part of managing the company's cash position. The major reasons for fund transfer activities are to maintain target balances or to fund operational (usually disbursement) needs, whether controlled by the central treasury manager or requested by another company location.

Target Balances

To manage bank balances effectively, the treasury manager must establish and maintain an effective target balance system for the overall banking network. This is true no matter what form of compensation is undertaken, because, at worst, the target for any given bank could be zero. For the purposes of this discussion it is assumed that compensation has taken the form of balances. Figure 3-9 illustrates the major aspects of target balance management.

Two basic activities are associated with bank target balance management: setting (and resetting) bank target balances and monitoring daily performance against the target. The target for each bank reflects the overall compensation for all activity with the bank, including credit and non-credit services. Credit services

Figure 3-9
Target Balance Management

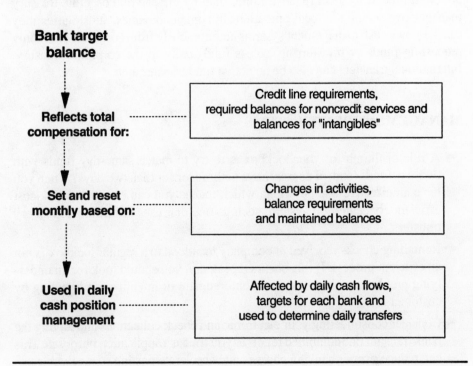

are usually set at a percentage of the line of credit, and the required balance changes only when the credit facility changes. Non-credit services, on the other hand, vary with the activity in the account; therefore, they are more difficult to measure on an ongoing basis. However, the process of reviewing bank account analyses monthly and reevaluating the overall target for each bank can indicate the need for changes in the targets to reflect any recent changes in activity. Obviously, the review process depends on the timely receipt of account analyses and the ability to process them quickly so that the overall performance in maintaining the bank target can be measured.

Funding Accounts

Maintaining target balances at major banks often requires a daily decision as to whether funds should be moved in or out of key accounts at each major bank. Similarly, operating banks usually require daily transfer decisions for covering clearings of payroll and accounts payable disbursement fundings or for concentrating deposits at a major bank. Short-term investments or debt repayments require fund transfers as well. Internally, local plant operating or payroll accounts are often funded by local request, rather than by the central corporate treasury manager overseeing the local operation. In some companies, subsidiaries may run their own cash management systems autonomously from corporate staff, only requesting funds or transferring excess funds daily to the corporate treasury. International transfers can also be an active fund transfer area.

MANAGEMENT REVIEW ITEMS

➡ A rule of thumb for your lockbox is to try to match same-day funds with two-day funds (and, of course, have nothing longer than two days). Then you have an effective one-day float, which means you can establish a low-cost efficient concentration system, such as one that uses electronic depository transfers.

➡ Remailing checks received at company locations to a regular lockbox is not an efficient process. If this occurs repeatedly, you should look for an underlying problem, such as lax credit enforcement or intentional misrouting by customers.

➡ Consider consolidating your electronic and check collections and having the bank transmit one combined report to you for cash application purposes. This can reduce overall banking charges and accelerate posting of receivables.

➡ Consider using a lockbox network as an enhancement to a single lockbox system, not as a replacement for multiple lockbox points.

➡ If you have established a concentration system that uses electronic depository transfers or paper DTCs, you should be prepared to use wire transfers as back-up in cases of errors. All collection points should be set up on your funds transfer initiation system, grouped together if the system offers such a feature, so they can be accessed automatically and will incur the cheapest bank service charge.

➡ If you are using wire transfers to concentrate funds from many locations, you should consider using wire drawdowns, which may be priced more attractively than centrally initiated wires and may be easier to use if you have limited personnel to initiate wires.

➡ If you are considering using anticipatory DTCs for concentrating local deposits, you should schedule a review of the arrangements with your auditors (internal and/or external, as appropriate) and representatives from the bank.

➡ Monitor the amounts of each of your controlled disbursement notifications, looking for such things as average amount of the first notification, the average time the second notification is received, and any regular peak days (of the week).

➡ If you have operations nationwide or over a wide geographic expanse, you should consider using multiple drawee checks to consolidate your payroll into one bank account. This will entail arranging with one or more local banks to honor your payroll checks, but is often cheaper than using many local banks for payrolls.

➡ If you are planning to make electronic payments, you should be sure that your systems department or systems analyst is supplied with full technical specifications and formats for possible ACH transaction types.

➡ If you are planning to make ACH debits (e.g., for tax payments), consider establishing a separate bank account for this purpose. Then, depending on how easily the payments are handled, you can decide to make this account a zero balance account at a later date.

CHAPTER 4

CASH MANAGEMENT STRATEGIES

Effective cash management does not happen by accident. Too often, financial managers have focused on the more tactical issues associated with cash management, such as techniques for better cash collections or improved use of disbursement float, rather than considering the bigger picture. A cash management strategy provides the appropriate framework for the pieces of the cash management puzzle. Without it, a company's cash management function becomes reactive, undervalued, and inefficient. Companies that have successfully developed and maintained sophisticated cash management functions have done so because their strategies have been simply formulated.

This chapter addresses the fundamental parts of a successful cash management strategy:

- Managing cash flows
- Managing working capital
- The impact of EDI
- Analyses and decision support
- Relationship management
- The global cash management environment
- Formulating treasury management policies

MANAGING CASH FLOWS

Cash flows come in more than one medium: paper (i.e., checks) and electronics. Although their primary focus has been how to increase their effective use of paper-based checks, corporate treasury managers have to consider how to handle both kinds of payment flows in the current changing environment. Handling flows involves cash collections, concentration, and disbursements.

Collections (Paper-Based Flows)

While the basic design of a collection system depends upon whether the funds are received over the counter or in the mail and whether the funds are received at company locations or can be directed to a third party (e.g., a bank), all collection systems have to satisfy a basic group of objectives (shown in Box 4-1).

The nature of customer payments has an influence on a company's collection system. A primary distinction in collection systems is whether the payments are largely wholesale or retail, although many companies have both kinds. In the former, corporate customers generate payments in response to company invoices with possible adjustments in the paid amount because of allowable discounts, returns, or allowances. Often, wholesale check payments cover more than one invoice. Thus, a collection system characterized by a majority of wholesale check payments will focus on float reduction and the accurate and timely handling of information related to the payments.

Retail payments are usually made by consumers or small businesses. Retail checks are generally much smaller in amount (per check) than wholesale checks. They typically represent recurring payments (e.g., installment payments) for an ongoing financial transaction, service, or single invoice. There are also many more retail payments, and, accordingly, processing cost is a more important consideration in system design than float reduction.

Concentration

Cash concentration, which is essentially moving funds from many accounts with smaller balances into one or a few cash pools, has several basic objectives:

- **Simplified cash management**: An effective concentration system can enable the treasury manager to focus on one balance (or at least a few) for the sources of the company's liquidity. This also provides better control over the company's banking network and can reduce the number of accounts that need to be actively monitored.

- **Pooled funds**: Creating larger amounts of funds from many smaller accounts makes it possible for a treasury manager to obtain more attractive investments or avoid needless short-term borrowing.

- **Decreased excess balances**: Concentration systems help reduce excess balances in a company's banking network.

Box 4-1
Objectives of Collection Systems

Mobilizing funds: A collection system has as its primary goal getting funds from the company's payors into the company's banking system as effectively and economically as possible. For this reason, collections and concentration must be fully integrated.

Updating accounts receivables: Customer accounts receivable files must be updated on a timely and accurate basis. If not, there may be a loss of further sales as well as a deterioration in customer relations. Accordingly, collections must be effectively coordinated with the credit management function and, if separate, the accounts receivable processing function.

Accessing deposit information: A collection system should provide timely, accurate cash receipt information and the resulting impact of receipts on bank balances. The information should be easy to integrate with other company information systems. A collection system is a major part of treasury management information systems.

Providing audit trails: A collection system should provide appropriate control points in coordination with the company's internal and external auditors.

- **Lower funds transfer expense**: Concentration systems, if designed properly, should optimize the costs of transferring funds between company accounts.

Corporate treasury managers usually have a choice in methods of concentration: wire transfer or depository transfer check (electronic or paper). The former method is used to move large blocks of funds that are immediately available or accumulate as good funds over time. The latter method, especially the electronic version, is used to move smaller amounts of funds routinely. It is the method of choice usually because it is economical, easy to establish, and does not require constant intervention, as wire transfers often do.

Determining the optimal break-even point is relatively simple. It is the amount of transferred funds that will provide a return better than the transfer cost. Since the all-in costs for DTCs are far less than the full costs of wire transfers, DTCs can be used for moving smaller amounts of funds. In deciding which method to use, corporate treasury managers should use their typical banking costs and the internal opportunity cost of funds (e.g., short-term investment or borrowing rate).

Corporate treasury managers do not often mix methods. For example, if an electronic DTC system is appropriate for most points (i.e., the amounts of the deposits are small), then it will probably be used for *all* deposit transfers unless there are significant exception situations. If one or a few points show substantial amounts of immediately available funds (i.e., funds that are good on the *same* day that they are deposited), the treasury manager may decide to set those points up to wire out the good funds daily. However, too many exceptions ruin the simplicity and efficiency of the collection system.

An advantage in using DTCs is that they can usually concentrate funds with the same timing as wire transfers if the deposits take at least one day to clear. In such situations, corporate treasury managers usually wire out the cleared funds the day *after* deposit. Since a DTC is created the *same* day as the deposit and usually takes only one day to clear, it has the same effect as the wire — having the funds available at the company's concentration bank on the next business day after deposit — at a fraction of the wire transfer cost. In addition, since most bank DTC services provide transfer information late in the same day as the deposit, the corporate treasury manager has time to react to problem situations before losing use of deposited funds. For example, if a location has not reported its deposit by the end of the day or by an earlier deadline, the corporate treasury manager can still use other means to move funds (e.g., wire transfer on the next business day) if he or she determines that there are funds in the local deposit account.

Cash Disbursements

Disbursement systems are linked to the company's cash collection and concentration systems. As part of the company's overall cash flow system, disbursement banks should be located at efficient points (i.e., where information can be managed efficiently and where funds transfers are possible without excess expense). To be effective, disbursements should be considered as a system.

Disbursement system design is influenced by corporate structure and objectives. Some of the most relevant aspects are:

- Resolving conflicts between disbursement float and relations with payees
- The degree of centralization in the company's banking system
- The degree of local autonomy

A major influence in designing an effective disbursement system is a company's policy regarding disbursement float. It is critical to determine if the company wishes to extend the float to its maximum, which may be at the expense of the company's vendors or other payees, or to maintain strong vendor/supplier relations by paying locally or by using a bank to which checks can clear quickly. It should be noted that most companies do not have formal policies regarding disbursement float, nor do they attempt to maximize disbursement float in employee payroll or shareholder dividend accounts. Such policy decisions should be discussed with senior financial decision-makers and local financial managers so that an appropriate system can be developed.

Another key factor is the degree of centralization in the company's paying organization as well as in its banking network. For instance, check-writing, account reconciliation, and other activities are usually performed at a local level in decentralized disbursement systems. Checks may not be drawn on a local bank unless the bank is a major part of the company's overall banking network. If the local manager has full autonomy, checks will probably be drawn on local banks. The primary advantages of this latter arrangement are better relationships with local vendors or suppliers (because checks are drawn on local banks) and an increased ability to resolve payment disputes quickly. However, this may also result in idle local disbursement account balances or possibly some difficulty in estimating daily clearings or in using effective disbursement tools (e.g., controlled disbursing). Also, if the local operation is paying many suppliers that are not located in the local area, the advantages of using a local bank are questionable.

In centralized disbursement systems, check-writing, reconciliation, and other disbursement activities are usually performed at a central location. It is important that optimal disbursement banks are chosen and that payees are paid from the appropriate disbursement accounts in accordance with the company's overall cash management strategy. Advantages of these centralized systems include:

- Minimal bank and internal company costs
- No idle cash balances at local banks
- Better control over disbursement float

On the other hand, since local invoices may have to be sent to the central location for processing, payments to suppliers may be delayed, and the company may miss attractive payment discounts. Relationships with suppliers may be adversely affected because their collection float may increase and any payment disputes may not be resolved quickly.

Managing Disbursement Systems

The most basic method of managing a disbursement account is probably through staggered or delayed funding, which uses a formula for transferring funds to the account. The transfer amount is usually based on historical clearing patterns. As long as these patterns continue to be predictable, this method can be simple, effective, and economical in controlling disbursement account balances.

Many treasury managers cannot accurately forecast the amount of daily clearings against disbursement accounts. In this case, using zero balance accounts (ZBAs) or controlled disbursement accounts can mitigate this weakness. Typical uses of ZBAs are for divisional accounts payable payments and for other types of payments, such as payroll and stock dividends. These accounts are useful because the treasury manager can control the balances and funding of a single master account without having to worry about funding all the subaccounts that are tied to that master. ZBA master and subaccounts are almost always managed through branches of a single bank. This reduces idle balances and eliminates unnecessary multiple transfers, which can be a significant cost savings. Also, with this approach, local financial managers are able to retain disbursement authority. With controlled disbursement, the early notification of the day's funding requirement helps eliminate idle balances by giving the treasury manager sufficient time to invest surplus funds or to obtain additional funds while the money markets are still active and investment rates are attractive.

Originally, banks, especially those with branches located in geographically isolated locations (**remote points**) offered significant float gains if a company used the bank for its disbursements. However, this "technique," which took advantage of soft spots in the check-clearing system has been discouraged by the continuing improvements in the check clearing system and by a shift in corporate emphasis to information management. The Federal Reserve has also effectively outlawed the practice of "true" **remote disbursement**. It has defined remote disbursement as

> ... *Arrangements that are designed to delay the collection and final settlement of checks. Users of delayed disbursement arrangements draw checks on institutions located substantial distances from the payee or on institutions located outside of Federal Reserve cities where alternate and more efficient payment arrangements are available.*

Electronic Payments

One of the most debated topics in payments systems is the relatively sluggish pace at which corporations and individuals are moving from paper to electronic payments. There are several reasons for the slow growth of EFT/ACH transactions. In the first place, EFT is not challenging a static or inefficient check system. In fact, the paper-based, check payment system is still growing. Furthermore, for

EFT to grow, the float inherent with check payments has to become a non-issue. This float is still regarded by too many companies as a tremendous benefit.

Consumers and many companies prefer paying by check. Also, paying by check has been recognized as a legal method of payment (possibly the preferred method). Checks have been recognized by the Uniform Commercial Code (UCC) for many years, while EFT has only been recognized since the development of Article 4A in 1990. Finally, the lack of generally agreed-upon standards or too many confusing types of transactions have inhibited the growth of EFT.

The ACH network may be at the same critical juncture that automated teller machines (ATMs) were in the early 1980's. For ACH use, banks must find ways to use the network to competitive advantage as they did with ATMs. They must understand the corporate customer's needs, educate customers further and then go out and meet the customer's needs.

Applications of Electronic Payments
The fundamentals of EFT are simple and straightforward. The automated clearing house (ACH) network allows regional ACHs to interface electronically with each other, thereby linking a member of any clearing house with other members.

Transactions can be **value dated**. This concept of value dating is very different from value dating as used in non-domestic payments systems, which is discussed in Chapter 12. The value dated or warehoused transactions are transmitted to the system prior to the day when the funds will be available to the recipient. This offers attractive options to companies that make transfers for similar or predetermined amounts on a regular basis.

For example, by using direct deposit of payroll services, companies can pay their employees around the country electronically without worrying about physically delivering paychecks or setting up special check-cashing arrangements at local banks. Other electronic applications of interest to corporations include electronic depository transfer checks (for cash concentration) and routine funds transfers for corporate trade payments.

Some applications are used by fewer companies. These include preauthorized debit and credit transfers, utilized by large insurance companies for collection of monthly premium payments (debits) and payments to annuity holders (credits). Several other companies have also begun to use the ACH network for preauthorized credit transfers to local dealers as part of an overall EDI strategy, although not without some problems. Other companies have also begun to use the ACH for payment of periodic dividend payments to shareholders and routine payments to retirement and pension fund recipients, in a similar manner as the U.S. government has done with monthly social security payments.

EFT Myths and Influences

There are a few myths surrounding EFT, and they may also be partially responsible for its slow development. The first one is that corporations are "obsessed"
with the generation and extension of float and will resist anything that works
against this process. Although this may be the case in a few companies, most
corporations already are involved in EFT to the extent that they are frequent users
of wire transfers. Many companies have also converted their cash concentration
systems to the ACH network. In addition, many companies routinely depend on
electronic transfers for international payments.

Another myth involves the costs of EFT and paper-based functions. Unfortunately, many well-meaning analysts have produced studies showing that EFT
is considerably cheaper than paper with little in the way of actual experience or
verification of the cost factors used. This has created a great deal of skepticism.
Empirical work in this area is necessary to improve the quality and reasonability
of approaching EFT on a cost-benefit basis. In addition, EFT will probably
compare more favorably if the general value of the use of funds (a company's
internal cost of funds or opportunity rate of investment) remains at a low level.
Then, EFT and paper systems can be evaluated on a level playing field (i.e., not
skewed by a high value associated with the float).

One common myth concerns employee acceptance of any electronic service.
Many companies reported early resistance to any such arrangement. However,
much of this response seemed to have been created by a general lack of understanding by the employees. Many companies have successfully implemented
direct deposit of payroll, for instance, by replacing costly mailing procedures with
electronic transfers. In such cases, the employees were indifferent to the means
of receipt because they did not personally handle their paychecks anyway.

In assessing the feasibility of EFT for the company, the treasury manager
may encounter several counterbalancing forces. These forces, may be either real
or perceived (by the treasury manager). In either case they will influence any
decision regarding EFT. The first one, economic impact, is the natural starting
point. The second force, suspicions about technology, reflects some of the
skepticism or mistrust of automation still present in the treasury departments of
many companies. Salesmanship and bank relations can become larger forces if
not handled effectively and need to be considered seriously. Finally, the auditors'
acceptance and understanding can exert much influence over the decision if the
audit group does not have a good grasp of EFT principles or the potential
application has not been reviewed with them in some detail before final design
has been completed. The familiarity of both internal and external auditors with
EFT and with treasury management fundamentals has increased substantially in
recent years, so this force may not be as important in the future.

In summary, EFT has shown signs of moving from its slow-growth posture and should develop at a much faster rate in the near future. The impact of rising costs for paper-based systems, reduced value of paper-based float, improved technical and data security capabilities, and more efficient clearing options for the ACH network should serve as catalysts in that development.

MANAGING WORKING CAPITAL

Historically, treasury managers have spent much of their time managing a small portion of the cash flow timeline. Typically, they are occupied with the payment portion and are involved with banks and the payment system. However, improved management of corporate payables and receivables can provide substantial savings to the corporation.

It is important for the treasury manager to develop an appropriate cash management discipline. The objective is to broaden the scope from the narrow *cash management* concept to the broader one of *working capital management*. The key targets are corporate payables and receivables, but any corporate area that is involved in making or receiving payments could be ''attacked.''

Treasury managers have focused more on receivables than payables because there has been a stronger link to receivables through the credit function, which is often a part of the treasury function. On the other hand, there is rarely a comparable link to accounts payable; it almost always reports to the accounting (controllership) function. Treasury managers should still have regular contact with the payables managers, and they should use this contact to improve the cash management efficiency of the payables function.

Making changes is not easy. Typically, purchasing managers work hard to negotiate the best price and quality of the products and services that the company needs. However, they often do not negotiate the payment terms. The treasury manager should get involved as the payment expert to make sure that the purchasing manager understands the financial tradeoffs of purchasing decisions (e.g., the effect of taking the discount or paying on net terms).

There are a number of questions that should be answered before going too far in trying to review procedures and policies. Are the company's financial systems centralized or decentralized? Who is responsible for payables and receivables? Who makes the decisions to pay or allows customers extra time to pay? It also is a good idea to determine where they report - to the accounting side or the treasury side. This will be helpful if changes are recommended.

Payables

The objective in improving the company's payables management is to extend the current payment period (or even use all of it) or to increase discount terms. One fundamental requirement is a good description of the current system, procedures, and policies (if any) for handling vendor invoices. A standard questionnaire or checklist is best for this purpose. A sample is shown in Box 4-2.

One technique to improve payables payment time is to negotiate extended terms to reflect transit time delay. Often, a vendor will be flexible in this area, although the vendor's credit manager may not know how long the transit time is for specific shipments. In such cases, it is beneficial to study the process beforehand to estimate transit time or offer to accept an average transit time delay. This approach can add time to the payment due date for these items while still allowing the payor to stay within credit terms.

The last item to determine is whether the company's payables processors have a **preferred vendor list**. This is a list of vendors that get paid early, sometimes as soon as their invoices or statements are received. Usually, this has been the result of overly aggressive collectors, but such lists exist in many companies.

Paying too early costs the company use of the funds. It is unlikely that a preferred vendor list can be eliminated, but it should be possible to shorten it by questioning why certain vendors are on it. In addition to an early-pay list, the treasury manager should look for vendors that are receiving their payments by courier. This extra expense should be justified, as should the accelerated clearing.

Receivables

The major objectives here should be enforcing terms, collecting payments sooner, and measuring outstanding receivables more effectively. Timing is very important in receivables processing. This includes the timing of:

- Invoicing (preparation and distribution)
- Posting of invoices to receivables
- Initial collection efforts
- Follow-up collection efforts
- Payment receipt

Many concerns about receivables processing will be the mirror image of payables concerns. For instance, the treasury manager should review the com-

Box 4-2
Checklist for Vendor Invoice Handling

Please provide the breakdown of invoices:
_____ % by mail
_____ % hand delivered
_____ % by EDI

What department (or group) first receives the invoices?

How are invoices logged in or controlled?

As invoices are being processed, how is the due date or payment date determined?

Who is responsible for matching up the invoice to shipping or receiving documents and purchase orders?

Is the due date for payment taken from the invoice date or determined from the receipt of the goods or the receipt of invoice?

What type of review process is currently in place to ensure that the vendor terms are met?

List the names of vendors who are on an exception or preferred list (i.e., who receive preferential treatment when it comes to payment of invoices).

Who is responsible for answering telephone inquiries from vendors pertaining to the status of invoices?

Have any vendors indicated that they will permit payment of their invoice beyond the terms indicated on the individual invoice (i.e., internal grace periods or processing time)?

On how many days during the average week are checks prepared?

When checks are mailed to vendors, at what time during the day are they delivered to the post office?

Does the mail room or mailing agent/department sort the vendor checks or envelopes in any special way?

Describe the internal procedure that has been established for those special circumstances where checks are not mailed but instead are given to someone within your organization to be held for pickup or distributed by hand to the vendor.

If checks are prepared and held overnight for an extended period of time, where are they held and who is responsible for their safekeeping?

(continued on next page)

Box 4-2 (continued)
Checklist for Vendor Invoice Handling

What procedures are in place to ensure that checks are received by vendors in a timely fashion (i.e., within their terms of payment)?

Describe the treatment of the checks (i.e., dollar amount), when checks are held over for a month-end or fixed-cycle reporting period.

Describe the auditing procedures that are in place to ensure that your company/subsidiary/division is paying vendors in a timely fashion or within the terms of payment shown on either your purchase order, the vendor's acceptance of your purchase order, or the invoice.

If payments are made to vendors earlier than the stated terms or later than those terms, who within the organization has the authority to authorize the abnormal payment?

Are vendors paid via manual checks? If so, what type(s) of vendor?

Describe the backup system currently in place if you are unable to prepare computer checks because of system failure.

Are checks ever delivered to vendors by Express Mail, et al., (such as overnight delivery)? If so, please explain.

What is the average length of time between month-end cutoff and actual reconciliation of the checks issued during the month? What department has this responsibility?

What type of account reconciliation is performed (i.e., full, partial, from a bank, or internally reconciled)?

Please describe how your accounts payable/vendor payment process could be improved to make it more efficient or more responsive to your vendors by meeting their needs for timely payment.

---

pany's policies regarding grace periods, transit time extensions, and anticipation discounts.

Delving into payables and receivables processing isn't easy. It's often moving onto the turf of another department. However, as treasury managers look for bigger float issues to tackle, they will have to broaden their horizons. There are much larger float issues involved in payables and receivables than in payments alone. Marginal improvements can bring big returns to the company. In addition, understanding how payables and receivables are being handled is vital information for the future — when electronic data interchange or other payment technologies will be common practice.

THE IMPACT OF ELECTRONIC DATA INTERCHANGE

Electronic data interchange (EDI) is changing how companies do business. With new inventory management techniques and widespread computer-to-computer links to facilitate the order entry process, companies are no longer mired in a growing mountain of paper. Although the main savings in switching to EDI lie in the non-treasury areas of the company, EDI can have an impact on treasury and cash management. Selecting the method of payment to settle EDI transactions should involve the treasury manager. It is helpful to differentiate between *EDI* and *financial EDI* and between *financial EDI* and *EFT*.

EDI refers to *all* information that is exchanged in computer-readable form between two trading partners. This does not necessarily involve a bank unless it is one of the trading partners. Examples of EDI items include purchase orders, remittance details, and regular invoices or statements. **Financial EDI,** on the other hand, involves banks because it encompasses the information that is exchanged between a company and its bank. Examples of financial EDI are bank account statements and transaction confirmations. **EFT** is more restrictive yet. It involves the exchange of information between banks (not companies directly) resulting in the transfer of value from one party to another. Typical EFT applications include direct deposit of payroll, corporate trade payments, preauthorized payments, and regular wire transfers.

Most corporate treasury managers know that EFT means replacing their paper check with an ACH transaction or other electronic equivalent. Most also know that EDI means replacing the accompanying paper payment advice with an electronic equivalent. However, they must determine how to assess whether EFT/EDI is right for their companies. This entails considering the basic costs and benefits of EFT/EDI and identifying the key decision points.

Costs to Consider

Although costs may differ from one company to another, there are a number of costs that are common to most companies. These include:

- **Setup:** These include exploring the EFT/EDI alternatives as well as converting internal systems, such as billing, receivables, and payables, to create or receive electronic payments once a decision is made.

- **System maintenance**: Maintaining the system is an annual fixed cost. Moreover, these maintenance costs will be required for a dual system. Until most U.S. businesses have converted to electronic payment methods, the early converters will need to keep their paper-based systems.
- **Education**: Customer/vendor education costs are both direct and indirect. Direct costs include educating customers and vendors about a new payment system and why they should convert. Indirect costs will arise if a customer's bank or a vendor's bank does not have the appropriate EFT capability.
- **Renegotiation of credit terms**: Costs of negotiating new payment/credit terms include deciding how to select customers and ensuring that the company does not violate fair trade laws, such as the Robinson-Patman Act. Negotiating will cover more than trade terms; a customer may perceive a loss of control by agreeing to pay electronically.
- **Transactions costs**: Processing costs for individual transactions may change with EFT. There may be additional costs associated with low volume applications. Also, banks may impose charges for initiating or receiving payments.
- **EFT risk**: EFT risk implies costs as well. In EFT systems it is not always clear who bears the risk of payment failure. According to the Federal Reserve, the ACH system was not designed for large payments. Therefore, large dollar payments may subject the initiating bank to significant risk.
- **Float**: As EFT usually means large dollar payments, the value of float gained or lost can dwarf all other transaction costs. Of course, this value depends on the company's opportunity cost of funds. Because of the certainty of when payment will occur, sometimes a float loss can be tolerated.

Benefits

The benefits of EFT/EDI are easy to quantify using actual company data. First of all, EFT/EDI immediately provides improved cash forecasts because exact transfer dates are known in advance. If there is sufficient lead time, this can eliminate excess balances or unanticipated borrowings. Companies should experience lower bank costs for account reconcilement, lockbox processing and information reporting. These savings will result directly from the elimination of paper

Box 4-3
Key Financial EDI/EFT Questions

For EFT payments, will the company pay one or multiple invoices with each payment? A single invoice can use the CCD+ format — the same format used in the U.S. Treasury's Vendor Express program. Otherwise, the CTP or CTX format must be used.

Will the payment advice accompany the value transfer, or will it use a separate EDI system, perhaps the one used for transferring invoice information?

Will the EFT program be for customers, vendors, or both?

Will the company negotiate new payment terms with customers and suppliers? If so, will it be done case by case, or will all customers and vendors be changed to a new standard? Will this affect any discount policy for prompt payment? How will the company handle the regulatory issues?

Will customers pay with an ACH credit transaction, or will the company draft their accounts with an ACH debit transaction?

Does the company want its bank to combine customer EFT payments with lockbox (paper) payments into a single format? Conversely, does the company want its bank to translate its electronic payments into different formats to meet vendor specifications?

Will the company have a broad-based program involving large numbers of customers and/or vendors, or concentrate only on the largest ones?

handling. The same thing internally will mean lower costs for accounts receivable posting.

Offsetting the cost of float lost by payers is the reduced float to receivers because customers adhere to payment terms. Negotiated payment terms not only help the float equation but also affect cash forecasting. Finally, there is a benefit to the corporate image of a company that is perceived as a player in EFT/EDI. This may position the company's treasury department to participate in other corporate EDI initiatives.

Key Decision Points

In analyzing all the data collected on costs and benefits, it is important to keep a time line in mind. Timing is critical for implementation and operations as well as for financial analysis. No company can make a successful transition to electronic payments without taking into account when its vendors and customers will convert to EFT.

This directly affects all the items detailed under costs and benefits. Because of the long lead time in converting to EFT, the most appropriate way to measure the financial impact on a company is to adapt the capital budgeting framework and try to determine if the implementation is a positive net present value project. This way, the dollars associated with costs and benefits will be treated equally over the length of the conversion project. Box 4-3 presents a series of questions to consider before selecting an EFT system.

Some environments and some situations will be more conducive to EFT than others. Favorable circumstances include:

- Where a company has economic power over customers or vendors, such as large oil companies and oil jobbers, franchisers and franchisees and the U.S. Treasury and government suppliers.
- Where a small number of customers or vendors comprise a large proportion of payments. Sears' program, for example, involves only a few hundred of its 10,000 vendors, but they account for 45% of all payments (measured in dollars).
- Where an industry has already committed itself to EFT/EDI, such as the automotive industry.
- Where aggressive float games are not the rule. The grocery industry, for example, is not a conducive environment for EFT.

Financial EDI Planning

Depending on the company's approach, developing a pilot plan and overall strategic plan for financial EDI can be difficult. Two typical checklists for these plans are shown in Box 4-4. They highlight the items to consider from the buyer's or seller's viewpoint.

ANALYSES AND DECISION SUPPORT

A Treasury Automation Strategy

Developing an automation strategy is an important consideration as part of the company's overall cash management strategy. The first step is to chart the major flows of information into and out of the treasury function. The sources of

Box 4-4
Checklists for Financial EDI

Buyer's viewpoint

Can our purchasing and materials management systems:

- Generate copies of electronic purchase orders (POs)?
- Make PO information available to the accounts payable department in electronic form?
- Generate electronic records of materials received?
- Make receiving documents available to accounts payable in electronic form?

Can our data processing system match POs, receivers,and invoices electronically?

What modifications are required in our accounts payable system to issue:

- ANSI X12 payment order/remittance advices?
- NACHA-formatted payments?

In order to implement financial EDI as a buyer, what modifications need to be made in the following internal applications systems:

- Purchase order system?
- Materials management system?
- Accounts payable matching?
- Accounts payable computer processing?
- Accounts payable output?

What are the estimated costs of making these changes?

What will our implementation goals be in terms of number of trading partners and number of payments? Over what period of time?

To what extent will operating costs be reduced as a result of achieving these goals?

Seller's viewpoint

Can the order entry system:

- Accept input of electronic payment orders?
- Make order information available to the production or shipping department in electronic form?

(continued on next page)

Box 4-4 (continued)
Checklists for Financial EDI

Does our shipping system:
- Generate electronic shipping documents?
- Make shipping information available to the billing department in electronic form?

In order to issue electronic invoices to customers, what modifications to the billing system are required?

In order to receive and apply electronic remittance information, what modifications to the accounts receivable system are required?

What are the implementation goals in terms of number of trading partners and number of remittances? Over what period of time?

To what extent will operating costs be reduced as a result of achieving these goals?

Source: *Journal of Cash Management.* Reprinted with permission.

---

information are probably the same ones for cash forecasting and scheduling. In addition, external sources or users of information should be charted (e.g., banks and financial markets). Typical flows and systems in the treasury function that affect a company's cash management include cash forecasting and planning, cash position management, financial market administration, cash accounting, and banking network administration.

Control and Information Management

For any system to function properly, some form of control must be established and, if needed, must be exerted on the system from time to time. Corporate treasury management systems are no exception, but the establishment of control over this function can sometimes prove difficult. As is the case for many corporate functions, the inequality of responsibility with authority can pose substantial barriers in establishing control. Thus the treasury manager may possess a great deal of responsibility for the company's cash management and related financial operations but little in the way of recognized authority.

This section discusses the nature of control in treasury management and considers its logical links with information management. More specifically, the discussion deals with an operational definition of control, the essential elements of control and information, accounting influences and requirements and a conceptual approach to decision support systems for treasury.

Before considering what control means in operational terms, it will be useful to review what *cash* means in a treasury sense. When treasury managers talk about cash, they mean the actual working funds of the corporation, funds that are available to the company through its banking system and related sources of credit (excluding trade-related transactions). This definition of cash does not consider any accounting aspects of cash and is much more flexible in nature in order to reflect more accurately the pragmatics of the treasury function. Working from this basis, control is, therefore, the ability to establish, identify, monitor, and mobilize flows of funds throughout the entire organization. It entails the organization of relevant cash management and banking data, the documentation of financial transactions, and the establishment of effective sources and uses of cash. Centralization of this control function has become more commonplace, thereby providing companies with the economies of scale associated with this form of financial consolidation.

Elements of Control

The essential elements of control are integrally linked with information systems. Bank information reporting systems, internal corporate projections and financial reporting procedures and other external sources are fundamental components of an overall control system. The major elements of a control system are funds flows, data flows, analytical functions, and organizational interactions. These elements must be integrated if an effective control system is to be created.

Funds Flows

The flows of funds are the basic determinants of the nature of the control system. They affect the scope and complexity of the system and, depending on their size, frequency, and occurrence, will often dictate the level of control necessary or even possible.

To integrate the flows of funds into a control system, a treasury manager must be able to determine how much of the total flows can be effectively incorporated into a central system. For example, if the company's organization is quite decentralized, it will probably be a major project for the treasury manager to consider taking over all payment and receipt transactions. On the other hand, an effective control system may be designed to upstream receipts automatically. from a network of corporate lockbox collection points into a central concentration account and to convert major local disbursement accounts to controlled disbursement accounts with a major corporate bank. In this manner, the treasury manager

Figure 4-1
Major Treasury Data Flows

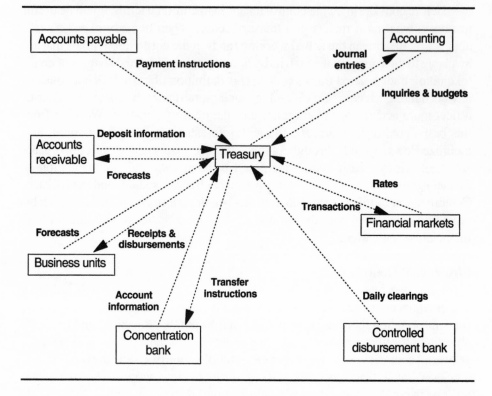

has established control over the funding of disbursements and the concentration of receipts without taking on the detailed initiation of the billing or paying functions.

Data Flows

The flows of data, on the other hand, should be handled in a different fashion. To establish an effective control system over the company's cash management activities, the treasury manager will have to construct an accurate, timely and comprehensive information system that incorporates much of the relevant flows of cash management data. Data flows should be controlled or incorporated into the control system to a much greater degree than funds flows. This is also the link between control and information management.

The data flows (see Figure 4-1) associated with cash management activities are both internal and external to the company. The internal flows encompass many of the types of information described in the cash scheduling and planning section, including estimates of cash flows and cash funding requirements. Other types of data may vary from company to company. Data needed include the investment and borrowing levels and rates, bank credit line arrangements, and major bank operating relationships.

Also, the interchange of data between the treasury manager and a financial manager at an independent subsidiary can be very educational for both. Each side can keep the other informed as to developments in the banking or money markets, and each one can readily compare the terms or details of their financial transactions to determine the feasibility of prospective transactions or the realized benefit of ones already completed. Receiving and reviewing the data and controlling some or all of the company's cash flows are important aspects of control, but they lose much of their impact if not tied together through an analytical function.

Analytical Functions

Analytical functions can vary in complexity, depending on the scope of the company's cash management system. In smaller systems with relatively few operating locations and banking arrangements, these activities can easily be incorporated into the daily cash position and target balance routines and the periodic evaluation of the cash estimates.

In more decentralized or larger systems, the analyses will require more effort and supporting tools. As the number and diversity of operating points in the system increase, the need for some automated assistance increases as well. For example, the timing requirements for cash funding decisions in such systems cannot be deferred while laborious manual computations are performed.

Organizational Interactions

The final set of major elements is that of organizational interactions. Throughout the preceding discussions, there has been a continuing theme of information exchange and intracompany communications, both of which are in large part determined by historic and ongoing organizational interactions. In the past, the interchange between treasury and the operating locations may not have been well developed and, consequently, has imposed a barrier to any system of control over cash management activities.

Measuring Treasury Performance

Until recently, the role of treasury was limited. With low and stable interest rates, keeping high cash balances in corporate checking accounts was considered prudent treasury management because it demonstrated solid corporate liquidity and served as bank compensation for credit lines and the other (few) services available to companies. Considering the high degree of decentralization and local autonomy, treasury was not a particularly exciting place to work. Today, all that has changed. Current financial conditions, high levels of leverage, and a profusion of new treasury tools have taxed the skills of the treasury professional, and companies have been discovering the importance of treasury as its role has expanded.

With this expansion has come the need for better evaluation of the treasury management function and its impact on the corporation. To do this properly requires reliable methods of measuring treasury performance.

To measure treasury performance, its effect on the entire corporation must be considered. Most areas that have a direct effect on the bottom line require some kind of performance measurement. In an operating area, it may be the net operating profit, for instance. However, treasury does not have a true "product line" relationship with the rest of the company. Often, its role is changed or even created by external activities (e.g., financing a merger or liquidating an asset).

By establishing an effective treasury performance measurement procedure, a company should be able to:

- Recognize the quality of treasury decisions
- Quantify treasury's impact on the company's bottom line
- Determine how well treasury is fulfilling its goals of asset protection and liability management
- Avoid managerial "second guessing"

Even in a highly decentralized company, there must be some central control over the treasury function of the company. (The problems of E.F. Hutton are a case in point.) However, the lines of responsibility and authority must be clearly defined so that treasury or any other area does not get falsely "blamed" for the other's error. These lines can be incorporated into the performance measurement system by having comparative benchmarks for operating units as well as major staff areas. The size of the company may also create the need for internal measurement of local treasury managers in addition to measuring the central treasury function.

One perspective is a *qualitative* one. Asset safety is the principal objective from this point of view. Treasury's role is essentially that of a caretaker. This old-fashioned view is very narrow and does not truly reflect the current state of treasury management.

The *quantitative* perspective, on the other hand, does it by the numbers. First, the appropriate performance criteria, including the sources for these criteria, must be identified. Then regular performance reports can be produced and reviewed. **Benchmarks** (e.g., internal goals tied to a level of investments, interest income

Box 4-5
Treasury Performance Benchmarks

Activity	Benchmark	Source
Regular Activities		
Short-term investing	90-day T-bill	_Wall St. Journal_
Short-term bank borrowing	Average prime rate	Bank reports
Short-term non-bank borrowing	Average of Fed composite rate	FRB of NY
Foreign exchange	Average spot rate	_Wall St. Journal_
Special Activities		
Lockbox study	Balances reduced	Consulting report
Disbursement study	Float improvements	Consulting report
Electronic payment study	Net cost savings	Consulting report
Treasury review	Net cost savings	Consulting report
New computer system	Reduced operating costs	Internal study
Inter-company Activities		
Bank compensation	Average balances/ fees paid	Account analyses
Unit's short-term borrowing	Average CP or bank rates	Internal reports vs. parent's

or expense, external interest rates or economic indices) can be used to set the standard for treasury performance. Anticipated cost savings, balance reductions or profit improvements can also be used as standards, but they tend to be more subjective than external benchmarks.

Establishing Performance Parameters
Typical benchmarks are shown in Box 4-5. It's not so important to find the benchmark for each treasury activity; the point is to select one that is relatively

easy to find and is understood by the treasury manager and management. In addition, how the benchmark will be used to define success or failure is important. That is, it should be decided whether beating or matching the benchmark constitutes satisfactory performance or whether results are within an acceptable range below the standard. For example, a satisfactory short-term borrowing benchmark could be for commercial paper to be ten basis points (0.1 percent) better (i.e., lower, if issuing) than the Federal Reserve composite rate for the same period. Similarly, a satisfactory FX benchmark could be for the average FX rate obtained for Japanese yen to be ten basis points within (below) the daily closing rates for the same period.

Special projects are more difficult. In some cases, such as lockbox or disbursement studies, it may be impossible to compute an accurate savings. In addition, the estimated savings decrease if future customer mix and payment performance change radically. Thus, it is important to try to allow for some means of measuring the final result of such studies. One method that is often used in estimating savings from such projects is to distinguish between hard and soft dollar savings. *Hard* dollar savings are actual, measurable savings, such as reduced staff or bank charges, while *soft* dollar savings represent equivalent dollar savings for non-financial improvements, such as faster decisions or reduced clerical time (but without any reduced clerical staffing).

Intra-company standards can be derived from similar standards for overall activity. For instance, if the benchmark for central treasury short-term borrowing is comparison of commercial paper rates with the Fed composite, then the same standard can be used for a major subsidiary. To be fair. the acceptable level of performance for the unit should be more liberal than for the parent.

Measurement reports should be prepared quarterly unless circumstances warrant higher frequency. A quarterly period is suitable as it does not allow a small deviation from normal to be exaggerated or overrated. Reports should also include some history to avoid the "what have you done for me lately?" approach. Performance reports cannot be too complicated and should be complementary to treasury objectives and responsibilities. Each report should also contain a brief narrative explaining any major variances (good and bad) or changes (improvement, worsening) from the last report.

Performance standards are not absolute; they may have to be changed over time. To accomplish this, there should be an annual review of the parameters to make any necessary adjustments.

Treasury as a Profit Center

Often, when senior financial managers are considering how to measure treasury performance, they contemplate establishing the treasury function as a profit

---

Box 4-6
Objectives of Cash Forecasting

Managing liquidity: necessary for timing the maturities of short-term investments, rolling over maturing loans (or commercial paper), or anticipating borrowing needs so that economical (or possible) financing can be arranged (e.g., negotiating adequate credit lines)

Controlling cash: computing variances between estimated and actual cash flows to identify financing problems or unanticipated developments in the company's financial (working capital) position

Strategic financial planning: help in determining how well the company's financial plans are being met; e.g., assessing how accurate estimates of future funding needs/surpluses have been

Cash budgeting: estimating revenues and costs (financial and nonfinancial) for potential projects as well as ongoing operations

---

center. The rationale is that measurement by profits and losses will provide incentives for treasury managers and optimize the return to the company. However, this method is dangerous because it downplays two of the primary roles of treasury: asset protection and liability management. Treasury may also function as a central bank for the corporation. Putting it on a profit basis may run counter to these objectives in that a treasury manager may make decisions that enhance return (e.g., by accepting a riskier investment) rather than ensure that funds are available for regular disbursements.

It is vital that the primary objective for the treasury function be the factor in choosing what to measure. Few companies (if any) have established their treasury functions as true stand-alone profit centers. The risks are far greater than the rewards.

Cash Forecasting, Scheduling, and Planning

Cash forecasting is concerned with estimating the company's cash positions over a defined period, ranging from one month to one or more years. Cash forecasting focuses on the overall cash position, not on daily position management. Its major objectives are shown in Box 4-6.

An important distinction is between **cash scheduling** and **forecasting**. It is common to label longer-term (one month or longer) cash flow predictions as cash forecasting and shorter-term predictions of cash flows as cash scheduling. This distinction is useful but not exact because there is considerable overlap between scheduling and forecasting.

An Illustration

All too often this part of the overall cash management process is overlooked or misunderstood. The monthly "forecast" can become "etched in stone," with the result that local financial managers inadvertently create large local pools of unused funds waiting to be disbursed according to an outdated (but mandatory) projection.

In one such instance, a corporate treasury manager was conducting a review with a local financial manager. The local manager was surprised and somewhat embarrassed by the size of his bank balances but explained them away by admitting that his boss would not let him change his monthly forecast, which called for funds each week. He readily agreed that these estimates were rough "guesstimates" but felt there was little he could do. His supervisor had been reprimanded for an erroneous sales and revenue estimate and was determined to prevent any further situations if at all possible.

Fundamental Forecasting Considerations

Forecasting cash flows over both the short- and longer-term is one of the most important tasks of the treasury function. There are a wide variety of techniques that can be applied to these problems. As well, there are a number of treasury management and corporate elements that influence the degree of success of any cash flow forecast.

An important consideration is the corporate organization. Cash forecasting usually involves gathering and evaluating information from many sources, both inside and outside of the company. In general, the more decentralized the company, the more difficult the forecasting will be. Longer projections (e.g., monthly forecasts) are often distributed outside the treasury area. It is important to establish effective communication between the treasury function and those using the estimates.

Another facet of cash forecasting is defined by the company's cash management system. Some products and services can simplify the cash scheduling and forecasting process, such as bank information reporting systems, which provide data on major balances and transactions, controlled disbursing services, which reduce uncertainty in estimating daily clearings against the company's accounts, and electronic (wire, ACH) payments, which reduce or eliminate the uncertainty in estimating check collections.

Cash Scheduling

Cash scheduling is the determination of the company's short-term cash position. It typically involves estimating cash collections and disbursements in order to develop an estimate of the daily net cash position over the forecast horizon, usually from one to six weeks. Its key purpose is to enable the treasury manager to manage the daily cash position efficiently.

Efficient cash position management has many benefits. For example, it enables the treasury manager to maintain cash balances near the target level with fewer transactions. It also enhances liquidity management. For example, the maturity of an investment might be extended if a cash surplus were predicted; under a normal yield curve, this would improve investment returns. Managing the cash position efficiently provides accurate information on cash flows to other areas of the corporation.

Cash scheduling operates by assigning known and expected cash receipts and disbursements within the forecast horizon at the time they will occur. The net cash flow for each day in the forecasting period is the difference between these receipts and disbursements. Examples of cash flows that can be scheduled are:

- Principal, interest and sinking fund payments
- Dividend payments (once they are declared)
- Contractual obligations, such as progress payments on new construction
- Corporate trade payments
- Payroll

Cash scheduling is often accurate but generally requires an extensive information system to compile and to consolidate the purchase, sales, investment, and borrowing data on which the cash schedule is based. Box 4-7 shows an example of the cash flow components used to develop the aggregate forecast. This part of the cash scheduling process is also dependent upon corporate organization. A centralized company has a much easier task than a decentralized company.

Cash Planning

The treasury function of the company should play a leading role in planning for a company's cash needs, and it is in this area that a short-term cash scheduling system may not provide enough support. The relatively short time horizons of typical scheduling systems hamper the ability of the company to look further out.

Box 4-7
Cash Scheduling Components

From corporate treasury

- Federal, state, and local taxes
- Corporate dividends
- Pension fund payments
- Income savings plan payments
- Insurance payments
- Staff payroll
- Vendor payments
- Foreign exchange procurement
- Interest and principal repayments
- Maturing investments
- External financing (market debt, bank debt, etc.)

From operating units

- Lockbox collections
- Local office deposits
- International collections
- Local payables and payroll funding
- Capital expenditures

Dividend and loan payments from subsidiaries

This need can be satisfied by some form of longer-term forecasting, and in this context the term forecasting is quite appropriate. Now there is indeed a useful application for more sophisticated statistical techniques. Also, with the longer time horizons, the differences between cash flows as shown in financial statements or measured by the actual flows of funds through the company's banking network are not relevant, because the results of the forecast will not be translated into daily activities.

A number of companies have established statistically based forecasting systems and have reported on their successes. Many of the standard quantitative techniques have been applied to this problem, but usually on a customized basis. It is logical that individual companies will tailor their forecasst to their own situations and the specific information important to them. Sources and types of data differ greatly from company to company, thereby making any standard method implausible.

The end uses for such forecasts typically include long-term financial strategies, such as the timing and relative size of long-term debt or equity issues, the establishment of short- and long-term debt mix, or the impact of acquisitions or divestitures. These forecasts are also used to assess the longer-term impact of changes in short-term and long-term interest rates. These few examples demonstrate the inherent difference between cash forecasting and cash scheduling and should be kept in mind when dealing with either function.

RELATIONSHIP MANAGEMENT

The importance of existing bank relationships increases as the current trend toward using fewer banks continues. Companies expect their major banks to be able to provide more services on a bigger scale, even though they may have separated their credit and non-credit (cash management) needs and often use different groups of banks for each type of service.

Credit relationships are important as sources of short-term funds or for backup to other sources (e.g., commercial paper). A major aspect of bank relationship management is ensuring that the company has sufficient lines of credit to support its business activities. This entails monitoring use or matching outstanding and projected commercial paper volumes with total backup lines. If more lines are needed, then steps must be taken to increase lines with existing banks or to add facilities with new banks.

Non-credit relationships have, in recent years, taken on as much or more importance as credit relationships. Part of bank relationship management involves the evaluation of current services, including dealing with problems and controlling costs. Special reviews, such as lockbox (collection) or disbursement studies, can be helpful in determining whether current services are adequate or must be changed. Also, regular review of monthly account analysis statements can be an important step in the evaluation process. The monthly statements offer valuable information on service use and costs. Careful review may also identify duplicate services or possibly unnecessary ones.

A corporate treasury manager functions as a purchasing manager when selecting bank services. Several common pitfalls should be avoided when purchasing bank cash management products:

- Too much reliance on bank reputation or prestige
- Too much influence from the credit relationship

- Too much influence from the individual doing the selling
- Comparing unequal products or institutions

In recent years, the financial stability of banks has become an important issue for corporations. Federal government bailouts and unforeseen bank failures have created new worries over the safety of corporate deposits (which often exceed the FDIC maximum insured amount of $100,000) as well as the stability of bank services. Corporations also face risk in their investments if they are purchasing bank CDs or commercial paper.

Bank Services

One of the mutual objectives of the corporation-bank relationship should be to assure that a bank earns a reasonable return on its credit and non-credit services. Attempting to construct a corporate cash management system based on utilizing various banks' loss leader services is at best imprudent and at worst doomed to failure. In addition, playing one bank against another in order to secure cut-rate charges for services will only be effective for a short time. Once this tactic has been exhausted, the imprudent treasury manager and his or her corporation will find their tasks far more difficult than if a more rational, reasonable approach had been adopted.

Senior financial management, the treasury staff, and other users of bank services should be aware (or made aware) that bank services have costs associated with them, no matter how trivial the service. It is the treasury manager's responsibility to optimize the company's banking costs, educating upper management as to the nature and level of these costs, while maintaining cordial banking relations. The key to succeeding in this endeavor lies in using a reasonable and systematic approach to bank compensation.

Bank costs must be identified, quantified, and monitored routinely. Historically, bank compensation essentially consisted of a gentleman's understanding between a corporate treasurer and the firm's bankers. Since interest rates were rather low and relatively static in nature, neither side felt the need to determine precisely the amount of compensation required. The system was quite simple — the treasurer and his treasury manager knew that they had to maintain 10-15% of the company's credit line in the form of "clear" balances with each of the company's banks. These balances could be established and maintained by keeping a separate account with the appropriate amount or, even simpler, by funding disbursements when checks were mailed. In this manner, the disbursement float generated would create sufficient balance levels to compensate the banks. These balances were also usually large enough to compensate the bank for the non-credit bank services it provided, thus creating the notion, especially in the minds of the local financial manager, that the bank services were being provided free. If the balances were short in any particular month, the company would raise them the next month. In any case, their bankers could be counted on to point out any serious deficits and recommend appropriate amounts of compensating balances.

However, interest rates did not remain either low or static in the 1960's, 1970's, and 1980's, and bankers, corporate treasurers, and treasury managers all grew sensitive to the levels of compensating balances. Corporations initiated large-scale studies, often with bank consultants, to analyze the levels of and reasons for the balances being maintained in the company's banking network. In addition, the need for massive credit lines was reassessed.

The result was a request for more precise measures of compensation levels, but still in the form of balances. In response, banks began to prepare and distribute statements that broke down the compensation levels required of their customers. These **account analysis statements** itemized the corporation's activities with the bank and showed the bank's service charges for each account.

By assigning a hypothetical value to the average collected balances maintained by the corporation with the bank and adjusting the balances for reserve requirements, the "value" of the balances could be compared with the accumulated service charges for the reported period (usually a month). Thus the corporate treasury manager could identify any deficits or excesses and make adjustments to the balances maintained with the bank. Balances required for credit lines were not normally shown on these statements, so the treasury manager had to add them in as well.

Some banks converted the charges to balances to make the comparison easier. The treasury manager also added all deficits and/or excesses to determine the net position for each bank, rather than attempt to balance each account. The underlying assumption was that if the value of the balances equaled the charges, the bank would not require any other compensation for non-credit services.

Account analyses have become more descriptive over time and have encouraged companies to compare similar charges among their banks. The account analysis statements have also proved to be extremely informative to treasury managers and have assisted them in devising appropriate compensation methods and strategies.

Bank Compensation

There are two basic methods used by companies to compensate their banks: fees and compensating balances. Actually, using a combination of both has become increasingly common, and is now used by a majority of companies.

Many companies use fee compensation for tighter cost control. Fees can be put into a budget and compared to other costs while balances are not as directly comparable. Conversely, some companies favor balance compensation because balances can hide certain costs.

It has been argued that since fees are a direct expense, they can be deducted from taxable income. While plausible at first glance, this reasoning is flawed. If a company switches from balance to fee compensation, balances are removed from the bank and invested in an interest-bearing asset. The taxes paid on income from investment typically offset the tax savings from the deductibility of the fees. Thus, taxes alone do not have any real effects.

In the past, banks have preferred payment via balances. Since one measure of a bank's size is its asset base, some bankers may view a corporate relationship more favorably if balances are used for compensation because balances add to assets and fees do not. This preference may be changing, as evidenced by one bank's (Wells Fargo) dropping of earnings credits entirely in 1992 and converting totally to fees.

While many larger banks have taken a more profit-oriented approach in recent years, balances may still be a critical factor for companies that depend on medium or small banks for cash management-related services as well as credit and financial advice. In the past, a few banks have such strong preferences for balances that they levy higher service charges, or surcharges, if they are to be paid in fees. However, this practice seems to be disappearing.

Fees vs. Balances

Fees prevent overcompensation; excess balances are a form of overpayment. There is a slight variation or alternative in balance compensation that some companies and banks have favored in recent years: non-interest-bearing certificates of deposit.

Non-interest-bearing CDs, or in some cases time deposits, are attractive for compensation purposes for two reasons. First, there are no longer any reserve requirements on this type of account, as compared with the current 10% assessed on regular accounts. This means that a dollar kept in a non-interest-bearing CD will be worth more in terms of the amount of service charges it covers. The other attraction of this form of compensation is that banks may offer an earnings credit rate different from the rate used on their account analysis. This rate used is usually the bank's own CD rate, one that is normally much higher than the money market rate used for account analysis purposes.

The main disadvantage with this sort of compensation method lies in its lack of flexibility because funds must actually be converted into the CD form, and this cannot be accomplished simply or for very short periods of time. It is quite probable that the conversion cost of attempting to switch between regular balances and CDs daily would far outweigh the differential in savings.

Thus this form of compensation is not used for regular operating charges that are related to collection or disbursement activities. Rather, it is used more often· in compensating the bank for special, distinct services provided to the corporation such as consulting-advisory services. In these cases, sufficient funds are segregated in the form of a CD, which is maintained for an appropriate length of time to provide the proper return to the bank for the service. During the period the corporation does not have use of the funds. This latter feature is often cited by treasury managers as the major drawback.

For most large corporations with access to the commercial paper market as a short-term source of funds, it will usually be cost effective for the company to pay for its bank services by fees. This is due to the cheaper cost of funds associated with commercial paper (even including the cost of backup lines of credit) as compared with the earnings credit rate, adjusted for reserve requirements.

Thus it is more attractive for the corporation to borrow the funds and pay the fees than to leave balances that earn a lower return. To the extent that the effective earnings credit (i.e. , reflective of reserves) approximates the cost of borrowing or alternative investments, the corporate treasury manager becomes indifferent as to the compensation method. The attractiveness of fees is also enhanced by the fact that most banks simply charge fees at the level shown on the account analyses without taking into account reserve requirements or differences or time lags in the money market rates used in computing earnings credit rates. By failing to do this banks have tended to underprice the fee method of compensation.

Another major factor increasing the popularity of fees is the ability of a corporation to reduce the amount of its disbursement float present in its bank balances. This is due to the general availability of controlled disbursing services, which allow the corporation to fund its disbursements on the actual day of clearing. This reduces the excess balances that were formerly present and that represented a portion of the disbursement float. This possibility has also given rise, at least in part, to the last major factor in increasing the popularity of fee compensation — the payment of fees for credit services.

Just as the use of fees for non-credit services has increased recently, so has the method of compensation for lines of credit. As more and more banks offer credit lines and even revolving credit agreements (committed lines) on a full fee basis with no compensating balance requirements, there is no alternative use for excess operating balances. Until recently, most U.S. banks would not consider relinquishing the percent compensating balance method. However, the aggressive entry of foreign banks in the U.S. marketplace and the desires or demands of major customers have changed this.

In summary, then, there appears to be a major change and conversion in the method of compensation for both credit and non-credit services taking place. This does not change the basic tools for information requirements of the treasury manager appreciably, but it probably heightens the need for timely, accurate bank data. Note that fee compensation virtually requires a streamlined, efficient cash management system, since the ability of the company to remove substantial amounts of its cash balances makes the conversion beneficial and attractive. The inability to do so will cost the company the full opportunity savings it seeks. By substantially reducing the amount of cash in the cash management pipeline, finer control and a simpler system are required.

The Combination Method

The great "compromise" seems to be to compensate banks by a mixture of fees and balances. Non-removable balances (transaction, dual and/or double-counted balances) could be used as a compensation base, with any deficiencies paid by fee. In this way, the maximum amount could be invested (or an optimal amount borrowed), and overcompensation would be less likely.

Thus, companies that successfully manage their compensation levels will wind up with a mixture of compensation methods. They will pay for the bulk of their activities at major banks through fees while maintaining a number of secondary relationships on a balance compensation basis.

Note that when companies negotiate a fee offset arrangement, whereby any collected balances maintained are converted to fee equivalents and subtracted from the total fee due, this conversion is typically done at the bank's earnings credit rate, which means that the company has lost a small amount in the conversion. This, however, seems to be an appropriate and equitable way to handle excess balances in such arrangements. There is still an impetus for the company to reduce its balances, but if balances do occur, it still has some applicable use for them. It is important, however, to remember this distinction when comparing costs or alternative methods of compensation.

THE GLOBAL CASH MANAGEMENT ENVIRONMENT

Corporate treasury managers who have explored the global cash management environment have encountered many similarities to the domestic cash management environment of the early to middle 1970's. For instance, many of the problems in initiating cash management overseas have arisen from a general lack of attention or awareness at the local level, as was also true in the United States. In any case, there are three common types of problems likely to be encountered by the treasury manager as he or she considers international or global cash management:

- Internal company-related problems
- Cross-border problems
- Banking system problems

Company-related problems stem from the internal organization itself, and they are probably the first ones that must be overcome in establishing any effective global cash management system. They are primarily educational and political. Educational problems are evidenced by the lack of awareness by overseas personnel, who tend to view cash management as nonexistent and banking as a necessary evil. The basic mechanics of funds movement and the principles of cash position management and effective short-term cash projecting in real terms (not in accounting terms) are typically absent overseas and knowledge of them must be instilled. Political problems arise from the real or perceived loss of autonomy at the local level. These problems are by no means monumental and can be overcome through repeated visits and mutual cooperation.

Cross-border problems may also involve internal company problems because there are many interactions between different foreign units of the same company, and these interactions can create problems in cash management. One method of dealing successfully with this type of problem is to use a multilateral or bilateral netting system. Essentially, these systems, whether run by the company itself or by one of its banks, legislate the inter-subsidiary payment mechanism and set up a common, logical network for funds transfer throughout the corporation.

Other types of cross-border problems involve the timely and accurate receipt of export collections from overseas points and international funds transfers in general. Typical problems of this sort are misguided transfers, the use of checks instead of some form of electronic means, payment with foreign or "mixed" currencies, and lack of documentation with the transfer. The use of foreign currency checks or mixed ones (e.g., a U.S. dollar check drawn on an overseas bank must be cleared back to that bank and back again to the United States before the funds are good) can pose major problems.

Banking system problems arise when treasury managers try to superimpose U.S. cash management practices on foreign subsidiaries or expect to find U.S. cash management services overseas. It takes time to understand any banking system, so international treasury managers must invest time learning about foreign banks and the products and services they offer.

Most of these problems can be easily handled by review and analysis, and then by enforcing effective standards worldwide. The S.W.I.F.T. network has greatly improved international transfers, while documentation standards are generally improving in most major banks around the world.

FORMULATING TREASURY MANAGEMENT POLICIES

Policies must have a purpose (at least one) if they are to be of any value. Simply writing down some rules and regulations is not enough. Creating a nice looking binder that gathers dust on every bookcase in the treasury department is not worth the effort, either. Before embarking on the mission to develop new policies or to update old ones, treasury managers should write down why the current procedures are being practiced.

One objective might be to document operating procedures in a very decentralized treasury environment for better control or for effective performance measurement or to be able to establish reasonable measurement criteria for senior management to evaluate treasury management activities. Many policies are completed as a kind of protection of last resort. That is, the idea is to set up parameters before any problem situations occur, so the treasury manager can evaluate the situation or be evaluated in an objective manner. Effective policies can help do this.

The policies should be divided into major areas. Although the categories should be tailored to the specific case, it is typical to start with three general areas: bank relations, short-term liquidity, and organizational (see Box 4-8). Others can be added, such as credit management, receivable/payables processing, risk management, or other related activities.

Bank Relations Policy Items

Formal bank relations policies help the firm deal fairly with its banks and assure that everyone in the company understands and agrees with the stated approach to bank relations. If the firm is going to deal with a relatively large number of banks (e.g., more than 10), the firm usually establishes a tiered structure for its banking network. The first policy consideration is then to determine what each tier consists of (i.e., what the characteristics, such as level of credit and non-credit services, are for each bank in that tier) and how individual banks can move into or out of each tier (e.g., this may be linked to performance measurement or financial stability or both).

Bank financial stability parameters are now an integral part of overall bank policy. These include basic credit standards as well as how often the bank's financial performance must be reviewed. It should include what steps must be

---

Box 4-8
Treasury Management Policy Items

Bank relations
- Bank tiers or levels
- Bank stability
- Bank performance measurement
- Bank compensation methods, limits and horizons
- Bank target balances
- Responsibilities for bank relations
- Regular bank reviews

Short-term liquidity management
- Investments
- Borrowing
- Foreign exchange
- Hedging and risk management

Organizational
- Use of consultants, outside managers, RFPs
- Responsibilities for bank relationship management
- Responsibilities for bank communications
- Bank documentation
- Personal banking

---

taken when an existing bank fails to meet the company's standards. It is important to remember that the standards established here may be independent from the investment standards (described below). The key concerns in this case should be risk for the company's assets and whether the bank can provide adequate credit services when the company needs them. In addition to financial performance. It may include operating performance measurement parameters. These can help in determining how often a bank is reviewed or is included in new business opportunities.

Bank compensation is a key aspect of the bank relations policy. First, it is important that the firm select an appropriate method of compensation. There may be exceptions for specific situations or for banks in certain tiers, but there should be a general policy statement on compensation. Other items to consider include compensation horizons (i.e., time limits for achieving target compensation levels), the mix of fees and balances, types of services that can be paid for by fee, and those that can be paid for by compensating balances, and procedures for maintaining bank target balance levels (e.g., how often each bank's balances are to be reviewed). Finally, the policy should specify the expected "regular" time periods for bank reviews with the firm's major (top tier) banks.

Short-Term Liquidity Management Policy Items

Firms that are active in short-term investments market should have established a formal investment policy. Borrowing policy should cover the borrowing options, how much "cushion" to allow in the company's total lines of credit, the form of credit agreement and how often credit services must be reviewed. Foreign exchange (FX) and hedging are often included in this area of treasury policy. Establishing operating parameters, such as how much FX exposure will be covered or which locations are permitted to purchase FX contracts, will vary from company to company.

The final item in this section is interest rate risk management. The firm should establish financial parameters for covering corporate interest rate risk, such as which instruments can be used, how much of each type can be used, and how often the protection programs will be evaluated.

Organizational Policy Items

This area can include many items. For instance, this may be the area that covers the policy on using outside third parties for assistance in treasury management. Third parties can include management consultants (either from a bank or non-bank consulting firm) or money managers. It may also include a formal policy on the use of request for proposal (RFPs) for bank cash management services. Other major items in this policy area include identification of responsibilities for bank relationship management and bank communications This includes who is responsible for maintaining bank documentation (e.g., signing authorities, signature facsimile plates) and how often this is to be reviewed. Treasury disaster plans and systems policies also can be included in this section. Back-up procedures and related systems needs can be supplied by the systems group.

All levels of financial management should be involved in policy formulation. Active participants in treasury activities should be polled for their input on how things work now, what improvements they would make and what's missing. A senior treasury manager (e.g., an assistant treasurer) should be responsible for creating a review draft of the overall policy. This is not a small task if nothing has been done in the past. The first version or versions of the draft should be

Box 4-9
3M's Cash Management Mission Statement

Mission: To operate a world class professional cash management organization; to meet the cash requirements of 3M's operations by positioning investments in approved securities or by borrowing as required; to receive and disburse funds efficiently; and to minimize operating costs.

Principles:

To incorporate the highest levels of ethics, competency, innovation, and technology into 3M's cash management practices.

To work closely with selected banks and financial organizations and 3M's divisions, subsidiaries, and staff departments to provide highly responsive services and a keen awareness of state of the art cash management practices.

To accurately forecast sources and uses of funds and take appropriate actions to insure the availability of sufficient cash to meet day-to-day and long-term needs at the best price.

To establish and monitor a network to receive, process, and concentrate monies owed to 3M as rapidly and efficiently as possible.

To establish and monitor systems that insure timely payment to vendors and employees and maximize the benefits of legitimate float without taking improper advantage of system or mechanical delays.

To invest excess cash according to policies established by 3M's Board of Directors with the objective of providing appropriate levels of safety, liquidity, and yield in that order.

To provide accurate and timely accounting records to 3M's operations.

To continuously review financial services vendors and internal controls to insure sufficient security for the protection of 3M's cash, securities, and investments.

To fairly compensate banks and financial vendors for service provided.

Reprinted with permission from *The Treasury Pro.*

reviewed and revised before circulating to higher levels of treasury management and to interested outside functional areas, such as accounting and internal audit.

After gaining general consensus on a draft internally, the policy-maker should then circulate the policy statement to senior management and outside-treasury areas for review and sign-off. By getting various areas of corporate financial management involved, the treasury management policy has a good chance of becoming an effective working document. In addition, a plan should be established for the next update when doing the current one to assure that the policy is updated on a timely basis. Box 4-9 gives a specific example of a cash management policy statement.

MANAGEMENT REVIEW ITEMS

➡ Segregate your cash flows by type and dollar size for a more effective review. You then should be able to decide whether to use specific cash management services, such as controlled disbursements or retail lockboxes.

➡ Look beyond the treasury department for costs associated with preparing checks or receiving customer payments.

➡ Add your electronic requirements to company receivable and payables systems, so they will be added whenever the systems are updated.

➡ Review accounts payable practices as regularly as you do collections. Look for discounts not taken and other items on a vendor checklist that you customize to your needs, based on the standard checklist shown in this chapter.

➡ Become known as the ''payments'' expert, not the ''float'' expert, so you'll be automatically included in EDI planning and development sessions.

➡ Look for EDI efforts in your company's main business lines by contacting industry trade association and industry action groups or by reading industry trade publications.

➡ Categorize your treasury information flows in standard groupings, such as type of control item.

➡ Establish treasury performance benchmarks as a separate project with representation from all parts of treasury participating. make sure there is a final, written product from this endeavor. Use Box 4-5 as a guide.

➡ Don't ask for written cash forecasts unless you absolutely need them. Tailor your very short-term needs to your cash flow system, depending on the users and providers of funds for key information over the phone.

➡ Establish a regular report on variances to each user and provider of funds, not just to treasury management.

➡ If you have a decentralized cash flow system (i.e., payments and collections are handled at a local level), routinely circulate excerpts from monthly account analyses to appropriate managers to verify volumes, check for reasonability, etc.

➡ Develop a simple spreadsheet program to monitor your bank costs for major relationships over time. Review each bank at least monthly.

➡ If your opportunity cost of funds or the rate at which you normally invest funds in the short term (e.g., overnight) is better than 90% of your bank's earnings credit rate or the average of the 90-day U.S. treasury bills (a usual rate used for earnings credit rate), then you'll be better off compensating with fees as much as possible.

➡ If interest rates are dropping quickly, you may be better off by leaving larger compensating balances with your banks. This works if you use the combination method of bank compensation.

➡ Divide your treasury policies into specific areas, so you van work on and review them separately. Different pieces, such as bank relations, short-term investing, and short-term borrowing, can then be circulated to different reviewers for comment.

➡ Ask other treasury managers or bankers for sample policies, and offer to share your policies.

CHAPTER 5

MANAGING TREASURY INFORMATION

Corporate treasury management is still a relatively young field, as compared with many other corporate financial disciplines. Corporations are at different levels of sophistication or are still undergoing changes in the way they approach the subject. In addition, as cash management develops and incorporates more technology into its fundamental practices, corporate treasury managers will be faced with alternative ways of managing the information related to the treasury function.

Analytical studies provide information that is a basic part of the developmental structure of treasury management. Supplemented by decision support systems, especially those that can be implemented on the personal computer (PC), this analytical side of cash management plays a significant role in providing an efficient framework for the corporate treasury function.

This chapter considers the major analytical aspects of cash management:

- Collection and disbursement studies
- Other analytical studies, including automation feasibility studies, overall treasury reviews, and treasury audits
- Fundamental treasury information management
- Cash scheduling and forecasting

COLLECTION AND DISBURSEMENT STUDIES

Corporate treasury managers have used quantitative methods and standardized approaches to determine where to locate their collection points and how to optimize their disbursements. Collections and disbursements are not static, however; they require periodic review and possible fine tuning because of

---

Box 5-1
Steps in a Collection Study

Quantify float associated with the current system

Set constraints/limitations on lockbox "solutions" (e.g., number of possible lockbox points, excluded collection locations, restricted groups of banks, use of lockbox networks)

Identify one or more optimal lockbox solutions

Determine float for alternative solutions being considered by the company

Compare the alternatives to the current system and to each other

Make decision to change the current system (or not)

---

changes in corporate working capital practices, shifts in the company's lines of business, and economic conditions (e.g., interest rates) in general.

Collection Studies

Collection studies use quantitative methods to determine a company's optimal collection points. These points may or may not include any of the current locations where the firm collects funds. A normal by-product of the study is an estimate of the improvement in collections to be obtained from making the optimal changes. The main objective of a collection study is to define an improved collection system to reduce overall float (i.e., mail, processing, and collection float) associated with processing checks into available cash. This usually entails considering potential lockbox solutions to the collection problem. The main steps in a collection study are shown in Box 5-1.

Most larger companies already have some lockbox system in place, so their reasons for conducting a study are in fine tuning the existing system. Other companies, as they grow in size and/or sophistication, often decide to perform an initial collection study.

In either case, it is important to determine the relevant information to help in making the decision to initiate a study. For a firm with an existing lockbox system, this usually takes the form of a monitoring system. The major factors that affect the complexity of the system are shown in the checklist in Box 5-2.

Box 5-2
Lockbox Monitoring System Checklist

How involved is the treasury manager with daily lockbox processing?

How many lockboxes does the company currently use?

How old is the current system?

How often are lockbox arrangements and lockbox banks reviewed?

How involved is senior treasury management?

How are lockbox errors identified, reported and resolved?

When was the last personal visit to the current lockbox banks? Who made it?

How is float tracked?

When were Lockbox Profile reports reviewed for each lockbox bank?

The Lockbox Profile

Collection study standards for the industry are provided by Phoenix-Hecht. It provides each participating bank with an individual *Lockbox Profile* report. Each profile (see Figure 5-1) contains four parts:

- Total Float Comparison
- Deposit Impact
- Operational Features
- Nationwide Comparisons

These reports can be very helpful in monitoring bank lockbox performance. For example, the float comparison offers a brief picture of the bank's processing and how it compares with other banks. Treasury managers can use the Deposit Impact section to determine how often deposits should be made and to evaluate the potential effects of early deposit cut-offs. The description of operational features is a concise listing of key aspects of the bank's lockbox services. While not a replacement for an actual on-site visit, it does describe basic operating procedures and special aspects (if any) of the bank's service.

Other Study Considerations

If the current system depends on significant manual office processing of receipts, it is important to quantify the delays resulting from in-house handling of checks. Typical office processing with over-the-counter deposits at a local branch bank will inflate both float and per item processing costs. Some high-volume retailers

Figure 5-1
Sample Lockbox Profile

Lockbox Operational Features

A unique zip code is used for lockbox mail.

Automated image processing is available.

Saturday processing and clearing is available.

Standard service includes a negotiated number of daily deposits.

Availability assigned on an item-by-item basis.

Daily telephone reporting of total items and dollars deposited offered.

Wholesale lockbox data capture for remittance updating offered.

Comparison of Bank ABC with National Average Smoothed Results

Sending State/ZIP		Bank Results Total Float	National Average Total Float	Bank Is Faster/(Slower)
Ohio		3.94	4.05	0.11
432	Columbus	3.86	3.90	0.04
436	Toledo	4.33	4.33	0.00
437	Zanesville	4.08	4.37	0.29
441	Cleveland	3.76	3.68	(0.08)

---

and insurance companies have established their own dedicated processing facilities, operating the same check sorting and encoding equipment as bank lockboxes. When high-volume, low-dollar payments characterize the receipts, an in-house center can be a viable alternative to a bank facility. Since the relative mail and availability performance of each city would still apply, selecting the location of an in-house facility would follow the same procedure as selecting a bank location.

Internal Study Data

A collection study is usually based on a typical month's receipts. Photocopies of all checks received during a one-month period and their envelopes provide the necessary data for the study (see Box 5-3). Payments from a subsidiary or another corporate division should be excluded because any advantage gained from

Box 5-3
Collection Study Data

Typical inputs

Postmark date and zip code of sender (from envelope)
Dollar amount of check
Transit routing symbol of drawee bank
Name of customer
Depositing bank

Typical outputs

Listing of dollar amounts by zip code and drawee bank location
(Fed city, RCPC, etc.)

Quantification of current system float (mail float measured versus
theoretical time, clearance float)

Optimal lockbox arrangements/simulations (up to four or more points)

Net benefit of each arrangement (includes direct costs but not
conversion costs)

reducing float on these checks is achieved at the expense of another area of the corporation and does not represent a real economic gain. Foreign payments are also excluded, since mail and collection times may not be available for foreign locations. In addition, a dollar cut-off is established for including checks (e.g., $1000) since 45-50% of the items typically represent 85-95% of the dollars in corporate-to-corporate payments. A retail payments study would require a more detailed statistical sampling procedure.

It is important that the study checks represent at least one-twelfth of the annual corporate receipts or the projected float cost savings will be distorted. In addition, a study is only useful when a corporation's customer mix remains fairly stable from one billing cycle to the next. If there is variability in the zip code sources of checks, a lockbox system that is optimal for one set of customers may not be appropriate for another. Usually a corporation has the same customers from month to month, but a study should be based on a sample that includes a typical geographic mix of remittance sources and drawee banks. The largest customers should also be represented appropriately. These preliminary adjustments are important because concentrations of remittance sources or drawee banks among the receipts will affect the dollar-weighted calculations of float for various networks.

The ability of an efficient lockbox system to minimize collection float depends on a number of characteristics of remittances:

- Geographic concentration of the check's zip code sources
- Geographic concentration of the check's drawee banks
- Proximity of check source and drawee bank

Strong concentrations of drawee banks and remittance sources can mean that a lockbox system with locations near those concentrations is very efficient. The correlation between the two types of concentrations will allow a configuration to minimize both the mail and collection float simultaneously. For example, if half a corporation's remittances are mailed from New York and the other half are mailed from San Francisco, two lockboxes (one in New York and one in San Francisco) will minimize the float for the system only if the checks mailed from New York are drawn on New York banks and the checks from San Francisco are drawn on San Francisco banks. However, if the checks mailed from San Francisco are drawn on banks in Montana and Texas and the checks mailed from New York are drawn on banks in Georgia and North Carolina, the most effective lockbox network may include Chicago, Dallas, Atlanta, and Charlotte. Even these four locations may not minimize mail and collection float completely, since one kind of float may be minimized at the expense of the other. A customer may deliberately engage in this type of activity in order to extend its disbursement float.

External Study Data

Once the basic characteristics of the receipts are determined, float for the current and alternative systems is calculated based on a matrix of mail and collection times between cities. Mail float is a function of the geographic location of payee and payor. Mail times are measured by Phoenix-Hecht between 106 primary zip code sources and approximately 50 potential lockbox sites three times a year. Mail times are expressed in both the latest times and smoothed average times, which capture trends in performance. Phoenix-Hecht times are utilized by most banks performing float analyses to form a data base for projection of mail times for current, alternative, and optimal systems.

Some studies show actual mail float calculations determined from the postmark date and the date of receipt and/or deposit. However, since projections of mail times for all alternative systems are based on Phoenix-Hecht times, this procedure can be misleading. Actual mail times can exceed Phoenix-Hecht times by as much as 1.5 days because of:

- Stale meter marks on predated mail

- Illegible postmarks obscuring the date mailed
- Holidays that interrupt normal mail service
- Cancellation date errors in transit
- Skewed percentages of mail in transit over a weekend
- Different measurement procedures (banks usually measure time in days, Phoenix-Hecht measures in tenths of a day)

Processing float can involve several hours or days in an office processing environment or two or three hours in a lockbox processing environment. Usually a lockbox model will include processing time when calculating an item's ability to meet an availability schedule cut-off time. Collection float is calculated for each item based on a matching of the check's receipt time to the availability schedules for the banks on which the check is drawn.

A collection study will determine the optimal system based solely on float considerations, compare it to alternative solutions that may include cities where corporate banking relationships already exist and evaluate the opportunity cost of one system versus another. The model will project float, number of items, and dollar amounts for items routed to each location in these simulated systems. Routing is performed by the model based on the zip code source and the drawee bank of the items. Sometimes substantial benefits can be achieved by simply rerouting customers within the current system, since they may be sending checks to a suboptimal location as a result of haphazard lockbox location assignment, a change in corporate accounts payable operations, or a lack of explicit directions by the receiving company. A collection study will recommend a final collection system to the corporation based on the float advantages available and the constraints of the corporation's banking network.

Lockbox Bank Selection

The end result is the identification of one or more potential lockbox locations. Some of the lockbox models also pinpoint specific banks as well, but the selection of the ultimate lockbox bank is usually left up to the company. There are a number of major criteria that can prove to be quite helpful in selecting a new lockbox location (see Box 5-4).

Most of these criteria deal with each potential bank objectively and suggest different measures of the sophistication and quality of the respective bank's service. This is quite evident in the criteria dealing with the processing, availability, direct-send programs, float assessment, and error rates. In cases where new relationships are being established, these factors are critical. If a treasury manager

---

Box 5-4
Lockbox Bank Selection Criteria

The type of lockbox service desired (e.g., retail or wholesale)

Cost of services

The bank's availability schedule(s) for the mix of items to be sent to the lockbox

Overall bank relationship (i.e., existing services with the bank, including past experience with the bank's lockbox area especially)

Existence of accelerated collection methods, such as direct-send arrangements, and whether improved availability is passed on routinely to corporate customers

Processing cutoffs for reporting deposits and processing daily check receipts, including number and frequency of daily mail pickups

Error rates (e.g., percentage of errors as compared with total items handled) and the means by which errors are detected and relayed to the company

---

discovers major discrepancies or deficiencies after initiating a lockbox, it is time consuming and usually costly to change to another bank. The time required to convert most of the company's customers to sending their remittances to a new lockbox configuration usually is in the 60- to 120-day range, and the decision to switch to another bank adds to this.

Many companies survey banks to determine the best bank for a new lockbox. To make objective comparisons among banks, they may use a request for information (RFI), a request for proposal (RFP), or a standardized questionnaire, such as the BAI/NCCMA Wholesale Lockbox Questionnaire.

The cost of the service can, of course, be an important factor in selecting a bank for lockbox services, but in many cases it will only be a minor influence. In cases where the volume of items tends to be relatively small while the size of the individual items is quite large, the major benefit of the lockbox comes from the faster check clearance, and this improvement usually far exceeds the differences in the costs for the services among several banks. In other cases where item volume is extremely large and the individual item's value is quite small, lockbox cost will be very important.

Disbursement Studies

Disbursement studies have two basic forms. The first is essentially a quantitative estimate of current clearing times for corporate checks. It may not suggest any major changes in the banking network and may only be used in establishing funding procedures or in developing predictive factors for short-term cash flow scheduling. The other type of disbursement study identifies disbursing locations to optimize the company's disbursement float.

The primary objective of a disbursement study is to identify a disbursement system that will maximize clearing float within the parameters of corporate financial policy and banking relationships. In some industries remote disbursing is still a prevalent and tolerated practice. In other industries (e.g., natural resources) remote disbursing is accepted because the country banks are located near corporate headquarters. However, in most industries, intentional remote disbursing is unacceptable and compromises the corporate image.

The typical steps in a disbursement study are:

- Quantify the float for the current system
- Rank potential disbursement locations based on projected float
- Identify the projected benefits of using multiple disbursement locations

A disbursement study is based on a typical month's payments or a full payables cycle. As in a collection study, it is important that the sample contain one twelfth of the annual corporate disbursements. In addition, study recommendations are most effective when the payee composition is consistent from month to month. Intracompany payments, payroll checks, tax payments, dividend checks, and other "nonfloatable" items are excluded from the study. A dollar cut-off is also determined to eliminate smaller items.

The data required for a study will vary with the sophistication of the study procedure. A customized study approach will examine the actual disbursement options to obtain the type of data shown in Figure 5-2. A less refined procedure would involve calculating dollar amounts sent to payees in the 106 primary zip codes, assuming that the deposit bank routing code corresponds geographically to the payee zip codes. This is a reasonable assumption, since a payee will generally not receive a check in one city and deposit it in another. In fact, corporate payees are usually collecting these disbursements in a lockbox, which acts as the company's agent.

Projected clearing times for various disbursement location alternatives are usually based on the average times published in the Phoenix-Hecht check clearing studies distributed twice a year. These studies determine the current and smoothed

Figure 5-2
Sample Disbursement Study Output

Disbursement Profile For:
Gotham National Bank

Contact:
John Smith
Vice President
Gotham National Bank
P.O. Box 12345
Gotham, NJ 07123

Federal Reserve RCPC Point
Routing Transit No.: 0212-1234

Name that appears on checks:
  Gotham National Bank
  Gotham, NJ

(201) 833-1234

Site is branch of contact bank.

Receives a second cash letter presentment
Average daily total controlled disbursement dollar presentment
is $25,000,000
Same-day notification made by: BankLink In-house system NDC
                                Telephone TWX/Telex Fax

Last Fed cash letter received at 9:30 (EST)
  — Usual first notification time window: 8:00-8:30 (EST)
    (76% of total dollars received)
  — Usual second notification time window: 9:45-10:00 (EST)
    (100% of total dollars reported)
  — Over-the-counter presentments not accepted for same-day credit
    after the first daily notification cutoff
  — Correspondent direct sends not accepted for same-day credit
    after the first daily notification cutoff

Customer funding options: ACH Item Automatic Credit Line Drawdown
                               Internal Bank Transfer Wire Transfer

Same-day funding upon notification (so that the company always has positive
collected balances by the end of the day) is required
Second presentment alternatives:
  — Two notifications – one for each presentment
  — One notification – after second presentment
  — Split funding – fund first and second presentments separately
  — Delay funding for second presentment
  — Delay funding for both presentments
  — Account reconcilement product may be used with controlled acct.

Usual number of business days after month-end at which full account
reconciliation statements are sent out: 10

Safekeeping of checks offered

---

smoothed average clearing times for $1.00 checks between 113 potential deposit locations and 113 potential drawee locations. Some cash management groups develop a supplemental data base of clearing times based on the clearing times of large dollar deposits, since those checks are often processed more rapidly than smaller checks.

If the data set includes only dollar volumes sent to each deposit point, the study is fairly straightforward. Clearing times for a disbursement account in each of the 113 potential drawee locations are projected based on the configuration of dollar volumes in the current deposit locations for the company's payees. In addition, the best two-location and three-location configuration are provided. It is interesting to note that with disbursements there are usually minimal gains available by expanding beyond two locations, and even a two-location system usually provides substantial benefits only to the Fortune 100.

Once the disbursement locations are ranked on the basis of projected clearing times, the company can choose the location with the longest clearing times that is also compatible with corporate banking relationships and control requirements. The potential gains available from selecting a given location are expressed in terms of the value of available balances associated with the clearing float.

The core of a disbursement analysis remains the projected clearing float for alternative drawee locations. Disbursement studies assume that the mail and processing float remain constant, since accounts payable functions tend to be centralized and the payee tends to collect and deposit a check in the same place. Nevertheless, it is interesting to note that the payee may subsequently conduct a receivables analysis and change a remittance location for particular disbursement checks. As the process is dynamic, a company should perform receivables and disbursement studies at regular intervals to achieve and maintain optimal float advantages.

OTHER ANALYTICAL STUDIES

Other analytical studies cover a wide range of treasury activities. For instance, they include studies with a narrow focus, such as assessing the feasibility of ACH applications or evaluating the costs and benefits of financial EDI, and those with a broader focus, such as overall treasury organizational reviews or cash management system studies.

Figure 5-3
Cost of Paying an Employee

Item	Check	EFT/ACH
Paid item charge	$0.070	$0.050
Check signer	0.001	-
Storage	0.014	-
Paper cost	0.028	0.006
Bank charges	0.030	-
Accounting dept	0.016	0.010
Start-up costs		0.020
Total direct costs	0.159	0.086

Feasibility of Automated Treasury Applications

An illustration of determining the feasibility of using an ACH transfer for paying an employee is given in Figure 5-3. The costs shown are typical but should not be taken literally. This type of analysis can be completed by the treasury manager with the help of the payroll processing personnel and can put the cost/benefit decision in proper perspective. Additional costs for either alternative can be added as the individual situation warrants. In addition, the computer start-up costs can be expressed as a fixed amount, rather than a per item cost as shown.

To the extent that float loss and/or early funding does not exceed $.073 (.159 - .086) per check, then the EFT/ACH route is cheaper. These comparisons are based on an *either/or* situation. If only a percentage converted, the potential savings would only be 0.073 times the percentage converting to ACH.

Costs and Benefits of Financial EDI

Another example of a specific analysis is comparing costs and benefits to a company from implementing financial EDI. More treasury managers are getting involved in this type of analysis, either as a major participant in a cross-functional task force or as the payments expert for the company. The cost-benefit checklist shown in Box 5-5 can help a company identify the relevant benefits and costs.

Box 5-5
EDI Cost/Benefit Worksheet

Benefits of eliminating paper-based system
Personnel

- Keying operations $_____
- Reconciliation of payments, purchase orders, etc. _____
- Filing   _____
- Retrieval   _____
- Preparing to mail   _____
- Reports   _____
- Telephone   _____
- Error resolution   _____
- Overhead   _____

Error consequences

- Misdirected orders   _____
- Loss of business due to errors   _____
- Spoiled merchandise due to errors   _____

Sales staff effectiveness

- Preparing purchase orders   _____
- Following up order status, payments, etc.   _____

Mail, paper and storage costs

- Postage   _____
- Envelopes and paper   _____
- Storage of paper documents   _____

Total estimated savings   _____

Costs of implementing EDI system
Hardware

- Computer systems   _____
- Communications hardware   _____

Software

- File conversion   _____
- Translation   _____
- Communication   _____

(continued on next page)

Box 5-5 (continued)
EDI Cost/Benefit Worksheet

Bridging

Personnel
- Additional (if any) to maintain EDI system $ _____

Training
- Internal – firm users   _____
- External – trading partners   _____

Time value costs
- Costs of earlier payments to suppliers   _____
- Network or third party   _____

Total estimated costs   _____

The detailed answers to each point may differ depending on the individual company's business lines and commitment to EDI development.

Reviewing Treasury Organizations and Procedures

In broader treasury reviews, the reviews encompass most aspects of the company's treasury activities. The recommendations may involve substantial revisions in regular operating procedures and the banking network. Their intent is usually to improve the efficiency of the company's treasury management system. They also can provide corporate blueprints for major reductions in banking arrangements and for greatly simplifying corporate cash management systems in the process. The major steps in such overall corporate treasury management reviews include:

- Determine appropriate performance criteria, which should be consistent with overall corporate performance standards.
- Review and document current flows, banking arrangements, and responsibilities.
- Analyze historical bank balances from major operating banks, comparing balances maintained with required compensating levels.
- Review and compare bank service charges.
- Study collections and disbursements in detail.

- Develop and recommend alternative systems for the company, estimating potential costs and benefits.

These major analytical activities must then be tailored to the company's individual situation and objectives. For instance, the company may wish to evaluate the feasibility of centralizing its cash management functions. In this case, the documentation of the current systems is a critical first step and may require a substantial investment by the company. In addition, the alternative solutions should consider the full impact of organizational changes and the possible reduction of local banking arrangements.

Obviously, the enormity of the tasks involved in reviewing the total cash management activities is determined by a number of critical factors. The most important factors and their primary characteristics are shown in a more detailed checklist (Box 5-6).

The organizational structure of the company can have a direct bearing on how complex and time-consuming a study will be. Often, a major study will be undertaken as part of a major corporate-wide reorganization. Current channels of communication, reporting relationships, and the strength of the financial activity throughout the company can all affect the study by creating organizational or informational barriers. In addition, the successful implementation of the study's findings will be dependent on these factors. The overall appreciation for treasury management within the company, not just the treasury manager or treasury staff, can significantly impact the study as well.

The geographic spread of major locations and the degree of local autonomy are two other major considerations in performing a treasury management review. More localized autonomy and decision making will require more detailed study on-site and the concurrence of local financial managers before any changes can be implemented.

The company's information systems can provide important support to a review if the treasury area possesses a substantial degree of automation. Lacking this, the regular systems may not be very useful in a review. The review then must be accomplished by using the manual records of the treasury function, thereby creating additional effort for the group conducting the review. In any case, the potential use or availability of in-house data processing resources should not be overlooked in conducting the review. The treasury is too often ignored as a user of data processing, although it has many needs that can be satisfied by small, in-house applications. It is quite probable that much of the current interest in microcomputers by banks and treasury managers alike has come about by the historic indifference of data processing toward the treasury function.

Box 5-6
Checklist of Major Items in a Treasury Review

Treasury organization

- Is a current organization chart for central treasury available?
- How centralized or decentralized are the company's treasury operations?
- How long have they been that way?
- If decentralized, is there a complete list of local company contacts?
- Do any of the company's operating units borrow and/or invest?
- Have there been any recent acquisitions? If so, how have they been integrated into the overall system?

Treasury policies

- Is there a formal procedures manual for treasury?
- Is there a short-term investment policy?
- Is there a bank relations policy?
- Are there job descriptions for treasury staff positions?

Treasury documentation

- Are lists of authorized signers available?
- Are copies of bank instruction letters (and enclosures) available?
- Is there a complete list of bank contacts?
- Are board resolutions available for review?
- Are there treasury management information reports, such as investment and borrowing maturities or portfolios available?
- Is there a list of credit line banks showing the amount of each line and current borrowing levels?

(continued on next page)

Finally, the scope and effectiveness of current cash management services throughout the company can greatly influence a review. If there is an absence of common services, such as lockboxes or balance reporting, the review will become more time-consuming and fundamental. If more sophisticated services are already in place, the review will tend to fine tune the existing system by adding other services or modifying procedures as appropriate.

Box 5-6 (continued)
Checklist of Major Items in a Treasury Review

Treasury technology

- Does treasury have its own computer system, such as a bank treasury work station or local area network?
- If yes, how is the system maintained?
- How are new system improvements handled?
- Is the company actively involved in electronic data interchange?
- Is treasury actively involved?

Banking network

- Is there a master list showing complete services by bank?
- Is there a flow chart of the current system?
- Are any changes to the system currently being implemented or planned?
- Are account analyses from the past year available for review?

Bank credit

- What are the compensation terms for credit lines?
- How often do the amounts or banks change?
- Are these regular lines, revolvers or other types of credit?

Recent studies

- Are copies of any recent consulting studies, internal audit reviews and/or external audit reports available?

Other investing and borrowing considerations

- Does the company issue commercial paper?
- Are historic outstanding volumes available?
- Are sales through one or more dealers or directly?
- Is there a short-term investment portfolio?
- What performance measurement benchmarks are currently used?

Treasury Management Consulting

Given the rationale and requirements for a major treasury management review, it should not be surprising that most companies must turn to outside experts for assistance. Many of the larger commercial banks, particularly those located in the major money centers, the large public accounting firms and other independent consulting firms all offer such arrangements for a fee or, in the case of many of the banks, for compensating balances. Most larger corporations faced with the task of selecting a consulting group will usually secure several proposals from one or more of the types of companies mentioned above. The final selection may depend on the company's demonstrating a solid understanding of the company's problems and a distinguished track record of performing such studies.

Structuring and refining an integrated, effective cash management system is one of the major tasks challenging corporate treasury staffs. When cash collection, disbursement, mobilization, investment, and forecasting procedures work efficiently, the company can realize substantial working capital benefits. However, it is often difficult to gauge the efficiency of an existing system or to determine areas for improvement. Bank treasury management consulting departments or specialized treasury consulting services are among the most valuable resources available to assist in the evaluation process. As corporations have grown more sophisticated in their treasury management requirements, commercial banks have been active in developing services and products that facilitate corporate treasury management operations. In addition, many management consulting firms now maintain dedicated staff with the necessary technical expertise to provide treasury consulting services. These two sources offer various skills at varying costs to help solve the corporate treasury manager's problems.

Treasury consultants can perform two types of analysis. They can conduct a general audit of the entire cash management function, which usually documents existing systems, discusses the strengths and weaknesses of those systems, and recommends further specific float or technical studies and/or basic structural improvements in the company's cash management. Also, they can perform detailed float analyses of operating cash management systems (e.g., collections, disbursements, funds concentration, or information mobilization) and indicate optimal float management decisions within the parameters of existing corporate bank relationships and internal information systems.

A Numerical Example

Float analyses measure float in terms of dollar-days and translate those days into uncollected balances. The costs associated with supporting those uncollected balances is calculated by multiplying the number of float days by the average amount collected or disbursed daily and valuing that amount by the company's cost of funds.

If a corporation collects $73 million annually and its receipts have an average of four days mail, processing, and collection float, the average uncollected balance associated with this float is:

($73,000,000 x 4)/365 = Average daily receipts = $800,000

For a company with a cost of capital of 12%, the annual cost of collection float would be $96,000 ($800,000 X 0.12). When float costs for alternative systems are compared, the differences represent the opportunity cost of using one system configuration over another.

Evaluating Consultants

Consultants can often be outside catalysts for change. Frequently, the internal resistance to restructuring a system can slow down the process and consultants can facilitate the movement toward innovation by providing an analytical framework for decision making.

Selecting consultants can be a difficult process, but it is worth the time and effort to talk to several groups before selecting one. The best consultant is one who can explain the methodology that will be applied and the rationale for that methodology. In addition, the consultant should be sensitive to the internal constraints of the organization as well as the structure of the corporate banking relationships. The optimal solution for maximizing short-term profits may not be the optimal solution for maximizing the long-term value of the firm if it disrupts existing banking/credit relationships. Developing an ongoing relationship with cash management specialists at several banks will keep the treasury manager aware of technological developments in the field as well as educate the banks of trends and concerns in the corporation's treasury policies.

During the study process, the corporate treasury manager has to stay involved, contributing to the direction of the analysis and guiding the recommendations. This involvement serves to:

- Evolve realistic solutions compatible with corporate policies
- Ensure basic data integrity
- Tailor the study procedure to the corporation
- Educate the corporate treasury manager in the current cash flow patterns and the implications of alternatives

A treasury study should produce not only recommendations for improved systems and procedures but also a valuable data profile of the corporation's cash flow (e.g., day-of-the-week patterns, geographic patterns, etc.) that can be utilized in other areas of treasury decision making. Working together, the corporate

---

Box 5-7
Reasons for Conducting a Treasury Audit

Financial exposure: Is the treasury function a financial area that has significant exposure for the corporation? How will the risks be minimized? Are sound internal controls are in place? If not, what controls should be added?

Financial contribution: Does the treasury function have the potential to make a significant contribution to the company's bottom line? What steps can be taken to maximize the efficiency of the treasury function?

Management assurance: Does senior management understand the treasury function? Will the audit (conducted by an impartial third party) assure management that the treasury function is working properly?

Update: Has the treasury function been reviewed in the past five years or less? Does management need an update on past problems or a progress report on the implementation of major projects?

Technology: Does the company need the newest technology? Are there new products that will expand the limits of treasury? Will they make the treasury function more efficient?

Regulatory changes: Are there new Federal Reserve regulations that may pose problems for the smooth functioning of treasury operations? Is the company's wire transfer processing creating daylight overdrafts?

Practice: Are there better ways to manage the company's cash flows? Does the company have too many (few) collection points? Does it have too many (too few) banking relationships?

---

treasury manager and the consultants can achieve significant ongoing benefits for the company.

Auditing the Treasury Function

Corporate treasury managers often have to deal with audit reviews of their activities. Usually, these reviews focus on specific transactions or documents. However, complete audits of the treasury function are becoming more common. Treasury managers can even help structure the audits beforehand. Some of the reasons many companies conduct treasury audits are listed in Box 5-7.

A treasury audit is different from a regular, annual audit of the company's financial condition by the company's independent auditors (or internal auditors). While some parts of treasury and some of its activities (e.g., credit lines,

---

Box 5-8
Treasury Organization Checklist

What are the specific functional areas within the overall treasury group?
> How long has treasury handled these functions? Which areas (if any) have been added or deleted recently?

How centralized or decentralized is the treasury function?
> How long has it been this way? Does this arrangement differ from other areas of finance? If so, has this posed any problems for treasury?

How much involvement with international does the treasury group have?
> Is this likely to change in the near future? If so, what effect will any change have on the current treasury function?

Where is the treasury located within the corporate organization?
> To whom does the treasurer report? Is the treasury staff able to influence actions that affect the cash flows of the money? If so, how?

How important is the treasury function to the overall firm?
> Does senior management consider it a valuable member of the financial team? Does it play a leading role in financing or other major activities?

How does the treasury function relate to other financial units in the company?
> Specifically, how does it interact with budgeting and planning, general accounting, accounts receivable, and accounts payable?

---

investment portfolios) are included in the annual audit, a comprehensive review as described below is not routinely performed. In addition, conducting a treasury audit requires expertise in corporate treasury generally and in the company's industry specifically.

If a treasury audit is to be conducted by an internal audit staff, it will require planning and coordination between corporate treasury management and internal audit supervisors. Here again, the audit team will need additional preparation and training for a special audit.

A treasury audit should identify control problems in the company's banking system. However, this may not be easy because auditors generally lack full familiarity with treasury practices, services, and regulation and because the treasury function tends to be incompletely documented.

Conducting the Audit

The first step in conducting the treasury audit is to gain an overview of the treasury function. This entails understanding the organization of the treasury function and how it interacts with the other financial groups throughout the company. It is also important to determine how important the treasury function is with regard to the overall company and how much attention it is likely to receive from senior management. A checklist of key organizational items to be reviewed at this step is shown in Box 5-8.

The next step is a specific review of treasury policies and the controls needed to comply with those policies. The review covers the overall process, including how information is routinely reported within the treasury function and to outside locations. It also covers actual inspection of typical documents, such as regular computer reports, transaction confirmations, and standard bank account agreements. Typical policies to be reviewed include:

- Bank relations and cash management services
- Short-term investments
- Foreign exchange exposure management
- Hedging interest rates and foreign exchange positions
- Forecasting cash flows
- Short-term debt instruments
- Overall corporate liquidity requirements
- Management reporting

Given these policies (or some portion of the total), the treasury audit should include a review of related controls. For example, the audit will cover who in the treasury function has the authority to enter into contractual arrangements with the company's banks and how heavily these transactions are documented. It is also important to identify which staff members can actually execute specific transactions, such as short-term investments, foreign exchange contracts, and short-term loans. The review may consider who has the authority to establish the level of hedging transactions and whether there are adequate foreign exchange guidelines that complement the hedging activities. The other major control item to be reviewed is overall signing authority: How many people have it (by account)? Where is the master list of signing authorities maintained? How often is the list reviewed or changed?

The final step in a treasury audit is a detailed review of the procedures established to carry out treasury policies. This should be combined with a review of the actual practices (which should follow the prescribed procedures) and materials gathered from various sources. Typical sources of information are shown in Box 5-9. It is in this step that the effectiveness and efficiency of the treasury function can be measured and the contribution of the function to the overall company can be determined.

Box 5-9
Treasury Audits: Sources of Information

Treasury for: bank records and agreements, loan covenants, transaction data, short-term investment portfolios, short-term debt outstanding, policy manuals, previous studies, and proposals.

Accounting for: bank statements, policy manuals, financial compliance, intra-company transaction data, previous audits

Operating units for: local transaction data, bank records, previous studies and proposals

Independent sources for: new products and services, new procedures, financial data

---

By working together with internal or external auditors, the treasury manager can benefit from an audit and get more than just a clean bill of health. If the treasury manager has been unable to get anyone's attention (at a senior level) about a potential problem area, the audit may, because the report is coming from an objective third party, have more impact on an otherwise reluctant senior executive.

FUNDAMENTAL TREASURY INFORMATION MANAGEMENT

Managing information has become the primary activity for most corporate treasury managers. However, the treasury management function can generate mountains of data, much of which must be sorted through and organized so that timely liquidity decisions can be made. This entails establishing effective decision support systems, an effective treasury information structure, and the appropriate bank-supplied information.

Decision Support Systems for Treasury

Efficient structuring of the company's payment systems and banking arrangements, in conjunction with the essential elements and influences discussed earlier, suggests the need to consider some form of decision support for the treasury operations involved with the company's cash management.

Conceptually, it is possible to devise a decision support system for essential treasury management activities in order to assist treasury in establishing and

---

Box 5-10
Major Building Blocks for Treasury Decision Support

Bank balance reporting data base

Money market operations data base

Cash projection data base

Bank compensation data base

---

maintaining control. The decision support system should tie together the diverse activities of the treasury manager and offer him or her the ability both to control the corporate cash management system and to utilize analytical techniques effectively.

There are several major building blocks in a conceptual system. These blocks establish the framework for the system. They encompass the various cash management activities, and in so doing they offer standard analytical and reporting opportunities. Also, by taking advantage of technological advances, they can increase the relative productivity of the cash management function substantially. This should allow the cash management function to extend its control over much of the corporate activities without major increases in central staff resources. The major building blocks can be thought of in terms of individual data bases for each major function (see Box 5-10). Each data base has its own characteristics, the extent of which is defined by each corporate case. However, there are common aspects that will tend to be applicable in most cases. The bases alone will not be very effective without additional analytical capabilities and regular operating reports for the treasury manager to use.

The **bank balance reporting data base** represents a central repository for bank transaction data, gathering all relevant balance and transaction detail from the company's banking network regularly. While the reporting systems differ in format and content somewhat, the data base offers a uniform medium for this information. The means of gathering numerous bank balance reporting system data is by no means simple. The use of personal computers to accomplish this task has been increasing steadily, and some companies have begun establishing direct computer link-ups with their major banks to gather data automatically. Once input into the data base, the use of the data for target balance or cash position management is possible. This data base also will support the funds movement activity, as the funds initiation services offered by most bank balance reporting systems can be accessed in conjunction with this data base. Analytical reports can suggest short-term target balance changes and funds movements to accomplish them. Also, when integrated with the other data bases, they can be used to record and effect funds movements for local account funding, cash concentration, and liquidity management activities.

The **money market operations data base** comprises the short-term liquidity operations for the company. It records daily investment and/or borrowing transactions and uses these data, together with data from other data bases, to project the net cash needs or excesses of the company. In situations where the money market activity is substantial, involving different sources of short-term borrowings, this data base plays a key role in integrating the treasury manager's activities. In such cases, analytical capabilities and comparative reports, such as those that were outlined earlier, are essential. The captured data with future maturities also can be of great use in analyzing the company's projected cash position and can help in formulating short-term borrowing or investment strategies. Regular operating reports generated by this base should include accounting reports and maturity schedules for the treasury manager. At present, most of the data to be input into this base is, unfortunately, not available in machine-readable form and must be input manually.

The **cash projection data base** takes the cash estimates and converts them to a common format, allowing the treasury manager to analyze differences and make modifications efficiently. Data can be input manually if not too voluminous, or tie-ins to local computer systems can be of help in handling data input. To incorporate the telephone type of system discussed earlier, manual entry would probably be the method chosen. Again, developments in microcomputer applications offer considerable help. The projection data base provides the expected cash flow data to compare with the actual data reported by the bank balance reporting systems. As such, it is an integral part of cash position management activities. It is also used in analyzing possible future cash positions or anticipated money market transactions and assessing their impact. By linking this data base with the others, sophisticated analytical techniques can be incorporated into the treasury manager's tool kit.

The last data base is **bank compensation**, which provides the historical tracking from the monthly account analysis statements and data from the balance reporting data base. This base provides overall analyses of bank compensation performance. In addition, it computes appropriate bank target balances and compares bank costs for similar services. This data base offers many analytical possibilities, drawing from historical data, and it can be valuable in investigating new services or in resolving problems with the company's banks. When structured to include the balances from independent subsidiaries, it also provides a

---

Figure 5-11
Fundamental Components of Treasury Information Systems

General level

- Overall system security
- System access protocols
- Data base manager (e.g., dBase IV)
- System communications programs (e.g., CrossTalk)
- Word processing programs (e.g., Word)
- Graphics programs (e.g., Harvard Graphics)
- Spreadsheet programs (e.g., Lotus, Excel, Quattro Pro)

Specific level

- Bank relationship manager
- Cash balance worksheet
- Bank balance/transaction reports
- Funds transfer initiation
- Investment portfolios
- Short-term borrowing reports
- Cash forecasting and scheduling
- Accounting/general ledger interface

---

means of monitoring their performance in a manner similar to the rest of the corporation. Some large companies have now linked this data base with their major banks by establishing electronic transmission of account analysis information monthly as a standard EDI transaction.

These data bases encompass the major areas of cash management that must be included in any control system. The conceptual decision support system can be considered as a beginning, a blueprint for the treasury manager in constructing and maintaining an effective and beneficial system of control over the company's cash management activities.

Components of a Treasury Information System

Building a comprehensive treasury information system was not a top priority for treasury managers or their company's systems staff for a long time. That seems to have changed at present. As PCs have proliferated in corporate offices, the treasury function has also enjoyed the benefits of automation.

There are several fundamental components of treasury information systems (see Box 5-11). It is useful to consider them in two levels, general and specific functions. The general level includes such functions as system access, security and other general tools, many of which may be simple off-the-shelf software products, like spreadsheets. This is particularly true if the treasury information system is part of a local area network (LAN). The more specific functions can represent treasury work station products offered by a few software vendors or customized systems developed in-house. The types of specific functions will depend on the individual company.

Banks and corporations can interact electronically to develop further treasury information system integration. The most common way to do this is by using treasury work stations, which are PC-based systems. The end result enables the treasury manager to receive summary and detailed bank balance and transaction data directly into a PC. After this, the data can be reformatted, analyzed, reported or transmitted under the treasury manager's own control.

Reports can be sent to outlying units through the company's internal communications system, for instance, or different areas of corporate treasury and accounting can have access individualized reports for their functions. Using a PC can eliminate many of the manual procedures that were for so long a normal practice in treasury. Typical treasury work station applications include:

- Balance reporting
- Bank relationship management (contacts, signing authorities, etc.)
- Investment or debt management
- Daily cash ledger/worksheet
- Wire transfer initiation
- Cash forecasting

Bank Information

Banks provide a great deal of information to companies daily. Types of data that are available are shown in Box 5-12. Treasury managers on most large companies have been long-time users of these systems for most of the information shown, especially the previous-day type. Many access the systems for same-day information as well, although it does entail an additional cost and not all banks can provide comprehensive same-day data on a timely basis.

Box 5-12
Bank Information Reporting

Previous-day reports

- Account balances, showing ledger and collected balances at the close of business on the previous day for individual accounts and summarized for the company, as well as balance histories for specified past time periods
- Detailed debits and credits (deposits, transfers and clearings) for selected accounts and total transaction summaries by account and for the company
- Deposit information, including lockbox totals, showing one- and two-day float amounts
- Adjustments for errors or other changes in past reports
- Borrowing reports, such as credit line usage, commercial paper issuance
- Custody/safekeeping reports on securities held
- DTC registers showing amounts by sending location (may also be available late on the same day)

Current-day reports

- Account balance summaries
- Specific incoming transfers (usually over a certain minimum amount)
- ACH reports
- Controlled disbursement notifications (may also be by telephone)
- Outgoing wire transfers

CASH SCHEDULING AND FORECASTING

Developing a responsive, effective approach to projecting cash flows can be a difficult challenge for the treasury manager. This is because the true nature of what is to be projected and for how long may differ substantially from company to company. In addition, establishing an efficient network of information flow between users/providers of cash and the preparer of the cash flow projections can be overwhelming. Treasury managers have to forecast cash flows for three major reasons:

- **Planning**: Determining a sense of direction for the company's short-term cash needs, as well as its longer-term working capital requirements
- **Monitoring**: Understanding the nature of the company's cash flows, how their change could affect the company's overall liquidity, and what safety precautions are called for
- **Control**: Ensuring that the company's short-term assets are protected and its short-term liabilities are managed prudently

To accomplish these broad objectives, the corporate treasury manager must consider developing a cash scheduling and forecasting system. We use the term *scheduling* to differentiate between short-term cash flow projections, where many of the flows are known or are typically estimated without the aid of sophisticated models but by experience and consensus, and longer-term cash forecasts (for time periods of one month to several years).

Developing a Cash Scheduling System

There are a number of logical steps in developing a short-term cash scheduling system. The typical treasury manager faces a sensitive task in developing and establishing an effective company-wide cash scheduling system. While individual corporations may possess some distinct idiosyncrasies, the fundamental approach to establishing such a system does not vary significantly from case to case. A treasury manager often will find it necessary to adopt a rational, systematic approach to this estimating problem.

The first major step in the development process is a definitional stage. That is, before the treasury manager can begin to design and receive periodic estimates of the company's cash flows, the basic parameters surrounding the estimation process must be defined. These basic parameters (see Box 5-13) provide the essential framework and heavily influence the operating requirements and procedures of the scheduling system.

Whatever the final list of data elements looks like, it should encompass all the different uses and sources of funds for the company. The elements should be clearly described so that the provider of the estimate can understand precisely what is needed. For instance, cash collections should be broken down further into lockbox and local office deposits for estimating purposes. Breaking the elements down into smaller units will make the estimates more useful. The identification of variances and the reasons behind the variances will also be far easier.

Once the list of data elements has been formulated, it should be relatively straightforward to identify the best source for providing regular estimates of each

---

Box 5-13
Basic Cash Scheduling Parameters

Description of data items to be estimated

Identification of the source(s) of estimates

Frequency of regular estimates

Time period(s) covered by regular estimates

Method and format for transmitting estimates

Procedures for modifying estimates

Means of gathering data

Level of accuracy required or expected

Consolidation and reporting procedures

Expected use of consolidated estimates

---

item. The potential sources will, in large part, be dictated by the corporate organization. For instance, in a decentralized company the local financial managers will usually possess a great deal of control over their individual collections and disbursements. As a result, these managers should be the logical sources of regular estimates, as they are in the best position of knowing the characteristics of their flows.

Impact of Decentralization

Even in decentralized companies, however, there may be several centralized activities, such as consolidated tax payments, central pension fund payment processing, corporate insurance payments, or other corporate staff functions. Furthermore, the treasury area itself may often control various items, such as investments or debt, and should provide the estimates of these variables.

At this point of review, it should also be possible to identify any preliminary problems in supplying estimates. For example, the decentralized unit may be unable to provide estimates in a form that the treasury manager can readily use. This may often be the case for disbursements that are funded centrally by the treasury manager but are prepared and sent out by the local financial manager. In these instances the local manager is not concerned with and usually does not track the clearings in his or her disbursement account. Therefore, the central treasury manager must be able to translate the local manager's estimate into terms

Figure 5-4
Sample System for Cash Flow Estimates

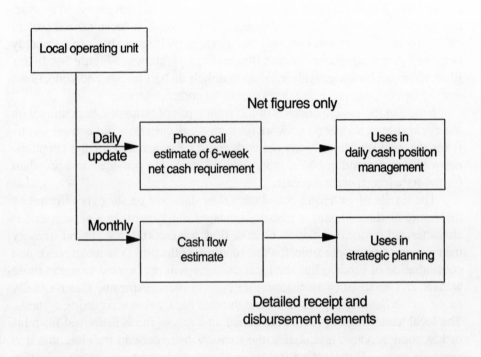

that are meaningful to the treasury manager. This can be done by various methods, the most common one being a disbursement clearing analysis. Historical patterns and percentages are often provided by the company's commercial banks in their full reconciliation program and can be used to update the factors regularly.

However, the company's own internal processing systems must be capable of providing accurate issuance data to the reconciliation program for this tool to have any application at all. If this alternative is not available to the treasury manager, he or she must rely on personal experience or construct a rudimentary system. This can be done by receiving daily figures of disbursements mailed and estimating clearings on a proportional basis in a similar fashion to the staggered funding procedure described in Chapter 3.

The next three major parameters — frequency, time periods covered, method and format for the estimates — can be treated as a related package when establishing them. For example, if the frequency is weekly or more often, then the use of the mails may not be timely enough. The time periods covered in such a case will also be affected in that an extremely frequent reporting system will probably not be able to accommodate very lengthy projections. It should be noted as well that the degree of decentralized inputs will have a direct bearing on these parameters. This means that the treasury manager should not expect to receive, nor for that matter should he or she attempt to establish, a decentralized system calling for numerous input variables on an extremely frequent basis (e.g., weekly or better). A typical system for cash flow estimates is shown in Figure 5-4. In this illustration local units provide estimates of their disbursements and collections, and the treasury manager translates them into common terms.

Note that the system consists of different types of estimates, beginning with a very short-term telephone network for intra-week cash flow projections — this is for the cash schedule. A fax network could be substituted for the telephone network. On a monthly basis, more detailed items are provided in a standard format for a longer-term forecast.

The means of gathering actual cash flow data will be strongly affected by the nature of the company's treasury management system. In a system that is characterized by local initiation of cash flow transactions, the central treasury manager is often responsible for the funding, collection (via lockboxes), and concentration of funds. Thus the local manager will not be able to report those actuals, and the treasury manager must establish alternate means. This is usually based on the detailed reports available through bank balance reporting systems. The local manager can provide the actual amounts of funds disbursed from his or her point of view, and, again, the treasury manager can translate this into common terms. This is often treated in the same manner as the modification process discussed earlier. This is another instance in which the decentralization of the cash flow system can create estimating problems for the treasury manager. Thus the need for keeping the estimating system quite simple and for establishing a frequent and easy method of transmitting data is quite important and must figure prominently in the establishment of the estimating procedures.

Consolidating and Reporting

Finally, the consolidation and reporting of the estimates and the expected use of the consolidated estimates must be considered in conjunction with one another. The primary user of the consolidated estimate will be the treasury manager or the member of the corporate treasury staff who manages the daily cash position for the company. This person needs the estimate expressed in terms of the net effects on the daily cash position, extended out through the normal short-term planning horizon. This latter time period may vary from company to company but must be established in the regular procedures for processing and analyzing the estimates.

Summaries of the short-term estimate are typically provided to treasury management, especially in larger companies, where other areas of treasury are responsible for financing or investment transactions. Longer projections, such as monthly ones, are often summarized as well and distributed outside the treasury area to other financial areas. The use of these reports will tend to vary from company to company but should be established formally when creating a cash scheduling system.

Once the cash flow estimates are received or prepared regularly, some form of analytical review will be required. This can take the form of simply tracking historical estimates and actuals to more elaborate variance analyses. The purpose of the review is to determine the effectiveness of the system in its ability to provide meaningful estimates within the accuracy guidelines expected for it and to identify operating or communications problems at an early stage. Obviously, the analysis should identify possible sources of the errors, and future reviews should be able to demonstrate the effectiveness of actions taken to resolve the problems identified. Care must be taken, however, not to treat the analysis as a report card on the providers of the estimates.

The expected level of accuracy in the estimates must be kept in mind as well as the way variations are treated. That is, there may be logical, reasonable causes of large variations, and overreaction may create different problems for the analyzer. In any case, the analysis process should be kept in the proper perspective: Its objectives are to maintain a sound estimating system and resolve problems as effectively as possible without becoming one itself.

Cash Flow Forecasting

In most cash flow forecasting problems, the most efficient approach is to break down the cash flows into their major components. This is done because the determinants for each component can have different effects and, consequently, can call for different forecasting techniques. For example, it may be appropriate to split disbursements into large-sized trade payables, small payable payments, corporate interest, shareholder dividends, payroll disbursements, etc. It is often useful to group the cash flows by their degree of predictability. For instance, three groups can be chosen:

- **Certain flows**: Many cash flows are known in advance and do not therefore have to be estimated. If these flows are not separated from other less certain flows, it may be difficult to develop a reasonable forecast. Examples of certain cash flows include consolidated tax payments, interest on long-term, (or even short-term debt if it is "long" enough), and preferred stock dividends, which are often funded well ahead of the payment date.

- **Forecastable flows**: Many flows are not certain but can be estimated with reasonable accuracy based on another variable. For example, cash receipts from regular customer payments can usually be forecast within narrow ranges. Based on regular collection times and historical credit terms, these estimates can be used to predict actual deposits in corporate lockboxes.

- **Unpredictable flows**: Other cash flows will remain uncertain and cannot be forecast successfully. For example, an unanticipated receipt or unplanned major disbursement might pop up without warning. The presence of many of these items can create major obstacles for an effective cash flow forecasting system. It is obvious that the treasury manager needs to spend a great deal of time working on this group of cash flow components to be able to shift them to one of the other groups.

There are a number of techniques that enable the treasury manager to develop short-term cash forecasts. The basic format used for cash scheduling, the receipts and disbursement approach, can also be used for a cash forecast.

The Distribution Method

While there are a variety of statistical and hybrid approaches, one specialized technique, the distribution method, is used in many cash forecasting situations. Cash flows that are thought of as single entities are often received or paid out over several days. For example, payroll checks may take several days to clear even though they were all issued on the same date. The distribution method of forecasting cash flows can be used to spread the total amount over the days on which the cash flow will occur. The input variable for the distribution forecast is the total estimated cash flow to be allocated to the days of the forecast horizon. The total is spread over the days in the forecast horizon by multiplying the total by estimates of the proportions that will occur on each day.

For example, to apply this technique to determine the funding of monthly payroll, the total cash flow would be the total dollar amount of the payroll. The distribution method would estimate the percentage of the total that would clear on the first, second, third, etc., business days after the payroll date. See Figure 5-5 for an example of forecasting using the distribution method. The distribution method is accurate, allows seasonality and trends to be incorporated and is relatively easy and economical to prepare. However, it usually calls for a large

Figure 5-5
Forecasting with the Distribution Method

A company has used a regression model to estimate the proportion of dollars that will clear its disbursement account on a given business day. It has determined that the proportion depends on the day of the week and on the number of business days since the checks were distributed. The estimated proportions are as follows:

Business Days Since Distribution	Pct. Expected to Clear	Day of the Week	Incremental Percent
1	13%	Monday	-2%
2	38	Tuesday	0%
3	28	Wednesday	2%
4	13	Thursday	1%
5	08	Friday	-1%

For example, if $100,000 in payroll checks was distributed on Thursday, June 1, the estimated dollar clearing on each day is as follows:

Date	Percent clearing	Dollars clearing
June 1 (Thurs.)	13% + 1% = 14%	$14,000
June 2 (Fri.)	38% - 1% = 37%	$37,000
June 5 (Mon.)	28% - 2% = 26%	$26,000
June 6 (Tues.)	13% + 0% = 13%	$13,000
June 7 (Wed.)	8% + 2% = 10%	$10,000

---

amount of data to estimate the proportions used to distribute the amount to be predicted.

The Percentage-of-Sales Method

Projected profit and loss statements (P&Ls) and balance sheets can form the basis of predicted cash flows over a longer forecast horizon. Most techniques are based on the percentage-of-sales method, in which financial statements are projected, based upon future sales and the historical relationship between sales and balance sheet items. A significant number of balance sheet items are linked to sales in this way: cash, inventory, accounts receivable, accounts payable, etc. Items that are not proportional to sales are treated on an individual basis; they are typically

---

Box 5-14
Preparing a Percentage-of-Sales Forecast

Prepare sales forecast.

Identify which balance sheet and income statement (P&L) items can be estimated as a specific percentage of sales, i.e., which can be based on historical averages or more sophisticated statistical approaches, such as regression.

Simply project or estimate other balance sheet and P&L items that are assumed to be constant or updated with available information, such as projecting the level of long-term debt on the basis of the current amount outstanding plus scheduled changes.

Project net worth at its current level plus any additions to retained earnings and planned new issues, less dividends.

---

assumed to be constant unless more specific information is available. After generating these projections, it is usually the case that total assets do not equal total liabilities and equity. If the assets are larger, then the company has a cash surplus; if the assets are smaller, the company has a cash shortage that will have to be financed through debt or equity. Several versions of the forecast may be prepared under different assumptions to indicate the range of possible cash flows.

The percentage of sales method requires the steps shown in Box 5-14. This can be a useful approach because sale forecasts are often readily available to the corporate treasury manager. Thus, if a link between sales and key treasury items can be established, a meaningful cash forecast can be developed.

Either of two methods can be used to obtain a cash flow estimate from projected financial statements. The first approach is known as the **adjusted net income approach** and involves the following steps:

- Cash flow from operations (net income plus all non-cash deductions, such as depreciation) is calculated.
- Decreases in assets (except for depreciation) and increases in liabilities are determined.
- Increases in assets, decreases in liabilities and dividends are computed.

The difference between the first two categories (the sources of cash) and the third category (the uses of cash) is the net cash flow.

Figure 5-6
Example of a Percentage-of-Sales Forecast

Income Statement		Pro forma	
Sales	1,000	Sales	1,250
Cost of sale	800	Costs *(80% of sales)*	1,000
Taxable income	200	Taxable income	250
Taxes (@ 40%)	80	Taxes	100
Net income	120	Net income	150
Retained earnings	80	Retained earnings	100
Dividends (assuming a dividend payout of 1/3)	40	Dividends	50

Balance Sheet

	Amount	Pct. of sales		Amount	Pct. of sales
Cash	160	16%	Accts payable	300	30%
Accts receivable	440	44	Notes payable	100	
Inventory	600	60	Current liabilities	400	
Current assets	1,200		Long-term debt	800	
Fixed assets	1,800		Common + surplus	800	
			Retained earnings	1,000	
Total assets	3,000		Total liab. + equity	3,000	

Pro forma

Cash	200	Accts payable	375	
Accts receivable	550	Notes payable	100	
Inventory	750	Current liabilities	475	
Current assets	1,500	Long-term debt	800	
Fixed assets	1,800	Common + surplus	800	
		Retained earnings (from previous amt. of 1000 + this yr's 100)	1,100	
Total assets	3,300	Total liab. + equity	3,175	

The difference between Total liabilities and equity and Total assets – 125 – represents the net financing requirements.

In the second approach, the amount by which projected liabilities and net worth exceed or fall short of projected assets represents a cash surplus (inflow) or a cash shortage (outflow). Figure 5-6 illustrates a forecast based on the percentage of sales method, showing the forecast in the form of pro forma financial statements. Note that the projected balance sheet does not balance. The difference between total assets and total liabilities and equity (if positive) represents the firm's financing requirements.

Statistical Forecasting

Statistical approaches to cash forecasting have had greatly varying degrees of success. There have not been very generic solutions available since the characteristics of each firm's cash flows are so important in determining the statistical approach. The statistical approaches briefly reviewed below provide an introduction to the complex issue of time series forecasts.

Time Series Forecasting

Simple moving averages are *extrapolative* methods in that they base a forecast on a simple average of past values of the variable to be predicted. A one-step ahead forecast is prepared by calculating the average of some number of the most recent actual values for the cash flow or cash flow item in question. Because each observation used in the estimation has the same weight, the speed with which the forecast adjusts to trends or seasonal variations depends on the number of observations. When this is large (e.g., over 50), then the most recent cash flow has very little influence on the forecast. In any case, a forecast prepared using a simple moving average will *always* lag any trend in the actual cash flow.

Exponential smoothing assigns declining weights to each observation in the sample. A simple exponential smoothing forecast is shown in Figure 5-7. This equation shows that the exponential smoothing forecast for the next period is equal to last period's forecast plus a correction (a constant, times the forecast error) for the most recent forecast error. A large smoothing constant has the same effect as a small sample in a simple moving average forecast; for both, the most recent observation exerts more influence on the direction of the forecast. As in simple moving average forecasts, a simple exponential smoothing forecast will lag any trend in the data. To correct for this, and to allow seasonality in the forecast, there are extensions of exponential smoothing that allow the user to incorporate trend and seasonality.

In this example, for days 6 through 8, two types of forecasts are generated. The first is a simple moving average using the past five days. For example, the forecast for day 6 is:

Figure 5-7
An Example of Exponential Smoothing and Moving Averages

Day	Cash Flow	Moving Average		Exponential Smoothing	
		Forecast	Error	Forecast	Error
1	110	-	-	-	-
2	120	-	-	-	-
3	115	-	-	-	-
4	122	-	-	-	-
5	126	-	-	-	-
6	124	118.6	5.4	118.6	5.2
7	129	121.4	7.6	120.8	8.2
8	133	128.8	9.8	124.0	8.4

$$F_6 = (110 + 120 + 115 + 122 + 126)/5 = 118.8.$$

The resulting forecast error (also called the **residual**) is the difference between the actual value and the forecast:

$$U_6 = X_6 - F_6 = 124 - 118.6 = 5.4.$$

For the exponential smoothing example, the general formula is:

$$F_{t+1} = X_t + [X (X_t - F_t)].$$

It is necessary to initialize the forecast; in this case the moving average forecast is used. In this example, a value of .4 was used for α, so that the forecast for day 7 is:

$$F_7 = 124 + .4(124 - 118.6) = 120.76 .$$

More Complex Approaches
Regression analysis is a statistical technique that establishes the best linear relationship between the cash flow to be predicted (i.e., the independent variable) and one or more input (i.e., explanatory) variables. It is often used in conjunction with the distribution method for forecasting cash flows. A computer is necessary to develop regression models of any practical size. G. Box and G. Jenkins developed a systematic approach to identifying, estimating and testing time series models. These models are often called **Box-Jenkins** or **ARIMA** (autoregressive integrated moving average) models and are among the most sophisticated time

series approaches. Moving average and exponential smoothing models are special cases of ARIMA models.

Statistical techniques can provide accurate forecasts for those cash flow components that (at least approximately) meet the technical assumptions of each model. Computer software is available for all of the techniques described, and, especially for the averaging models, forecasts can be generated quickly at low cost. On the other hand, the more sophisticated approaches (such as regression and Box-Jenkins) require specialized knowledge and often a large amount of data to develop a suitable model.

MANAGEMENT REVIEW ITEMS

➡ Don't panic over announced mail time changes. Too often, treasury managers rush out to conduct collection studies before the standard mail time surveys have measured and incorporated any changes (if there were any) into their standard values. Remember that many mail time changes affect retail mail more than wholesale (i.e., company to company) mail.

➡ Remember that postmark dates are not always accurate (error rates of 10%-12% have been found).

➡ Availability times can be misleading because banks may have different availability cutoff times. If there is any doubt, ask your bank for a report that shows exactly what your availability has been over a period of time. (Any bank that is serious about offering collection services will have such a report.)

➡ Ask your current lockbox banks for their Phoenix-Hecht Lockbox Profile Reports. Also, ask any prospective bank for this report. If the bank does not have a report, consider whether it is serious about lockbox services.

➡ Be careful with the scale of your check size when doing a collection or disbursement study. If not, large dollar items can make small fractions of a day significant, thereby skewing the findings.

➡ If a disbursement study has not been conducted in several years and your system is several years old, consider doing one currently. You may not be interested in finding a new disbursement location or even lengthening your disbursement float, but you may wish to quantify current disbursement float for forecasting purposes or to determine whether there are any obvious inefficiencies in the current system.

➡ Use common sense when studying disbursements. Setting up a system that utilizes banks that are not part of the overall corporate network may not stand up in the long run and may not offer true *control* over disbursements.

➡ Incorporate the results of collection or disbursement studies into requests for proposals for bank services.

➡ Before launching an EDI cost-benefit analysis, review expense and benefit items with other (non-treasury) areas to customize your approach.

➡ Sit down and draw a flow chart of the company's treasury systems, including the banking network — as it is supposed to be. Then review this chart with treasury staff to identify any discrepancies, omissions, or possible problem areas. If it is impossible to flow chart the systems, a bigger problem has been identified. Then, try to develop a flow chart with help from those staff members responsible for the functions.

➡ Insist on building in an *ad hoc* reporting capability for all treasury data bases. The ability to develop reports quickly in response to management requests will be well worth the investment.

➡ Cash management functions and corresponding bank services can reduce the complexity of a company's cash forecasting system. Analyze forecasting requirements in light of the cash management services already in place or those that could be established.

➡ Forecasting methodology does not mean selecting a canned statistical package and feeding it mountains of historical data. It involves the matching of possible sources of reliable information, subject to acceptable levels of precision and accuracy.

➡ The method of bank compensation can also affect the forecasting system methodology. If you use balances, you may not require as fine a level of accuracy in the forecast because you may have sufficient funds "in the system" to cover emergency shortfalls. This is not the case if you pay by fee.

➡ Short-term cash forecasting (and probably medium-term forecasting as well) always should take the form of a receipts and disbursements projection, using as the focal point the consolidated forecasting entity, usually corporate treasury.

➡ Before attempting to use a more formal forecasting technique, such as statistical routine, split receipts and disbursements into two separate pieces to be attacked individually. Then use the "eyeball" approach by graphing the data and trying to determine if there is an obvious pattern to the flows. If one is not evident, don't expect much from the statistical programs.

CHAPTER 6

DEALING WITH BANKS

One of the most important tasks of the treasury manager, regardless of his or her level in the treasury organization, is managing bank relationships. This is something that a treasury manager, even if he or she becomes the senior treasury executive will always be involved in. Similarly, companies of all sizes must face issues of bank relations, both on the credit and non-credit sides.

This chapter describes the types of activities involved in managing bank relations:

- Managing the banking network
- Bank compensation
- Bank documentation
- Measuring bank performance
- Dealing with bank risk

MANAGING THE BANKING NETWORK

As companies grow in size and sophistication, so do their banking needs. As a company grows, its banking arrangements are usually arranged into a hierarchical structure. Designing, evaluating, and maintaining a banking network takes time and effort. One of the most fundamental tasks is bank selection.

Bank Selection

In establishing new banking relationships and in assessing or modifying existing ones, a logical framework of workable criteria is necessary. Several general criteria that can assist the treasury manager are shown in Box 6-1.

Box 6-1
General Criteria for Bank Selection

Role of the bank

Services needed

Sophistication of services

Quality of services

Location

The role of the bank is the overall guide for selecting or modifying the relationship. The treasury manager must first decide whether the bank is to play a major role as one or the only concentration bank for the company, thereby fulfilling a substantial portion of the company's banking needs. On the other hand, the bank may only be expected to be a regional collector of funds or even a local payroll bank. The banks may also play a major role in the credit requirements of the company and can become an important financial resource and advisor for the company. The number and complexity of such relationships will usually be dependent on the size of the company and the nature of its organization and relative internal autonomies.

Banking relationships must be developed in a consistent, logical manner. They represent major commitments from both the corporation and the bank and are not typically changed haphazardly. The lead bank relationship is something continually sought by most banks, and, when established, it is relatively stable. From the company's point of view, it is desirable to have relatively few major relationships in order to concentrate its cash efficiently and to take advantage of more advanced services and techniques. The attractiveness of a stabilized, effective banking network is also a major factor in establishing major roles for a company's banks.

In the past, there was a tendency on the part of the treasury manager and the lead bank to become complacent in that the lead relationship was viewed as sacrosanct. In recent years this has changed. In either case, once a lead relationship has been developed and the bank (or banks) and the company are satisfied that a proper level of compensation has been established, that bank (or banks) will have an advantage over other banks. This is due to the willingness of the company's treasury staff to discuss problems and needs with its major banks first and the ability of a major bank to consider the overall profitability of the company to the bank in instituting new services. If, on the other hand, the bank plays a minor role in the overall corporate network, this should be understood by the treasury staff and the bank at the beginning of any new relationship. In fulfilling this secondary role the bank should be certain that it will receive the proper level of compensation. As the bank does not have many different services to be able to "bundle up" its charges, each one it provides should be able to stand on its own. These secondary banks often provide essential services, such as providing key collection points in the corporation's overall cash management system. As such, their selection becomes an important decision in establishing an effective cash management system and supporting bank network.

Finally, banks may be needed at the local level for plant payrolls or small, operating accounts. The selection of these banks is less critical than that of the types of banks previously discussed, but it does require some attention. Often local plant personnel will recommend one or two banks because the banks are located conveniently to the plant, have offered personal banking services to local company personnel, or have provided financial assistance to incoming employees or in local financial matters. In states with widespread branching, it may be possible to utilize a local branch of one of the company's major banking relationships, thus keeping that local banking point "in the family."

Implicit in the consideration of a bank's role is the assumption that the corporate treasury manager has identified the services required from each bank. Credit and non-credit services offered by banks may be influenced by their size, location, or internal resources. For instance, if a corporation desires substantial lines of credit, it will probably first look at larger banks, which can offer more credit than smaller banks. Likewise, if a lockbox service is needed, banks located in regional cities with more advanced lockbox services will offer a more attractive alternative than banks located in other non-city locations.

Just as important as the type of service needed is the degree of sophistication of that service. If a company requires an automated lockbox service, for example, it must seek out those banks that can provide such a service efficiently and cost effectively. Closely related to the degree of sophistication is the issue of the quality of the service, which is measured by:

- Relative error rates
- Completion of daily workload on a timely basis
- The ability of the bank to provide customized services to various customers economically and efficiently

The last aspect of bank selection is that of the location. Because the U.S. banking system does not yet permit interstate branching, a corporation doing business in various parts of the country or, more especially, a corporation with one or more plants located in different areas of the country will probably have to

---

Box 6-2
Standard RFP Items

Bank contact(s)

Corporate contact(s)

Authorized signers and users of the account

Current system data: average transaction volumes, basic
operating procedures, existing provider(s) of services

Format for projecting average expense of new service
(e.g., account analysis format)

Timetable for decision-making

Information on error handling

Emergency or special situation procedures

Format and deadline for submission

---

establish some sort of local operating relationships. These arrangements may be quite minor or relatively significant, depending on the company and location involved. The more decentralized a company's treasury is, the more important local bank relations will be. Thus, location can, of its own accord, become a substantial decision criterion in bank selection.

Using RFPs

Many companies have formalized their selection process by using request for proposals (RFPs) for banking services. As companies have gained experience with fundamental bank cash management services (e.g., lockbox, controlled disbursements), they regard many of these services as "commodities." That is, they are indifferent, as long as the quality of the service is comparable, as to which of their banks provides the service. Price and service performance become the pivotal issues. To make a decision in as objective a framework as possible, many companies have turned to the request for proposal as a vehicle.

The standard items in any RFP are shown in Box 6-2. As companies complete RFPs for specific services, they would obviously add their specific requirements to this list of basic points.

Figure 6-1
Bank Compensation Summary

Banks	Average Balances Year-to-Date ($000)			
	Ledger	Collected	Required*	Fees Paid
Bank A	2,000	1,500	3,000	5.00
Bank B	1,400	1,400	3,200	6.00
Bank C	1,000	650	3,500	9.50
Bank D	500	150	150	0.00
Bank E	2,350	100	5,100	16.67
ALL	7,250	4,800	14,950	7.17

*In this example, balances are valued at 4% per year or .333% per month.

BANK COMPENSATION

Bank compensation requires time and effort on the part of the treasury manager. This area of treasury management has taken on a significant role in determining the overall corporation-bank relationship. Account analyses provide basic data to the corporation and are the building blocks for bank target balances as well as a bank compensation information system. As bank compensation arrangements drift more toward explicit fees, the need for an effective information system that can incorporate current data will increase. Thus the bank compensation aspect of treasury management encourages the establishment of more effective control over corporate treasury activities and requires a higher degree of information reporting than in previous times.

As bank compensation becomes more complex, it is monitored on an ongoing basis. Figure 6-1 shows a sample tracking report for a company compensating its five banks with a fee-balance combination. In one case (Bank D), the balances offset the requirements, so no fee has been paid. The collected balance column represents the average collected balance maintained, and this amount is used to offset the fees (at the bank's earnings credit rate) before the actual fees (shown in the fees paid column) are remitted. This type of report is often maintained on a computer spreadsheet.

Understanding Account Analyses

The most common reports received by a company from its banks are the **bank account analysis statements**, usually referred to just as **account analyses**. An account analysis is a detailed statement prepared by a bank for each corporate account, normally on a monthly basis. The report shows the service charges associated with the activity for each account for the period and computes a theoretical profit that the bank ''earned'' on the average balances in the account over the period. These statements have long served as a fundamental information source between a bank and its corporate customer. Increasingly, however, as more companies convert to fee compensation, the account analysis is becoming the backup to an invoice for services — or the invoice itself. Consequently, more importance has been placed on the accuracy, format, and timely delivery of the statements.

Account analysis statements have not yet been produced in a uniform format. However, there have been efforts to standardize account analysis statements by individual companies and the Treasury Management Association (formerly NCCMA: National Corporate Cash Management Association). The latter group released its standard in November 1987. By surveying a sample of corporations, the association developed a format that incorporated the desired features from the users of the statements. The effort was also supported by 26 commercial banks. The participating banks contributed financially to the project as well as technically by discussing differences among the banks in handling account analysis information.

The basic sections are shown in Box 6-3. The sections break up the pieces of an account analysis statement into logical sections, showing as much detail and history as possible. Box 6-3 also displays the other feature of this standard — the categorization of service charges into families. The individual service charges from the participating banks were coded (numerically) to the standard. In this way, corporate treasury managers can compare charges easily. New banks can have their service charge components coded by submitting them to the association.

Unfortunately, this approach is a slow one; banks are not prepared to revamp their account analysis systems overnight. Many banks will be taking steps to accommodate the standard gradually. In the meantime, corporate treasury managers must continue with many varied paper-based formats. A development that may accelerate the standardization of account analyses is the **electronic transmission standard**. In 1991, the Treasury Management Association, in conjunction with the American National Standards Institute (ANSI) released a standard transaction set for account analysis transmission. For corporations with many

Box 6-3
Standard Account Analysis - Section Titles and Families

I: Customer Information – account information, bank contact ,and other identifying information

II: Current and Historic Balance and Compensation Information – average balances (ledger, float and collected), earnings credit rate, fees paid and other compensation data by month, on a year-to-date basis

III: Adjustment Detail – detailed descriptions of all adjustments made to a bank account during the reporting period

IV: Management Summary of All Accounts – recap of key information, such as average balances and service charges for each account with the bank

V: Service Description and Cost Information – summary and details for each service charge, grouped by standard service charge family

Service Charge Families :
- General account services
- Depository services
- Lockbox services
- Disbursement services
- Funds transfer services
- Reconciliation services
- Information services
- International services
- Securities services
- Trust services
- Credit services
- Miscellaneous services

banks and, accordingly, many account analyses, this may be very useful. The largest banks, which participated in the development of this standard, should be able to transmit the information electronically in the near future.

Main Features

Although the formats for account analyses differ widely from bank to bank, the main elements usually include the following:

- **Average balances**: These are calculated on an average calendar basis and include ledger, float, and collected balances.
- **Earnings allowance:**This is the rate used to value the average collected balance for compensation purposes. It is usually tied to a money market, such as the average 90-day T-bill rate.
- **Reserve requirement**: This is the rate charged to the bank on corporate demand deposits by the Federal Reserve. As of 1992, it is 10%.
- **Service charges**: These are itemized by more detailed activity components for each account, with a total for each account. These may be shown as charges only, or they may be shown as collected balances required. Few banks show only required balances for the service activity.

Typically not shown on individual account analyses are such items as required compensation for lines of credit, "intangible" bank services, such as employee mortgage assistance, or arrangements for the double counting of operating balances for both service charge activity and lines of credit. These items may be included on an overall company summary or detailed in an accompanying cover letter from the bank officer in charge of the company's accounts.

It should be noted that the existence of double counting of balances is all but extinct currently. Formerly, banks would allow companies to apply the average collected balances maintained with the bank toward the compensation of service charges and apply the same balances toward compensation for credit lines. Usually, the company did not maintain sufficient operating balances to cover the compensation requirements for lines of credit, normally 10% of the line. Thus the companies had to keep additional balances with the bank. However, double counting was really lowering the effective percentage of compensation, and as these effective rates were offered directly, it was not surprising that double counting should disappear. Intangible services used to encompass many services that were not itemized on the account analysis.

As most banks have improved their internal reporting and incorporated inputs from individual operating areas of the bank, the number of services that cannot be included on an account analysis has been reduced dramatically. Currently, these types of services tend to be in the mortgage assistance or related area. However, as many companies have their own programs for relocation assistance or even mortgage assistance, the need for additional bank compensation has diminished. For all practical purposes, intangible services currently can be considered as corporate good will balances.

Earnings credit or allowance rates differ from bank to bank in the way the rate is set each month. This practice varies widely, ranging from a mysterious rate with no identification of the underlying bases to various averages (30 days to 3 months; simple and moving) of a money market rate, usually the T-bill rate. In addition, some banks show a deduction for reserve requirements whereas others adjust the earnings allowance for it.

A simplified sample account analysis statement is shown in Figure 6-2. The top portion of the statement shows the balance history for the month and the earnings allowance calculation. The uncollected funds (or float) represent the average daily amount of funds deposited that have not yet cleared and become good funds to the company. The available or free balance is the average daily balance after the bank has assessed the account for its reserve requirements. In practice, of course, the bank does not do this account by account, but it settles its position in aggregate with the Federal Reserve Bank weekly. This computation represents an apportioning of this overall reserve figure.

The next portion of the statement details the service charges for the account and itemizes the activity for the account for the month. This itemization includes the monthly volume, a unit charge for the type of activity, and the total charge for the activity for the month. Also shown in this illustration is the collected balance equivalent for the total service charge for each type of activity.

Summing the total service charges shows whether the account created a profit or a loss to the bank for the period. The sum of the collected balance equivalents shows the excess (if a profit) or deficit (if a loss) in terms of average collected balances. This figure represents the amount of extra or insufficient balances that are in this particular account. Most account analyses describe this amount as being available to support other services, since the calculation is a theoretical and historical one. This is due to the fact that the position of just one account cannot fully reflect the overall position of the company with its bank. Thus this type of computation must be made over all accounts the company maintains with the bank to determine whether, in aggregate, the bank was sufficiently compensated for the services, both credit and non-credit, it provided the company. This overall computation is often included by the bank in a customer summary, which looks like a regular account analysis.

The summary shows the total balances maintained in all accounts, the balances required for non-credit services, and the compensating balances required for credit services. If the balances maintained equal the required amount, the bank should be adequately compensated for the services it provided to the company. To the extent that excesses exist, the company can treat them as good

Figure 6-2
Sample Account Analysis

GOTHAM STATE BANK–MONTHLY ACCOUNT ANALYSIS
Customer Acct. No. 141-62-2481
For Feb. 93
Title: General Account
Customer: VIP Company, Inc.
New York, NY

Balances	$150,000
Average ledger balance	50,000
Average float/uncollected funds	50,000
Average collected balance	100,000
Reserve requirement (@10.0%)	10,000
Average available (free) balance	90,000
Earnings credit allowance (6.0%, or 0.5%/month)	450

Services and Charges

Service	Volume	Unit Charge	Total Charges	Required Balances
Checks deposited	250	$0.10	$25	$5,000
Deposits	20	0.45	9	1,800
Checks paid	150	0.16	24	4,800
Wire transfers—in	5	10.00	50	10,000
Wire transfers—out	15	8.00	120	24,000
Account maintenance	1	15.00	15	3,000
Grand total			$ 243	$48,600
Net profit/(loss) on account			$ 207	
Excess collected balances available for other services:				$41,400

At this earnings credit allowance rate, $1.00 of service charges requires
$200 in collected balances.

will balances, or, as is more often the case, deal with this net position on an average basis.

Companies used to be able to compute a rolling average over the most current year or treat the net position on an average year-to-date basis, resetting to zero at the beginning of each calendar year. However, with the increased use of fees and fee offsets (in fee-balance combination methods), this is no longer the norm. Banks now expect their corporate customers to *settle up* on compensation amounts monthly, or at most quarterly.

Calculating Balance Equivalents

The balance equivalent of one dollar of service charges was shown on the sample account analysis. This conversion is possible by using the monthly earnings credit and reserve requirement rates as follows:

$$ECB = SC/[EC \times (1.0 - RR)]$$

where:
ECB is the collected balance equivalent
SC is the service charge to be converted
EC is the monthly earnings credit rate (computed by dividing the annual rate shown on the account analysis by 12)
RR is the bank's reserve requirement as shown on the account analysis.

When the reserve requirement has been incorporated into the earnings credit rate, the divisor of the formula simply becomes the monthly earnings credit rate. This conversion formula is useful in reviewing account analyses that only show service charges. These charges can then be converted to determine the excess or deficit in terms of collected balances. If many such conversions are to be made, computing the collected balance equivalent of $1.00 is helpful in that this answer can then be easily multiplied by the amount of service charges for each account to determine the balances required for each account or activity.

The purpose of converting to equivalent collected balances is associated with the treasury manager's need to know what amount of balances must be maintained on average with the bank for compensation purposes. This compensation will be accomplished by establishing an overall target balance for the bank and attempting to maintain that target on average over time. Therefore, the treasury manager must find a common denominator for compensating all banks, and collected balances are the usual means.

Collected balances are used for this purpose, not ledger or free balances. Ledger balances are not used because they also include float and, accordingly, do not reflect good balances to the bank or the company. On the other hand, free

Figure 6-3
Bank Compensation Report

Bank	Average Collected Balance	Average Required Balance	Average Over/ (Under)	Nov. O/(U)	Dec. O/(U)	Jan. O/(U)
A	$532	$594	($61)	($670)	($46)	$533
B	1369	1183	186	(100)	235	423
C	338	77	261	231	167	385
D	485	369	115	(235)	190	390
E	406	235	171	200	150	163
F	546	385	161	(340)	620	203
Total	$3,676	$2,843	$833	($914)	$1,316	$2,097

balances are collected balances less reserve requirements, and such balances are not normally reported by banks daily. Thus collected balances represent the most appropriate measure, being good funds and usually reported daily by the bank to its corporate customer.

Bank Compensation Information System

Unless a corporation has very few banking relationships and fully understands and trusts its major banks implicitly, it will find itself in need of some form of information system regarding its bank compensation. With a relatively small number of banks (e.g., under five) this can be accomplished fairly easily on a manual basis. However, as the number of banks increases, the ability of the treasury manager to deal with each relationship on an effective and timely basis diminishes rapidly. It is natural, then, to consider an information system for bank compensation. Most corporate treasury managers have such individualized requirements that the development of a customized system seems advisable. The costs of doing so have decreased so much recently that it no longer represents a major system development cost to create an in-house system.

The major components for such a system are easily defined. The major ones include descriptive bank data, account-identifying elements, fundamental decision rules, and periodic account and bank data. Descriptive bank data include such items as the bank name, monthly earnings credit, reserve requirements, and overall bank target or the target for credit services. Account-identifying elements include the account number, type of account, operating unit responsible for the

Figure 6-4
Bank Compensation: Float in Days

Bank	Account	October	November	December
A	Lockbox	0.80	1.55	1.14
B	Lockbox	1.76	0.92	5.43
C	Lockbox	1.25	2.04	1.55
D	Lockbox	1.08	1.57	1.05
E	Lockbox	1.22	1.34	1.31
F	Deposit	2.87	2.73	3.34

account, and method of compensation for the account. Fundamental decision rules lay out guidelines for converting service charges to balances, how to handle bank targets, how to treat different methods of compensation, and how to summarize balances. Periodic account and bank data are inputs from the monthly account analyses.

Usually, only the total service charges or required balances are used, together with average balances. Putting these components together, one can create a bank compensation information system to monitor and report on bank activity. Basic reports can provide the treasury manager with an in-depth profile of the banking activity for the overall corporation, and the performance in any given period should suggest changes to individual bank targets.

The overall bank compensation report (see Figure 6-3) can show a trend in excess-deficit-balance positions for the latest six months. This can show the treasury manager how well the target balances have been maintained and whether any further changes are warranted.

The calculation of a float factor for each depository or lockbox account (see Figure 6-4) is possible by using data from the account analyses for such accounts and internal data. The latter are the total funds deposited in the account for the month. Dividing this monthly deposit figure by the number of calendar days in the month yields the average daily deposit. Then if this average daily deposit figure is divided into the average daily float (either shown directly on the account analysis or computed by subtracting the collected balance from the ledger balance), the answer is the average number of days deposits are taking to clear. Performing this computation for all major depository accounts, whether lockbox or local depositories, can provide a simple and effective means of monitoring check clearance float in various corporate banks. The float factor can pinpoint problem areas where further review or analysis is suggested. If the computed factors show a marked increase over time, it may indicate a shift in customer remittance habits or the expansion of that particular business into newer geographic areas. In either case, further detailed review is called for and is highlighted in the report.

Evaluating Bank Charges

The methods of charging for non-credit services vary substantially from bank to bank. The trend is toward the unbundling of service charges, that is, breaking down services into smaller units of activity and charging for each portion of the overall service. This way the bank charges a company only for the steps it requires, rather than assessing each customer on an average basis regardless of the extra activities associated with any one customer. This newer approach can make the account analyses quite lengthy and make comparisons between banks for "similar" services all but impossible.

Even without this breakdown into subcomponents, comparing service charges between banks is difficult because banks compute their charges in different ways. There are usually two types of major components of service charges: standard charges, which occur fairly commonly on any account analysis, and nonstandard charges, which are usually created by an individual bank for its service charges.

Sound treasury management practice calls for regular review of bank service charges. Although this review should be ongoing (aided, of course, by monthly account analyses), treasury managers should perform a more formalized review at least on an annual basis.

One of the major parameters affecting bank service charges is the bank's location. This is demonstrated clearly in Figure 6-5. This figure shows services for each of the five regional groupings (Northeast, Southeast, Midwest, West, and Money Center) used in the 1991-1992 Phoenix-Hecht Blue Book of Bank Prices. Only the charges that showed differences of 50% or more from the national average were included on the list. The service charges are the average price paid for each service on a per item or flat basis. Money center banks are by far the most expensive for cash management services. There are nine services shown for Money Center banks, and they all have positive differences (i.e., are higher) from the national average. In fact, three services (general account maintenance, maintenance for electronic balance reporting, and non-repetitive manual outgoing wire transfers) are more than double the national average.

The greatest negative differences are shown in the Southeast banks for concentration maintenance and deposit charges. In general, using independent

Figure 6-5
Bank Service Charges

Service	Pct Diff.	Region	Avg ($)
Account maintenance: general	133%	Money center	21.94
Balance Reporting	108	Money center	75.09
Outgoing wire (nonrepet. manual)	106	Money center	14.47
Deposit	94	Money center	1.02
Debit posting	86	Money center	0.31
Concentration maintenance	85	Money center	73.94
Return items	69	Money center	3.17
Partial account reconciliation	51	Money center	55.65
Wholesale lockbox monthly	50	Money center	96.26
Controlled disbursement monthly	71	West	93.44
ARP check paid	53	West	0.06
Debit posting	-55	West	0.31
Full account reconciliation	-51	Midwest	86.06
Current day balance & activity rep.	-51	Northeast	0.22
Debit posting	-60	Southeast	1.02
	-62	Southeast	0.31

Average bank service charges

Account maintenance	$21.94	Checks paid - regular	
Collected overdraft (per occurence)	25.53	Checks paid - controlled disbursement	0.15
Debit posting	0.31	Stop payment	14.94
Credit posting	0.58	Concentration maintenance	73.94
Deposit	1.02	ACH debit	0.11
Checks deposited	0.11	ACH credit	0.14
On-us & affiliates	0.07	Incoming wire transfer	6.69
Controlled disbursmt maint.	93.44	Outgo. wire/repet., autom.	6.25
	96.26	Outgo. wire/repet., manual	10.93
Return items	3.17	Outgo. wire/nonrep., autom.	7.86
Lockbox items processed	0.35	Outgo wire/nonrep., manual	14.47
Lockbox photocopy	0.11	Concentration DTC per item	0.54
Full account reconciliation	86.06	Concentration ACH	0.24
Partial acct. reconciliation	55.65	Bal. reptg electronic maint.	75.09
Acct. reconciliation check pd.	0.06	Bal. reptg: curr. day activity	69.78
Acct. reconciliation sort & list	0.04	International incoming wire	10.56
Curr. day bal. & activity reptg.	0.22	International outgoing wire	25.32

Source: 1991-1992 *Phoenix-Hecht Blue Book of Bank Prices*

data about bank service charges can be very useful in evaluating bank charges. The independence removes much of the subjectivity you would otherwise face and probably represents a far wider sample of banks than your own banking network encompasses.

Charging for Uncollected Overdrafts

In the past, most banks did not charge their corporate customers for collected balance overdrafts. Recently, however, this has changed. Many banks have now been assessing a funds usage fee. These charges are assessed by the bank for the use of uncollected funds. Many treasury managers believe that this is unfair, especially if they maintain a positive average collected balance for most of the month and end up with many thousands of dollars of positive collected balances.

In the past, banks were not concerned about an "occasional" day or two of collected overdrafts. They looked at the average collected balances for the month, which were almost always positive. There were not many banks whose systems were capable of capturing a daily collected overdraft since the systems were designed to look at the monthly average. Banks are not required to charge for the use of uncollected funds. This is a pricing decision that individual banks have made. In the mid-1980's, a few large banks began tracking daily uncollected funds positions and assessing a charge for the use of those funds, even though current regulations do not allow them to pay interest on the positive balances. This does not appear to be an even-handed treatment of negative and positive balances. Charging for uncollected overdrafts is an example of how banks have unbundled their pricing and now often charge for every component step of the service that they provide to their customers. There is no reason to expect this trend to disappear in the future. This means that corporate treasury managers will have to be able to evaluate their bank services effectively and understand the charges better to be able to purchase bank services that are cost effective.

Banks have justified their charges to customers for collected overdrafts because collected overdrafts are in fact extensions of credit that require the bank to address several issues and incur several substantial costs:

- **Credit risk**: Collected overdrafts represent a credit exposure to the company.
- **Funding cost**: The bank incurs a funding cost when covering a customer's overdraft position. These costs exceed the bank's monthly earnings credit rate. Also, the overdrafts are not predictable.
- **Opportunity cost**: Collected overdrafts are non-earning assets, and, as such, they have a direct negative impact on the bank's return on asset performance.

- **Administrative cost**: The bank incurs administrative costs in approving, monitoring, reporting, paying, and collecting funds that are greater than normal because collected overdrafts do represent an extension of credit.

Many banks have concluded that only charging the earnings credit rate for overdrafts and allowing this to be paid for in "soft dollar" compensating balances does not properly compensate the bank. As a result, some banks charge the difference between the earnings credit rate and the prime rate on the amount of the overdraft and show the charge on the monthly account analysis statement. Any adjustments that affected previous balance levels could also result in charges for collected overdrafts.

Interest on Corporate Checking Accounts

Currently, corporations do not earn explicit interest on their bank checking accounts. This is prohibited by Federal Reserve Regulation Q. There is some debate over whether this ban should be lifted and, if so, what effect its elimination would have on bank balances and, in turn, bank compensation.

Because corporations move funds to concentrate them for investment or other short-term purposes, it is thought that fewer transfers would be required if corporations could earn interest on their checking account balances. This would help in reducing the amount of daylight overdrafts and would possibly simplify many corporate cash management systems. It would also clarify bank compensation, as balances now would earn interest, not earnings credit, although it would probably be possible to select an interest-earning account or a "regular" business account that would not earn interest.

On the other hand, many companies already have approximated this arrangement through the use of bank sweep arrangements. With sweep services, companies automatically invest excess balances on a daily basis. Thus, it can be argued that there would be little impact on corporate cash management practices if interest could be earned on corporate accounts. It should be noted that larger corporations, those that maintain significant balances that are not currently earning interest, are not heavy users of sweep accounts because, it is argued, they are able to obtain better rates on short-term investments than offered by the sweep accounts. If, however, they were satisfied with the interest rates offered on regular checking accounts and did not have to pay for funds concentration, they might shift their balances to interest-earning accounts. This shift would have a heavy impact on bank relations.

BANK DOCUMENTATION

Bank documentation is one of the "necessary evils" of the treasury manager's responsibilities. Influenced by the company's accounting function, bank documentation is a routine but important activity.

Most treasury control systems are heavily influenced by the corporate accounting function and must have the ability to satisfy accounting reporting and audit requirements. These latter requirements may consist of both internal and external obligations in the sense that the corporate accounting function needs transaction data while internal audit (perhaps) and the company's independent auditors need to be able to review control points and confirm the financial transactions and bank balances of the company. The accounting function, considered broadly, influences the cash management function in that it normally sets forth its requirements in the form of standard transaction confirmation procedures and documentation, bank statement and reconciliation procedures, official documentation for banking relationship authorization, and necessary details for periodic audit evaluation. Often the treasury manager must discuss possible system changes with his or her accounting representatives to ensure that corporate standards are not violated or that the potential service will provide adequate levels of detail.

Account Documentation

Corporate treasury managers cannot open bank relationships without authorization from senior management. This usually takes the form of a company **board resolution**. Companies vary in how they authorize bank relationships. Corporations generally use one of two approaches. They either authorize generally, bank by bank, or specifically — account by account. The form of the board resolution varies greatly.

Most banks have a standard board resolution form that they will supply. If the form is generally the same as the corporation's form, it can be used. However, many corporations have their own form and format for board resolutions. In this case, they supply their documentation to the banks. Smaller companies may not have standard forms or may feel that they have less influence over their banks and, therefore, are resigned to using the bank form. Although the detailed wording may differ slightly from one form to another, the general items do not. They include:

- Name of authorizing person (usually the corporate secretary)
- State of jurisdiction

- Bank name
- State of resolution
- Titles of authorized signers or persons who can transact the company's business via the bank account
- Official witness and date of signing the resolution

Corporate treasury managers also must deal with **bank service agreements**. Just like account analyses, these agreements differ from bank to bank. In fact, some very large companies have been able to use their own form of agreement, instead of dealing with the many different forms from all their banks. Box 6-4 provides a checklist for bank service agreements.

Transaction Documentation

Transaction reporting documents should encompass all types of financial transactions that the treasury function handles or is involved with, even if only partially. Individual confirmation letters or reports can take many forms, including individual letters sent to the company's banks to document funds movements from corporate accounts or the concentration of funds into a central account. Accounting should receive independent confirmation of these transactions from the banks. These reports can be individual debit or credit tickets or detailed bank balance reporting system outputs, as described earlier. Similarly, short-term investment and borrowing transactions are usually confirmed by letter to the broker/dealer, with the latter independently reconfirming the transaction.

In each of these instances, the accounting department should have received both internal and independent, external records for each transaction, thereby satisfying the requirements of the corporate checks and balances. Bank statements and related account reconciliations provide financial data to the accounting function so that it can properly complete its normal account monitoring and check disbursement reconcilement responsibilities. Sometimes the bank account reconcilement responsibilities have remained in the treasury area, but this is generally viewed as a control weakness in an accounting sense as the initiators of financial funding transactions, for instance, should not be able to handle the reconciling of their bank accounts.

The working agreement documents represent official, written communications between the company and its bankers or other financial institutions. The accounting function is normally involved in establishing most of the financial arrangements and often must supply financial reports to corporate lenders. Thus the need to provide this information to accounting is self-evident. For example, accounting must understand the details of a revolving credit agreement, since it must know whether to treat the borrowings as short- or long-term and what regular financial information must be supplied to the lending institutions.

Periodically, the audit confirmations of credit lines and bank balances must be handled by the treasury area for the review of these data by internal or independent auditors. This typically occurs after the end of the company's fiscal year during the annual financial audit and requires special written communications with each corporate bank to send responses to the audit group independently.

These accounting requirements present another set of conditions for the treasury manager in establishing an effective control system. The control system must possess the capabilities of producing all transaction reports routinely on a timely and accurate basis. In addition, the system must provide for a centralized source for all bank documentation so that it can be reviewed easily and modified in an orderly and timely basis due to changes in procedures, policies, or personnel. The requirements may exert influence directly in dictating the form and level of transaction detail needed in the system and indirectly in making it quite costly in terms of manual effort to maintain a substantial number of bank accounts or relationships. Obviously, the latter consideration can be a minor one if the benefits of such a system are significant.

UCC 4A

One recent regulation that has impacted corporate-bank relations has been Article 4A of the Uniform Commercial Code. This article clarified liabilities in electronic payments. Many observers felt that it shifted most of the liability onto corporations.

A recent survey of the major cash management banks by the *Journal of Cash Management* (1991) showed that the following changes were occurring because of UCC 4A:

- Less flexibility in non-repetitive transfers
- Stricter wire transfer and system security by both banks and their customers
- New drafts of bank-corporate service agreements

MEASURING BANK PERFORMANCE

It used to be that corporations had little to say about how a bank performed operationally or financially. The biggest statement it could make was changing

Box 6-4
Checklist of Key Items for Bank Service Agreements

Operating procedures

- Are all procedures understood (by the bank) and documented?
- Are exception situations identified?
- Are company contacts provided for these situations?

Reporting requirements

- Are reporting cutoffs clearly stated?
- What if there is no activity on a day?

Performance measurement

- Have service quality standards been agreed to by the bank?
- Can they be regularly reported?
- Who will be in charge?
- Have the (new) BAI standards been used?

Liabilities and indemnification

- Are service agreements in conformance with UCC?
- If not, has corporate counsel signed off on any waivers?
- How will damages be identified and handled?

Compensation

- How will the bank be compensated for this account?
- How long is the compensation period? Monthly? Quarterly? Longer?

- Is this account tied ito an overall corporate summary?

Ability to audit

- Do the company and its auditors have authority to visit the bank?
- Are there any restrictions on access to corporate data or other materials?

Notifications

- How much lead time must there be for notifications of change?
- Are all changes in procedure and in the service required in writing?

Authorized activities

- Are all activities (i.e., transactions into and out of the account) defined?
- Are preauthorized transactions, such as ACH debits, included?

Authorized persons

- Are all authorized signer current?
- Are signers to be restricted in any way, or can any signer initiate or confirm any type of authorized transaction?

Document flow

- Is the expected flow of documents (both ways) defined?
- Is each document identified sufficiently?

Box 6-5
Bank Evaluation Matrix – Definition of Categories

Level of service: Organizational structure of bank; capabilities of contact persons; willingness to suggest improvements and expansion of present services

Operations: Responsiveness of branches; frequency of errors; ability to deliver timely service

Problem solving: Ability of contact persons to "trouble shoot" within the bank; ability to detect errors early and resolve quickly

Fees: Fees for account and cash management services

Growth potential: Capacity of existing facilities; presence in other states

Professionalism: Manner of handling the relationship, including sales calls, proposals, and operations

Technology: Availability of state-of-the-art services and data processing capabilities

Conversion: Ease of establishing new banking relationship

Bank stability: Operational stability, including personnel turnover; mergers and acquisitions activity; financial stability

Market share: Percent of market accounted for by the bank

Importance to bank: Importance as evidenced by representatives from bank; relative size of the account

---

banks or rewarding more business to banks who had performed well, as measured by unsophisticated, subjective measures. That has changed. Today, a treasury manager cannot afford to make subjective decisions.

Evaluating Operating Performance

Evaluating a bank's performance requires a sufficient number of objective parameters. Box 6-5 shows a number of items that form a bank evaluation matrix. The matrix can be used to evaluate each major bank or can be tailored to reflect the company's banking network.

Box 6-6
Thomas & Betts: Bank Tiering Philosophy

Tier 1: These banks are the company's three or four major banks on a worldwide basis. In addition to supplying operating services, the primary purpose of these banks is to supply credit to the company, specifically a large unexpected amount of credit during a time when credit is scarce.

Tier 2: These banks either supply a critical service or are banks of the highest quality and reputation with which the company does significant business. These banks would move up to Tier 1 should the company need an additional Tier 1 bank or if it is necessary to replace one of the current Tier 1 banks.

Tier 3: These are high quality banks with a good reputation. The company's limited banking needs precludes giving them more business. There is a large gap between Tier 2 and Tier 3 banks in the amount of banking business allocated.

Tier 4: The company does business with these banks because of circumstances. Only under unusual circumstances will these banks obtain additional business.

Bank Report Cards

Many treasury managers formalize the evaluation procedure and generate bank report cards. These report cards measure the operational performance of a bank over a fixed time period, usually quarterly or monthly. The results are then reviewed individually with the bank. Some companies distribute their report cards among all their banks, so each bank can see how it compares with other bank service providers.

Illustration: Thomas & Betts Bank Report Card

The following discussion is adapted from a presentation by Donald D. Aquila, manager of treasury operations for Thomas & Betts Corporation, at an annual treasury management conference of the Treasury Management Association of New Jersey. This report card has been used for many years and has been an effective bank relationship management tool. To understand how Thomas & Betts uses its report card, it is first important to note some background on the company's banking philosophy. Thomas & Betts organizes its banks into a four-tier system (see Box 6-6). The primary banks are in the top two tiers, with the first tier being more important. The tiering instills a spirit of competition among the banks for additional business with the company. The third tier contains banks that may work their way into the company's "regular" bank group. The fourth-tier banks play relatively minor roles. Only banks in the top two tiers receive quarterly report cards.

The company looks to its top-tier banks as the primary banks for a part of its annual credit requirements, paying them with compensating balances or equivalent fees. These banks are also be expected to participate in any formal revolving credit agreements. In addition, the company gives the primary banks a chance to participate in all significant credit transactions, such as short-term financing (e.g., money market loans, bankers acceptances), intermediate transactions (e.g., leasing, long-term debt, industrial revenue bonds), and miscellaneous transactions (e.g., sale of lease credits).

The company expects its top-tier banks to provide the company with the same credit terms it offers to its best customers. Thomas & Betts also expects the banks to handle any unforeseen emergency credit requirements, even in tight credit conditions.

On a quarterly basis, the company prepares a report card for its top banks. A sample report card is shown in Figure 6-6. Each bank is graded on accuracy and timing, according to problems and response time. The possible grades that can be attained are affected by the number of problems according to the following rules:

- 4: No problems during the quarter
- 3: One problem during the quarter
- 2: Two or three problems during the quarter
- 1: Four or more problems during the quarter

The key to making the report card work is defining a *problem*. For example, a lockbox problem is recorded if the bank returns *actual* checks to the company instead of check copies or if the bank does not send lockbox information in the correct format for credit/receivables processing (the company and bank have agreed on a set format for remittance information, check copy, and envelope to accelerate internal company processing). Problems in wires and DTCs might involve a misrouted transfer, transmitting erroneous information, or failure to call in a lockbox deposit for concentration. Balance reporting errors usually are failures to report on time (by 9:30 A.M.) to the company. A similar error can occur with controlled disbursements.

Response time errors are somewhat different. Banks are measured by how soon they return calls to the company when an error or other problem has occurred. The standards are:

Figure 6-6
Thomas & Betts Corporation: Bank Report Card

Bank	Lock-box	Disbrs-mts.	State-ments	Wires/DTCs	Bal. Reptg.	Inv./Borr.	Other	Resp. Time	Cash Appl.
A	1	3	4	4	2	3	4	2	-
B	4	-	4	4	4	4	4	4	3
C	4	-	4	4	3	-	4	4	4
D	-	-	4	4	3	-	4	4	-
E	4	-	4	4	1	4	3	4	3
F	-	4	3	4	3	-	4	4	-
G	-	-	4	4	-	-	4	4	-
H	4	4	4	4	3	4	4	4	3
Avg.	3.4	3.7	3.9	4.0	2.7	3.8	3.9	3.8	3.2

- 4: Same day
- 3: One day
- 2: Two days
- 1: Three or more days

The banks are then rated by the treasury staff for each operating service provided. Final results are sent to each bank's credit and operations contacts and are circulated internally throughout the company. The banks also receive documentation for each error incurred during the performance period. Copies are attached to the report card. The treasury staff also prepares a banking summary quarterly for internal distribution and annually for its top banks. This is useful in monitoring how much bank services cost and how much each bank is providing in dollar terms.

The combination of these reports is a solid foundation for effective bank relationships. Thomas & Betts has taken steps to quantify what — in many companies — is a subjective, qualitative activity. This quantification is a positive development, as long as the criteria are applied uniformly and objectively. For example, the report card shown in Figure 6-6 does not show a computed overall bank average. This is because not every bank supplies the same number of services and, consequently, an overall rating would be misleading. Each treasury manager must decide what performance measurement guidelines are appropriate for his or her case.

DEALING WITH BANK RISK

Concern about risk and financial performance used to be the primary concern of the banker. Now it is just as important to the treasury manager. There are even risks in the traditional non-credit (or cash management) services.

Risks in Non-credit Services

Risk exists in any cash management or bank transactional service. Any corporation whose funds have been tied up in a bank liquidation, failure, or near-failure knows this. So do bankers who have been involved in charging off losses from operational services. Operational credit risk is the risk of loss of money or its use stemming from the insolvency of one of the parties in a funds transfer. Operational credit risk is mainly created by timing differences between the point where one party gets credit for funds it is receiving and the point where the other party gives up the right to funds it is disbursing. A good example is a daylight overdraft. Money is wired out early in the day, in excess of the company's available balance, in anticipation of a wire coming in later that day to fund it. There is a timing mismatch of several hours. In paper funds transfers (e.g., checks), this mismatch can be several days.

Deposits
A deposit is a check or draft physically transferred to a bank. The bank takes possession at deposit, but it doesn't take **title** to the check until final settlement. The depositor/bank relationship is initially one of principal and agent — the depositor owns the item until final settlement. At deposit, the bank gives the depositor provisional credit in the form of a book entry. At final settlement, the bank becomes the owner of the item. The relationship then changes from one of principal/agent to one of creditor/debt. This distinction is crucial when a bank fails and checks are in the process of collection.

Collected credit occurs when the bank gives a corporation the use of the money based on its estimate of when final settlement will occur. However, the item may be returned instead of going to final settlement. This is a major point of risk for banks offering cash management services. **Final settlement** occurs when the item is paid by the drawee bank. The depository bank does not know when this happens. It only knows if final settlement doesn't occur (i.e., the check is returned). Basically, final settlement happens by default: If nothing prevents it, final settlement takes place.

On a timeline, if a check is deposited on Monday, **provisional credit** is given for it on Monday and perhaps **collected credit** from the bank on Tuesday. The check is sent back to be paid by the drawee bank. If it is presented for payment on Tuesday, this would be final settlement. Final settlement could even be Wednesday. If the drawee's account has insufficient funds, the check is returned but may not arrive at the depository bank until Wednesday, Thursday, or possibly Friday. Based on the collected credit given on Tuesday, the depositor may have wired that money out. The bank then faces four or more days at risk for that item. If, meanwhile, the company doesn't have the funds or goes into receivership, the bank is taking a credit risk. In short, for banks, collected funds do not equal good money. As banks and the Federal Reserve reduce the time for settlement, whether payment is made by check or through the automated clearing house, they reduce the level of potential credit risk they face.

Disbursements

If a disbursement bank fails before the company's checks are presented for final payment (i.e., the cash letter hasn't arrived at the bank), those checks will be dishonored and returned. If the company's funds are in the disbursement account, the company is at risk because it has been unable to use the funds to pay for the checks. Instead, the company's money is tied up in an insolvent bank, and it still must pay the suppliers to whom it originally sent the checks.

If the cash letter did arrive, the checks will be paid, drawing down the account to a less exposed position. The company, of course, is liable for any checks that were paid in overdraft. That is, if the checks were posted, the FDIC would be responsible for collecting the overdraft as receiver of the failed bank. If the bank did not let the checks be posted, they would be returned as NSF. Note that the FDIC usually closes banks at the end of business (that is, it does not let the bank open on the next business day) so that all checks can be posted through the (last) business day. If the cash letter is in the bank but hasn't been opened or processed, the FDIC would probably consider that the checks had been presented for final payment. This is subject to interpretation, but there hasn't been a court case over items in the process of collection since before World War II.

Risks from Bank Failures

When a Federally insured bank fails, the FDIC determines what happens in its role as conservator of failed bank assets. The most drastic scenario is a payoff situation, where the bank is closed. The accounts are frozen, the insured depositors are paid off, all the loans are called, the FDIC writes a check to the insured depositors (within three days, one hopes), the FDIC sees what assets can be salvaged to pay off other creditors, and it closes the bank. The FDIC tries to estimate the value of other bank assets, such as vault cash, government securities, and bank premises. This amount is then distributed on a pro rata basis to the uninsured depositors, those with over $100,000 in deposits. Operations are disrupted; employees are out of work. Freedom National (NY) was an example of this drastic situation. It usually happens only to small banks.

The second possibility, one the FDIC seems to prefer, is called purchase and assumption. More than 80 percent of FDIC actions are of this type. The FDIC arranges for another bank to buy the good assets and assume all of the liabilities (i.e., deposits), while the FDIC takes the other assets. The bank simply reopens the next day and continues doing business. The new bank honors all checks written on the old bank. There's no loss to depositors and no disruption. This is less expensive for the FDIC, which is mandated to find the least-cost solution. This approach is often tied to the FDIC's **too-big-to-fail doctrine**. Examples of this doctrine were the Bank of New England and several of the Texas banks. Because deposit brokers know the FDIC prefers the second solution, they used to have no qualms about placing deposits in shaky banks and S&Ls at high rates. The depositors knew the FDIC would arrange a purchase and assumption if the bank went bad. To instill some market discipline, the FDIC developed modified purchase and assumptions, sometimes called insured deposit. Good assets are transferred into a good bank, which also assumes only the insured deposits.

A final way the FDIC helps in a bank failure is by not closing the bank but, instead, giving it open-bank assistance. The FDIC arranges a capital injection, a restructuring, a merger, or a recapitalization, and the bank remains open. A number of large banks have benefitted from this approach.

What Constitutes a Depositor?
The FDIC defines a depositor as the holder of an account engaged in a bona fide independent activity. So any legal entity or subsidiary with a bona fide purpose (not simply to circumvent the insurance cap) is a separate depositor. The criterion is legal entity, which a subsidiary usually is and a division is not. Another criterion is whether the accounts are held in the same *right and capacity*. The FDIC looks at the purpose of the account and the relationship between the owner and the beneficiary of the account. If any fiduciary relationship exists between the company and the beneficiary of the funds, then those funds are considered to be held in a separate right and capacity from, say, a payroll account, a general payables account, a dividend account, or a company pension plan. The fiduciary relationship must be stated in the account name. In their own right, these accounts

---

Box 6-7
Bank Soundness Criteria

Choose strong banks, insured banks, and large banks, which are all less likely to be closed.

Limit accounts that are in the same "right and capacity" to $100,000.

Wire out all collected funds daily (maintain ZBAs).

Borrow from the bank. (Some state laws may let a depositor offset its loans against its deposits, which a bank would do if the company went bankrupt, or this provision could be negotiated into borrowing agreements, presuming, of course, that the FDIC would allow it.)

Have the bank redirect lockbox mail to an alternate processor.

Prepare an alternate disbursement site.

---

are insurable up to $100,000 and don't have to be included with the company's other accounts.

Minimizing Corporate Risk

Companies can evaluate their banks, either internally or by subscribing to a rating service that analyzes and grades banks. A bank is only as good as its assets. If the bank's loan portfolio cannot be thoroughly examined, it is difficult to make an informed judgment. This is one weakness that is common to all rating services.

Some companies have established formal criteria for dealing with banks that could possibly be in trouble soundness (see Box 6-7).

If a check is deposited in a bank that then went under and final settlement had not occurred, the firm could ask the writer of the check to stop payment on it. Then the check would be returned to the FDIC. For a valid stop-payment, however, a good business reason is required. Otherwise, the FDIC would probably view the action as an attempt to circumvent the conservation of the assets of the failed bank. For a large check, the FDIC would come after the firm. The risk to companies is really very small because only small banks fail. A local depository may be vulnerable, but a firm is not likely to keep $100,000 there. However, there's always a chance that the too-big-to-fail doctrine will be eliminated by the FDIC. Then the risks will change. In summary, there are no such things as non-credit operating services. Timely and complete monitoring of the whole relationship is essential to see what the total exposure is. A loan, a letter of credit, a lockbox, a disbursement account all of these need to be added up to get a complete picture of a company's credit exposure.

The risks are increasing. The deposit balance turnover at banks has increased over the last ten years by tenfold. The average account turnover used to be about 40 times a year. Now money in accounts turns over more than once a day.

Bank Safety

A safe bank is one that is efficient and profitable — with costs down and revenues up. In the past, higher revenues outweighed the hefty overhead being built up by banks. But the early 1990's has been a time of bad loans and non-performing real estate assets, which together cut into net interest income. The mega-mergers of this same time period and the continuing toll of failed banks have simply aggravated the jitters that corporations have about bank safety.

The focus is now on comparing the old rules with the new rules. Up to now, the FDIC had the option of paying off large depositors when a big bank failed. The failed bank's buyer would simply pay a premium in order to get the failed bank's franchise. Then the FDIC would turn around and use that premium to pay off large depositors. The justification for this approach was that it would cost less than liquidating the bank.

The new rule, as of 1995, mandates that the least costly route be pursued when dealing with a failed bank — not one that was merely less costly. Paying off large depositors not legally insured (beyond the $100,000 FDIC cap) would not be in the spirit of a least-cost resolution. While there may still be room for the FDIC to pay off large depositors in cases where not doing so would harm the economy or the financial system, this kind of exception isn't likely to help small and middle-sized banks. The FDIC would be hard put to justify many such rescues.

Bank Rating Agencies

The Securities and Exchange Commission (SEC) has certified six bank rating agencies (see Box 6-8). These six are part of what the SEC calls the **NRSRO (Nationally Recognized Statistical Rating Organizations)**. These bank raters offer information and forecasts about the safety of specific banks usually for a regular fee. Most of them also offer some free information.

Illustration: the Bertelsmann Case
This section illustrates how a large corporation — Bertelsmann, Inc. — regularly evaluates its bank risks. This section is based on a presentation by Bertelsmann

---

Box 6-8
Bank Raters

Duff & Phelps/MCM (incorporates the former bank ratings arm of McCarthy, Crisanti & Maffei.)

Fitch Investors Service

IBCA Banking Analysis

Moody's

Standard & Poor's

Thomson BankWatch, Inc.

Treasurer Basil P. Mavrovitis at a meeting of the Treasury Management Association of New Jersey.

With the U.S. banking system showing few signs of a strong and rapid rebound from its economic malaise, corporate treasury managers cannot afford to take anything for granted. This includes the ultimate safety net for big banks — the Federal Reserve's too big to fail doctrine — or FDIC insurance for smaller banks. Relying on these protections can be costly in another way: The treasury manager cannot afford to have his or her professional credibility questioned when a bank fails — even if the company's exposure is under the FDIC limit.

Bank risk is formally reviewed quarterly at Bertelsmann. Most large companies like Bertelsmann deal with many banks of various sizes, so even with regularly scheduled evaluation there has to be an emergency procedure. Bertelsmann's rationale is that banks and companies, regardless of their size, will always face exposure to depository or counterparty risks.

The company uses outside services and relies heavily on one of them for input on their banks. The treasurer subscribes to an expanded service that allows him contact with an analyst directly at any time if he has a question or concern about a specific bank. The firm's basic risk assumptions and outlook are shown in Box 6-9.

The treasurer prepares a formal, written quarterly report that is circulated throughout financial management in the U.S. and at the parent German company. An integral part is the detailed bank risk analysis report. This report shows current and historic ratings for all major Bertelsmann banks. This is accompanied by a written narrative that points out rating changes, discusses general banking news (e.g., recent bank mergers, failures, or other noteworthy financial reports), and highlights significant company transactions (e.g., new cash management

Box 6-9
Bertelsmann's Assumptions on Bank Risk

Don't test or rely on the too big to fail doctrine or the Fed chairman's belief in free markets with limited government intervention.

The current credit crunch is a byproduct of the current weakness in the U.S. banking system.

Many money center, regional and local banks do not have much lending capacity because their capital to risk asset ratios are poor.

Long-standing bank relationships should not stand in the way of objectively analyzing bank risk.

Bank mergers and consolidations will not solve the U.S. banking system's problems overnight.

Bank ratings and perceived bank risk should be formally reviewed via internal analysis quarterly and should be monitored on an ongoing basis.

changes) or bank concerns (e.g., commentary on a specific bank that is experiencing difficulties). The narrative is written for an audience that is concerned about Bertelsmann's assets but is not in constant touch with the U.S. economic and banking situation on a daily basis.

MANAGEMENT REVIEW ITEMS

➡ Group banks by level of importance to be able to deal more effectively with each of them. Meetings should be held with major banks at least quarterly.

➡ When using a request for proposal, do not include banks as a courtesy. Remember you will have to inform all the banks that were not selected for the service, and it may be extremely time consuming to have to tell many banks why they were not selected.

➡ Set up a spreadsheet model to summarize overall bank compensation levels. Allow for monthly input of account analyses summary, with the ability to look at monthly totals for at least the latest six months.

➡ Ask banks when or whether they will be providing their account analyses in a standard format or whether they are capable of transmitting account analysis information electronically.

➡ Review bank account analyses faithfully every month. This should be considered "must" reading and cannot be avoided. Look especially for obvious errors, large swings in balances and/or service charges, changes in services, and questionable services that you don't understand or recall establishing.

➡ Select a small group of banks to review in detail with other treasury members monthly. This "bank of the month" review session should look at errors, problems, and historic balance levels and service charges.

➡ Compute float factors to cross check your depository and lockbox accounts. Look for wide swings from month to month. Be sure to check your input data first before challenging the bank over an apparent error.

➡ Weigh incurring a charge for uncollected overdrafts versus paying "full freight" for controlled disbursing. For example, many banks charge extra for a controlled disbursement account, and this charge can be two or three times the amount of an uncollected overdraft charge.

➡ Review bank account documentation at least annually. Replace outdated agreements and be sure to bring all signing authorities and other related information up to date. It may be instructive to do this before the annual financial audit.

➡ If you use more than three or four banks for the similar groups of cash management services, consider initiating a simple quarterly bank report card. The procedure in preparing the report card will be beneficial in documenting processing errors and training the treasury staff to track bank performance.

➡ Establish a treasury risk review group. This group should meet quarterly or semi-annually to discuss the risks posed by the company's banks and to recommend any appropriate actions. Try to get members from functional areas outside treasury, such as internal audit, involved with this group.

➡ Establish an emergency offset procedure to be used in case of bank financial troubles in those states where it is permitted. Then you can initiate this procedure if a fiscal emergency arises.

➡ Prepare a regular (quarterly) bank report for senior management, incorporating operating and financial performance results. This will keep senior management informed and help establish a reputation for treasury as banking experts.

CHAPTER 7

GRANTING CREDIT

One of the central issues in modern financial management is the proper evaluation of risk and return. Within the realm of short-term corporate finance this is especially important in the management of accounts receivable. The profitability of many corporations and financial institutions depends very heavily on the institution's ability to evaluate and control credit risk.

However, in many companies, the credit department has traditionally been out of the mainstream of the finance function. The credit department was often very loosely monitored, often on the basis of simple measures of delinquencies and bad debts. As long as out-of-pocket costs were considered "reasonable," credit managers were left alone. In many companies this fostered a very static credit organization, often indifferent to developments that could dramatically improve its performance. This complacency survived in many companies through the relative prosperity of the 1980's.

The economic environment of the early 1990's changed this perspective. Corporations realized the importance of the credit function, not only because of its impact on costs, but, more importantly, because careful management of credit risks can greatly enhance revenues. Recognizing that credit terms are part of pricing clarifies its impact on the company's revenues. Innovations in computer and information technology together with new credit information products have provided an extensive array of new management approaches that can be applied to the corporation's and the financial institution's credit function.

This chapter analyzes credit granting — the first stage of accounts receivable management. The types of corporate decisions include the following:

- The kind of information on companies and consumers that is available in making credit-granting decisions
- The legal and regulatory factors that influence credit granting

- How credit grantors "process" available credit information to make value-maximizing decisions

This chapter also develops the structure for credit-granting decisions. It discusses how corporations and financial institutions manage the credit function. The primary sections are:

- Cost/benefit analysis
- The credit contract
- Legal and regulatory aspects
- The credit analysis process
- Credit information
- Credit granting methodology
- Emerging trends

In this chapter, as well as in the remainder of this text, credit management is primarily addressed from the corporate credit grantor's viewpoint. The modifications required when considering the credit management decisions of a financial institution are not complex and may even simplify the analysis. Also, while it is feasible in some industries to sell only on cash terms, this chapter addresses this option only indirectly as one possible (and relatively uninteresting) form of the credit contract. The numerous possibilities for risk shifting (i.e., "selling" all or some of the credit risk to a third party) are deferred until the next chapter.

COST/BENEFIT ANALYSIS

Credit decisions fall into three basic categories:

- **Domestic trade credit**: credit extended to companies in the credit grantor's home country
- **Export trade credit**: credit extended to companies outside of the credit grantor's country
- **Consumer credit**: credit extended to individuals

While there is considerable commonality among these three categories, each is typically handled differently because of the variations in risk, in type and availability of credit information, and in regulation. However, the primary cost/benefit analysis is similar for all three types of decisions. International credit is discussed further in Chapter 12.

As is so often the case in corporate finance, the firm is faced with the determination of costs and benefits that are, to a reasonable extent, quantifiable (such as the costs of credit information, costs of bad debts, etc.) and those that are very difficult to quantify (such as the impact on sales of differing credit and collection policies). This hybrid nature of the credit decision, combined with the rapidly evolving dynamics of the business environment and information technology, has led many companies to adopt a relatively simple framework for their credit evaluation. In many cases this is an adequate solution to a complex problem; however, in other cases it may fail to take advantage of the many powerful tools currently available to manage the credit function.

In addition, as with almost all other problems in corporate finance, optimal credit decisions are determined by net present values. In the case of credit granting, this is seldom simple. Some costs are out-of-pocket (such as costs of credit information and bad debts); others are opportunity or investment costs (e.g., costs of investment in receivables and extended financing of delinquent accounts). Still others represent less tractable factors. Determining how customers will react to changing credit policies is a very inexact science. For example, one of the major reasons for offering credit is its impact on sales. The capital budgeting analysis requires reasonable estimates of all of these components, including the proper evaluation of risk.

It is often the case in practice that credit decisions are not fully integrated with the revenue/marketing aspects. As noted earlier, the performance measurement of liquid asset management is especially difficult. There are numerous examples of corporations where the sales/marketing staff is compensated based on some measure of total sales, while the credit staff is evaluated based on the ratio of bad debts (or delinquencies) to total sales. Naturally these two viewpoints are not easy to reconcile. Furthermore, consider the credit function of a company that produces and sells computer hardware and software (or any other business for which the gross margin on different products is very dissimilar). The gross margin on hardware is often a small fraction of that for software. This should imply that the credit standards for purchasers of hardware should be much more stringent than for purchasers of software. Also, accepting credit risks requires an accurate evaluation of both sides of the cost/benefit equation: revenues and losses.

While a complete integration of the credit and marketing viewpoints is difficult to attain, it is a vital aspect of the credit granting function. The cost/benefit analysis developed here provides a usable framework for the evaluation of different credit policies and performance.

Estimating Credit Costs and Benefits

The major costs for a company maintaining its own (in-house) credit operations fall into four general categories:

- Financing costs
- Delinquency and bad debt costs
- Costs of initial credit evaluation
- Costs of ongoing credit monitoring and collection efforts

Financing Costs

Financing costs of receivables can be determined either explicitly as the cost of financing the assets or indirectly as the opportunity cost of capital tied up in the assets. For a company with a significant portfolio of outstanding receivables, these costs can be substantial and volatile. For instance, the head of credit operations at Sears, Roebuck, and Company has observed that for an increase in interest rates of one percent costs increase approximately $20 million annually.

Most companies establish an opportunity cost of capital, such as its pre-tax cost of capital, and apply this to the outstanding level of accounts receivable (A.R.) to evaluate the cost of A.R. investment.

Delinquency and Bad Debt Costs

In extending credit the corporation is adopting the role of a lender and is subject to the corresponding risks. A major part of this risk is the possibility of "unsatisfactory" payment behavior — ranging from delinquent payments to write-off or default. Professor Edward Altman provides a methodology for estimating the latter in the context of bank loan charge-offs. For a sample of large banks he finds that the average recovery (percentage of charged-off balance collected) on loans that have been written off is 30%, depending on the bank and the loan type. The cost of delinquencies include the additional investment in A.R. due to accounts that are past some target due date. Consider the following example.

Illustration

Suppose a company uses 15% as its cost of capital. It has an average of $3,800,000 outstanding in A.R. with annual sales of $30 million on net 30 terms (i.e., the entire invoice is payable within 30 days). The *total* opportunity cost of investment in A.R. is estimated to be $0.57 million (15% of $3.8 million). However, a substantial percentage of this figure is due to accounts that are not paying within the stated terms.

Since the average day's sales are $82,192 ($30,000,000 over 365), and DSOs are 46.23 ($3,800,000 over 82,192), the cost of delinquencies is the investment in the additional 16.23 days of sales, the difference between the actual and the target DSOs, (46.23 - 30). This amounts to $200,096 (16.23 X $82,192 X .15). This figure represents the potential gain from improving the performance of

---

Box 7-1
Factors Affecting Realizable Asset Value

The **security interest** the seller has in the asset.

The **realizable value** of the asset: For example, if the asset is relatively inexpensive or is difficult to recover, it may not be worthwhile to initiate legal proceedings to recover it.

The overall **creditworthiness of the debtor**: If the debtor is already experiencing severe financial distress then the prospects of recovering a significant amount of the asset's value diminish.

---

delinquent accounts, although, as noted earlier, the marketing impact of this tightening of credit policy impacts the decision.

Cost of Bad Debts

Companies differ widely in their handling of write-offs and bad debts. In many cases write-off policy is dictated by accounting practices, in particular, the goal of having assets correctly (or at least conservatively) valued. For example, a receivable that is more than 90 days past due may be "written down" using a contra-asset allowance account. The eventual realizable value of the written-down asset depends on a number of factors (see Box 7-1).

Costs of Credit Evaluation

The cost of credit evaluation can represent a very large part of the total credit department budget. The major components are the cost of acquiring and analyzing external credit information. The credit reports obtainable from consumer and commercial credit companies differ widely in costs and content; it is not uncommon for a firm to incur upwards of $30 in credit information costs in order to make a business credit decision. Some companies that perform extensive financial statement analysis when making credit decisions estimate the cost of making a credit decision at over $100.

A key judgment is the relative value that this costly information has in making superior credit granting decisions. In an attempt to control these costs, recently many credit grantors have developed automated credit systems. (These are discussed in a later section.)

Box 7-2
Reasons for Credit Use

Convenience: On the consumer side, the buyer need not have the required cash for each purchase. On the corporate side, for repeated purchases the buyer has the advantage of accumulating these purchases into a smaller number of invoices.

Competition: In many cases, particularly on the corporate side, credit terms are well established for the industry, making it difficult for a credit grantor to offer less favorable terms.

Price discrimination: Because of the float generated in a retail credit card transaction, for example, it is often said that cash customers are subsidizing credit buyers. This has led to two-tiered pricing — one price for cash and another for credit — in a number of situations.

Credit rationing: This is related to the theory that grantors of credit have debt capacity that they share with their buyers. In periods of tight credit, buyers will prefer these "spontaneous" sources of credit rather than draw on other credit reserves.

Costs of Ongoing Monitoring and Collection Efforts

All accounts incur expenses in processing payments and in maintaining proper credit records. Many companies, especially those that rely heavily on manual credit operations, pay too little attention to the monitoring of relatively small or infrequent buyers. The costs of collection efforts include the effort devoted to pursuing delinquent accounts and the often extensive costs attached to accounts that require legal intervention to effect collection. For example, many creditors lose in bankruptcies because they consider the effort of participating in the bankruptcy proceedings not worth the potential return.

Benefits: The Marketing Impact

As noted earlier, it is difficult for companies to assess the potential benefits of varying credit policies. For example, many retailers often believe that they can improve profits by eliminating their credit departments but fear the effects on overall profits by a resulting drop in sales.

In order to evaluate the role of credit as a merchandising and promotional tool, the credit grantor needs to determine the significance of the diverse reasons for the use of credit by its customers (see Box 7-2).

The credit grantor must also consider the value of the information obtained by studying the data base of credit purchases. This information can be used to target mail promotions, for example, and, in some circumstances, can be sold to other parties. This data base of credit customers has also been used as a springboard for more targeted offerings of financial services. The following example illustrates one company's strategy in the credit-granting question.

Illustration: ARCO

On April 15, 1982, the Atlantic Richfield Company (ARCO), the eighth largest gasoline retailer in the United States, stopped honoring credit cards (its own, of which there were about three million, and all others) for retail gasoline purchases. It simultaneously lowered its prices by about 3 cents per gallon. This came at a time of nationwide surpluses in gasoline supplies and an increasing market share by independent ("discount") retailers. From *Newsweek* (March 15, 1982, p. 56):

> *ARCO spent about $73 million last year maintaining the credit card system— a bill that included everything from the postage to mail monthly statements to the salaries paid 150 employees at ARCO's computer center in Atlanta.*

Other sources estimated gasoline retailers' cost of credit operations to be 6-9 cents per gallon. (*Business Week*, May 10, 1982, p. 111) The cost savings from eliminating credit operations enabled ARCO to offer a lower retail price, which would presumably increase sales and profitability. It would also avoid the growing problems of bad debts and lost and stolen cards.

Because of the convenience of credit cards, many ARCO customers were expected to buy elsewhere, a move that was encouraged by ARCO's competitors. A number of them began accepting ARCO cards while issuing the holder one of their own label; SUNOCO even gave ARCO cardholders a $2.50 rebate on a SUNOCO card (*New York Times*, April 14, 1982, p. D14).

By August of 1982, most observers felt that the ARCO move had been successful. ARCO reported that sales at its service stations had increased by about 50%. A number of major competitors maintained their own credit operations and introduced a two-tiered pricing scheme with discounts of about 4 cents per gallon for cash sales. However, the Service Station Dealers of America filed a complaint with the Federal Trade Commission alleging that the companies had first raised their prices then offered the discount. This violation of truth in lending was denied by the companies involved. The competition also reacted in a diversity of ways. Shell installed computer terminals for credit verification at all of their gas stations to cut down on bad debt losses. Gulf, in conjunction with Mellon Bank, arranged to have customers pay by on-site electronic funds transfer.

Figure 7-1
A Simple Credit Risk Pricing Model

$$p(1+K) = 1+r$$

where:

p = probability that the debt obligation will be repaid
k = promised yield
r = required expected yield

If the required expected yield is 15% and the promised yield is 20%, then

$$p = \frac{(1+r)}{(1+k)} = \frac{(1.15)}{(1.2)} = 95.8$$

(This is adapted from Saunders (1993), where extensions of this model are
analyzed.)

The apparent success of ARCO in curtailing its credit operations holds a number of lessons for other retailers. First, it emphasizes the cost of credit operations and the components of this cost. It shows how price elastic consumers are when it comes to a product like gasoline, for which there is very little brand loyalty. Lastly, it has shown how powerful the marketing aspects of credit and pricing are.

Pricing Credit Risk

To formalize the relationship between the risk evaluation process and the estimation of return, it is useful to develop a simple model of pricing credit risk in a one period setting (see Figure 7-1).

In the example shown in Figure 7-1, the calculation yielded a probability of 0.958. This means that the debt needs to have a 95.8% chance of repayment before it makes sense to extend the risky credit.

Now assume that l represents the present value of the portion of the debt that can be recovered upon default. For example, if the debt is secured by high quality collateral, such as accounts receivable, then one would expect a value of nearly one for the present value of the debt. This logic can be incorporated into the simple formula developed above (see Figure 7-2). The first term represents the value of the debt obligation in case of default and the second term represents the value in the no-default case. The example shows that the debt now needs only a 79.2%

Figure 7-2
Additions to the Credit Risk Formula

$$I(1 + k)(1 - p) + p(1 + k) = 1 + r$$

Rewriting this expression in terms of p:

$$p = \frac{[(1 + r) - 1 \times (1 + k)]}{[(1+k) \times (1 - I)]}$$

Continuing the above example, if 80% of the receivable is the estimated recovery rate (I), then:

$$p = \frac{[1.15 - .8\,(1.2)]}{[1.2 \times .2]} = .792$$

---

chance of payment before it makes sense to grant the credit. These types of calculations, together with the loss estimates obtained from the credit evaluation process, form the basis for the credit granting decision.

An Example of the Cost/Benefit Framework

A simple example can help describe the basic cost/benefit structure. Consider the credit granting procedures that would be appropriate for Belloc Cellular, a new company with a franchise to sell cellular telephone lines (i.e., access to telephone lines; the equipment is sold by unaffiliated vendors that refer customers to Belloc or one of its competitors) to consumers and businesses.

The basic cost/benefit analysis for Belloc is shown in Figure 7-3. The problem is simplified considerably by dividing all potential customers into two risk categories.

Losses occur in cases 2 and 3. Adapting the usual statistical parlance, case 2 implies a type I error and case 3 describes a type II error. A type I error occurs when an acceptable customer is rejected. A type II error occurs when an unacceptable customer is accepted. The correct decisions are cases 1 and 4. Each of these four cases has a different impact on the company's profitability. Each is analyzed after making some simplifying assumptions:

- Costs and benefits are evaluated only over the first year. (This understates the total benefits and reflects a rather conservative approach to credit granting.)
- The first year's profit from an acceptable risk is $3,000.

Figure 7-3
Belloc Cost-Benefit Matrix

	Decision	
Outcome	Accept	Reject
Acceptable risk	Case 1	Case 2
Unacceptable risk	Case 3	Case 4

- The first year's loss from an unacceptable risk is $1,000.
- The fixed cost of processing an application is $20. (This is a temporary and unrealistic assumption. A later section describes the important (and difficult) issue of how changing the investigation effort can change the accuracy of the risk evaluation.)
- Belloc also pays a fixed commission of $400 to the vendor for each customer that it refers to and is subsequently accepted by Belloc.

The next stage is to determine the relevant costs of cases 2 and 3 and the relevant benefits of cases 1 and 4. With the above structure, the costs and benefits are as follows:

- Case 1: Benefit = (Profit from an acceptable risk) less (Fixed commission cost) less (Fixed cost of processing application)
- Case 2: Cost = (Lost profit from an acceptable risk) plus (Fixed cost of processing application)
- Case 3: Cost = (Loss from an unacceptable risk) plus (Fixed commission) plus (Fixed cost of processing application)
- Case 4: Cost = (Fixed cost of processing application)

The second, and often more complex, stage is to estimate the probabilities of each of these cases occurring and compute the total expected value. The total expected value is obtained by multiplying each of the costs and benefits by the corresponding probability. To add to the illustration, assume the following probabilities:

- The probability of accepting a good risk is .80.
- The probability of rejecting a good risk is .14.
- The probability of accepting a bad risk is .02.
- The probability of rejecting a bad risk is .04.

Box 7-3
Basic Types of Credit Accounts

Open book credit: Here goods are sold without a contract for each transaction. Most types of trade credit are in this category; the invoice provides an informal statement of the transaction. Billing is effected through this invoice or by a regular statement covering all purchases over the relevant period.

Documentary credit: This covers a wide variety of transactions (often international), where the seller places additional requirements, such as some type of bank support, on the buyer before authorizing shipment.

Installment credit. Here repayment is made by a series of regular installments for interest and amortization of principal. Most of these arrangements are for one-time purchases of expensive items, for example, a vehicle or dinner at a good New York restaurant.

Revolving credit: The usual bank credit card (Visa or MasterCard) is an example. The debtor has the flexibility of paying off differing amounts, ranging from the entire outstanding balance to the minimum payment required to remain current (usually a fraction of the outstanding balance).

Note that these are not **conditional probabilities**. Cases 1 through 4 represent the four possible outcomes. We would interpret case 1 as meaning that Belloc rejects *and* the customer is an acceptable risk. On the other hand, the conditional probability would be .80/(.80+.14), or .851, which is the chance that Belloc would reject a customer, *given that* it was an acceptable risk. (These definitions are covered in any good probability or statistics text; e.g., Hoag and Craig (1985).)

In the example, the total expected value would be calculated by the following:

$$\text{Expected value} = .66(\$3000) - .82(\$400) - .02(\$1000) - \$20 = \$1612$$

This expected value is positive, meaning that with these numbers, Belloc's credit operation expects to make an average of $1,612 in the first year on each submitted application. Belloc will have an acceptance rate of 82% (.80+.02, the sum of the probabilities of accepting a good risk and accepting a bad risk) and a percentage of acceptable risks of 97.6% (.80/.82, the proportion of accepting good risks over all acceptances).

In this example the acceptance rate does not vary. However, it is crucial to optimize this "model" over different acceptance rates. In this instance, the high return/risk ratio suggests that a more lenient credit policy should be considered.

THE CREDIT CONTRACT

Credit contracts typically offered by corporations vary enormously in scope. Some are largely informal, describing little more than the terms of sale and an address for invoice remittance. For transactions of significantly higher value and/or risk (e.g., equipment leasing), the contracts can become more complex, eventually beginning to resemble bond indentures.

Credit agreements common in the United States all contain two basic types of information: the account category and the credit terms.

Types of Credit Accounts

There are four basic types of credit accounts (see Box 7-3). The first two are generally applicable to corporate credit; the latter two are principally for consumer credit.

For example, American Express offers two types of cards to consumers. With the more common variety, purchases are accrued over the billing period and the total amount is due within a few days of receipt of the bill. This type of charge card transaction would most resemble an open account transaction. American Express also offers another card, the Optima card, which is of the revolving type.

The differences in risk in these two types of credit have recently been clearly spelled out in the context of the 1990-1992 recession. American Express said that losses from bad credit, most of which was extended through the Optima card, will cost it $155 million more than it had anticipated.

Credit Terms

The second major part of the credit agreement stipulates the terms on which credit is granted; these are called the terms of sale or the **credit terms** (see Box 7-4). While these are fairly consistent within a given industry, because of antitrust law, they must be set without collusion with other credit grantors. The **Robinson-Patman Act**, which restricts discrimination in terms of sales, considers terms of sale to be a part of pricing. In most industries terms of sale relate to the perishability, seasonality or turnover of the items.

One of the most common types of terms shown in Box 7-4 is called **ordinary terms**. These are stated as *net t* or, more generally, d/t_1 *net* t_2. The first example specifies that payment is due within t days from a given date (typically from receipt of goods). The second allows a discount of $d\%$ if payment is made by t_1 days; if the discount is not taken, full payment is due within t_2 days. For example, *2/10 net 30* specifies that if payment is made within 10 days, 2% may be discounted from the stated price; otherwise the full invoiced price is due within 30 days. For example, food products are often sold on *net 7* or *net 10* terms, while longer-lived assets, such as jewelry may have terms approaching six months.

One of the most subjective areas of accounts receivable management relates to the degree of enforcement of stated terms. Many buyers with considerable market power attempt to "stretch" payables beyond stated terms or take a discount when one is not warranted. This practice also falls under the purview of the Robinson-Patman Act, discussed further below. For example, a company should be careful not to grant a discount to a customer for payments later than the discount time period as this action may be regarded as favorable to one customer or "prejudicial" to others and would potentially violate the Robinson-Patman Act. The other key components of the credit contract are shown in Box 7-5.

Changing credit terms and standards

While sellers tend to offer trade credit terms that are within the norms determined by the industry, an interesting question is the impact of changing credit terms. This involves evaluating the impact on sales, bad debts, and, perhaps less obviously, the impact on the other components of working capital. In practice, the issue of changing trade credit terms is less important than the day-to-day issue of making individual credit decisions (accept/reject or determining credit limits).

Trade Credit: The Economic Rationale

Trade credit remains a critically important source of financing for almost all companies. There are a number of motives for the prevalence of trade credit in the domestic and international credit markets. Some of the most important include the following:

- **Allocation of debt capacity**: The basic story is that the suppliers of trade credit are often larger than their buyers. In order to help these smaller, and assumedly less creditworthy, buyers finance their purchases, the seller extends its borrowing capacity to its buyers. For example, General Motors Acceptance Corporation is one of the largest domestic borrowers. It uses its extensive short- and long-term borrowing resources to offer financing to buyers of GM vehicles.
- **Contracting costs**: Trade credit avoids costly contracting between seller and buyer.
- **Pricing motive**: Trade credit terms can offer a way to circumvent restrictions on prices and price discrimination. While it is illegal,

Box 7-4
Common Domestic Terms of Sale

Cash in Advance (CIA): These terms require payment before the order is shipped. They are typically used if the buyer is viewed as a credit risk. Another name for these terms is **Cash Before Delivery** .

Cash on Delivery (COD): These terms mean that the buyer must pay upon delivery of the goods. Like CIA terms, they are also used to reduce the seller's risk.

Cash Terms: These terms mean that the buyer generally has a week to ten days to make the payment. They are frequently used for sales of highly perishable items.

Documentary Collections: These terms cover a broad class of transactions, especially common in international trade. Transactions are handled through a bank, which controls the release of the goods. The basic transaction requires a bill of lading and an acceptable payment or promise of payment. These terms are very safe because the bill of lading (hence, the shipment) is not released until the bank is satisfied that payment is or will be made.

Bill-to-Bill: These terms are used in items with regular (typically weekly) deliveries. The invoice for the previous delivery is payable when the next shipment arrives.

Ordinary Terms: These terms include a net due date, by which date the full amount must be paid, and often a discount date, by which the payment must be received in order to take advantage of the discount. These dates are usually calculated from the invoice date, although other dates, such as the delivery date, may be specified. These variants are expressed as **R.O.G.** (receipt of goods) or **A.O.G.** (arrival of goods). R.O.G. terms are often used for products requiring water shipment, such as sugar.

Monthly billing terms: With these terms, a monthly statement is issued for all invoices issued prior to a cutoff date. Payment is usually due on a fixed date in the following month. For example, *2/10th, Prox net 30th* means a discount of 2% can be taken if payment is made by the 10th day of the following month; the full amount is due on the 30th day of the following month. Terms can also be written as **E.O.M.**, for end-of-month or, more maternally, terms may also be stated as **M.O.M.**, for middle of the month.

Seasonal billing terms: With these terms, due dates are based on the seasonality of the given product. For example, with toys, it is common to ship in the early fall; the invoice would be payable in thirds: one third upon delivery, another third in mid-December and the final third in mid-January. A variety of other highly seasonal products — textbooks, sporting goods, etc. — have similar credit terms, in which the payment terms attempt to match the buyer's cash flow.

Box 7-5
Other Components of the Credit Contract

Collateral: To increase the seller's security, assets are often pledged as security. The assets are typically the most liquid, although fixed assets are sometimes used.

Guarantees: In many cases, the seller insists on the guarantee of a related entity (as opposed to credit enhancement, discussed in the next chapter). For example, when extending credit to a small company, the credit grantor may request the principals of the company

Penalties for failure to adhere to credit terms: Most credit agreements are explicit about penalties that are payable for failure to meet specified terms to personally guarantee the debt. Verifying the explicit nature of the guarantee is critical. In a recent ruling on a $9.6 million loan (*Wall Street Journal,* December 16, 1991), Banc One Leasing Corporation was ruled negligent for not obtaining independent verification of a loan guarantee; the bank's guarantee documentation was subsequently found to be a forgery.

Payment form: The seller, especially in international transactions, may require that the payment be via a specified payment mechanism, such as wire transfer, or in a pre-specified currency.

Remittance location: In many cases, the seller uses a lockbox, and payments are directed to this bank post office box rather than to a corporate address.

Other specialized conditions: As the transactions become more complex, a variety of additional conditions can be included. These could relate to inspection of the goods, insurance for the goods in transit, etc.

---

certain credit grantors are known to be more lenient in enforcing credit terms with favored customers.

While discounts are very common, it is usually the case that the implicit borrowing terms are significantly higher than prevailing borrowing rates, which seems to favor the debt capacity argument.

Trade Credit: Implicit Borrowing Costs

For the buyer, trade credit provides a flexible source of financing. It often has the added advantage that it is a borrowing source that often circumvents other debt covenants and limits. Thus, when deciding whether to pay a $100,000 invoice offered on *1/10 net 60* terms versus borrowing against an existing bank credit

Figure 7-4
Formula to Determine Implicit Borrowing Rate

Assume the terms are d/t_1 net t_2

Implicit borrowing rate $= \dfrac{d}{1-d} \times \dfrac{365}{t_2 - t_1}$

For terms of *1/10 net 60*, the calculation is

Implicit rate $= \dfrac{.01}{1-.01} \times \dfrac{365}{(60-10)}$

$$= 7.374\%$$

---

line, a treasury manager should also consider the effect of using the existing debt capacity and the potential tightening of debt covenants, in addition to the implicit borrowing costs.

The calculation of the implicit borrowing costs follows the paradigm used for other borrowing calculations shown in Chapter 9. As shown, one determines the "interest" paid (here the forgone discount) divided by the loan amount (here the amount net of discount), and annualize. The effective borrowing period is the difference between the net date and the last date that the discount could be taken. For example, credit terms of *1/10 net 60* means that one percent of the invoice can be considered the amount of interest paid to borrow the discounted purchase amount from the supplier for 50 additional days — from the discount date to the net payment date. The formula is shown in Figure 7-4.

The buyer would compare this annual rate of 7.374% with alternative sources, considering the additional factors noted above. Figure 7-5 shows the implicit borrowing rate for discounts ranging from .005 to .025 with effective borrowing periods, ranging from 10 to 60 days. Note that *2/10 net 30*, for example, implies an effective borrowing rate of 37.2%.

Stretching Payables

The practice of stretching payables (paying significantly past the stated credit terms) can strain relationships with suppliers. The impact of this practice naturally depends on the relative bargaining power of the two parties. As companies move further toward EDI/EFT and its attendant closer relations between buyer and

Figure 7-5
Implicit Borrowing Rates with Trade Credit

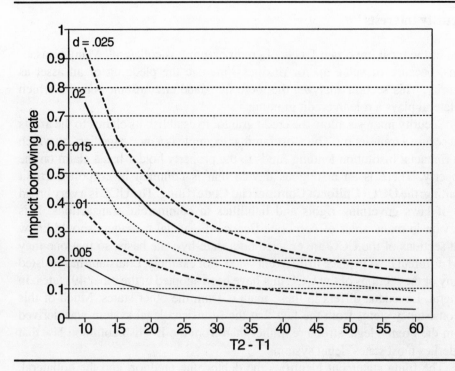

seller, this practice should decline. Another important factor is the effect that the reporting of this delinquency may have on the buyer. As will be clarified, the commercial credit bureaus maintain extensive data bases of corporate and consumer trade experiences. These experiences become a very important factor for many companies in determining whether or not to grant credit. Finally, it has become increasingly common for companies to assess penalties for late payment. In the worst case, trade creditors can institute legal action to collect funds owed. This is discussed in the following section.

LEGAL AND REGULATORY ASPECTS

The credit grantor must be aware of the complex and dynamic regulatory structure surrounding credit operations. A sampling of the relevant U.S. laws on credit (see

Box 7-6) illustrates this point. While the majority of these laws focus on consumer credit, most apply equally well to corporate credit granting.

Security Interests

One of the most important facets of credit granting is collateral. Many transactions, because of value and/or riskiness, involve the pledging of an asset as security. This section analyzes the more mundane circumstances under which collateral plays a role in credit granting.

Security interests allow the credit grantor to establish its claims to the assets that secure a transaction. The most familiar example is a mortgage lien, by which the financial institution lending funds to the property holder has a claim on the property. There is an analogous device that is common in corporate credit granting: the **UCC (Uniform Commercial Code)** filing. The UCC is a very broad set of laws governing rights and liabilities in commercial transactions. It is relevant in many areas of corporate finance. Financial managers should know that sections of the UCC are enacted on a state-by-state basis, so that one may find different laws in place in different states. For example, Louisiana has resisted many of the sections of the UCC that have been adopted in the other 49 states. In general, Louisiana differs in these matters from the other states. Much of this inconsistency stems from the fact that the Louisiana legal system was derived from the French legal structure, rather than from the English common law that underlies most states' legal systems.

The filing statement identifies the debtor, the creditor, and the collateral. Analogous to a mortgage lien, a creditor will file a UCC-1, which then becomes a matter of public record. Suppliers of business credit data routinely include UCC filing information in their credit reports on corporations.

A UCC-1 filing, together with a **security agreement** (a general document in which the debtor outlines the nature of the assets pledged to the creditor) allows the creditor to seize the secured asset if the debtor fails to satisfy its payment obligations. The filing of the UCC *perfects* (makes enforceable) the debtor's security interest.

Knowing about a company's previous collateralized debts is important in evaluating any further collateral that can be pledged. A **lien search** is often used to uncover whether or not a debtor has other secured creditors.

Box 7-6
A Sampling of U.S. Credit Legislation

Consumer protection

- *Truth in Lending Act* (1969): requires meaningful disclosure of credit terms (notably dollar amount of finance charges and annual percentage rate)
- *Credit Card Issuance Act* (1970): prohibits unsolicited credit card issuance
- *Fair Credit Reporting Act* (1971): requires justification of rejected credit
- *Fair Credit Billing Act (*1975): controls inaccurate billing
- *Equal Credit Opportunity Act* (1975 and 1976): prevents discrimination on the basis of sex, marital status, race, color, religion, national origin, age, receipt of income from public assistance, exercise of rights under the Consumer Credit Protection Act
- *Fair Debt Collection Practices Act* (1978): protects against improper (harassing, deceptive, etc.) collection practices
- *Electronic Funds Transfer Act* (1978): prohibits making credit extension conditional on EFT payment
- *Debt Collection Act* (1982): allows the federal government to report delinquent debtor information to credit bureaus

Antitrust legislation

- *The Sherman Act* (1890): prohibits restraint of trade in interstate commerce
- *The Robinson-Patman Act* (1976): an amendment to the Clayton Act (which was designed to update the Sherman Act), restricting price discrimination

Note: In parentheses is the effective year of the legislation. All of these entries are titles of the Consumer Credit Protection Act except for the Fair Credit Billing Act, which is an amendment to the Truth in Lending Act.

Source: Nelson (1990) and Cole (1988)

THE CREDIT ANALYSIS PROCESS

Previous sections have developed the credit grantor's basic cost/benefit and regulatory parameters. The next thing to consider is the evaluation of the customer's creditworthiness. The key questions that have to be answered in evaluating business risks for a commercial credit are shown in Box 7-7.

The credit granting process usually operates in a tightly defined set of parameters. In addition to the cost/benefit framework as outlined earlier in this chapter, there are several other key factors:

- **Competitive position**: In highly competitive settings, such as in small-dollar leasing, credit grantors may have to accept weaker credits and perform the credit evaluation function more quickly than they would otherwise.

- **Type of customer**: The size or type of company has an impact on the credit granting process. For example, dealing with smaller companies may necessitate performing the credit function with a relatively small amount of credit information. In addition, selling into a narrow industrial base leads to a riskier credit portfolio because of the lack of diversification.

- **Regulatory considerations**: Consumer lending in particular is influenced by a diverse collection of laws, differing by state and constantly evolving.

- **Nature of the product or service being sold**: This gets into issues of market power and relative competition, but other matters should also affect policy. For example, in some instances the company is selling a partially or totally customized product. This affects its eventual recovery value in case of nonpayment. It also requires the company to make at least a preliminary credit evaluation before proceeding too far with a new customer.

The lending process operates within these parameters. It sets out procedures for obtaining the appropriate credit information and using it to make the credit assessment and then (potentially) modifying the credit agreement so that the risk-return tradeoff is acceptable to the credit grantor.

Prescreening

A recent development in commercial credit has been the use of **credit prescreening**. In this technique, a company isolates a potential market, such as a certain industrial group in a given section of the country, and applies credit criteria to

Box 7-7
Identifying Business Risks

Production
- Does the business rely on one or several key suppliers?
- What are the main components of production costs?
- How sensitive is the company's cash flow to changes in production costs?
- Is the company exposed to technological change?

Marketing
- What factors affect industry sales?
- How sensitive are sales to price changes?
- What are the strategies of competitors?
- Are buyers more powerful than suppliers?

Personnel
- How dependent is the company on certain key individuals?
- What is the outlook for labor relations?
- When will existing labor contracts expire?

Source: Adapted from Hale (1983)

weed out those potential customers that lack the specified level of credit quality. This has been common in consumer credit for a number of years. Creditworthy consumers are regularly inundated with unsolicited preapprovals for credit cards.

One of the first major applications of commercial prescreens was carried out in 1989 for a major corporate credit card solicitation. The company had a statistical model built from a sample of its corporate customers. This model was then applied to a group of corporate accounts that had already been preselected on demographic and Standard Industrial Classification (SIC) parameters. The result was a rank ordering of potential corporate customers. The companies that scored sufficiently high were sent pre-qualified applications, essentially guaranteeing that they would receive a credit card merely by filling in the enclosed application. This type of pre-approved solicitation typically results in a much higher response rate than the usual solicitations to apply for credit. Note that this type of pre-approval greatly simplifies or even eliminates the credit approval process for the solicited companies.

CREDIT INFORMATION

There are many types of information that the credit grantor has at its disposal to make credit decisions. The cost (in terms of acquisition or in terms of required analysis) differs greatly, as does its value in making informed credit evaluations. A basic distinction is between **internal** and **external** sources of information. The former refers to information that is essentially costlessly available at the time of the credit evaluation. The latter refers to information that is purchased or otherwise obtained from sources outside the credit granting company. The most important sources of internal and external information are shown in Box 7-8.

These and other relevant data are not costlessly acquired. Even if some information is obtained from credit applications, there remains the cost of verification and processing. More credit information does not necessarily mean a better credit decision. The basic issue is the marginal value of the information versus the cost of acquiring it. While this can become a rather subtle statistical point, it is a very important practical issue.

Consumer Credit Data

Consumer credit reports are available on virtually all individuals in the U.S. and Canada through the major consumer credit bureaus. In the U.S., the market is dominated by three: TRW, Trans Union Credit Information Corporation, and Equifax. A credit grantor with significant volume pays approximately $1 to $3 per report, is typically connected on-line to these three credit bureaus, and often has software designed to extract (parse out) the individual elements of the data report most relevant to its credit granting process. These extracted elements are then fed into an automating credit decision system. The majority of these are based on statistical models, although other forms of decision-making techniques are used in practice. For an additional charge (typically less than $1), the credit grantor can also receive a prediction, based on one or a set of statistical models, of the individual's probability of bankruptcy or severe delinquency.

In North America, the credit grantor must have received written permission from the credit seeker to obtain these reports. (However, this is not required for obtaining business credit data.) The data bases are accessed through the individual's social security number. Recent questions about the accuracy of consumer credit reports have prompted regulatory scrutiny. A 1991 *American Banker* survey noted that 48% of the reports examined contained errors.

Box 7-8
Sources of Credit Information

Internal Sources

- **The applicant's previous credit history** (if any): It is a generally accepted fact that more "seasoned" credits tend to perform better than new credits. The company granting credit has a valuable source of payment information.

- **The new customer's credit application**: While this information is not likely to have much value without independent verification, it can be used to access trade or bank references. In order to expedite application handling and minimize credit costs, some companies make small-dollar credit decisions solely on the basis of a statistical model or expert system generating a recommended decision based only on the application data. Consumer bureau reports are also used in making decisions on some applicants.

External sources

- **Local and nationwide credit reporting agencies**: These organizations collect, evaluate and report information on credit history, including past payment history, financial information, high credit amounts, length of time credit has been available and any actions that have been necessary to achieve collection.

- **The customer's bank**: This can also be a valuable source of information about the customer's financial condition and available credit. Although in most cases the information received is not detailed and is often only transmitted through the mail, which is unacceptable in some credit granting circumstances.

- **Trade references**: These describe other companies' experiences with the customer and are an excellent indicator of when payment will be made.

- **Financial statements**: These provide important information on corporate credit applications. Financial statement analysis is almost always done on large credits, often based on the evaluation of standard financial ratios.

Business Credit Data

In the U.S. and Canada, the market for business credit data is dominated by Dun & Bradstreet Corporation, through its Credit Services Division. Its revenues from the sale of business data approach $1 billion annually. TRW is its major competitor, although other, usually industry specific, credit reporting companies exist. Although Dun & Bradstreet and other companies collect business credit information on companies outside the U.S. and Canada, in general, the level of information available is much less than would be obtainable domestically. This has a number of implications for granting credit to non-North American entities. A simplified outline of a business credit report is shown in Figure 7-6. Figure 7-7 offers a brief explanation of the D&B rating and outlines D&B's measure of composite payment behavior — the **Paydex**.

Very roughly stated, there are reports with relatively complete information available on approximately 1.5 million U.S. companies. Less complete data can sometimes be obtained on several million more companies. Although very few companies with sales approaching $1 million are not represented in TRW's or D&B's data bases, other companies can be missing from these data bases if they are very small or young, are in an industry that does not typically seek credit broadly (e.g., agriculture or consulting), or are not actively seeking credit.

One of the most useful devices used in making credit decisions in the U.S. is the D&B rating. It is similar in spirit to bond and other financial instrument ratings. Unlike financial instrument ratings, it is not initiated by the company, nor is the level of analysis nearly as comprehensive. It has two components: an analysis of the *financial strength* of the company and a *composite payment rating*. These ratings are often used as a benchmark for credit granting. For example, a company may stipulate that any buyer with a rating of 1A1 or better, will receive an initial credit line of $10,000. Also, companies that experience a downgrade in rating may be subject to more scrutiny than others. In certain industries (e.g., textiles) a credit rating is very important in order to have wide access to suppliers.

While a full description of the data collection process is well beyond the scope of this book, it is critical to be aware of the manner in which the data are collected. Some of the data (e.g., company age, sales, and financial statements) are typically obtained voluntarily from the principals of the company itself. Naturally this can lead to problems of veracity and timeliness.

Other data are not obtained from the principals of the company. These data include *public filing data* (which is information drawn from the courts on suits, liens, judgments, and bankruptcies) and *trade data*. These trade experiences are crucial to the credit granting process and consist of trade experiences submitted to the credit collection company by major domestic corporations. For example, a large transportation company would give the credit agency its A.R. tape, from which the credit agency would extract the experiences that correspond to companies in its data base and append these to that company's available data. The process for collecting trade experiences and public filing data for consumers is analogous to what is described here.

Figure 7-6
A Simplified Business Credit Information Report

Copyright notice	Date report written
Firm identifiers	Firm industry description
	Primary and secondary SICs
Address	Year started
	Sales
	Rating
	Number of employees

Trade Data

Record Date	High Credit	Owes	Past Due	Terms	Last Sale
3-12 Discount	25000	1000	0	2/10 net 30	1 mo.
5-12 Prompt	34213	0	0	Net 30	6-12 mo.
3-01 Slow 30	500	250	0	Net 30	1 mo.
...					

Financial statements and updates

Bank account data (e.g., average balance)

Public filings

Suits
Liens
UCC filings

Other information

Detail on principals and directors
Branches and subsidiaries
Description of premises

CREDIT GRANTING METHODOLOGY

The basic goal of the credit granting process is to evaluate credit applicants with the objective of determining the appropriate risk-return tradeoff. The problem can be considered as a forecasting question: *Given the credit applicant's char-*

Figure 7-7
D&B Rating and Payment Index

D&B Rating

			Composite Credit Appraisal		
Estimated Financial Strength		High	Good	Fair	Limited
5A	$50,000,000 and over	1	2	3	4
4A	$10,000,000 to $49,999,999	1	2	3	4
3A	$1,000,000 to $9,999,999	1	2	3	4
2A	$750,000 to $999,999	1	2	3	4
1A	$500,000 to $749,999	1	2	3	4
BA	$300,000 to $499,999	1	2	3	4
BB	$200,000 to $299,999	1	2	3	4
CB	$125,000 to $199,999	1	2	3	4
CC	$75,000 to $124,999	1	2	3	4
DC	$50,000 to $74,999	1	2	3	4
DD	$35,000 to $49,999	1	2	3	4
EE	$20,000 to $34,999	1	2	3	4
FF	$10,000 to $19,999	1	2	3	4
GG	$5,000 to $9,999	1	2	3	4
HH	up to $4,999	1	2	3	4

Absence of rating: A rating of -- is commonly assigned when D&B does not have sufficient data to establish a rating. Ratings of NQ (not quoted) or INV (under investigation) are usually interpreted negatively.

D&B Payment Index: Paydex

Paydex	Payment
100	Anticipate
90	Discount
80	Prompt
70	Slow to 15 days
50	Slow to 30 days
40	Slow to 60 days
30	Slow to 90 days
20	Slow to 120 days

Paydex requires at least four trade experiences within the last 13 months from different credit grantors.

Box 7-9
The Five C's of Credit

Character: the perceived integrity of the individual applicant or the officers of a corporate applicant

Capacity: a measure of the customer's resources to pay the obligation

Capital: a measure of the customer's long-term financial resources that could be called upon if the immediate cash flow is insufficient

Collateral: the assets secured to satisfy the obligation if payment is not made

Conditions: the economic conditions of the customer and the seller

---

acteristics, what will future payment behavior be? As such, many of the issues raised in general forecasting applications are relevant here, particularly the costs of errors in prediction, the relevant characteristics for prediction, and the complexity of the forecasting method, relative to the anticipated benefits.

Qualitative Analysis

The type of analysis naturally depends upon the type of information available and the cost/benefit tradeoff. The traditional qualitative approaches are based on the ancient five C's of credit (see Box 7-9). Many credit grantors have attempted to distill the expertise of the individuals that make credit decisions using variants of *expert systems*.

Figure 7-8 provides an example of a qualitative credit scoring *scorecard*, which is analogous to the scorecards that are common in consumer credit scoring. It was taken from a major computer manufacturer's procedures for allocating lines of credit for requests under $75,000.

Quantitative Analysis

Many credit grantors face the problem of making numerous, relatively small-dollar credit decisions. In order to make these decisions efficiently, it has become common to adopt quantitative approaches that automate the decision-making process. While the methodology used to develop the decision-making procedure varies, once implemented, these **credit scoring models** function in a similar manner and offer comparable advantages.

Credit scoring is a very common and often a very effective technique for making credit decisions involving relatively low-dollar or repetitive transactions. The first applications of consumer credit scoring began in the 1950's as banks that were processing substantial volumes of credit cards sought operating efficiencies. The enactment of legislation against discrimination in credit granting accelerated its dissemination.

Currently, its major users include all the major grantors of consumer credit, such as credit card companies, retail department stores, consumer credit companies, major banks, utilities, and leasing companies. On the commercial side, its applications have only become important in the last few years. The initial proponents of commercial credit scoring were leasing companies, telecommunications companies, and manufacturing companies.

A credit scoring model is a procedure for weighting characteristics (assumed relevant to payment behavior) to obtain a numerical score, which can then be used to determine whether or not credit should be granted or the amount of credit that should be granted. For credit decisions with relatively low value or risk or with a need for rapid application processing, credit scoring is very commonly used. Almost all companies and financial institutions granting retail credit use one of its many variants. On the commercial credit side, its applications began seriously in the late 1980's and are growing very rapidly.

The structure of a credit scoring model can be precisely that of a linear regression model. The model has a set of *explanatory* variables, which are related to the creditworthiness of a given applicant. For consumer credit, these variables may measure past payment history, number of credit requests, incidence of derogatory trade experiences, time in file, annual income, years at current address, and so on. For commercial credit, years in business, rating, presence of public filings, and measures of payment performance are important. Corresponding to each explanatory variable is a weight that determines how much each variable contributes to the total score.

Generally, the higher the score the more creditworthy is the applicant. In many applications, the scores are partitioned into ranges with each range having a recommended decision. For example, if scores ranged from 0 to 100, with higher scores indicating greater creditworthiness, scores above 75 may mean automatic approval, scores below 50 may mean automatic rejection, and intermediate scores would be referred to an analyst for further analysis. This type of structure leads to a more efficient allocation of analysts' time, concentrating their attention on the borderline cases.

Figure 7-8
A Qualitative Credit Scoring System

---

1. Average checking account balance

3 figures and less	-5 points
Low to medium 4 figures	1 or 2
High 4 to medium 5	3 to 5
High 5 to medium 6	6 to 8
High 6	9
7 figures and above	10

2. Unsecured bank line of credit

Moderate 4 figures & less	0 points
Medium 4 to low 5 figures	1 to 2
Moderate 5 to medium 5	3 to 4
High 5 to low 6	5 to 6
Moderate to high 6	7 to 9
7 figures and above	10

3. Secured line of credit from a bank

Moderate 4 figures & less	-3 points
Medium 4 to low 5 figures	0
Moderate 5 to medium 5	1 to 3
High 5 to low 6	4 to 5
Moderate to high 6	6 to 8
7 figures and above	9 to 10

4. Percent of line of credit extended (used)

100% extended	-5 points
50 - 99% extended	-2
10 - 49% extended	0
Less than 10% extended	2

5. Total gross sales

Less than $500,000	-5 points
$500,000 - $1,000,000	1 to 3
$1 million to $5 million	4 to 6
$5 to $15 million	7 to 9
More than $15 million	10

6. Total employees

Less than 6	-5 points
6 to 20	1 to 2
21 to 50	3 to 5
51 to 150	6 to 7
151 to 250	8
251 to 1000	9
More than 1000	10

7. Trade payment history

Average >90 days late	-5 points
Average 61 - 90 days late	-2
Average 31 - 60 days late	0
Average <30 days late	1 to 3
Current	4 to 5

8. Total years in business

Less than 1 year	-5 points
1 year	0
2 to 3 years	1 to 2
4 to 5 years	3 to 5
7 years	7
8 years	8
9 years	9
10 years	10

9. Public filings

1 filing	-3 points
0 filings	3

10. Premises

Leased/rented	-2 points
Owned	2

Source: Credit Research Foundation

Techniques

Some of the basic statistical techniques used in predicting company failure are also important in credit scoring. However, for a wide variety of reasons, statistical methods are not the only important methodology. Two others are important. Both are under the rubric of artificial intelligence although the approaches are radically different. In all of the applications, the objective is to determine how to weigh the observable data in order to make a prediction of creditworthiness. While the particular choice of technique may seem like a largely technical point, in practice it plays an important role.

Figure 7-9 presents an overview of three important approaches:

- Expert systems
- Neural nets
- Statistical systems

Expert systems. The term *expert systems* in this area lacks a precise meaning. In the majority of applications in credit management it means the computer implementation of decision rules determined by one or more "experts." In essence, these processes are merely automating the manual steps that a human credit analyst might perform. Naturally, if the system is replicating the process of a mediocre analyst, it can do little more than mimic this level of decision-making expertise. However, in practice, many applications have been quite successful since the basis of creditworthiness is reasonably apparent to experienced credit analysts.

Neural Nets. Neural nets are examples of "knowledge engineering." This terminology refers to a group of techniques that purport to imitate the human learning process. Like expert systems, many variants exist. The fundamental approach is initially the same as a statistical approach: Take a set of observed outcomes and a set of variables observable at the time the credit decision is made and try to build a model that can explain the observed outcomes. Where neural nets differ from statistical approaches is in the manner in which the models are developed. Neural nets take the input (data observable at the time the credit decision is made) and the output (the eventual classification of the debtor as an acceptable or unacceptable risk) and through a number of possible channels the neural net "learns" which inputs lead to which responses. The resulting net is often a nonlinear representation of this input/output relationship.

Statistical Systems. Credit scoring is an important application of a general group of statistical techniques called *classification analysis*. In classification

Figure 7-9
Credit Scoring Process Flow

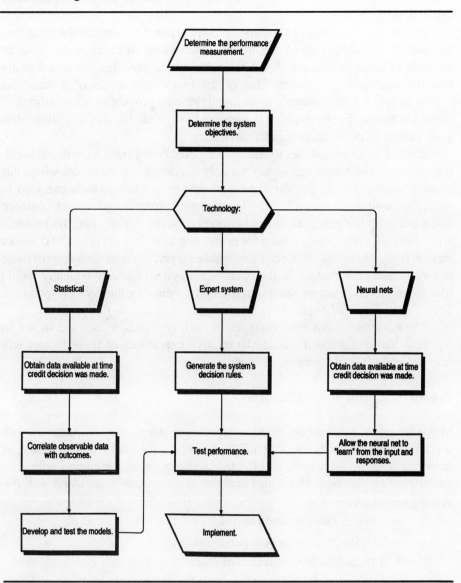

analysis, the statistician is attempting to use measurements (such as financial ratios and business characteristics) to classify an observation into one of a number, most often two, discrete categories. For example, in a consumer credit scoring application, the statistician will examine the consumer's financial characteristics at the time of the credit application together with the applicant's eventual performance.

Probably the majority of systems currently in place use statistical approaches to generate the weighting of the initial observations in order to generate an estimate of creditworthiness. As in the other two approaches, there are many possible statistical approaches. One of the major advantages of a statistical approach is that it can (directly or indirectly) create probability distributions of creditworthiness. For example, it is possible to say that this credit applicant has a 3% chance of being an unacceptable risk.

Each of these approaches to determining creditworthiness have corresponding advantages and disadvantages. One very important consideration, which has no easy solution, is the problem of *reject inference*. This obstacle can lead to significant estimation bias, difficulty in estimating projected system performance and a host of other practical and estimation problems. Simply put, the problem arises because the population used for estimating a credit scoring model does not include rejected applicants (since there can be no performance measure for these observations). Nonetheless, in the operational system the user typically would like the model to generate scores on the entire "through-the-door" population. Several statistical techniques have been suggested to handle this problem.

The advantages and disadvantages of each type of approach are shown in Figure 7-10. In any specific case, the relative importance of these factors will help determine which technique to pursue.

Benefits of Credit Scoring Models

Major issuers of retail credit, such as department stores, use quantitative credit scoring models, often developing a different model for each billing region. The quantitative approaches are cost effective and can aid in complying with consumer credit legislation. The major benefits to a company from using a credit-scoring model are:

- Gains in management control
- Benefits in training new personnel
- A reduction in loan applicant processing costs
- A more legally defensible system for denying credit
- Increased input to the company's management information system

The first benefit arises from the ability to quantify objectives. More stringent credit can be interpreted as raising the cutoff score. Based on historical information, the impact of this can be assessed. The second benefit comes from summa-

Figure 7-10
Approaches to Credit Scoring: Advantages and Disadvantages

	Technique		
Criterion	Expert Systems	Neural Nets	Statistics
Development effort	Low to high	High	Medium
Updating effort	Low to high	Low	Low
Comprehensibility	Medium to high	Low	High
Implementation effort	Low to high	Low	Low

rizing the credit grantor's past experience and highlighting in the credit-scoring model those characteristics that have proved most significant in discriminating between good and bad credit accounts. After the initial development stage, a successful credit-scoring system is clearly simpler, cheaper, and faster than having a credit analyst interpret the available credit information. As previously mentioned, U.S. credit legislation requires informing rejected credit applicants of the reasons for credit denial. A credit scoring scheme simplifies this procedure.

A credit scoring model should weight heavily a characteristic that discriminates well between good and bad accounts. The selection of an appropriate performance measure to categorize accounts into good and bad is important. For example, there are two types of errors generated by choosing a particular cutoff score:

- Type I: rejecting a good risk (lost revenue, an opportunity cost usually)
- Type II: accepting a bad risk (bad debt loss and/or delinquency costs)

As the cutoff score increases, meaning granting credit to fewer applicants, the probability of a type II error decreases while the probability of a type I error increases. The cost/benefit analysis outlined previously helps the company determine the optimal cutoff.

Credit scoring using subjective weights is often used, as was illustrated in Figure 7-8. However, in 1941 David Durand suggested the use of discriminant analysis (a close relative of linear regression) as a statistical method to identify and weight the factors that distinguish paying customers from non-paying customers.

Roughly stated, the statistical credit scoring procedure follows three stages:

- Standard and high-risk accounts are defined (based on historical data), and information is compiled to discriminate between the two types of accounts. This information includes variables available at the time the credit decision is made and plausibly (from an economic and a statistical sense) correlated with customer performance.
- The characteristics are weighted (using statistics, artificial intelligence, or a less formal approach) in the way that best distinguishes between the two classes of accounts, thus creating an aggregate credit score that measures creditworthiness. The precise meaning of "best" varies according to the particular application.
- Two cutoff scores are typically set; an applicant with a score above the higher cutoff is granted credit while one below the lower limit is denied credit. An applicant with a score between the two limits is usually referred for further analysis before a decision is made. In many cases, these cutoff scores will depend upon the value and type of credit transaction.

These three steps ignore one important component of credit scoring. In practice, the statistician has to determine the effect of applicants that were previously rejected. That is, the data used for estimation consist primarily of accepted applicants (otherwise one could not assess whether or not they had been acceptable risks), however, the eventual model will be applied to the entire universe of applicants, which can be statistically very different from the sample used for estimation.

It is also important to note that the credit score should incorporate the key components of the credit decision: an estimate of the creditworthiness of the applicant and an evaluation of the cost/benefit relevant to the transaction being evaluated. Thus it is often the case that a particular credit applicant would be accepted for one type of transaction but rejected for another transaction that has different risk/return characteristics.

EMERGING TRENDS

This chapter has outlined the key features of the corporate credit granting decisions. Due to rapidly evolving computer technology, improvements in information processing/decision-making methodology, and new information products, this area is evolving quickly. Key trends that are emerging include:

- Superior use of external credit information. Credit information providers, both on the consumer and the corporate side has responded to sophisticated credit grantors by offering a wider variety of credit information packages. One interesting example is DunsLink, a product of Dun & Bradstreet that offers computer-to-computer exchange of data elements. By using this product, a credit grantor can select the data elements it chooses from the D&B data base and have them fed directly into a decision-making procedure or data base. This is not only efficient; it can offer substantial savings in credit information costs because only the targeted data elements are transmitted and paid for.

- Better analysis of the cost/benefit tradeoff. Formerly there was often too great a separation between the "defensive" function of credit (minimizing delinquencies and bad debts) and the marketing function of credit. Better credit-making procedures have allowed credit analysts to adapt the credit contract for higher risk transactions in order to make the deal acceptable to both parties.

MANAGEMENT REVIEW ITEMS

➡ Review credit management operations to define all of your credit costs, trying to classify each cost as out-of-pocket or opportunity. Keep your results in a computer spreadsheet file if possible, and repeat the review annually.

➡ Calculate the total opportunity cost of investment in accounts receivable using DSO figures not credit terms.

➡ Use the credit risk formula (from Figure 7-2) to determine the minimum acceptance level for granting credit. Compare this with your actual receivable collection experience. If it is higher, initiate a major credit review aimed at tightening credit standards. If it is lower, you may not want to anything, or it may be a sign of too stringent credit standards.

➡ Calculate the implicit borrowing rate for credit terms offered by your business lines. Calculate for terms offered and average actual experience levels. Compare your results with your cost of funds, and review your findings with credit management.

➡ Check for customers, especially large ones, that routinely violate credit terms, either taking discounts after the discount cut-off date or assuming a grace period. Consider instituting a penalty program for late payers.

➡ Adapt consumer credit standards to small corporate customers.

➡ Keep records of your D&B use. Make sure that all credit managers are notified when updates are received or if new services are available. Look for duplicate use of D&B services, such as using banks for credit reviews that are nothing more than D&B reports (you can often see these charges on your monthly account analyses).

CHAPTER 8

MANAGING
ACCOUNTS RECEIVABLE

The previous chapter described the process of initial credit granting. This chapter focuses on the next stage: the monitoring and control of accounts receivable (A.R.). These are the activities that companies undertake to maximize the value of existing consumer and corporate receivables, in addition to enhancing future revenues. As in the case of credit granting, the company faces the tradeoff between the costs (principally delinquency and bad debts) versus the less tractable benefits of enhancing customer relations. A related topic analyzed in this chapter is management of credit risk, describing the tools available for reducing or even eliminating risk in the A.R. portfolio.

The basic objectives of A.R. management include:

- **Managing delinquencies**: This objective relates to controlling accounts that delay payment beyond stated terms. One of the basic facts of A.R. management is that the more delinquent an account becomes, the more difficult it is to collect. The intent of this function is to manage accounts so that relatively few become delinquent and to identify those that will become problem accounts as early as possible. Naturally this is closely related to the second objective of controlling risk.

- **Managing credit risk**: The goal is to minimize the company's losses on accounts that will not be fully collected. Unlike the objectives of managing delinquencies, here the possibilities for continuing business relations with the delinquent company are relatively small. It is necessary to initiate appropriate actions on overdue accounts. Conversely, it is important to be able to efficiently change credit limits and other credit policy variables on accounts that are not overdue. For example, many companies annually review credit lines on all accounts, adjusting credit limits (upward or downward) based on purchase and payment behavior.

- **Forecasting objectives**: This has many aspects. The most important are estimating the cash flows from the A.R. portfolio and estimating bad debt losses.

This chapter is organized into the following sections:

- Measuring A.R. performance: This section describes the primary tools for evaluating the individual and aggregate performance of A.R.
- Managing credit risk: This section describes the mechanisms available to reduce or eliminate the risks of maintaining a receivables portfolio by using letters of credit and guarantees.
- Factoring and credit insurance: This section analyzes techniques that can totally or partially eliminate credit risk either through selling the receivable to a financial institution or purchasing insurance against severe delinquency.
- Collection policy: The final section analyzes the steps companies take to manage severely delinquent accounts.

MEASURING ACCOUNTS RECEIVABLE PERFORMANCE

This area of the credit function deals with the accounting and statistical measurements that try to evaluate A.R. performance. This monitoring should occur on an individual account basis and in the aggregate.

It is necessary to monitor individual accounts for compliance with payment standards in order to initiate appropriate actions when customers delay payment beyond agreed-upon terms. Also, even though a customer's observed payment behavior has not shifted, there may still be material changes in the customer's financial condition that affect its ability to make timely payments. An example of this would be when the seller is providing a raw material or leasing an asset essential to the customer's daily operations. The customer may be experiencing severe problems but will continue to pay this supplier on a timely basis for fear of losing all cash flow generation potential. Another example would be in retailing where the store is careful to pay its wholesalers while delaying payment to other credit grantors.

In many corporate and consumer credit settings, one of the key policy aspects is the determination of a customer's credit line. As was discussed in Chapter 7, an initial credit line is established when the customer first applies for credit. One of the key aspects of monitoring is then to use the customer's track record of purchases and payments, together with external information, to adjust this credit limit upward or downward. On the aggregate level, monitoring is important in setting overall policy guidelines with respect to risk and return and in forecasting cash flows and bad debt losses.

Monitoring on both the aggregate and the individual level is very commonly based on one of several approaches:

- Aging schedule
- Days sales outstanding (DSO)
- Receivables balance pattern
- Behavior scoring

Aging Schedule

In the **aging schedule** approach, accounts are categorized according to their payment status. A very common categorization would be into inactive, current, one-month overdue, two-months overdue, etc., although sometimes finer categorizations are used.

The aging schedule is a very important way to analyze account performance. It is a list of the amounts or percentages of outstanding accounts receivable in specified categories, frequently 30-day increments. One distinction that occurs in practice is between total and partial aging. In the latter, an account may be represented in more than one aging category. This can occur, for example, if the account has one invoice current and one that is two months overdue. With total balance aging, an account would be in one category only, typically based on the longest outstanding receivable. Its main use is to identify the aggregate quality of accounts receivable. This is important because the more overdue a receivable becomes, the more difficult it is to collect. The aging schedule can be a more informative breakdown than DSOs because it provides information on the distribution of accounts, not just a single average. However, the aging schedule suffers from the same potentially misleading signals as DSO when sales vary. As well, its interpretation is difficult if the data include sales made on differing credit terms. The following example provides an illustration of these properties.

A Sample Calculation

Assume the aging schedule shown in Figure 8-1 for a company that sells on net 30 terms. All figures are computed at the end of the month, and all receivables are written off when they reach 121 days overdue. These figures are generated

Figure 8-1
Sample Aging Schedule ($ millions)

| Month | Sales | Current | Overdue | | | | Write-offs* |
			1-30	*31-60*	*61-90*	*91-120*	
January	130	110	30	20	30	10	5
February	150	120	35	20	15	20	10
March	200	160	40	25	15	10	15
April	220	200	45	30	20	15	10
May	250	230	40	40	25	15	15

*Written-off receivables are included here since they will be used in subsequent calculations. They are not considered part of accounts receivable.

by categorizing each account receivable according to its status: current (meaning less than 30 days since the sale was made) or into its number of months overdue.

A more common way to express the aging schedule is in terms of the percentage of total receivables in each category. For example, to generate the figures for January, first compute the total A.R.:

$$200 (= 110 + 30 + 20 + 30 + 10)$$

and then divide the dollar amount in each of the aging categories by this figure. For this example only 55% (110/200) of the accounts are current; 15% are overdue less than one month; 10% are overdue between one and two months; 15% are overdue between two and three months and 5% are overdue more than three months. The percentage aging schedule is shown in Figure 8-2.

Overall these data tend to show a slightly improving aging schedule. The percentage of current accounts is rising from 55.0 to 65.7%. However, this interpretation may not be warranted; the fact that sales are increasing over this period tends to inflate the percentage of current versus accounts.

Days Sales Outstanding

Days sales outstanding measure the average turnover of A.R. One important implication of these types of categorization is that different sales and collection policies will apply to accounts in different categories. The simplest method of calculating DSOs is to divide accounts receivable outstanding at the end of a time

Figure 8-2
Aging Schedule (in percentages)

Month	Total A.R.	Current	Overdue 1-30	31-60	61-90	91-120
January	200	55.0%	15.0%	10.0%	15.0%	5.0%
February	210	57.1	6.7	9.5	7.1	9.5
March	250	64.0	12.0	8.0	10.0	6.0
April	310	64.5	14.5	9.7	6.5	4.8
May	350	65.7	11.4	11.4	7.1	4.3

period (month or quarter) by the average daily credit sales for the period. DSOs are easy to calculate and give a figure that can be compared to stated credit terms or to a historic average.

However, DSOs are very sensitive to the pattern of sales. For example, if sales are decreasing, DSOs will tend to fall even if there is no change in the payment behavior of the customers. This happens if the denominator (daily credit sales) does not completely adjust to the falling numerator. Thus changes in DSOs may be misleading if sales vary, such as with seasonal sales. Fortunately, several modifications of the basic calculation have been developed that mitigate this problem.

In the following example, we illustrate these characteristics and show three different methods of calculating DSO. The first is the simplest, but may lead to distortions if sales are not reasonably constant. The second, the LIFO approach, tries to adapt to changing sales. The third, the weighted average method, uses the most information. We use the A.R. and sales figures shown in Figures 8-1 and 8-2 for these calculations.

DSOs: Method 1
The first approach to computing DSOs merely uses some estimate of the day's sales relevant to the period for which DSOs are being determined. For example, to compute April's DSO, we could naively use the previous four months of sales to estimate what the average day of sales is:

$$\text{Day's sales} = \frac{130 + 150 + 200 + 220}{4 \times 30} = \frac{700}{120} = 5.83$$

Figure 8-3
Three DSO Calculations

	Method 1	LIFO Method	Weighted Average Method
March	46.9	40.0	36.0
April	53.1	43.5	36.8
May	55.3	43.6	36.9

Then, we calculate April's DSO:

$$\text{April DSO} = \frac{200 + 45 + 30 + 20 + 15}{5.83} = 53.2 \text{ days}$$

DSOs: The LIFO Approach

A second approach uses the LIFO (last in, first out) principle of allocating the receivables to the most recent month of sales. For April's DSO, we reduce the total amount of receivables, 310, by the most recent months of sales until the total is accounted for:

$$310 = 220 + 90 = \text{April's sales} + \frac{90}{200} \text{ of March's sales}$$

Thus

$$\text{April DSOs} = 30 \text{ days} + (.45 \text{ X } 30) \text{ days} = 43.5 \text{ days}$$

DSOs: The Weighted Average Approach

This method takes the aging fractions and multiplies each by the corresponding average age. In this example, if there is no monthly pattern in sales, the average current receivable would be 15 days old; the average 1-30 day overdue receivable would be 45 days old, etc. Thus, the April DSO is calculated as:

$$\text{DSOs} = (.645 \text{ x } 15) + (.145 \text{ x } 45) + (.097 \text{ x } 75) + (.065 \text{ x } 105) + (.048 \text{ x } 135)$$
$$= 36.8$$

Comparing the Three Methods

The table in Figure 8-3 shows the DSOs in March, April and May using the three methods. Note that the first method seems to indicate that payment behavior is

Figure 8-4
Receivables Balance Pattern

End-of-Month Receivables Balance (in $ millions)

	Sales	Jan.	Feb.	March	April	May	June
January	130	110	35	25	20	15	5
February	150		120	40	30	25	15
March	200			160	45	40	20
April	220				200	40	35
May	250					230	80

End-of-Month Receivables Balance (in percentages)

	Sales	Jan.	Feb.	March	April	May	June
January	130	84.6%	26.9%	19.2%	15.4%	11.5%	3.8%
February	150		80.0	26.7	20.0	16.7	10.0
March	200			80.0	22.5	20.0	10.0
April	220				90.0	18.2	15.9
May	250					92.0	32.0

---

worsening, but the other two methods, because of their ability to adjust to changes in sales, indicate a fairly stable pattern.

Receivables Balance Pattern

A method that has been suggested as an alternative to the aging schedule is the **receivables balance pattern**. It specifies the percentage of credit sales in a time period (usually a month) that remains outstanding at the end of each subsequent period. This set of figures is usually compared to a benchmark balance pattern, which is identified by examining a sample of the company's collection history. The company's collection experience at any point in time can then be compared to the normal payment experience.

The balance pattern gives a more complete distribution of the collection experience. Furthermore, it is not directly affected by variations in sales. Thus, it is not subject to misleading signals if sales have seasonality. The balance pattern can also be used to project accounts receivable levels and collections as a basis for preparing cash flow forecasts.

An Example of the Receivables Balance Pattern

Expanding upon the previous example presented, Figure 8-4 categorizes receivables (in both dollars and percentages) into the month in which they were created. These numbers can be determined from following the diagonals in the aging schedule. For example, for January, the aging schedule indicates that 110 of outstanding receivables are current; this becomes the 110 in row one of the table. The aging schedule indicates that 35 of February's receivables are 1-30 days overdue; these are sales that must have been made in January. This is then the second entry in row 1 of the exhibit. Similarly, the third entry, 25, is the aging schedule's March 31-60 day overdue amount.

In summary, the table shows that of January's sales of 130, 110 were still outstanding at the end of January; 35 were outstanding at the end of February; 25 were outstanding at the end of March; 20 remained uncollected at the end of April. Finally, 15 were still outstanding at the end of May. Conversely, one can take the amount by which the receivable balance has been reduced to determine the amount that has been collected in the given month. In this table, the numbers that could not be obtained because of the incomplete aging schedule are in italics.

It is often easier to interpret these patterns by rewriting the percentages in terms of months since sale. This is shown in Figure 8-5. Figures that cannot be ascertained are shown as N/A. The first column of percentages corresponds to the percentage of customers that are (reasonably enough) not paying before the due date. The second column of percentages represents customers that are between 1 and 30 days late in payment. The table shows that this averages 25.2%, but no trend is obvious. Similarly, 18.8% of sales are between 31-60 days past due, etc. Because these figures are expressed as percentages, they are not subject to the distortions inherent in either DSOs or the aging schedule.

Behavior Scoring

One of the areas that has grown very rapidly in recent years is the statistical management of existing credit accounts. The basic approach is to assign a score to each account being monitored on a periodic basis, such as a month or a quarter. This score could relate to the account's creditworthiness, or it could be a recommended credit line. While credit lines and active accounts are typically monitored on a periodic basis, the key difference here is that quantitative approaches are used to assign these scores.

Figure 8-5
End-of-Month Receivables Balance Pattern by Months Since Sale

	Sales	Current	1 Mo.	2 Mos.	3 Mos.	4 Mos.
January	130	84.6%	26.9%	19.2%	15.4%	11.5%
February	150	80.0	26.7	20.0	16.7	10.0
March	200	80.0	22.5	20.0	10.0	N/A
April	220	90.9	18.2	15.9	N/A	N/A
May	250	92.0	32.0			
Overall Average		85.5	25.2	18.8	14.0	10.8

As with credit scoring, the original users of behavior scoring were credit card issuers. They were interested in monitoring the behavior of existing credit card holders. Since then, its application has spread to the scoring of corporate accounts.

While the benefits of behavior scoring are quite diverse, two of the most important are:

- **Effectively controlling risk**: Users believe that statistical systems represent the most cost-effective approach to control risk for the large numbers of relatively small-dollar accounts they manage. In many respects, the benefits outlined in Chapter 7 for credit scoring apply equally well here, the key point being that it allows credit analysts to focus their attention on the most sensitive accounts, leaving the more routine decisions to the automated system.

- **Automating payment authorization**: In some cases the statistical systems were designed to automate the payment authorization process. For example, the system might monitor each credit purchase and evaluate the expected revenue impact of the transaction based on recent payment and purchase patterns. While the primary goal of the system is usually to optimize the expected revenues versus expected delinquencies and bad debts, some systems are more narrowly focused on fraud detection. These techniques essentially are looking for transactions that do not match the buyer's profile. For example, if it detected one cardholder purchasing five VCRs in one day, it would probably flag this as anomalous behavior.

Credit Alert Systems

While many business credit users of behavior scoring use statistical models to assign scores, many of the benefits can be realized with more simple systems that monitor external data bases for material changes, such as the presence of suits, liens, judgments, or a decline in credit rating.

For example, through Dun & Bradstreet, a user can designate a set of accounts to be periodically monitored for significant changes occurring in the D&B data base. This information can be transmitted on-line from D&B to the credit grantor using an electronic mailbox. For example, for all accounts with over $10,000 in credit extended, a company might have the business data provider check for material changes to the company's creditworthiness. In a simple system this might include checking if any suits, liens, or judgments have been filed against the company or if its D&B credit rating has declined.

This external information, combined with the credit grantor's own observations of the customer's payment and purchase activity, can provide very accurate and timely surveillance of important accounts.

MANAGING CREDIT RISK

One of the most important facets of managing credit is controlling the different components of risk. In most settings, the most important element is the risk of nonpayment. Other important aspects of risk include the risk of severe delinquency, and in international settings there is foreign exchange (FX) risk and country risk stemming from receiving payments in other than the domestic currency. Controlling FX and country risk is treated in Chapter 12. Delinquency risk is partially controlled by the initial credit granting decision, which manages the overall risk levels.

Many domestic and international settings involve selling to companies that fall short of the credit grantor's usual standards of credit quality or companies whose creditworthiness is very difficult to assess. Rather than turn down the proposed deal, there are a number of options the seller has to restructure the credit contract so that it can be mutually acceptable.

In this section we consider ways to manage credit risk through mechanisms that improve the creditworthiness of the buyer: guarantees and letters of credit. The next section considers methods that shift all or part of the risk onto a third party, such as a factor or credit insurer.

Guarantees and Letters of Credit

In many cases when the seller's credit quality is insufficient, it is possible to obtain a guarantee from a more creditworthy entity. In some cases this will be the company's parent or some type of government agency that has a stake in the buyer's success. Much more commonly the guarantee is through a bank. This can be via an actual **bank guarantee** of the debt or somewhat less directly through the bank's issuance of a **letter of credit (L/C)**. While in the U.S., banks are not permitted to explicitly guarantee another entity's debt, bank guarantees are quite common in Europe.

The role of letters of credit in international trade typically incorporates substitution of creditworthiness, but has many further aspects that can facilitate transactions, in particular, international transactions.

In general, an L/C represents the obligation of a bank to remit funds when clearly prespecified terms and conditions are met. This is known as the **Wichita Rationale** (see Dolan (1991)), stemming from a case in which the court ruled that the bank document, although called a letter of credit, was in fact not a letter of credit since its contingencies rested on performance, rather than on the presentation of documents. This generality has been tested in the courts in terms of how broad these terms and conditions can be. The argument gets into rather subtle areas of law, but the key aspect of any letter of credit transaction is that performance or nonperformance must be determinable through the presentation of documents. Furthermore, the courts have on occasion interpreted bank commitments as letters of credit even though neither the bank nor the lender has used such terminology. One such case, discussed in Dolan (1991), related to Toyota's use of **floor planning**, a form of inventory financing. The court ruled that the agreement between the floor planner and its customers' suppliers was indeed a letter of credit because the loan agreement required the bank to honor drafts drawn against invoices.

The flows involved in an international transaction (on L/C terms, net 180 days) are described in Box 8-1. A schematic representation is shown in Figure 8-6. Note that in this illustration the L/C bank is playing two important roles in guaranteeing of payment and in verifying that the transaction is as the buyer has specified.

Properties of Letters of Credit

While L/Cs are often assumed to be guarantees of payment, in reality, their structure is quite complex, often a blend between the credit substitution role and its function as an expediter of payment. A key distinction is between **standby**

Box 8-1
A Letter of Credit Transaction

Assume the L/C transaction is structured as follows: A foreign buyer wishes to purchase goods from a domestic seller. The seller (often called the **beneficiary)** and buyer have set the terms as net 180 days with payment through an L/C. Although the stages can be more complex and the timing may not be precisely as shown below, the following are the steps in a typical transaction.

1. The buyer places an order on net 180 L/C terms, payable in $US.

2. The buyer applies to its bank (called the **issuing** or **opening** bank) for a letter of credit to back the transaction. Often this transaction is facilitated if the buyer's bank is in the seller's country. While it is common to obtain an L/C to secure a single transaction, many companies actively doing international business will establish a line of credit facility much like a line of credit, and individual transactions will create (time or sight) drafts to draw down this line.

3. The buyer's bank, after establishing the creditworthiness of the buyer, determines the price it will charge the buyer for issuing the L/C. (In most cases this would already have been done.)

4. The buyer's bank issues the L/C and forwards the relevant information to the seller's bank (called the **advising** bank).

5. The seller's bank informs the seller of the L/C.

6. The seller ships the ordered goods.

7. The documentation required to transfer the goods (usually a bill of lading) and to fulfill other of the buyer's requirements (such as insurance and inspection certificates) are forwarded to the seller's bank.

8. The seller presents to its bank a draft drawn on the buyer's bank.

9. The seller's bank transfers these documents to the buyer's bank. The buyer's bank inspects the documents to confirm that the goods shipped are in satisfactory condition and are as specified in the buyer's order. At this point the buyer's bank **accepts** its obligation to honor the time draft, creating a bankers acceptance. This is the crucial stage in the process. There may be several iterations between the buyer's and the seller's banks until the buyer's bank is satisfied with the documentation. Also, although much of the work at this stage involves correcting spelling and other relatively minor fixes, if the buyer's bank has begun to be uneasy about the creditworthiness of the buyer, it can often be looking for any way out of its obligation.

10. Depending upon the agreement between the seller and its bank, at this stage the buyer either makes or promises to make payment to its bank.

11. When the buyer's bank is satisfied with the buyer's commitment to pay, it forwards the bill of lading and other documentation to the buyer, allowing it to take possession of the goods.

12. The buyer's bank then forwards the acceptance to the seller's bank.

13. The seller's bank forwards the acceptance to the buyer. At this point, the seller can hold the acceptance until its maturity date and receive the full face value of the draft, or it can discount the acceptance to receive immediate funds.

Figure 8-6
Steps in a Trade Letter of Credit Transaction

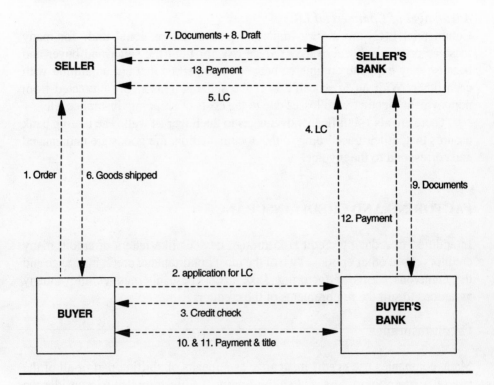

L/Cs and **commercial** (**trade** or **documentary**) L/Cs. According to Dolan (1991):

> *The merchants and bankers that use the credit distinguish those that serve the sale of commodities and those that guarantee the performance of an obligation, calling the former a commercial credit and the latter a standby credit.*

Standby L/Cs are primarily bank guarantees that come into play in the case of non-performance. They can be used to guarantee commercial paper and other securities. In these cases, the creditworthiness of the issue would ultimately depend on the credit quality of the guarantor (the bank) rather than the original issuer of the security.

Commercial L/Cs often combine these credit aspects with a broader role in facilitating trade. Unlike a standby L/C, which is issued with a relatively small probability of being used, a commercial L/C is issued with the expectation that the bank will have to honor its obligations. The key characteristics of a commercial L/C are shown in Box 8-2.

Advantages of Commercial L/Cs

Commercial L/Cs are a very important part of international trade for many reasons, primarily because they reduce risk for both the seller and buyer and because they expedite commerce between two parties that are unfamiliar with each other. With an irrevocable L/C, the seller is reasonably protected from nonpayment together with losses due to the costs of shipping, insurance, etc.

There are also significant advantages to the buyer as well. The issuing bank ensures that, at least according to the documentation, the goods are undamaged and correspond to the invoice.

FACTORING AND CREDIT INSURANCE

In addition to reducing credit risk through devices like letters of credit, many creditors chose other options. Two of the most important are credit insurance and the numerous forms of factoring. Like L/Cs, these alternatives allow many variations to suit the requirements of the creditor.

Credit Insurance

Many companies use **credit insurance** as a means of shifting part or all of the risk of "extraordinary losses" to a third party. To illustrate its use, consider the following simple example.

Birney Inc. is a manufacturer of chairs. Its 1991 profits were $400,000 on annual sales are just over $10 million. It sells 40% of its output to 90 relatively small, regional furniture stores. The remainder is sold on credit terms of net 90 days to five major nationwide retailers. Two of these retailers have recently experienced considerable financial distress and Birney is concerned about collecting on these receivables.

One possibility is to contract with a credit insurance company. There are three significant major credit insurance companies in the U.S. The largest, American Credit Indemnity, is a subsidiary of Dun & Bradstreet and has approximately 75% of the market. The other two companies are Fidelity and Continental. The three companies offer comparable services. In this case, Birney would submit a list of the buyers and typical outstanding amounts to the credit insurer, which would then reply with a maximum insurable amount for each buyer (and a price for the policy). A number of details of the agreement, such as a deductible amount,

Box 8-2
Characteristics of a Commercial Letter of Credit

Revocability: One of the most significant attributes of an L/C is whether or not the L/C issuing bank is committed to honoring drafts drawn on the L/C. A **revocable L/C**, which is much less common than an **irrevocable L/C**, provides no guarantee of payment. The main purpose of a revocable L/C is to facilitate international payments, often between subsidiaries or when there are controls on the flows of a given currency.

Confirmation: The seller's bank often **confirms** the issuing bank's L/C. This is done for a variety of reasons, the most important being the seller's wish to reduce its risk by having a bank of its choosing also guarantee payment. This has been the case, for example, with an American seller dealing with a buyer using an L/C issued by a bank in the Philippines. Because of the country and bank risk, the seller may request its American advising bank to confirm payment.

Documentation: As noted earlier, one of the key aspects of any commercial L/C is the set of documents that determine performance or non-performance. In international trade, these documents typically include:

- Invoices: These are necessary in order that the issuing bank can verify that the goods are as specified by the buyer.

- Drafts: These must be drawn on the correct beneficiary and must correspond to any limits defined in the L/C.

- Bill of lading: This document verifies receipt of goods by the shipper and permits the holder to take possession.

- Insurance and inspection certificates: Typically the buyer requires that the shipment be insured and often stipulates that there must be an inspection certificate to warrant the quality of the shipped goods.

Transferability: A transferable L/C permits the initial beneficiary to transfer the credit to other parties. This is typically used when the original beneficiary is acting as a middleman.

Revolving: Many L/Cs have a revolving feature to facilitate repeated purchases. In this case the L/C specifies a maximum amount of credit availability.

coinsurance of credit losses above a predetermined amount, etc. would be negotiated in this agreement. With this type of policy in place, Birney would refer any receivable (from these covered buyers) to the credit insurer once it had reached 60 days past due. The credit insurer would remit to Birney the face value of the receivable within a few days. The responsibility of collecting the receivable would reside with the credit insurer.

This illustration points out a few key characteristics of credit insurance:

- It is generally used by medium-sized and smaller companies that are uncomfortable with their credit exposure to a number of (usually large) buyers. In most cases, the company seeking insurance is not large enough to perform a detailed credit analysis of its customers. Most users of credit insurance have sales under $50 million.

- Since the credit insurer needs to make a profit on its coverage, for the insurance to be economically rational, either the credit insurance company must be superior in evaluating the creditworthiness of buyers or must have some diversification or economies of scale advantage.

While credit insurance is still a relatively small market in the U.S., it is much more important abroad, especially in Europe. One industry source estimates that in Europe more than 50 percent of all companies carry some credit insurance. In the U.S., the corresponding figure is under 5 percent. One of the key reasons for this is the comparative lack of credit information available in countries like France, Austria, and Germany, which rely heavily on credit insurance. In these countries, the major credit insurers have very extensive data bases of corporations. In fact, the government often relies on the credit insurer to provide information about corporations. This is in contrast to the U.S. and Canada, where the business credit information companies maintain extensive data base on almost all significant companies, making it cost-effective for companies to do their own credit analysis.

While there is a fair amount of flexibility in contract structure, the basic contract with a credit grantor specifies a list of approved buyers, each with a pre-specified credit limit. For example, American Credit Indemnity (ACI) will often base its coverage on the D&B rating. It may also have a contractual deductible amount and a 10 to 20% coinsurance (sharing of the loss by the seller) of any loss above this deductible amount.

Naturally enough, credit insurers must be skillful in estimating creditworthiness. As such, they are active users of commercial credit data. For example, ACI actively uses on-line updating of business credit data from Dun & Bradstreet on accounts it is insuring.

Credit insurance has recently experienced significant growth. One reason is the 1986 change in tax laws, which phased out the deductibility of bad debt reserves.

Factoring

Another important risk shifting option is **factoring**, the sale or transfer of title of accounts receivable to a factoring company. Factoring is highly industry specific. The major users are in manufacturing, particularly finished apparel and textiles. It is also prevalent in wholesale, especially sporting goods, toys, and furniture.

The factor, usually a subsidiary of a financial services company or bank, performs the credit and collection function and provides a number of options to the selling company. The key ones include:

- **With or without recourse**: With recourse means the seller is liable if the factor cannot collect on an account. Most factoring is without recourse.
- **With or without notification**: With notification means that the buyer knows that its account has been factored and is required to remit directly to the factor. Most factoring is on a notification basis.
- **Maturity or discount factoring**: With maturity factoring funds are available to the seller on the average collection date. With discount factoring, funds are remitted to the seller sooner than the average collection date. The majority of users desire the speeding of cash flow and opt for discount factoring.

Pricing
Factoring is generally considered an expensive financing option. Most of its users fit the profile and have a motivation similar to that outlined earlier for buyers of credit insurance. One exception is that factoring may have positive impact on cash flow.

Pricing usually features a fixed percentage (about 1%) of the invoice as a commission. When using discount factoring, the interest rate is frequently prime plus two or three percent. In addition, there is typically a reserve of about 3 to 5% for returns, disputes, etc. Recently a number of factors have also required users to share bad debt losses on certain larger receivables.

Advantages and Disadvantages
According to a recent survey of factors (Farragher (1986)), the main reasons for using a factor are (in decreasing order of importance):

- Credit analysis and collection: Having the factor perform the credit and collection function is very useful for companies without expertise in this area.

- Bad-debt loss exposure: Relatively small companies are often undiversified in terms of their buyers, having a large percentage of receivables from one of two companies. Factoring (or credit insurance) can mitigate this exposure.
- Cash advance: Many companies using factors have highly seasonal sales; the ability to accelerate cash flows can be very beneficial.
- Accounting: It is important for some companies to have the factor perform the basic accounting function.

There are some aspects that partially offset these advantages:

- Cost: As noted earlier, especially for non-recourse factoring, this can be significantly more expensive than bank borrowing or credit insurance.
- Control: Since the factor controls the credit and collection function, the seller may lose the ability to enhance revenues through adopting more lenient credit and collection procedures.
- Dual systems: Since the factor will not accept all credits, or may place a limit on its exposure to a certain buyer (such as a large retailer), the seller is still stuck with performing the credit and collection function on some of its customers.

COLLECTIONS POLICY

This section addresses the problems inherent in collecting funds from "substandard" accounts. The key points are:

- **Promptness**: As the previous section has shown, delinquent accounts tend to perform much worse if not attended to properly.
- **Cost/benefit analysis**: Certain accounts may not respond to a particular form of collection procedure. It is important to understand which procedures make economic sense at a given stage in the collection process. If it can be established that the goods were received as ordered, at this stage the credit manager should not be as interested in preserving customer relations as with attempting to recover as much of the invoiced value as possible.

In this area there are a variety of approaches available to speed the collection of delinquent accounts. There are both **internal procedures** — the credit department's strategy toward collection — and **external** — for example, selling the receivable to a collection agency. These are discussed below.

Internal Strategies

Different credit grantors pursue very diverse approaches to the collection of delinquent accounts. Their rationales should be consistent with the cost/benefit analysis performed for the initial credit granting decision. That is, there should be a determination of the tradeoff between the sales impact versus the cost impact of collection policies. However, as the age of the delinquent account becomes greater, the potential benefits begin to diminish.

It is important at an early stage to distinguish those accounts that are actually delinquent from those delays that are caused by some dispute over the merchandise being invoiced. It is prudent for the credit grantor to confirm in writing that the goods as ordered were received.

Most companies begin with relatively mild reminders so as not to agitate customers that are, in the longer-term, profitable. As the delinquency increases, the long-term revenue potential of the customer diminishes.

External Strategies

There are relatively few external strategies available once a debt has become severely delinquent. The only major third-party channels are collection agencies, which are often part of a more complete receivables management offering, and adjustment bureaus.

Collection Agencies

Collection agencies are frequently used for the collection of severely delinquent consumer or business accounts. Their activities are restricted by the Fair Debt Collection Practices Act. On the business credit side, the creditor typically sells the collection agency the receivable once the company has exhausted its usual collection weapons. While the company may turn a receivable over relatively infrequently, many companies routinely assign delinquent accounts.

While methods of reimbursement vary significantly, usually the agency charges 30-50% of the collected amount as its fee. For companies that have an ongoing relationship with a collection agency, the charges are based upon some historical recovery rate.

Adjustment Bureaus

Another possible third-party method of collecting delinquent accounts is an adjustment bureau. The first bureaus have been in existence for over 100 years. They are typically organized by a given industry group for the benefit of their members. The National Association of Credit Management (NACM) has been important in their development.

MANAGEMENT REVIEW ITEMS

➡ Conduct annual credit reviews, maintaining a record of customer credit limits (possibly on a computer spreadsheet).

➡ Be sure to check whether receivables are aged partially or totally. Investigate all partial past dues as though they were 100% past due.

➡ Check your sales volumes before when computing A.R. performance measures. If sales are increasing, measures like the aging schedule will be inflated and must be taken into account when comparing with past performance.

➡ Check with the Credit Research Foundation or NACM for standard DSOs for your company's business lines, being sure to check how the ratios are calculated.

➡ If sales decrease, DSOs may decrease even if there is no change in customer payment practice. This is because the numerator and denominator of the DSO calculation are changing but not in proportional amounts.

➡ Set up a spreadsheet model to calculate DSOs several ways monthly. Compare similar methods with each other and with other methods over time to look for trends and problems. Investigate any major swings (e.g., plus or minus 10%).

➡ To check L/C costs, shop around among your major banks or with major foreign banks from the countries where you may be doing business. Look for pricing differentials between commercial and standby L/Cs because some banks may be trying to sell one form more than the other.

➡ Even if U.S. operations are not interested in credit insurance, investigate it for foreign subsidiaries.

➡ Look for special cases (e.g., highly seasonal sales) where factoring may be available (or may be a regular industry practice) to diversify sources of short-term funds.

CHAPTER 9

SHORT-TERM BORROWING VEHICLES

One of the most critical tasks in corporate treasury is the management of short-term borrowing. It is the most important source of liquidity for many companies, and for almost all companies it is an essential element of debt policy. In managing corporate liquidity, companies need to be aware of the diverse and rapidly evolving sources of short-term credit and the explicit and implicit costs of these credit sources. Perhaps most important, corporations need to recognize how these credit mechanisms interact with company characteristics in formulating, implementing and monitoring a company's overall debt management and capital structure.

This chapter begins the analysis of how liquidity is managed through short-term debt and investment. It focuses on the vehicles used for corporate short-term borrowing. The next two chapters describe investment vehicles and how borrowing and investing tools are managed within the company's overall liquidity policies.

Short-term borrowing instruments can be broken down into three categories:

- **Bank sources**: These are the major means by which banks can supply short-term credit to corporations.

- **Money market sources**: These funds are obtained by bypassing the banking system and accessing the financial markets directly.

- **Other sources**: In addition to these two sources, there is an assortment of other possibilities for raising short-term capital. These arise from trade credit and various methods of asset-based financing. The latter include pledging or selling current assets for financing. While these often involve either banks or capital markets, they are analyzed separately in this chapter.

This chapter and the next two — describing short-term investing vehicles and borrowing and investing strategy — are closely linked.

AN OVERVIEW OF SHORT-TERM BORROWING

One of the most hotly debated issues in corporate finance is the effect of the overleveraging of the 1980's. Corporate indebtedness from 1950 to 1983 hovered around 130% of GNP, but it reached 186% in 1990. The peak was 225%, reached in the depths of the 1930's depression. While various authors hailed this greatly increased leverage as imposing necessary discipline on corporate management, others expressed grave fears of the effects that these greatly increased debt levels would have in any economic downturn.

While junk bonds provided an outlet for the credit requirements of some larger companies, this window greatly narrowed in 1990 with the collapse of Drexel, Burnham Lambert and junk guru Michael Milken. As the 1980's closed, commercial banks increasingly found themselves unable or unwilling to fulfill their traditional credit demands. Also at this time, the financial markets seemed responsive to new issues of longer-term financing. Figure 9-1 shows the supply of new long-term debt, equity (through initial public offerings), and hybrids. Hybrids here are preferred stock and convertible bonds and preferred. Three important trends are present:

- A greater reliance on financial markets for long-term financing: While bank loans to corporations have decreased significantly over this period, as the graph shows all three major sectors of corporate funding grew from 1989 to 1991.
- A general trend to greater equity financing: While this graph only shows initial public offerings, a more general pattern has been to reduce the high levels of leverage many companies took on during the 80's.
- A continuing *flight to quality*: Banks and money markets are continuing to supply credit to good risks while reducing their exposure to weaker credits.

These trends are important in understanding the current environment for debt management, which places a high priority on the ability to access financial markets, often through the application of diverse techniques of internal and external credit enhancement (to raise the credit quality of a given security). These concepts are introduced in this chapter and are developed further in the next two chapters.

Figure 9-1
Supply in U.S. Debt and Equity Markets

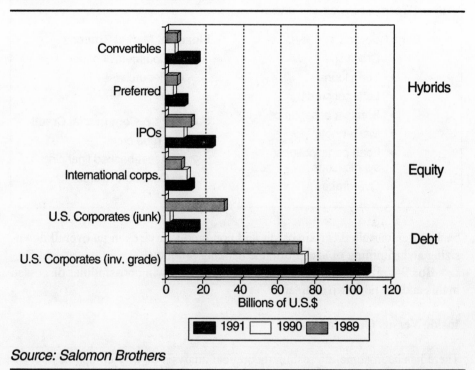

Source: Salomon Brothers

Although it is not a wholly satisfactory definition, short-term sources of funds are interpreted as "loans" that have a maturity of one year or less. These are funds typically used to finance inventory, receivables, or other working capital needs. In addition, they play a very valuable role in providing a reserve of borrowing capacity to be drawn down because of unanticipated demands.

The major source of financing for all but the largest, most creditworthy companies remains commercial banks. Although their traditional dominance has been eroded by the expansion of commercial paper, foreign sources, and securitization, banks remain a vital supplier of capital.

Much of the blame for the recession of 1990–1992 has been blamed on the *credit crunch*. According to Federal Reserve figures, from the beginning of 1990 to mid-1991, bank lending to business fell by 6.2% to $480.6 billion, which is still a substantial figure. The well publicized problems that many banks were experiencing (primarily with real estate and low-grade debt) led to expanded regulatory scrutiny including a tightening of capital adequacy guidelines. In turn,

---

Box 9-1
Short-Term Sources of Funds

Bank Sources
- Credit line
- Term loan
- Letter of credit
- Bankers acceptance
- Master note
- Loan participations/ syndications
- Overdrafts

Financial Market Sources
- Commercial paper
- Repurchase agreements

Suppliers & Commercial Credit
- Trade credit
- Asset-backed financing
- Commercial credit

---

banks often curtailed certain credit and non-credit services in an overall downsizing and trimming of less profitable banking products.

Box 9-1 presents an overview of the chief borrowing possibilities discussed in this and the next two chapters.

Inside Versus Outside Debt

There has been some interesting theoretical analysis of why companies opt for bank versus money market debt. It is useful to distinguish between **inside** and **outside** debt. The former refers to loans where the lender (typically a bank) has access to non-public information; the latter refers to traded debt (e.g., bonds and commercial paper) where lenders base their lending decision on publicly available information. In general, smaller companies depend more on inside debt than larger companies.

There are certain advantages to a borrower to use inside debt:

- **Less information asymmetry**: Inside debtholders should have better information about the borrower's prospects. This reduced uncertainty should reduce the borrower's costs.
- **Reduced flotation costs**: Since flotation costs are (on a percentage basis) much higher for smaller public issues, inside debt should reduce this cost component. In addition, the costs of registering a public issue with the SEC are eliminated.

- **Improved monitoring**: Banks should be in a better position to monitor the borrower's prospects and to structure the debt contract to provide better protection from material adverse changes.
- **Confidentiality**: In many cases it is in the company's best interest to maintain confidentiality about its future plans.

Empirical research into market reactions to financing announcements has found two-day abnormal returns to announcements of public straight debt, private placements and bank loans. Market reaction to straight debt is insignificant. Reaction to private placements is significantly *negative*, while reaction to announcements of bank loan agreements is significantly *positive*. The analysis suggests that the market associates some value with bank lending arrangements.

BANK SOURCES

This section analyzes the major forms of bank credit. The most important short-term borrowing vehicles are bank revolving credit lines, which are essentially short-term (usually annual) agreements between a corporation and a bank, permitting the borrowing company to draw down funds at its option up to a specified maximum. This type of borrowing is similar in many respects to bank term loans, although the latter are usually longer term, used for a more specific purpose (such as financing a long-term asset), and typically involve a fixed amortization.

This section also introduces one of the most important types of credit enhancement, the letter of credit. While its role in financing trade is discussed in other chapters, here the emphasis is on its role as a kind of bank credit guarantee. Closely related to this form of bank borrowing is the bankers acceptance, which started with companies having substantial international trade. Finally, two borrowing vehicles, master notes and loan syndications, provide good examples of an emerging trend in large corporate borrowing. Both are designed to minimize the involvement (read expense) of third parties, such as investment banks, by bringing the investing and borrowing companies into closer contact. Because this requires the investor to make the credit assessment, these two types of borrowing are restricted to relatively large, creditworthy corporations.

Bank Credit Lines

All lines can be considered as **revolving credit lines** in that they are usually offered on a continuing (or "revolving") basis. There are several types of

---

Box 9-2
Types of Credit Lines

   Uncommitted line (guidance line)

   Committed line

   Commercial paper backup line

   Revolving credit agreement

---

short-term bank credit lines (see Box 9-2), differing primarily by the degree of commitment the bank makes to the company.

Uncommitted or **guidance** lines are offered by banks to companies without any expected compensation and can, accordingly, be withdrawn at any time, even without notification. Foreign exchange (FX) lines and daylight overdraft lines, which banks establish for their customers, are examples of uncommitted lines. A company may not even know how big such lines are unless, of course, it exceeds the limit.

A **committed line** is probably what most treasury managers think of as a "regular" line of credit. This type of line is one of the most significant short-term sources of funds for companies of all sizes. A committed credit line is an agreement between the company and its bank (or a syndicate of banks if the credit is large enough) with a fixed maturity, specifying that the bank will provide funds at the borrower's option, up to a specified maximum amount. These credit lines are typically used to meet short-term seasonal needs, to provide a liquid reserve (a buffer for uncertain cash flows), and to provide temporary (bridge) financing before longer-term debt agreements are put into place.

Companies, especially larger ones that usually can obtain top short-term debt ratings, do not depend on their banks as a short-term source of funds; they are active borrowers in the commercial paper market. However, in order to borrow successfully, they are required to back up their issued commercial paper with bank lines of credit, which can be used to replace commercial paper that cannot be rolled over (i.e., resold at maturity). **Commercial paper backup lines** provide the necessary "insurance" commercial paper issuers need. For all practical purposes, these lines look just like regular lines, but they are "tagged" to the company's commercial paper issuance, and their amounts and bank providers are reported regularly to the public rating agencies. Some of the very large direct issuers of commercial paper, such as the large finance companies, only maintain backup lines for a fraction of their total outstanding commercial paper.

Box 9-3
Key Credit Line Terms

Purpose	Maximum borrowing levels
Maturity	Loan covenants
Commitment	Events of default
Clean-up period	Reporting requirements
Collateral and security interests	

Many companies are not satisfied with "simple" committed lines of credit and negotiate **revolving credit agreements** (**revolvers**), which are legal contracts between a company and a bank or group of banks to provide credit lines to the company. These agreements also usually have a **term loan** option, which the company can use to pay back short-term borrowings over a longer period of time. Most companies negotiate the terms of the revolver with their lead bank (or agent bank). The company may choose to specify the banks to be included in the revolver (if it is a multi-bank agreement) as well as the amounts for each bank. The rates, commitment fees, and other items are usually agreed upon by the agent bank on behalf of all banks. Some companies do not want to control the revolvers to this extent and rely on the agent bank to find appropriate participants in the credit. Others have chosen to negotiate with each bank independently. In these cases, the agent bank functions primarily to finalize legal details and to administer borrowing levels once the revolver is in place.

Characteristics of Credit Lines
The key terms of credit line agreements are shown in Box 9-3. These terms may not apply to any one type of credit, but in cases of most committed forms of credit, most of the items will be applicable.

Most credit lines have a stated purpose, although it is often vague, such as "financing current assets." In many cases, the loan agreement contains restrictions on what the funds can be used for. Credit lines and related agreements are usually renewed annually, although revolvers are normally arranged for more than one year. Borrowing against the line is ordinarily in the form of notes drawn for varying maturities. Repayment is most often at the option of the borrower. This flexibility in the timing of drawdowns and repayment is a very valuable aspect of this financing source.

Committed credit lines usually define the conditions, called **material adverse change conditions**, under which the bank can refuse to honor its obligation to supply funds. Committed lines require compensation, often in the form of compensating balances or a **commitment fee**, usually based on the total amount of the commitment and on the bank's assessment of the company's creditworthiness. The fees can range from 20 basis points or less for low risks to well over 100 basis points for riskier credits. Commitment fees are usually only charged for the *unused* amount of the credit line, but this often has to be negotiated between the company and the lending banks. In certain cases, banks have waived this fee if the line is "sufficiently utilized." There is often a 30- or 60-day period during which the borrower must have reduced the amount outstanding on the line. This **clean-up period** offers some protection to the bank in ensuring that the loan is not really being used as a long-term source of funding. This provision is often waived for large customers.

Most large lines allow the lender to secure its interests by pledging assets of the company and/or its principals. These are usually current assets secured through UCC (Uniform Commercial Code) filings.

The maximum amount of borrowing is normally fixed in advance. In other cases, it is based on the amount of collateral the borrower has pledged. For example, it may be the sum of 75% of the value of receivables pledged and 50% of the value of inventory pledged. In these cases, the company is required to supply the lender with appropriate documentation on the pledged assets.

Collateralization is one form of lender protection; **loan covenants** are another. Loan covenants for credit lines are similar to covenants in a bond indenture. They often stipulate minimal levels of financial performance, such as maintenance of certain liquidity and profitability ratios. They may also restrict sale of assets, liquidation of assets, payment of dividends, and capital expenditures. As in the case of collateralization, they are often waived for larger companies.

Events of default specify the conditions under which the borrower will be considered to be in default of the agreement. They can include **cross-default** clauses that are triggered if the borrower defaults on other debt or if the borrower files or is forced into bankruptcy. False reporting of financial condition is also typically considered an event of default.

The **reporting requirements** for credit lines usually involve sending periodic financial statements to the lenders. For example, banks may require quarterly updates of the company's condition and audited annual financial statements. If collateral is specified in the agreement, the bank will probably require adequate reporting of its condition.

Box 9-4
Basic Components to Credit Line Pricing

Interest rate

Commitment fee

Compensating balances

Closing fees

Pricing Structure

The pricing of credit lines is usually the result of significant negotiation between the borrower and the bank. The borrower is interested in achieving the required funds at the lowest cost and with the fewest constraints on its operations. Similarly, the bank usually looks at the overall profitability of a given customer and its preferences for fees versus balances and other considerations. The four basic components to credit line pricing are shown in Box 9-4.

Interest rates are typically variable. The usual basis for computation is the lead bank's prime rate, although certain money market rates, such as a fractional percent over **LIBOR** (London Interbank Offered Rate), are also common.

Banks charge for providing a credit commitment, typically a fee, expressed as a percentage of the total commitment or the unused amount of the line. Banks may also charge a penalty if a minimum average amount of borrowing is not maintained. Some banks have also charged an additional commitment fee, sometimes called a **facility fee**, set as a percentage of the overall credit facility. Large, creditworthy companies are usually able to negotiate favorable terms that eliminate or minimize both facility and commitment fees. Alternatively or in conjunction with commitment fees, some companies pay for the credit line commitment through compensating balances, usually specified as a percentage of the average unused portion of the commitment. It is most often computed as a monthly average of available funds. It has become less commonly applied to larger credits. There can also be **closing fees**, which are one-time charges incurred at the signing of the loan agreement, comparable to mortgage closing fees. In addition, it has become more common for the bank to request a significant application fee (as much as $50,000).

An Illustration

An example may help clarify how some companies use committed credit lines. One noted treasurer of a major company gave a speech where he described his company's borrowing strategy. He observed that in the previous year his com-

Figure 9-2
Credit Line Pricing

	Revolving Credits	Regular Lines*
Interest Rate Basis		
Prime rate	68%	58%
LIBOR	26	20
Money market rate	18	35
Fixed rate	5	3
Other rate	9	5
Commitment Fee		
On unused portion	80%	55%
On total amount	20	45
Compensating Balances		
Not required on usage	72%	71%
Not required on total line	69	67
Size of Commitment Fee		
25-50 basis points (bp)	70%	70%
50-75 bp	22	23
75-100 bp	6	5
more than 100 bp	2	2

*Regular lines are less formal agreements than revolvers.

Source: *Journal of Cash Management* (1990)

pany had committed lines of credit for $50 million with a syndicate of ten banks. For this commitment, it paid 50 basis points on the total amount committed. He then chortled that he did not use any of these lines (and then waited for applause).

There are clearly two ways to view this situation. The first is to recognize that the treasurer spent one-quarter of a million dollars for nothing. (.005 X $50 million.) But probably a better way to think about it is as insurance: Committed credit lines give a company a safety net in case cash flows are not as good as anticipated. In this case, the company did well and did not need to draw on these funds. However, if the primary purpose of a line is this type of insurance, it may make sense to try to negotiate a lower commitment fee and a higher interest rate.

Pricing Surveys

Figure 9-2 summarizes some results from a recent survey of bank loan pricing. It shows that current agreements tend not to include compensating balance requirements and that the prime rate remains a key ingredient in loan pricing. Some percentages add up to more than 100% due to multiple answers.

Grid Notes

When a company uses its bank credit lines, it usually signs a note with the bank or banks for the amount of the loan. If the company plans to use its credit facilities regularly (e.g., daily), it can arrange to use a **grid note**, instead of signing many individual notes. The grid note is signed at the beginning of the credit facility,and all borrowings and repayments are recorded by the bank on the note.

Term Loans

While these are not primarily thought of as a short-term source of funds, they play an important part in the overall borrowing strategy of a company. Term loans and lines of credit can be interchangeable; often, a line of credit is converted into a term loan. A term loan is generally for a fixed amount, usually related to a specific project, such as the construction of a new manufacturing facility. The credit agreement is typically of longer maturity than a bank credit line and usually designates a fixed amortization schedule. Funds are typically disbursed on a fixed schedule, rather than at the borrower's option.

The pricing structure on term loans is generally simpler than with credit lines. The interest is often either fixed or based on the prime rate. Compensating balances are seldom imposed. Reporting requirements may be more onerous, and the bank usually spends more effort in obtaining a proper security interest on fixed and/or current assets.

Letter of Credit

This is a bank undertaking to make payment at a future date, if certain well defined contingencies are met. The structure is often very similar to a line of credit or it can be linked to a specific transaction. The letter of credit (L/C) is very common in international transactions, but also plays a significant role in domestic financing, particularly where the seller is concerned about the creditworthiness of the buyer and the amount of the transaction is large. This type of letter of credit is called a **trade** or **commercial letter of credit**. This chapter focuses on the standby letter of credit. A letter of credit is generally unsecured, but it may be secured by the assets involved if it is for a specific trade transaction.

Standby Letter of Credit

In addition to using commercial L/Cs to facilitate trade, the **standby letter of credit** is very important in borrowing and investment. With this type of L/C, the bank is offering its guarantee of payment in case the company covered by the L/C does not perform the given task. For example, in commercial paper transactions, as will be clarified below, an issuer may obtain an irrevocable, standby L/C to back its commercial paper. In this case, the bank is liable for repayment of principal if the company defaults on the issue.

A percentage of the amount of the maximum credit extended is usually charged as a commitment fee, to be paid whether the letter of credit is drawn on or not. Unlike the case of the trade L/C, with standby L/Cs, it is expected that it drawn on only under adverse conditions and not in the normal course of business.

Bankers Acceptances

Bankers acceptances (BAs) are another form of short-term borrowing provided by banks, originally to finance cross-border trade transactions (although they can also be issued for domestic trade). They are really a combination bank-money market instrument. BAs are issued at a discount in the form of negotiable time drafts, with maturities ranging from 90 up to 270 days, the limit for short-term securities. The major steps in issuing a BA are shown in Box 9-5. Bankers acceptances have unusually low credit risk because the bank has guaranteed payment even if the issuer is unable to pay.

Master Note

A master note is an agreement, usually between a large, creditworthy borrower and a bank's trust or pension unit, whereby the bank agrees to supply funds over a one to five year period. The key feature is that the investing bank can vary the amount invested on a daily basis usually within preset limits. For example, the master note may be written with a five-year maturity specifying that the minimum amount invested is $50 million and the maximum invested is $100 million. On a given day, based on its current levels of liquid funds, the lender decides how much it will lend to the borrower.

The interest rate is often set as a small premium (e.g., 10 basis points) over the borrower's commercial paper rate. The investor thus gains by obtaining a rate

---

Box 9-5
Major Steps in Issuing a Bankers Acceptance

The issuer (e.g., an importing company) asks its bank to provide a letter of credit to it for goods it is purchasing.

The issuer's bank (the issuing bank) approves the customer's credit and issues a letter of credit to the supplying company. This shows the bank's guarantee of payment, thus improving the creditworthiness of the issuer.

The supplier can draw a time draft against the issuing bank and take this to its bank to receive payment (at a discount).

The supplier's bank presents the time draft to the issuing bank for payment. Assuming that all documentation is in order, the issuing bank *accepts* the draft and pays the supplier's bank. In this process, the bankers acceptance is created.

The holder of the BA can sell it to investors, who may hold it until maturity or offer it for resale in the money markets.

At maturity, the issuer has to pay the full amount of the acceptance to the issuing bank.

---

that is significantly higher than the overnight rate, while retaining most of the flexibility of overnight investing. The borrower gains by having one more source of short-term funds. The borrower also gains because there is almost no difference between the investor's yield and the borrower's all-in cost.

Most borrowers that use master notes minimize the effect of the individual daily fluctuations in borrowing levels on a given master note by having a relatively large number outstanding.

Loan Participations

The loan syndication process is a traditional part of the bank lending process. A bank takes a loan, and, rather than retain all of it as a bank asset, it finds other banks willing to buy (a portion of) the loan. This device enables a bank to make loans that would otherwise exceed its legal lending limit. It also permits a bank to increase the diversification of its loan portfolio.

Loan participations are similar to loan syndications, but the participating entities generally have much less involvement in the origination or structuring of the credit. While the entities purchasing the loan pieces are usually other banks,

---

Box 9-6
Loan Participation Procedures

Before noon (EST) the company calls its banks for a quote on borrowing rates for the maturities it is interested in.

With this information (together with current CP rates) the company decides on maturities and amounts.

It calls the syndicating bank to place a particular transaction.

The bank wires the funds into the company's account.

The bank then looks for investors willing to purchase some or all of the note.

---

a market for short-term participations has evolved where corporations are the investors. Since their beginnings in 1985, they have grown to a viable alternative to commercial paper for many A-2/P-2 rated issuers. Their purpose and pricing are very similar to commercial paper, and the market mechanism is similar to a direct placement.

After the corporation has created an arrangement with one or more banks, the borrowing process is as shown in Box 9-6. The bank does not assume any credit risk. It is merely acting as a broker to place the note with potential investors, earning a spread between the borrowing cost and the yield paid to investors. The bank's risk lies in the possibility of not finding buyers for all of the debt and having to hold it. The investors typically have approved lists of borrowers whose notes they will purchase.

Overdrafts

Overdraft borrowing is very common outside the U.S. Essentially it is structured like an informal credit line. The bank merely establishes a cost for allowing the company's available balance to fall below zero. This is a very convenient way of borrowing, although it can be more expensive than more structured ways of borrowing. It is almost a necessity in some countries because of the difficulty in managing bank balances.

A version of overdraft borrowing does exist in the U.S. via what are usually called working capital accounts. These accounts are generally marketed to medium-sized corporations that lack the expertise or time to carefully manage the account. With the working capital account, the company is given a credit for available balances above a certain minimum and charged interest for any overdrafts up to a predetermined maximum. Many banks have developed a multi-faceted credit service that they offer to smaller, mid-sized companies. This service offers the company an investment sweep service for excess balances or an automatic overdraft line of credit to cover deficit balances, combined with a controlled disbursing account.

Other Bank Sources

Because of the continuing difficulties banks are having, some have come up with creative ways to create funding for their corporate clients. For instance, on June 11, 1991, Citicorp announced that it would begin a new financing program that would allow corporate customers to borrow up to $1 billion. Under this arrangement, corporate customers with strong credit ratings are referred to Premium Funding Inc. (PFI), owned by Citicorp and Merrill Lynch. Corporations will obtain short-term loans from PFI, which, in turn will fund the loans by issuing its own commercial paper (CP). Citibank will also provide a backup line of credit for 20% of the total CP issued. Companies are expected to pay about 25–75 basis points above the CP yield. This structure allows Citicorp to make very low-profit loans to high-quality customers without tying up scarce bank capital.

Debtor-in-Possession Financing

Filing for bankruptcy can be viewed as a liquidity strategy, albeit a desperate one. Because of the structure of bankruptcy law, it often makes much more sense for banks to lend to corporations after they have filed for bankruptcy rather than before. This usually takes the form of **debtor-in-possession** (DIP) financing.

A typical example is the toy retailer, Child World Inc., which filed for bankruptcy on May 7, 1992. Saddled with cash flow problems because of the lingering recession in the Northeast, it was forced into bankruptcy after bankers withdrew the company's $100 million credit line. Child World then renegotiated a $50 million DIP line, to allow it to operate in Chapter 11. In a further concession, the banks agreed to subordinate their secured debt so that suppliers could be paid.

MONEY MARKET SOURCES

Increasingly, large corporations are turning to money markets rather than banks to provide short-term credit. While accessing these markets is relatively easy for large, creditworthy companies, there also are a number of devices, such as credit enhancement and securitization, that allow other companies to enter the money markets more easily.

Commercial Paper

The most important source of short-term borrowing for large U.S. companies is commercial paper. Commercial paper (CP) is a promissory note issued for a specific amount (usually in $1 million denominations) with a specific maturity (usually between one to 90 days). It allows the borrower to bypass traditional bank borrowing channels and raise funds more directly from the investor.

This is a very large, rapidly evolving and steadily expanding market both in the U.S. and abroad. The key characteristics of a CP issue are shown in Box 9-7.

Like the majority of money market instruments, most CP is sold on a discount basis. The issuer promises to pay the face value of the security on the maturity date. On the date of sale, the issuer receives less than the face value - the difference representing the implicit interest rate. The discounted proceeds are calculated by multiplying the face value of the issue by the quoted interest rate and the annualized maturity (using a 360-day year) and subtracting this answer from the face value. For example, if a 30-day, 100 million, CP issue is quoted at a price of 5%, the discount is .416 million (100 X .05 X 30/360). Ignoring any selling costs, the issuer receives $99.584 million (100 - .416).

The effective borrowing cost can be expressed as a (bond equivalent) yield by considering the interest and the amount generated and annualizing.

$$\text{yield} = \frac{d}{F-d} \times \frac{365}{m}$$

For this example,

$$\text{yield} = \frac{.416}{100 - .416} \times \frac{365}{30}$$

$$= .00418 \times 12.7$$

$$= 5.09\%$$

These calculations need to be modified slightly for interest-bearing CP, which represents about 2% of the total amount issued.

While most CP is restricted to a maximum maturity of 270 days, most investors prefer shorter maturities. Overnight paper is common, and most maturities do not exceed 30 days.

The key aspect of commercial paper is that it is structured to avoid the necessity of SEC registration. There are three ways that this exemption is invoked:

- Section 3(a)(3) exemption: This section exempts "Any note, draft, bill of exchange, or bankers acceptance that arises out of a current transaction or the proceeds of which have been or are to be used for

---

Box 9-7
Key Characteristics of a CP Issue

Yield	Rating
Maturity	Selling approach
Structure	Credit enhancement
Credit backing	

---

current transactions, and for which has a maturity at the time of issuance of not exceeding nine months ... "

- Section 3(a)(2) exemption: This exempts securities issued by or guaranteed by a bank. This exemption is not granted to bank holding companies or to issues of a foreign bank through its home office. An insurance surety bond cannot create this exemption.
- Section 4(2) exemption: This exemption is typically used for repeated direct placements with a group of "accredited investors." In this case, the maturities can exceed 270 days.

Most CP is structured under the 3(a)(3) exemption.

Credit Backing

Since most commercial paper is "rolled over" (reissued) at maturity, backup credit is required in case the next issue of paper cannot be sold. The backup credit is usually a bank line of credit (often uncommitted). The amount of these lines, which usually exceeds the outstanding commercial paper borrowing, must be reported to the rating agencies quarterly.

For most corporations using a commercial paper dealer, there must be 100% backup; that is, outstanding commercial paper must never exceed the total lines of credit. For direct issuers and some of the most creditworthy corporations, only a percentage (e.g., 60%) of the outstandings are covered.

Commercial Paper Ratings

Default rates on many money market instruments can be somewhat deceiving. In the domestic CP market there have been very few defaults of significant size. The first major default was Penn Central Transportation Company in 1970, which defaulted with $82 million in outstanding CP. This led to the formation of CP rating agencies.

Figure 9-3
S&P's Commercial Paper Rating Definitions

A	Issues with the greatest capacity for timely payment
A-1	Overwhelming (A-1+) or very strong safety (A -1)
A-2	Strong capacity for timely payment; not as strong as A-1
A-3	Satisfactory capacity for timely payment; more vulnerable to adverse changes in circumstances than higher-rated issues
B	Issues with an adequate capacity for timely repayment; such capacity can be damaged by changing conditions or short-term adversities
C	Short-term debt obligations with a doubtful capacity for repayment
D	The issue is either in default or is expected to be in default upon maturity

In general, the following relationships hold:

Bond Rating	*Probable CP Rating*
AAA, AA+, AA, AA-	A-1+
A+, A	A-1
A, BBB+	A-2
BBB, BBB	A-3
Less than BBB	B or C

Source: Standard and Poor's Corporation

Like ratings for bonds and other long-term securities, CP issues have a letter rating from at least one credit rating agency. Figure 9-3 offers a brief description of S&P's CP ratings. There are several rating services that assign ratings to corporations issuing commercial paper. These include:

- Moody's (using a scale P-1, P-2, down to P-3)
- Standard & Poor's (using a scale A down to D)
- Fitch (using a scale F-1 down to F-4)
- Duff & Phelps (Duff 1 to Duff 3)

Ratings from at least two agencies are usually required. The higher the rating, naturally, the lower will be the borrowing rate. Annual yield spreads A2/P2 over A1/P1 (over the past 15 years) have ranged from 19 to 134 basis points with an average of 51 basis points.

A commercial paper rating is an estimate of the probability of repayment of short-term debt. The analytical approach is fundamentally the same as for long-term issues. The primary difference is the priority placed on liquidity and financial flexibility.

Sales Approach

Most issuers use one or more CP dealers who act as principals, buying the issuer's paper and reselling to investors. The spread between bid and ask is typically a "dime," or 10 basis points. Currently there are about 2,000 issuers working through dealers. The direct segment of the market is comprised of about 125 issuers, typically very high quality financial companies, such as General Motors Acceptance Corporation (GMAC) and General Electric Credit Corporation. For example, GMAC represents almost 10% of the total volume of CP.

Another consequence of the Penn Central CP default was a legal clarification of what CP really was. Further, it placed some burden of *due diligence* on the CP dealer. A third important consequence was the emergence of unused bank credit lines to back the CP; these lines were assumed to play the role of an alternative source of liquidity in place to pay off maturing paper, rather than the usual policy of re-issuing. Currently, the majority of CP is issued in **bearer form**. The procedures for the physical handling of a this type of "paper" CP transaction are outlined in Box 9-8.

One of the recent innovations has been the development of book-entry procedures, paced by heavy direct CP issuers. These allow for electronic settlement of transactions, which can greatly reduce the possibility of **fails**, which are caused by the failure to execute each of the steps in Box 9-8 in a timely fashion. In addition, issuance costs are reduced.

Credit Enhancement

Corporations sometimes use a letter of credit instead of a line of credit to support their commercial paper (or other) borrowing. They pay the bank(s) providing the letter of credit as discussed above. The credit rating of the bank is now looked at as supporting the borrowing, rather than the corporation.

Entities that could not access the commercial paper market for reasons of creditworthiness or size use this alternative because, even including the bank's charge for the letter of credit, commercial paper is a less expensive form of short-term credit. Indemnity bonds issued from mono-line insurance companies serve the same purpose.

Box 9-8
How a Commercial Paper Transaction Works

The issuer sells the CP note to an investor for an agreed-upon rate, principal and maturity date.

The issuer contracts with its issuing bank to prepare the note and to deliver it to the investor's custodial bank.

The investor instructs its bank to wire funds to the issuer upon delivery and verification of the CP note.

Upon presentation of the note the funds are transferred to the issuer's bank (this date is known as the **settlement date**). The note is held at the custodial bank until the maturity date.

On the maturity date the note is returned to the issuer's paying agent (which could be different from the issuing bank) and funds (typically the face value of the note) are transferred to the investor. The note is marked *Paid* and returned to the issuer.

Source: Rapin and Martino (1987)

Borrowing Costs

The effective interest rate (assuming there is no form of credit enhancement) is a function of:

- The issuer's size
- The issue's maturity
- The prevailing level of rates
- The creditworthiness of the borrower
- The nature of the backup credit

The cost of a backup credit agreement, with payment in the form of compensating balances or commitment fees, adds to the cost of the commercial paper. There are also rating, printing, and issuance fees.

The basic formula is as usual:

$$Effective\ annual\ rate\ = \frac{Total\ Annual\ Costs}{Usable\ Loan\ (Annualized)}$$

Note that it is often the case that the money market convention of using 360 days rather than 365 is adopted in this formula. In this case, then

$$Usable\ Loan\ =\ Face\ Value\ \times\ [\ 1 - Rate \times \frac{maturity}{360}\ ]$$

For example, assume the following structure for a CP issue:

- Face value is $10 million.
- Discount price is 6%.
- Issue has a 30 day maturity.
- The CP dealer charges 1/8% of face value (per annum).
- The backup line of credit costs 1/4% (per annum) on the $10 million.

$$Usable\ Amount\ =\ \$10\ million \times [\ 1 - .06 \times \frac{30}{360}\ ]\ =\ \$9.95\ million$$

In this case, since the backup credit and dealer costs are already given in yield terms, it is easier to compute the effective annual rate by noting it is the sum of the investor's yield and these two charges. The effective annual rate is:

$$Effective\ Annual\ Rate\ =\ yield + dealer\ percentage + backup\ cost\ percentage$$

$$=\ \frac{.05 \times 365}{9.95 \times 30} + .00125 + .0025$$

$$=\ .0611 + .00125 + .0025\ =\ .06485$$

Note that in this example, there is a gap of 37.5 basis points between the investor's yield (6.11%) and the borrower's all-in cost (6.485%). This gap is due to the cost of credit support and the dealer's fee. It averages about 47 basis points.

OTHER BORROWING SOURCES

This chapter has outlined the key bank and money market sources of short-term funds. Others can be important, especially for companies that are not large enough or lack the creditworthiness to have easy access to short-term borrowing.

Trade Credit

As discussed earlier, the ability to defer payment of goods and services received is a huge part of corporate short-term debt. To a large extent it is spontaneous, arising out of the normal course of business, but there are some opportunities to use trade credit as a source of borrowing. The most obvious is when the company is offered credit terms that include a discount. For example, the credit terms, *1/10 net 30,* mean that the buyer can defer payment 20 days if it chooses not to take the 1% discount the seller is offering. In most cases, this is an expensive source of borrowing.

Accounts Receivable Financing

Another effective source of short-term funds is through pledging or sale of accounts receivable. For the former, banks offer credit agreements called **asset-based revolvers,** where the bank establishes a collateral value for the receivables, such as 75% of face value. The borrower's credit then is limited by the amount of collateral pledged. In the second case, receivables can be sold to a factor in a wide variety of ways. While there are many reasons for using a factor, if the factor pays for the receivable before its expected maturity date, it effectively provides the selling company with another borrowing source. Another possibility involves using the company's accounts receivable to establish a separate entity that issues securities with these assets as collateral. This is an option for companies with large amounts of receivables.

Another variety is to finance foreign receivables internally. To do this large multinational corporations use off-shore holding companies with low tax or tax-free funds to purchase receivables form other foreign subsidiaries,similar to a bank asset-backed revolver. The foreign subsidiaries may be able to use this as a relatively cheap source of funds. There may be tax implications involved in such transactions, and these need to be clarified before initiating any such transactions.

Non-Bank Sources of Borrowing

A group with increasing importance in short-term borrowing are non-bank financial institutions, such as the credit corporations and finance companies. In the credit crunch of the early 1990's, they were able to provide credit to many companies that could not get adequate bank financing. They were also able to outbid banks in some cases for larger credits. Finance companies have made significant inroads into what has been the commercial banks' market, especially with mid-sized and smaller companies. Much of the lending is tied to product lines (e.g., automobiles, electronics, appliances).

One interesting example of the latter is the January 1991 deal between Federated Department Stores (at the time still under bankruptcy protection) and General Electric Capital Corporation. In this case, GECC's $1 billion loan had terms that were superior to the existing Citicorp line. In turn, GECC would fund the loan by creating a funding corporation that would issue CP backed by the collateral of Federated consumer receivables and a letter of credit. This deal was based on a similar transaction done earlier for Allied Stores.

MANAGEMENT REVIEW ITEMS

➡ Establish a list of short-term borrowing options (e.g., adapt Box 9-1), and use it as a checklist periodically to spark new ideas or investigations.

➡ Group short-term lines of credit by type: committed, uncommitted, revolvers, backup, and other. Then use this to match your borrowing needs as indicated by your medium-term cash forecast.

➡ Develop a *term sheet* for a revolver or for standard conditions you'd like in committed lines of credit, and keep it current even if you are not considering negotiating a new agreement or credit line at present. Modify it based on discussions with your credit line banks over time. Then, when you are ready to negotiate, you'll be prepared.

➡ Keep a master list of loan covenants, updating it each time a new agreement is completed. Also, use it to target those covenants you wish to get rid of in future agreements.

➡ Track average compensation for your credit lines (e.g, using a computer spreadsheet model), converting to a common denominator (balances or fee equivalents) if necessary.

➡ Ask your agent or lead bank for an estimate of closing fees or a cap on them before agreeing to loan terms.

➡ Discuss loan participations with your revolver banks. They may be amenable to setting up a loan participation arrangement.

CHAPTER 10

SHORT-TERM INVESTMENT VEHICLES

This chapter focuses on the key properties of the short-term (money market) instruments that are the most important to corporations with short-term funds to invest. Because of the great diversity in terms of risk, return, and taxability, it is important for the corporate investor to have a good understanding of the alternatives that are available. The next chapter describes how these instruments are integrated into corporate liquidity strategies.

The money market is the diverse marketplace where large quantities of the short-term debt obligations of governments, financial institutions, and corporations are traded. While its major hubs are New York, London, and Tokyo, buyers, sellers, dealers, and brokers are widely dispersed yet able to function effectively because of efficient telecommunications networks. The market works extremely efficiently in matching buyers and sellers of billions of dollars of diverse financial assets each day. The key reason that borrowers that are large enough try to issue in this market is *liquidity* — the depth of the money market allows participants to trade large amounts of securities quickly with relatively little price impact. There are enough players and ways of making securities homogeneous, such as rating agencies, so that one entity's trades do not overly influence market prices.

To understand how the money markets affect short-term corporate investments, it is necessary to consider the following key areas:

- Money market overview: volume, price relationships, and other common characteristics of this market
- Risk and return factors: the properties and fundamental theories of fixed-income investment
- Primary money market securities: key instruments issued by governments, banks, and corporations (from the corporate investor's viewpoint)

Figure 10-1
Make-up of the Money Market

Security	Percentage
Governments	41.3%
Tax exempts	17.0
Commercial paper	11.1
Time deps./certs. of deposits	8.7
Repos	9.5
Federal agencies	8.1
Money funds	2.2
Bankers acceptances (BAs)	1.4
Money market preferreds	0.4
Dividend captures/other	0.3
Total	100.0%

- Tax-advantaged securities: the varieties of government debt and preferred stock that are important in corporate investing

MARKET OVERVIEW

Money markets are different from capital markets largely by the former's focus on debt instruments that mature in one year or less. Money market instruments generally have a high degree of safety and liquidity, allowing investors to sell assets before their stated maturity. The money markets are also characterized by a high degree of innovation and variety. Such techniques as credit enhancement and securitization continue to evolve and change the access to and characteristics of the market. Regulatory and tax changes also cause significant changes in the money markets.

Market Statistics

Figure 10-1 shows the relative outstanding amounts of the key instruments (on average). The main market instruments are highly liquid, safe, government securities, such as U.S. Treasury bills (T-bills). The volumes for many instruments (such as repurchase agreements) can only be roughly estimated. Because

Figure 10-2
Money Market Rates

Security	10/10/90	6/10/92
Bank prime	10.0	6.5
Fed funds	7.9	3.5
Discount rate	7.0	3.6
T-bills (26 weeks)	7.21	2.9
T-bills (13 weeks)	7.19	2.89
Agencies (1-10 year index)	8.59	5.52
CDs (180 days)	7.80	2.78
CDs (90 days)	7.72	2.73
CDs (30 days)	7.65	2.68
CP (90 days)	8.00	3.0
CP (60 days)	8.05	3.05
CP (30 days)	8.13	3.08
BAs (180 days)	7.79	3.04
BAs (90 days)	7.90	3.02
BAs (30 days)	7.79	3.04

these instruments are relatively interchangeable for investment purposes, the volumes can fluctuate dramatically.

Figure 10-2 shows the market yields as of October 10, 1990 and June 10, 1992. Note the remarkable decline in rates over this relatively short period. The two rates administered by the Federal Reserve, the discount rate and the Fed funds rate, were less than half of their values only 20 months prior. These rates are important benchmark rates because they are signals of the Federal Reserve's actions to control the money supply.

Market Participants

The major players in the money market include borrowers, investors, banks, dealers, brokers, regulators, and rating agencies. Each is described in the following sections.

Because of the money market's efficiency and depth, it is a very attractive place to raise funds in large amounts. Thus, almost every borrower that can access

---

Box 10-1
Major Types of Borrowers

Governments: The most important issuing entity is the federal government, although foreign, state, and local governments also issue short-term obligations.

Banks: Domestic and foreign-owned banks (or bank holding companies) issue certificates of deposit, commercial paper, and bankers acceptances.

Corporations: Domestic and foreign-owned corporations issue commercial paper and tax-advantaged investments, primarily preferred stock. Corporate borrowers in this market are generally either well-known, creditworthy entities whose risk is easily assessed by investors or lesser known credits that have used some form of credit enhancement to improve the instrument's creditworthiness.

Dealers: These are the market makers for money market (and many other) securities. They borrow actively to finance their positions. They frequently use repurchase agreements to finance their positions in government securities.

---

the money market directly (that is, without resorting to credit enhancement) would consider it its cheapest source of capital. It is useful to categorize the major borrowers into four categories (see Box 10-1).

The same entities that borrow in the money market also use it for investment. For example, banks, corporations, and dealers actively participate in both sides of the market. In addition, money market funds are major purchasers of these securities, in turn, making them available to corporations and consumers on a retail basis.

In addition to playing a role on both the borrowing and investing side of money markets, banks can also serve as dealers and brokers. One of the results of the continuing deregulation of commercial banking is the eroding of the traditional barriers between commercial and investment banking.

Dealers provide liquidity by **market making**: being available to buy and sell large amounts of securities at relatively small transaction costs. Dealers earn a spread between the buying and selling price. This spread is a measure of the liquidity of the particular instrument. Dealers also act as **agents**. For example, in commercial paper, the dealer acts on behalf of the issuer finding buyers for the paper and assisting in pricing and other issuing decisions. Dealers also profit (at least sometimes) in managing their own position in securities. Their role in arbitraging away temporary price anomalies is important in ensuring the efficiency of the market.

The main function of a **broker** is bringing together buyers and sellers of a particular security. Unlike the dealer, the broker does not take a position in the securities; it earns a commission on the trade. This commission is often very small. For example, a Fed funds broker may make as little as $1 per million dollars brokered.

The major **regulators** of the money market are the Securities and Exchanges Commission (SEC) and the Federal Reserve (the Fed). The role of the SEC is to ensure that public markets operate in a equitable and open manner.

Formed about the same time as the SEC, the Federal Reserve is charged with regulating banks, controlling the payments systems, and managing the money supply. Thus, it plays a complex role in the money market. One of the most important is in its administration of two key money market rates: the discount rate and the Fed funds rate.

The **discount rate** is the rate that the Fed charges to member banks for short-term borrowing. Collateral is generally pledged by the borrower. While the number of banks using this source at any one time is very small, it is regarded as an important indicator of Fed policy. Since 1980, it has had long periods of stability interspersed with periods where the Fed is actively intervening to stimulate the economy. For example, in 1991 and 1992 the Fed vigorously reduced the discount rate in a (somewhat futile) attempt to move the economy out of the recession.

Fed funds are interbank borrowing, typically on an overnight basis. The main purpose of the market is to transfer bank reserves from banks with excess supply to banks that need additional reserve balances. The Fed encouraged the development of this market in the 1930's by not subjecting Fed funds to reserve requirements, considering them borrowing rather than deposits. Fed funds borrowing is typically unsecured.

Rating Agencies

An influential component of financial markets is the role played by the **rating agencies**. The two major ones are Standard and Poor's Corporation (a subsidiary of McGraw-Hill) and Moody's (a division of the Dun & Bradstreet Corporation). They assign a letter/number grade to a particular instrument from a given issuer. For example, with commercial paper almost all issues are rated by two rating agencies. The existence of a rating on an instrument allows the investor to gauge its default probability.

There remains some debate about the actual value of ratings. A number of articles have shown that stock prices anticipate bond-rating changes. While the rating agencies have responded to this criticism by developing more contemporary notices of falling credit quality, the major value to the borrower of having a rated issue seems to be the increased liquidity (due to more potential buyers of the debt). This is because investment guidelines are often formulated in terms of debt ratings.

Risk and Return Factors

The most fundamental properties of all investments typically used for short-term investing are the relatively short maturities and safety of the securities. Almost all of the instruments have a maturity of less than one year, although others (preferred stock) have longer (or no) maturities but have been adapted for short-term corporate investment.

Because of the generally conservative nature of short-term investment activity, most of the investment vehicles commonly purchased are relatively free of **default risk**. Due to their relatively short maturities, they are also relatively free of **interest rate risk** (i.e., their prices are not as prone to being affected by interest changes as are longer-term and lower-coupon debt obligations).

Even within the relatively narrow spectrum of issuers represented in the money market, wide variations in before- and after-tax yields still persist. Four factors explain the major differences in yields among potential investments:

- The yield curve
- Default risk
- Liquidity
- Taxes

The relationship between market yields and maturity is captured in the yield curve. Generally, longer maturities promise higher returns. Securities other than those issued with the complete backing of the U.S. government are subject to some degree of default risk. Rating agencies play an important role in assessing this threat. For example, because bankers acceptances have never defaulted, they are not rated, while commercial paper, even though defaults are very rare, is rated. Investment guidelines for short-term investment often use credit ratings to align investment decisions with the corporation's risk/return objectives.

Just as in the case of default risk, government securities provide the highest standard of liquidity. Securities that are traded in small amounts or are lesser known can create liquidity problems. One example is commercial paper. While

Figure 10-3
Selected Treasury Yields

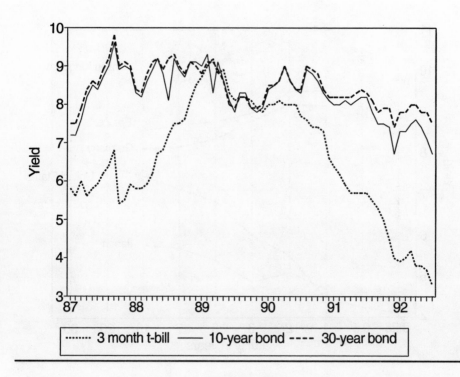

there is some liquidity in the short-term issues of the largest issuers, most commercial paper is difficult to liquidate before maturity. A better example is auction-rate preferred stock, which essentially trades only every 49 days. An important aspect of the money market's liquidity is the manner in which many of these securities are held. Most government securities and some other securities (e.g., some commercial paper) can be or must be held in electronic form, rather than paper certificates. This makes transactions very simple compared to physical delivery.

The tax treatment of certain government securities can significantly influence actual yields. For example, income from U.S. Treasury obligations is exempt from state income taxes. The income from obligations of state and local governments is exempt from federal income taxes. In addition, the preferential tax treatment of dividends received by a corporation can lead to investment opportunities in high dividend paying stocks, like many of the variants of preferred stock.

Figure 10-4
Yield Curves in Different Countries

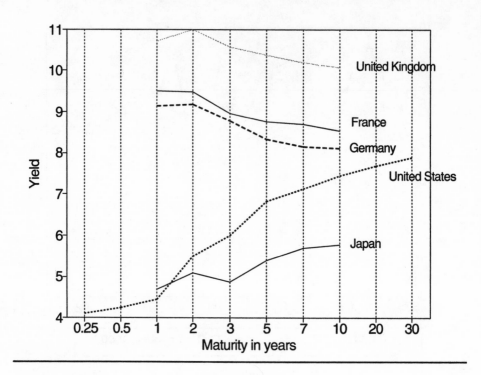

The Yield Curve

The widest **yield spreads** (differences between yields, usually measured against government securities) most often occur because of different maturities. This makes the maturity decision the most crucial investment decision. This conclusion is not generally true for longer-term investment, which gets equally involved with quality spreads. Figure 10-3 shows the yields for 3-month, 10- and 30-year treasuries from 1987 to 1992. This graph shows how unstable this relationship is. At the beginning of 1992, the spread is quite large for a period of low interest rates; the spread was close to zero at the beginning of 1989.

Treasuries are the usual basis for yield curve calculations because they retain their liquidity through a wide variety of maturities. Figure 10-4 offers an example of the U.S. treasury yield curve and the corresponding yield curve for four other countries. In this case, the yield curves for the United States and Japan are upward sloping: a **normal yield curve**. The yield curve for the European countries are downward sloping: an **inverted yield curve**. These differences reflect the different market forces and expectations in each of these countries.

Term Structure Theory

There are several theories that try to explain why the yield curve has a particular shape. Understanding these hypotheses can help the investor make rational decisions on the maturity of investments and on the future form of the yield curve. The basic theories are:

- **Market segmentation**: This theory suggests that certain investors have a preference for a particular maturity. For example, insurance companies may wish to match their long-lived liabilities by purchasing long-term bonds.

- **Pure expectations**: This theory asserts that risk aversion should not be built into the pricing of debt. Risk-neutral market participants will arbitrage away any differences in expected yields across different maturities. This theory suggests that when the economy is active, short-term rates are relatively high but are expected to fall. Conversely, in a recession, short-term rates are relatively low and the yield curve is normal. This phenomenon is clearly illustrated in Figure 10-3. In 1989 the short-term rates were high, and the yield curve was flat. After the recession began, short-term rates dropped quickly, but long-term rates fell much less, turning a flat yield curve into a relatively steeply sloped normal yield curve.

- **Liquidity preference**: This theory essentially assumes that the longer the maturity of a given asset, the riskier it is. This does not necessarily imply that the yield curve will slope upward. It merely suggests that the risk premium on debt will increase as its maturity increases. This risk premium is only one factor. Other important influences are market expectations and the market supply/demand relationship.

- **Preferred habitat**: This theory assumes that investors have a preferred maturity and need to be compensated by higher yields for shorter or longer maturities.

Empirical analysis seems to indicate that none of these theories in isolation provides a particularly good representation of actual yield curves. For example, it has been shown that the pure expectations theory does not provide an adequate explanation of actual yield curves.

PRIMARY MONEY MARKET SECURITIES

Figure 10-5 gives a broad overview of the money market instruments to be discussed in this and the following chapter.

Issues of the Federal Government and its Agencies

Financing the enormous federal deficit has led to a flood of government debt of all maturities. From 1975 to 1990, aggregate public debt of the U.S. grew from slightly more than $500 billion to more than $3 trillion. If this trend continues, the assumption that government debt is default free could be in jeopardy.

The federal government issues debt instruments in all the maturity ranges, ranging from treasury bills at maturities under a year to treasury notes and bonds for longer maturities.

Treasury securities are *full faith and credit* obligations of the U.S. Government, sold via regular auctions. This means that they are virtually free of default risk. A very active secondary market consisting of dealers, banks, and other financial institutions make Treasury securities the most liquid investment vehicles. Treasury securities are delivered and cleared electronically.

Treasury bills are issued at a discount with maturities of 13, 26, and 52 weeks. The investor's return comes from the fact that the security is sold at a discount from its par value and accrues to par value on the maturity date. The secondary market for T-bills is very active.

Treasury notes and **bonds** are coupon securities with interest paid semi-annually. Notes have maturities from 2 to 10 years; bonds have longer maturities.

Federal agency securities (agencies) are discount and coupon obligations of the federal agencies established by Congress to provide credit to specific sectors of the economy. Agency securities can also have very short to long maturities. Agencies are considered to be default-free even though only a few (long-term) securities are *explicitly* backed by the U.S. Government. Agencies usually have a slightly higher yield than Treasury securities of the same maturity because agencies are somewhat less liquid. Important examples of agencies include:

- Farm Credit Bank: issues notes and bonds whose interest income is generally exempt from state and local income taxes. The proceeds are used for agricultural loans.
- Federal Home Loan Bank: issues notes and bonds to fund loans to savings and loan associations.

Figure 10-5
Basic Characteristics of Money Market Instruments

Instrument	Maturity Range	Discount or Interest Bearing	Notes
T-bills	13, 26, 52 weeks	Discount	Obligations of the U.S. Treasury Active secondary market Highest safety
Agencies	5 days–20 years	Mostly interest bearing	Considered default free Slightly less liquid than T-bills
Domestic CDs	1 day ++	Interest bearing	Minimum investment usually $100,000 Yield depends on creditworthiness of issuer Can be fixed or variable rate
Eurodollar deposits	1 day–6 months	Interest bearing	Can be either time deposits or CDs Active secondary market
Bankers acceptances	30–270 days	Discount	Corporate time deposits "accepted" by banks Active secondary market
Commercial paper	1–270 days	Discount typically	Unsecured promissory note Structured to avoid SEC registration Typically rated Back-up source of liquidity required
Repurchase agreements	1 day ++	Discount	Sale of securities with an agreement to repurchase Typically collateralized by government securities Creditworthiness of seller a key issue Usually over-collateralized
Sweep arrangements	1 day	Interest bearing	Excess balances "swept" into predesignated security (e.g., bank CD or money market fund) Minimum amount required Rate reset daily

- Federal Home Loan Mortgage Corporation: issues guaranteed mortgage certificates to purchase mortgages from banks.
- Federal National Mortgage Association (FNMA or Fannie Mae): is actually a stockholder-owned corporation; it issues notes and bonds and uses the proceeds to purchase mortgages.

The last two agency securities are examples of **asset-backed securities**. In these cases, the security is backed by a pool of mortgages.

Government Securities

While the bulk of the public debt market is issued by the federal government, other government agencies issue short-term securities of significance to corporate investors. In particular, the tax status of these instruments makes them enticing to corporations with a high marginal tax rate.

Municipal securities (munis) interest-bearing notes and bonds issued by state and local governments and their agencies. The yield on a particular municipal security depends on the creditworthiness of the issuer. It is normally lower than the yield on T-bills because the interest income from munis is exempt from Federal income taxes. Most munis are also exempt from state and local taxes in the state of issue. There are two main categories of municipal securities:

- **General obligation** instruments are backed by the full faith and credit of the issuer and usually obtain higher credit ratings than other munis. Original maturities range from several months to one year.
- **Revenue obligations** are backed only by the revenues of a specific project. Often a guarantee is purchased by the issuer from a bank (a letter of credit) or from an insurance company (an indemnity bond) to improve the issuer's credit rating.

Municipalities also issue tax-exempt securities with floating rates and put options. These instruments include a variety of **variable rate demand obligations (VRDOs)**, which combine the benefits of short- and long-term securities. While their nominal maturity may be as much as thirty years, their interest rates are linked to money market rates, such as T-bill rates. These rates may float on a daily, weekly, or other basis. At each interest rate reset date, the investor has the opportunity to *put* the security back to the issuer, thereby receiving the principal.

Box 10-2
Key Characteristics of CDs:

Interest rate: **Fixed-rate CDs** can have an interest rate established at the time of issue. **Variable-rate CDs** have interest adjusted periodically to reflect prevailing market interest rates. The floating rate is usually adjusted every 30 or 90 days usually based on the **London Interbank Offered Rate** (LIBOR), which is a good proxy for an international bank's cost of funds. For example, a 6-month CD might offer interest 20 basis points above LIBOR. Each month, the interest due would be paid, and the next month's interest would be updated to the current LIBOR rate. Interest is typically computed on a 360-day year basis.

Issuing bank: **Yankee CDs** are U.S. dollar-denominated CDs issued by foreign banks through their branches in the U.S. market. **Eurodollar CDs** are U.S. dollar-denominated CDs issued by foreign banks abroad. Original maturities vary from 14 days to several years, but most have maturities not exceeding 6 months.

Secondary market: The jumbo CDs of major banks have an active secondary market. Credit rating agencies offer risk evaluations of these instruments, which make them more marketable.

Bank Securities

The most important securities issued by banks are:

- Certificates of deposit (CDs)
- Bankers acceptances
- Time deposits
- Commercial paper

Here the focus is on the first three vehicles. (Commercial paper was discussed in Chapter 9.)

Certificates of Deposit

Certificates of deposit (see Box 10-2) are instruments issued by banks certifying that a certain amount of money has been placed on deposit for a fixed time period. "Jumbo" CDs are usually issued in denominations of $1 million and more. These CDs are typically negotiable and trade in an active secondary market. **Domestic certificates of deposit (CDs)** are coupon instruments with original maturities of at least 14 days, issued by U.S. banks. They are usually traded in round lots of $1,000,000. The yield on CDs exceeds the yield on Treasury securities of the same maturity because CDs are not as liquid, and there is some default risk. A number of rating agencies rate the major issuers of CDs.

Bankers Acceptances

Bankers acceptances are short-term negotiable securities typically arising from international trade transactions. To illustrate, suppose an importer uses a letter of credit to finance a purchase of $5 million on net 90 terms. If the shipped goods meet with the bank's approval, the bank "accepts" the time draft, which specifies that it will honor the draft for $5 million in 90 days. The holder of this acceptance can choose to retain it until its maturity date, or it can sell it prior to maturity for a discount plus a commission (usually near 1%) from its face value. This discount is similar to the interest paid on bank CDs. Like CDs, there is an active secondary market for the large bank issuers of acceptances.

Time Deposits

Time deposits are often referred to as corporate "savings accounts" because they are similar to retail savings accounts. They offer fixed rates for fixed periods of time, and, accordingly, are less liquid than CDs or many other securities. Time deposits offer slightly higher rates than CDs. Just like CDs, there are Eurodollar time deposits as well as domestic (U.S.) time deposits.

Sweep Accounts

Sweep accounts are an effective tool in treasury management. There are two types of sweep accounts. One is called a **next-day account**; in this case, the bank determines the amount of funds remaining in a corporation's demand deposit account on the *following* day and invests this amount. The more common variant is called the **same-day sweep account**, which is activated after the day's activities to move funds into some investment the *same day*. The amount of money swept may be all the available funds, or the funds above a level required for bank compensation. On the following day, the company is credited with the swept funds together with interest.

The investments most commonly used are repos and the CP of the bank holding company. While the rates earned are relatively low given the overnight maturity and the scarcity of investment options, sweep accounts are especially important to small companies that do not have an active investment program or to companies that have significant flows arriving late in the banking day.

Corporate Securities and Repos

The most important money market instrument issued by corporations is commercial paper. Loan participations have also become a significant part of the market. See Chapter 9 for the details presented from the issuer's perspective. The major groups of CP investors include insurance companies, banks, mutual funds, and other corporations.

Repurchase Agreements

Repurchase agreements (repos or RPs) are a very important sector of the short-term investment market. Current estimates place the total market at about $500 billion. This is comparable to the size of the commercial paper market, but because the majority of repo transactions are very short-term, the repo market accounts for much more activity. While repurchase agreements are theoretically a matched pair of security sales, they are more accurately thought of as collateralized borrowing.

In a typical repo transaction, a dealer in government securities seeking to finance its portfolio borrows money from another dealer, corporation, bank, or other entity. The dealer pledges government securities as collateral. If this transaction is initiated by the investing company (e.g., a company holding a security under a repurchase agreement), the transaction is called a **reverse repo**. In a reverse repo, the investor usually deals with the repo dealer.

While in principle, any security can be used, because of default risk, the securities used are almost always government securities. Another reason is that government securities are generally held in book entry form, which makes the offsetting transactions simpler. Repos can be done overnight or for longer periods; the latter are called **term repos**. Securities involved in a repo can be delivered to a purchaser's third-party safekeeping agent or (for short-term transactions) they can be retained by the borrower. Although the purchaser nominally holds title to the securities whether or not delivery is actually taken, recent legal decisions have challenged this. When delivery is not taken, the courts have viewed the lender as another unsecured party. Therefore, the creditworthiness of the seller is a critical issue, despite the quality of the collateral.

Computing Risk and Returns

Risk and return calculations for money market instruments are somewhat complicated by the different methods for expressing prices and yields. Traditionally, for ease in converting from 30-, 60- and 90-day yields to annual yields, the convention of the 360-day year is used in almost all domestic cases when the

Box 10-3
Key Formulas for Discount Securities

Discount (D)

$$D = \frac{Fd}{360}$$

Selling price (P)

$$P = F - D = F[1 - (\frac{dt}{360})]$$

Bond equivalent yield (r)

$$r = \frac{(365 \times d)}{(360 - dt)}$$

where:

F = face value
d = quoted discount price (in %)
t = days to maturity

To compute the yield on a 13-week, $1 million T-bill selling at a 4% discount:

$$P = F[1 - (\frac{dt}{360})]$$
$$= 1[1 - \frac{(.04 \times 91)}{360}]$$
$$= [1 - .0101]$$
$$= \$.9899 \; million$$

The bond equivalent yield is:

$$r = \frac{(365 \times .04)}{[360 - (.04)(91)]}$$
$$= \frac{14.6}{356.4}$$
$$= 4.10\%$$

Box 10-4
Formulas for Arithmetic and Geometric Returns

Arithmetic return

$R_{t+1} = (Div_{t+1}/P_t) + [(P_{t+1} - P_t)/P_t]$

$\qquad = $ dividend (or coupon) return + capital gain

where:

$R_t \quad = $ return in period t
$P_t \quad = $ price in period t
$Div_t = $ dividend or coupon received in period t

Note that this is a mixture of realized (the coupon or dividend) and unrealized (the capital gain) gains.

Geometric Return from period 1 to period t:

$R_{1,t} = [(1 + R_1) \times (1 + R_2) \dots (1 + R_t)]^{1/t} - 1$

where R_i is the return in period i

---

price of a security is computed. However, to compute the yield to the investor, the rate is annualized to a 365-day year.

Yields on Discount Securities

For discount securities, the dollar price is equal to the face value less the dollar discount, which depends on the rate of discount and the number of days to maturity. Dollar discount and selling prices are computed using the formulas shown in Box 10-3.

The discount price is always less than the annual yield. This is because the amount invested is less than the face value and a year is not 360 days. To compare a discount security (such as a T-bill) with a coupon security (such as a CD), the discount rate must be converted to the **bond equivalent rate**.

The Mean-Variance Approach to Performance Evaluation

There are a number of alternatives for computing risk in a money market investment setting. The most basic approach is rooted in the seminal risk and return approach used in evaluating equity investments: the **mean-variance**

paradigm. It assumes that risk is measured by the variance (or its square root, the standard deviation) of returns and that investors are risk averse. Risk averse, in this setting, means that an investor choosing between two assets with equal expected returns will prefer the one with the lower variance.

There are two important ways to measure the return component: The **arithmetic (mean) return** and the **geometric (mean) return**. Their formulas are shown in Box 10-4.

While the formula for the geometric return may look strange, it is just the annualized holding period return. It considers the effect of compounding, while the arithmetic mean does not. That is, the arithmetic mean gives the best estimate of returns if the holding period is one year. A simple example of these risk and return calculations is shown in Figure 10-6.

In this very simple example, the two measures of mean return have shown approximately the same result. Over longer horizons, the geometric return will be lower than the corresponding arithmetic mean return. The calculations show that the strategy of holding the longer-dated T-bill has a higher return. Overall, the example shows that the longer-term strategy has slightly lower risk.

TAX-ADVANTAGED SECURITIES

Taxes are a major consideration in short-term investment. Many government securities are partially or totally tax-exempt. In addition, dividends received by a corporation are generally subject to preferential tax treatment.

The Effect of Taxes

When an investor is comparing the returns from two investments, the only relevant comparison is on an after-tax basis. This can create some interesting situations where investors with different tax treatments evaluate a given security.

Given a marginal tax rate of T percent on ordinary income and a tax-exempt yield of r, a taxable security must yield $[r/(1.00 - T)]$ for it to return the same after-tax yield as the tax-exempt security. For example, given a corporate tax rate of 34 percent, a tax-exempt yield of 6 percent is equivalent to a taxable yield of:

$$Yield = \frac{.06}{(1.00 - .34)} = 9.09\%$$

Figure 10-6
An Example of Investment Risk and Return Calculations

Assume a corporate investor is considering investing in T-bills over a one-year horizon. In order to assist in making the choice between holding 91-day versus 182-day
bills, the company is interested in knowing how the two choices have performed over
the past year. It has recorded the following prices for 91- and 182-day T-bills:

Day	91-Day Bill	182-Day Bill
1	8.0%	8.3%
92	7.5	
183	7.0	7.3
274	6.0	

This implies that the relevant yields are:

Day	91-Day Bill	182-Day Bill
1	8.28%	8.78%
92	7.75	
183	7.23	7.69
274	6.70	

To illustrate these figure, the details for the first rows are as follows:

$$8.28\% = \frac{(.08)365}{360 - (.08)(91)}$$

$$8.78\% = \frac{(.083)365}{360 - (.083)(182)}.$$

Mean returns

To compute the arithmetic returns on the two strategies:

$Mean_{91} = (.0828 + .0775 + .0723 + .067)/4 = 7.49\%$

$Mean_{182} = (.0878 + .0769)/2 = 8.23\%$

(continued on next page)

Figure 10-6 (continued)
An Example of Investment Risk and Return Calculations

To compute the geometric mean returns:

$$\text{G.mean}_{91} = [(1.0828)(1.0775)(1.0723)(1.067)]^{1/4} - 1 = 1.335^{1/4} - 1 = 7.49\%$$

$$\text{G.mean}_{182} = \sqrt{1.0878 \times 1.0769} - 1 = 8.23\%$$

To compute the standard deviation of returns

The variance is the average squared deviation from the mean value.
In this case:

Variance$_{91}$

$$= \frac{[(.0828 - .0749)^2 + (.0775 - .0749)^2 + (.0723 - .0749)^2 + (.0670 - .0749)^2]}{4}$$

$$= .000034$$

Standard deviation$_{91} = \sqrt{.000034} = .0058$

$$\text{Variance}_{182} = \frac{[(.0878 - .0823)^2 + (.0769 - .0823)^2]}{2} = .00003$$

Standard deviation$_{182} = \sqrt{.00003} = .0055$

There are numerous tax-advantaged government debt issues. For example, the interest on T-bills is exempt from state and local taxation. Many local governments issue tax-exempt securities. The next section focuses on a different type of tax-advantaged security: preferred stock. Though not strictly speaking a money market instrument, it is an area of importance to corporate investors because of the preferential treatment of dividends. This issue will be developed further in the next chapter, which discusses dividend capture strategies.

Preferred Stock

Intermediate between debt and equity financing is preferred stock, sometimes referred to as a **hybrid security**. The numerous variants of preferred stock are classed as equity by the IRS because they have no maturity. In case of liquidation of the issuer, they rank after debt and before common equity. However, because they are classed as equity, issuers are not permitted to deduct dividend payments from income. This reduces the number of potential issuers.

Basic Features

Like corporate debt, preferred stock can have a variety of features that are important to the corporate investor:

- Par value: Also called the **liquidation value**. Dividends are quoted as a percent of the par value.

- Cumulative: Dividends are typically cumulative. This means that if a dividend is missed, the cumulative total of unpaid preferred dividends (**arrearages**) must be paid before any common dividends can be paid.

- Voting rights: Preferred stock generally has no voting rights unless a predetermined number of dividends are omitted.

- Callability: Most preferred stock is callable at a small premium (often two to four percent of par), usually after a no-call period of five or ten years after issuance. Some issues have mandatory retirement through sinking fund provisions. A sinking fund provision is an important component of many debt contracts. It requires that the issuer retire (either through calling or open market purchase) a fixed percentage of the issue prior to maturity. Other preferred stock is known as **perpetual**, meaning that calls are not permitted.

- Risk: Investors generally view preferred stock as more risky than bonds, although the differential tax treatment may mean that preferred stock yields can be close to or even lower than the returns on long-term bonds of the same issuer. Preferred stock has bond-like ratings.

- Convertibility: Many preferred issues are convertible. This means that a share is convertible into a fixed number of shares of the company's common equity. Including this option gives the investor a chance to participate in the appreciation of the equity; because of the value of this option, it also reduces the dividend yield.

- Dividend setting: Prior to 1982, all preferred stock had a fixed dividend. Since then, a number of variants of preferred stock have devised different mechanisms to allow the dividend to adjust to current interest rates and market perceptions of the issuer's creditworthiness.

Advantages and Disadvantages of Preferred Stock Financing

Companies that issue preferred stock find the first major advantage is less cash flow restrictions (on dividends and on principal) than debt. Since failure to make coupon and principal payments on debt can lead to bankruptcy, the fact that on perpetual preferred there is no principal repayment and that dividends may be skipped gives the issuer greater freedom in cash outflows. Secondly, because preferred stock generally does not have voting rights, it leads to less dilution of control than common equity.

There are corresponding disadvantages to preferred stock financing, the major one being that dividends are not tax-deductible. This means that a highly taxed issuer that could issue debt probably would not choose preferred stock financing. Preferred stock also gives the issuer less flexibility in dividend payout than common equity.

The Dividend Received Exclusion

A wide variety of short-term investment vehicles have been designed to take advantage of the dividend received exclusion. This exemption shields a portion of any dividends received by a corporation from federal taxation. After being cut in 1986 and again in 1987, the percentage excluded is currently 70 percent. However, to qualify for this exemption, the corporate investor must hold the security for at least 45 days on a "risky" basis.

For example, on June 1 a company buys 1000 shares of ABC stock at $50 per share in order to capture its $1 dividend. The **ex-dividend date** (the date on which holders of the stock will no longer receive the current dividend) is June 15. If the company sells the stock after holding it at some risk for at least 45 days, the $1,000 of dividends received would yield taxable income of only $300. At the current maximum rates, this would generate a tax liability of $102. A convenient way to do this type of calculation is to note that, in this case, the effective tax rate on dividends is 10.2% (.34 X .30).

Preferred Stock: The Variable Rate Innovations

Due to corporate tax structure, corporate investors have developed an interest in preferred stock as a means of investing and as a method of raising capital. However, because preferred stock traditionally had a fixed dividend, it was unsuitable for short-term investments because of the price risk created by fluctuations in interest rates.

For example, suppose a (noncallable) straight preferred stock issue pays a yearly dividend of $5.00. If the relevant discount rate is 6%, one share of the preferred should sell for $83.33 ($5/.06). This valuation uses the formula for the evaluation of a perpetuity. If an asset is expected to yield a cash payment of $C per period forever, and the appropriate discount rate on future flows is r, the value of the asset is C/r. If the appropriate discount rate rises to 8%, each share will fall by:

$$83.33 - (\frac{5}{.08}) = 83.33 - 62.5 = \$20.83$$

This means that a rise in interest rates of two percentage points led to a 25% decline in the market value of the preferred. This high level of interest rate risk made preferred stock too risky for most corporate short-term investors, despite the favorable (at that time, much more favorable) tax treatment. Investment bankers addressed this flaw in the 1980's by a proliferation of preferred stock hybrids with various mechanisms that permit the dividend rates to adjust to market interest rates. This allows the *dividend* to adjust to market conditions, rather than the *price*.

Adjustable Rate Preferred (ARP)

ARPs were introduced in 1982 in an attempt to insulate preferred stockholders from the price erosion caused by rising interest rates. This was done by allowing the dividend rate to adjust quarterly to current treasury yields. The dividend rate is adjusted according to a predetermined spread, called the **reset rate**, above or below the highest of: the 3-month T-bill rate, the 10-year Constant Maturity Treasury Bond rate, or the 20-year Constant Maturity rate. This maximum is called the Treasury Base Yield. Early issues had a small or even positive reset; later issues featured resets of -600 or less, which meant that the dividend rate was more than 600 basis points below the treasury base yield.

Almost all ARPs have high and low interest rate **collars**, which restrict the issuer's and the investor's ability to benefit from large swings in interest rates. For example, an ARP issue with a collar of 15% and 8% means that the maximum and minimum dividend rates are 15% and 8% respectively. An ARP is also callable; that is, it can be redeemed by the issuer for a call premium (usually about 3% of face value) typically five years after issue. A number of issues were called in the late 1980's and early 1990's because they sank to their lower collar and because newer forms of variable-rate preferred began to replace ARPs.

The First ARP Issue

To illustrate this structure, consider the first issue, Chase Manhattan's 1982 AA-rated issue for $200 million. Its par value was $50. It was callable in five years at a call price of $51.50. Its reset was +50. At the time of issue the Treasury Base Yield was 13.62, which means that its initial dividend was $1.765 (14.12% of par, annualized). At this time the CP yield was 12.95%, which doesn't seem like too large a gap. However, on an after-tax basis the yield on the Chase ARP was 13.15%, versus 7.25% for CP, a substantial gap. (This calculation uses 1982 tax rates, which were a 46% corporate tax rate and an 85% dividend exclusion.)

Convertible Adjustable Preferred (CAP)

CAPs were created to further mitigate the price risk of preferred stock. A CAP gives the investor the option to convert into the par value of common stocks. This protects the instrument up to par value. This is unlike the usual convertible option, which allows the investor to benefit from the appreciation of the equity by allowing conversion into a fixed number of shares. There is only a very small volume of CAP still outstanding.

Auction Rate Preferred (AURP)

Auction rate preferred stock is better known under a variety of proprietary names such as MMP (Money Market Preferred) or DARTS (Dutch-Auction Rate Transferable Securities). Its initial dividend rate is usually set as a percentage of the 60-day commercial paper AA composite rate, which is published weekly by the Fed. A Dutch auction, which has become a popular in a number of other areas of corporate finance (e.g., share repurchase), is then held every 49 days. It is held for 49 days because that is the smallest multiple of seven (to ensure that the trading day does not fall on a weekend) larger than 45. This means that the stock does not really trade during these 7-week intervals, which greatly reduces its liquidity. However, there is no price risk since the share always changes hands at its par value.

An Example of a Dutch Auction

To illustrate how the Dutch Auction mechanism works consider the following simplified example. Suppose there are 10 shares — each with par value of $1 million. A few days prior to the dividend reset date, the existing and prospective shareholders have submitted the bids as shown in the first panel of Figure 10-7. The usual bid is a minimum required yield for the next trading period. Existing holders can also place hold orders (keep the stock at whatever the resulting yield ends up as) or sell orders (sell the stock at whatever the resulting yield ends up as). As with ARPs, there are usually collars that constrain the maximum and minimum bids.

In this example, bidder 6 wants to sell, irrespective of the promised yield. Bidder 5 wants to hold the security. The other 4 current shareholders have bid their minimum required yield. At this time bids from prospective buyers are also received. In this case there are 4 prospective owners, bidding from 3.8% to 4.7%. The trustee bank then takes the bids and attempts to allocate the available shares (9 in this case, since one shareholder has placed a hold order) based on the lowest bids. The lowest bid is 3.8%, then 4%, 4.1%, 4.2%, and 4.3%. At 4.3%, all 9 available shares have been allocated. Since there happen to be two bidders offering 4.3%, the tie goes to the existing shareholder.

Figure 10-7
An Example of a Dutch Auction

Bids from Existing Shareholders

Shareholder	Number of Shares Owned	Bid (Annualized Percentage)
1	2	4.0%
2	1	4.1
3	1	4.2
4	1	4.3
5	1	Hold
6	4	Sell

Bids from Prospective Shareholders

Bidder	Number of Shares Bid for	Bid (Annualized Percentage)
7	5	4.7%
8	2	3.8
9	2	4.2
10	1	4.3

Holdings After Dutch Auction

Bidder	Number of Shares
1	2
2	1
3	1
4	1
5	1
6	0
7	0
8	2
9	2
10	0

Market clearing bid = 4.3%

Unlike a treasury bill auction, here all bidders that end up holding the stock will receive the **market clearing bid**, which is 4.3% in this example. If there were not enough bidders to allow all shares to be allocated, the auction would fail. In this case, the dividend payment is fixed by a pre-established formula, usually 120% of the current commercial paper composite yield. While a failed auction is generally a negative signal, it is different from a default. A failed auction can continue to payout a relatively high yield for a considerable number of periods. In a default no one gets paid.

Both fails and defaults have happened in this market. A well publicized near miss occurred in October, 1990, when a Citicorp auction of a $75 million issue came within 5 basis points of failing. This issue had an upper bound on the dividend of 120% of the composite commercial paper yield. The market clearing bid was 9.4%, which was 115% of the CP yield.

Returning to the example in Figure 10-7, if there were only bidders 9 and 10 (not bidders 7 and 8) as prospective new owners, there would only be bids for 8 of the 9 available shares and the auction would fail. The existing shareholders would retain their existing holdings and they would be paid the pre-determined failed auction payout, such as 120% of the CP yield.

MANAGEMENT REVIEW ITEMS

➡ Keep a list of types of short-term money market instruments, and use it as a checklist when making investments. Include calculations, features, market-ability, or other key points you wish to remember.

➡ Keep a list of dealers and brokers even when you are not in the market to facilitate new investments.

➡ Periodically compare tax-free investments with your "regular" investments. Get routine updates from your tax department/advisor on the company's tax status.

➡ Consider Yankee or EuroCDs or time deposits instead of domestic CDs.

➡ Establish open-ended or rolling repos for simpler investments.

➡ Consider safekeeping with your dealer to allow last-minute substitutions and ease of investing.

➡ In times of changing interest rates, consider reverse repos instead of short-term borrowing. Try a reverse repo at a time when you are not in a crisis to test out the procedure. The small yield that you may have to lose will be worth the piece of mind.

➡ Try to review a new or different instrument each week, reviewing how it works, its calculations, market strength, and the best dealer(s) for it. This can help keep you current.

➡ Try to hold a meeting monthly with your major dealer (or one of your major dealers). This should help ensure that you're keeping abreast of the market.

➡ If you are not an active daily investor, consider using a sweep arrangement with your concentration bank. Review your sweep transactions weekly, and reevaluate investing excess funds as a separate transaction when they have reached a threshhold amount (e.g., $5 million).

➡ If you routinely receive sizable incoming wire transfers, especially from overseas, consider using a mid-day sweep service to invest the funds overnight.

CHAPTER 11

INVESTMENT AND BORROWING STRATEGY

One of the most important principles in finance is diversification: Don't put all your eggs into one basket. This is a very useful concept in choosing investing and borrowing strategy. On the investing side, diversification can smooth out the risk due to interest rate fluctuations, an issuer's credit deterioration, etc. On the borrowing side, it can allow a company to choose from a range of possible liquidity sources to take advantage of changing market conditions.

In this chapter, the pieces from the previous two chapters on investment and borrowing vehicles come together to form the basis for the company's overall liquidity management. The key sections of this chapter include:

- **Liquidity policy**: how borrowing and investment instruments fit into the overall liquidity strategy of the company
- **Investment guidelines**: how the diverse characteristics of short-term investment vehicles are put into an investing framework that is consistent with corporate characteristics and goals
- **Investment strategy**: analyzes key investing strategies: matching; riding the yield curve, a gambit based on the shape of the yield curve; and dividend capture, which is driven by the differential tax treatment of dividends
- **Borrowing strategy**: how companies can plan borrowings and enhance their access to short-term credit by using credit enhancement techniques like guarantees and securitization
- **Options and futures**: how options and futures can be used to mitigate risk

LIQUIDITY POLICY

One of the most crucial tasks of corporate treasury is determining and implementing liquidity policy. This involves the nurturing of the different sources of the required liquidity. These sources are ordered in terms of increasing impact on the company (see Box 11-1).

Broadly stated, the first two tiers represent liquidity that is relatively "painless," other than in the opportunity and/or insurance costs they generate. Tiers three through five are indicative of worsening levels of financial distress. The sixth level, reorganization through bankruptcy, can also be viewed as a (rather desperate) liquidity tool in that an otherwise viable firm can use the shelter of bankruptcy to allow it to restructure without excessive pressure from its creditors. Often, this protection is abused.

Primary Liquidity

The first two sources (in Box 11-1) represent the company's **primary liquidity**: sources that are expected to be drawn on to provide the company cash under normal operating circumstances.

The first source is formed by the short-term investments and cash reserves of the company. These assets provide liquidity with the least interference in the firm's operations. The determination of an optimal level of cash reserves naturally becomes an important part of this process. While this asset class is the most liquid, for the majority of companies holding cash balances and short-term investments is considered too expensive to constitute more than a minor share of the overall liquid reserve. The company's return on investment in productive assets should significantly exceed returns on short-term investment.

The second source, access to short-term borrowing, is probably the most important to most companies. The nature of this liquidity source depends greatly on the financial condition of the company and its size. Companies that stand a good chance of being denied credit would logically be far better off having committed lines of credit and diverse sources of funding than companies with broad access to credit.

Secondary Liquidity

In addition to the normal cash flows from a company's routine operations, there are numerous opportunities to adjust these flows to improve liquidity. For example, a company may delay paying its suppliers (with the resulting costs in terms of business relationships and credit record), or it may offer its products at

---

Box 11-1
Key Sources of Liquidity

The company's cash flow, cash balances and short-term investments

The company's access to short-term sources of credit

How the company manages its cash flows

Renegotiation of debt contracts

Liquidation of assets

Bankruptcy

---

lower prices or with less stringent credit terms in order to create cash flow. Management of inventory levels, such as by reducing order quantities, can also generate cash flows.

The modern view of the corporation is as a *nexus of contracts* between owners and management, managers and suppliers, debtholders and shareholders, etc. One of the most important contracts is that between the firm and its lenders, which include suppliers (through their granting of trade credit), banks, and investors in the firm's debt securities (such as bonds, debentures, and commercial paper). Across this diverse group, the possibilities for renegotiation vary greatly, ranging from requesting credit extensions from suppliers or relief from minor debt covenants that restrict the actions of the debtor. Many of these are rather minor and can be renegotiated without great difficulty; others materially affect the borrower's risk because they involve renegotiation of more formal agreements, such as bond indentures. The latter renegotiation presents problems because generally at least a two-thirds majority of bondholders must agree to certain changes in the debt agreement.

In the case of asset sales, the company is probably experiencing inordinate financial pressure and is forced to liquidate operating assets in order to create funds. In many cases these sales are a precursor to an eventual bankruptcy filing.

Bankruptcy refers to the option that a corporation has to file for Chapter 11 bankruptcy in an attempt to buy time to reorganize.

Differences
The major difference between primary and secondary liquidity is that the former can be used without disturbing the normal operations of the company. Secondary liquidity sources require varying degrees of disruption to the company. This can

---

Box 11-2
Current Asset and Liability Management as a Liquidity Source

Inventory: Reduce investment

Use smaller lot sizes
Reduce the number of items stocked
Discount prices to increase demand

Accounts receivable: Increase revenues

Reduce credit standards
More aggressive collection policy
Factor or pledge receivables to generate funds

Accounts payable: Delay payments

Slow payments
Pass up trade credit discounts
Renegotiate trade credit contracts

---

range from merely passing discounts in trade credit to liquidating operating assets. In this situation, current assets and liabilities can come into play, as outlined in Box 11-2.

This manipulation of the company's cash inflows and outflows can be done by trying to get buyers to accelerate payments. For example, in the third quarter of 1991, when most suppliers to the retail industry were suffering, many started offering price reductions of about 5% if merchants would pay in cash terms rather than about 60 days later. Retailers, on the other hand, were offering heavy price discounts in order to increase their own cash flows. On the disbursement side, cash flows can be improved by delaying payment to suppliers. This is why credit grantors focus on a company's payment record in making risk assessments.

This overview shows that an overall perspective of the company's credit-worthiness is essential to the formulation of a reasonable investment and borrowing strategy. It enables the company to prioritize the diverse objectives of borrowing and investment, including:

- **Impact on company profitability**: Higher expected returns on investments generally only come at the expense of higher risk and/or less liquidity. For borrowing, the cheapest source is ordinarily the least reliable in times of financial distress.
- **Liquidity requirements**: If the company's demands for liquidity are highly uncertain , the investment portfolio and the borrowing strategy

have to be flexible. Investments should have short maturities or an active secondary market and borrowing should be easily adjusted.

- **Tax position:** Many instruments are designed to offer tax advantages to corporate investors. The higher the corporate marginal tax rate, the more attractive are these instruments. Another aspect of taxation is the state of incorporation. Companies with large amounts of investment income often establish Delaware investment holding companies in order to take advantage of favorable tax treatment.

INVESTMENT GUIDELINES

As noted previously, the company's investment guidelines need to reflect the company's financial condition and its risk/return preferences. Another possible area of preferences relates to socially conscious investing: for example, avoiding companies that violate a company environmental standard. Investment guidelines are essential to maintaining this connection. They benefit both the company and the investment managers by clarifying the objectives of investment, by creating a game plan for implementing these decisions and by establishing performance measurement criteria.

The overall objective of short-term investment is often described as maximizing the after-tax return on invested funds over a predetermined investment horizon. In less aggressive companies, the objective may be the prudent investment of corporate assets to realize a "fair" return. These objectives are tempered by a series of constraints that control the level of overall investment risk as well as designating responsibilities and performance criteria.

Investment constraints depend on two primary factors. The first one is the corporation's attitudes on the risk/return tradeoff. That is, is the company in a position to "gamble," or is the short-term investment portfolio an important source of liquidity? The second factor is the characteristics of the company's cash flow. That is, are the flows sufficiently large or predictable so that longer-term investments can be assumed? What is the company's current and anticipated tax position?

Investment guidelines have a number of components:

- Restrictions on possible investments
- Restrictions on investment strategies
- Reporting requirements
- Performance evaluation and investment objectives
- Definition of responsibilities

Box 11-3
Investment Restriction Factors

Maturity

Quality

Marketability

Price Stability

Instrument Types

Constraints on the Investment Portfolio

To align actions with overall strategy, investment guidelines include constraints on the types of securities permitted. The limits are usually set on the factors shown in Box 11-3.

While longer-term securities generally offer higher yields, they are usually at the expense of higher overall risk and less liquidity. In addition, to mitigate the risk of relative yield curve shifts, it is prudent to diversify investments across different maturities. Often guidelines include statements of desired investments in given maturity ranges to ensure that investment return is not overly dependent upon one rate.

Quality limits are usually stated in terms of ratings made by Standard and Poor's, Moody's, or other agencies. For example, investments might be limited to commercial paper ranked A-1+ or A-1 by Standard & Poor's. Similar ratings occur for CDs, preferred stock, and other types of investments. While ratings have not traditionally been as important in Euromarkets, they are gaining in significance.

A security should be marketable so that it can be sold in large volumes quickly without making a significant price concession. An active secondary market for a security virtually ensures its marketability.

The prices of debt instruments fluctuate when interest rates change. An increase in market interest rates lowers the market value of outstanding fixed rate securities. A debt instrument's price is more sensitive to interest rate changes the longer its term to maturity. Trying to maintain price stability is another motivation for using maturity constraints.

As a safeguard over imprudent investing practices, it is usually a good idea to limit the types of instruments "eligible" for the investment portfolio. Some companies accommodate this by setting dollar or percent limits by type of instrument. While the majority of the investment portfolio is composed of short-term debt obligations, in many cases it is reasonable to include a broader range. One example is preferred stock because of the preferential tax treatment of the dividend. It is also possible that derivative securities (options, swaps, and futures) could play a role in managing the risk of an investment portfolio. Other constraints (for competitive or other reasons) may restrict the dealers, banks, or issuers that the company invests with, as well as the leverage that is permitted.

Constraints on Investment Strategies

Even with restrictions on possible investments, there is ample opportunity to take on risk. For example, one approach is **riding the yield curve**, discussed further in a later section. With this strategy (and a normal yield curve), the investor purchases securities with a maturity longer than its investment horizon with the intention of selling the instrument prior to its maturity. The idea is that for the period the investment is held it will be generating a higher return than shorter maturity investments.

An important risk reduction technique is diversification in terms of issuer, instrument, maturity, or other investment characteristics. For example, a typical constraint might stipulate that no more than five percent of the portfolio or $3 million can be invested in a single issuer's securities.

In order to prevent taking on excessive interest rate risk, many companies require that all investments be held to maturity. However, this restriction may overly curb the investment manager's ability to liquidate securities when otherwise appropriate.

Establishing Investment Guidelines
Box 11-4 provides a checklist that can be used in establishing guideline for short-term investments. The corporate treasury manager should take appropriate actions based on the answers to the questions.

INVESTMENT STRATEGY

The short-term investment decision for a corporate treasury manager handling a liquidity portfolio is very different from that of a money market dealer. The company's objectives are generally more conservative (with some notable exceptions) and focused on generating reasonable returns while meeting the company's liquidity requirements. Unlike other professional money managers, cor-

Box 11-4
Checklist for Investment Guidelines

Objectives/Purpose of the Portfolio

What is the purpose of the portfolio?

Is it a seasonal or permanent portfolio?

Does it represent very short-term excess funds, so that the investments should be quite short and very liquid?

How important is yield vs. safety or liquidity to the company?

Do these guidelines apply to all company portfolios? If not, are other portfolio guideline referenced in this document?

Responsibility for Making the Investments

Who (by job titles) are the authorized investors for the company?

Have the company's investment dealers been formally notified of the authorized investors?

Are there alternative investors who can make investments in emergency cases?

Types of Instruments

What instruments are approved for investments?

Are there specific instruments that are not approved?

How are new instruments handled?

Are descriptions of all instruments included with the guidelines or available for review purposes?

Have the following instruments been considered:

- U.S. treasury securities, Federal agencies, repos, reverse repos, bankers acceptances, commercial paper, certificates of deposit (domestic, Yankee, Euro), time deposits (domestic, Yankee, Euro), loan participation certificates, and tax-exempt securities?

Quality of Instruments

Are quality constraints shown for each type of approved instrument?

Are there minimum quality standards that must be applied to all new instruments?

What public or other types of ratings are used in the company's quality constraints?

Can the quality constraints be waived in specific cases? If so, how are waivers handled?

(continued on next page)

Box 11-4 (continued)
Checklist for Investment Guidelines

Maturity Limits

What is the maximum maturity any investment can be held?

Why has that limit been established?

Are there variations to the maximum maturities depending on the type of investment or name of issuer?

Maximum Positions by Type or Issuer

What limits are placed on the instruments or issuers that can be held in the portfolio?

Are foreign or other portfolios not administered by central treasury staff included in these limits?

Diversification Requirements/Limits

How do diversification limits compare with maximum positions?

Are there minimum diversification requirements for the portfolio?

Are there capabilities for special analyses or producing special investment reports?

Performance Measurement

What benchmarks are used to measure portfolio performance?

How often are the benchmarks reviewed or changed?

Who is authorized to make exceptions to the guidelines?

Who is responsible for regular review of the guidelines?

Who is responsible for assuring adherence to the guidelines?

If so, what procedures should be followed if this constraint conflicts with other constraints?

Hedging

Can the portfolio be used for hedging purposes?

If so, how are hedging transactions handled (e.g., segregated)?

If not, how are possible hedging "violations" monitored?

Reporting Requirements and Format

In what format should regular performance reports be presented?

Who should receive regular reports?

Figure 11-1
Safety, Liquidity, and Yields for Investments

Type of Security	Safety	Liquidity	Yield
U.S. T-bills	Highest	Highest	Lowest
Federal agencies			
Domestic bank CDs			
Yankee CDs			
Bankers acceptances			
Commercial paper (top-rated)			
Loan participation certificates			
Eurodollar time deposits	Lowest	Lowest	Highest

porate investors should seldom try to "beat the market" by anticipating shifts in interest rate or credit quality.

The corporate investor must establish an appropriate balance among the safety, liquidity, and yield of the securities held in the company's investment portfolio. For instance, concentrating too much on yield may create dangerous risks that might endanger the safety of an investment (and possibly the loss of a corporate asset) or reduce the liquidity of an investment below an acceptable minimum. The relative safety, liquidity, and yield for different types of investments are shown in Figure 11-1. The relative safety, liquidity, and yield for specific investments may vary because of credit quality, market acceptance, or other subjective factors.

A basic distinction in investment strategy is between **active** and **passive** investing. Active strategies include:

- Extending maturities (e.g., riding the yield curve) and credit quality ranges to capture additional yield
- Synthetically creating short-term investment vehicles by using cash and various types of derivative securities
- Investing globally to take advantage of interest rate and exchange rate differentials and to achieve further diversification

The more active strategies are typically used by large sophisticated investors like pension and mutual funds. However, while these *slick* strategies can outperform more passive approaches, it is also quite possible that they can substantially underperform more *naive* approaches. Potential gains and losses from active management increase as credit quality decreases. For example, during 1990 the spread between the average performance of the top half of A-rated bonds was 450 basis points (bp) higher than the lower half. The same figure for CCC-rated bonds was 6200 bp.

Passive strategies are often *do nothing* strategies. For instance, if all investments are made in overnight repos or bank sweep arrangements, the rate changes daily. It is possible with a passive strategy to obtain slightly higher yields by investing in riskier instruments overnight or by holding instruments to maturity as a standard policy, without regard to rates or matching needs.

In effect, however, such passive strategies are not really considered as strategies *per se*. There are three basic investment strategies used in short-term investment:

- Matching: purchasing a short-term investment whose maturity most closely matches the date an outflow of cash is expected
- Riding the yield curve: this means (assuming a normal yield curve) purchasing a security with a maturity longer than the date of the expected cash outflow
- Dividend capture: a strategy that takes advantage of the 70% dividend received exclusion

Matching

The matching strategy is a conservative approach to investments. It is usually considered more effective than passive strategies. This strategy requires coordination between cash needs and excesses and a reliable forecast. For instance, an investment might be made to coincide with a known tax payment (i.e., its maturity date would be the date the tax payment is due).

Another example of the matching strategy might be pre-funded dividend payments. In cases of preferred stock dividends, many companies are required to fund the succeeding dividend before paying the current one. The company would then make investments that mature on future dates when the dividend payment account is scheduled to be funded. These maturities would then become part of the cash forecast.

Using a matching strategy effectively does mean that the company's short-term forecasting has to be accurate. Otherwise, holding the investment to maturity may not be possible, thereby creating losses or other problems for the investor. In practice, the corporate investor only uses a matching strategy for some portion of the total portfolio. The amount will depend on the reliability of the cash

Figure 11-2
Riding the Yield Curve — Investment Alternatives

Alternative 1

Purchase 91-day T-bill at 98.75:

$$d = 1.25 \times \frac{360}{91} = 4.95$$

The bond equivalent yield is:

$$r = \frac{365d}{360 - dt} = \frac{365\,(.0495)}{360 - (.0495)(91)} = 5.08\%$$

Alternative 2

Assume the 182-day T-bill is selling at 97.30. As above, to compute the return on holding this bill to maturity, determine the discount:

$$d = 2.7 \times \frac{360}{182} = 5.34$$

The bond equivalent yield is:

$$r = \frac{365(.0543)}{360 - (.0543)(182)} = 5.66\%$$

Riding the yield curve — return on funds invested:

$$return = \frac{98.75 - 97.3}{97.3} \times \frac{365}{91} = .0149 \times 4.011 = 5.98\%$$

Return if interest rates rise after 91 days so that the price of the 91-day T-bill is 98.2, giving an effective yield of 7.46%. The return is:

$$return = \frac{98.2 - 97.3}{97.3} \times \frac{365}{91} = .00925 \times 4.011 = 3.71\%$$

---

forecast, timing of the company's cash flows, and the company's liquidity requirements.

Riding the Yield Curve

Riding the yield curve means deliberately choosing investments with maturities that do not coincide with the investor's intended holding period. In periods with a normal yield curve, this corresponds to buying assets with a maturity longer than the investing horizon.

With a normal yield curve, the maturity of the investment chosen is greater than the investor's investment horizon. In fact, it usually should be greater than twice the investment horizon to take enough advantage of the yield curve. If the yield curve does not shift (or if it shifts downward), the investor gains on two components:

- During the holding period the investor is holding an asset that has a higher return than other assets with shorter maturities.
- When the asset is sold, it gets a higher price than other assets with shorter maturities.

Illustration of Riding the Yield Curve

Assume a corporation has a 91-day investment horizon. It is considering investing in 91-day T-bills and holding them to maturity or in buying 182-day t-bills and selling after 91 days. First, assume that interest rates do not change.

Note that the longer maturity bill is yielding 58 basis points (bp) more. The yield curve ride strategy involves purchasing the 182-day T-bill and selling after 91 days (at a price of 98.75 in this case). Calculating the return on funds invested shows that the riding-the-yield-curve strategy returns 64 bp more than the matching strategy.

The offsetting risk is the uncertainty in interest rates when the 182-day bill is sold after 91 days. For instance, assume that the price of the 91-day T-bill changes to 98.2 (producing an effective yield of 7.46%). Then (as shown in the calculation in Figure 11-2) the return drops substantially to 3.71% This is considerably less (137 bp) than the original matching strategy.

This risk can be hedged by using interest rate futures or other types of protection against interest rate risk. Empirical studies of riding the yield curve seem to indicate that its return is slightly higher but more risky than matching.

Dividend Capture Programs

Dividend capture is a relatively risky investment strategy that is designed to take advantage of the 70% dividend received exclusion in order to generate high short-term, after-tax yields. As recent events have shown, however, these gains can subject the corporate investor to high levels of risk if the stock position is unhedged. The return on this maneuver is computed as shown in Figure 11-3.

This is equivalent to a pre-tax yield of 10.0% (.0657/.66). The problem is that if the stock price falls sufficiently over the 45-day period required to qualify

Figure 11-3
Dividend Capture Program

Purchase	-100.0	
Sale	+ 98.5	
Short-term loss	-1.50	
Net loss	-0.99	([1 - .34] x 1.50)
Dividend	+ 2.00	
Less taxes	- 0.20	(.34 x .30 x 2.00)
Net return	+0.81	

The after-tax return is:

$$return = \frac{.81}{100} \times \frac{365}{45} = 6.57\%$$

To compute the break-even stock price (S) at the end of the holding period:

.66(100 - S) = 1.80

S = \$97.27

---

for the dividends received exclusion, this return can easily vanish. Calculating the break-even stock price shows that the strategy will return a positive profit as long as the stock is above \$97.27.

There are several ways to hedge the risk of a dividend capture program. Among the most important are purchasing self-hedged instruments, such as preferred stock with adjustable dividends. Another choice is to develop a hedging program. For example, if a portfolio of utility securities is being held long, another group (with similar market risk) could be held short. Other strategies involve the use of options and futures.

Outside Investment Managers

One of the questions a company must answer is whether or not it should use outside investment managers. The first issue is the potential gain from inside versus outside investment management. If the company has a relatively small amount of investable funds, then it is unlikely that it makes sense to spend a lot of management effort on this decision. Passive strategies like using a money market fund or a sweep account are more efficient.

While many smaller companies lack the expertise or income potential to make short-term investment a major treasury activity, there are important advantages to maintaining investments in-house:

- **Investment management fees**: These figures can represent a significant amount of potential income. This is especially true in the current environment of low short-term rates. Management fees can range from 5 basis points to more than 80 basis points. The average, according to recent studies, is usually approximately 40 basis points.
- **Investment objectives**: It may be difficult to align the investment manager's objectives for investing cash with the company's. This is especially true if the investment manager is compensated based on performance.
- **Knowledge of cash flows**: The company should be better able to time investments to coincide with its timing of cash surpluses and shortages. For example, the safest way to increase investment returns usually is to extend maturities. An accurate forecast of cash requirements makes this feasible.

BORROWING STRATEGY

In establishing a borrowing strategy, it is vital to go beyond a consideration of possible borrowing vehicles to consider methods for enhancing the company's creditworthiness. In an economic climate of difficult access to credit, tools such as third-party guarantees (including bank standby letters of credit and insurance surety bonds) are important. Another device is securitization: carving out some of the company's best assets (usually receivables) and creating a bankruptcy-remote subsidiary to borrow using these assets as collateral.

Borrowing strategy also shares much in common with investment strategy. Diversification plays an important role. This diversification occurs both across maturities and across borrowing sources. Just as an investment portfolio should not overemphasize one particular segment of the maturity spectrum, the same is true of borrowing. Because future shifts in the yield curve and in investor demand vary, it is important for the borrower to keep open access to borrowing at different maturities. Similarly, the cheapest sources of financing (such as commercial paper) are usually the most volatile, making it vital that the corporation has alternatives. Finally, larger borrowers are actively seeking diversification across borders. This enables them to tap into different markets and potentially to take advantage of local differences in interest rates and FX rates. However, these differences can be quite small if fully hedged.

Borrowing Diversification

Companies that are primarily short-term borrowers should consider alternative sources of short-term debt. Prudent borrowers should investigate the availability of more than one source to tap when their companies need funds. If credit is squeezed, time spent beforehand can pay future dividends.

There are a number of options available. Getting started may require different actions, depending on the company's creditworthiness or external factors, such interest rates or timing (i.e., emergency cases vs. regular borrowings).

Bank Lines

Borrowing under a line of credit or revolving credit agreement (revolver) is probably the most common practice for smaller companies or those with lesser credit ratings. These forms of credit are also used as backup facilities by commercial paper issuers. If this is its major form of short-term credit, a company can diversify by negotiating several options for borrowing. For instance, it may be able to select among base rates other than the bank's prime rate, such as the London Interbank Offered Rate (LIBOR) or a rate tied to a money market rate. While some of these options may require a few days' notice, they also allow the borrower some flexibility. Obviously, the borrower needs to keep abreast of interest rates and their expected directions in order to use borrowing rate options effectively.

Negotiating bank lines and/or revolvers is a time-consuming task and does not happen overnight. However, if this is to be the main source of short-term funds, effective negotiations will provide major benefits. If a company expects heavy use of the facility, it may want to negotiate attractive rate options. On the other hand, if this is primarily a backup facility, it may want to negotiate more heavily for lower commitment fees. A borrower works out the terms and conditions for drawing down lines prior to actually borrowing, often in the form of a legal agreement.

Commercial Paper

Since commercial paper is the most popular form of corporate short-term borrowing and relatively easy to access for creditworthy companies, many companies feel comfortable with just a CP program for their short-term needs. Companies with sizable programs (e.g., more than $100 million in CP issued) will probably want to consider splitting their CP programs between two dealers (at

---

Box 11-5
Basic Documentation and Supplies for CP

Copies of the company's Certificates of Incumbency and Incorporation

A Treasurer's Certificate attesting that proceeds from CP issuance will be used for short-term working capital needs

A corporate board resolution authorizing the CP sales

A corporate board resolution authorizing the CP issuance by corporate authorized signers and the bank issuing agent

Corporate legal opinion assuring that the CP program complies with SEC Section 3(a)3

Blank CP notes

---

least). Split programs offer active, daily borrowers a cost-effective source of short-term funds. Setting up a CP program is not difficult, but it does require time and effort. A company will usually require:

- A short-term debt rating from one or both of the major rating agencies (Moody's and Standard & Poor's)
- A dealer to sell the CP (this is usually an investment bank or one of the large commercial banks that sell paper)
- An issuing agent for the CP notes (this is a commercial bank)
- Basic documentation and supplies (see Box 11-5)

For those companies without CP ratings (or with ratings too low to permit much access to the market), commercial banks can provide credit support through a backup letter of credit. However, some companies have found that their bank's short-term ratings have suffered in recent years, making credit support more costly.

Bank Loan Participations

If a company's credit ratings are lowered or if it is not an active CP issuer, it may want to look into bank loan participations as another source of short-term funds.

With the SEC directive (rule 2a7) effectively limiting the amount of lower-rated CP that the large money market funds can hold in their portfolios, companies with lower ratings have experienced increased costs and possible market limitations of for their CP borrowing. Many such companies have found loan participations to be very attractive. The basic documentation is simple as the borrowing is done through a bank **grid note.** The borrower can set up a regular bank group, such as its main revolver group, to bid for its daily borrowing needs. This has been an effective way to gain competitive rates and increased borrowing opportunities if the group is diverse and active, since some banks may not wish to participate every day.

Credit Enhancement

One of the most powerful tools that has developed in the last decade has been that of credit substitution, where an entity "buys" the creditworthiness of a bank or insurance company. Often, a relatively weak CP issuer can get a strong bank to issue a standby letter of credit to back its CP. With this structure, the issue's rating is based on the creditworthiness of the letter of credit bank and not the company itself. This can provide access to the CP market for companies that otherwise would be rated too low. A potential drawback is that the issuer is subject to changes in the creditworthiness of the guarantor. Insurance companies can perform the same role through the issuance of surety bonds. This has been an essential part of the municipal security market for several years, often called bond insurance.

Newer devices have been used in longer-term issues. These include:

- **Senior/subordinated structure**, which divides a debt into a number of classes (or **tranches**) with different rights to the cash flows backing the issue
- **Cash accounts**, which are reserves of cash set aside (in case the cash flows supporting the issue fall) and play the same role as a standby letter of credit or a surety bond

Securitization

Many companies have created financial subsidiaries whose major purpose is to generate cheaper funding than the parent could obtain. A recent example would be a major retailer's creating a bankruptcy-remote subsidiary (i.e., the subsidiary is structured so that the ownership of the assets lies clearly with the subsidiary) to purchase the parent's receivables and issue securities using these receivables as collateral. This can lead to less expensive funding because the subsidiary will have an easily identifiable credit risk. This credit risk can be reduced by using various forms of credit enhancement.

A material issue is the overall effect this type of reorganization can have on the company. While the newly created company is creditworthy, what effect does

---

Box 11-6
Mattel Funding Corporation's
Asset-backed, Auction-rate Preferred Issue

Value: 625 shares with liquidation preference $100,000 per share

Collars: The rate resulting from any auction cannot exceed 110% or be lower than 58% of the 60-day AA composite commercial paper rate.

Eligible Assets: Receivables, cash, and short-term money market instruments

Dividends: The initial rate set at 5.4% (annualized) and then set each 49-day through a Dutch auction.

Credit Support: A surety bond in the amount of $71,875,000 issued by Financial Security Assurance Inc.

Assets: A random selection of receivables from "eligible debtors." Which essentially are solvent domestic companies not more than 90 days past due. The purchase price of the receivables will consist of a discount (prime + 1) corresponding to the average maturity of the receivables, plus .5% bad debt allowance.

Corporate structure: The company is structured as a wholly-owned, bankruptcy-remote subsidiary of Mattel Corporation.

---

stripping out the best assets have on the viability of the remaining entity? This is usually called the principle of **value additivity**: the company can't be worth more than the individual pieces. If this is true, can the company really gain value by this type of split? At this point one is reminded of the classic Yogi Berra thought on value additivity. Yogi allegedly walked into a pizza parlor and requested a whole pizza. When it was delivered he was asked if he wanted it cut in six or eight pieces. "Eight," Yogi replied, "I'm really hungry."

An Example of Asset Securitization

An interesting example of a securitized issue is Mattel Funding Corporation's asset-backed, short-term, auction-rate preferred stock (see Box 11-6). This issue uses the Dutch auction process to set its dividend every 49 days. Like most new variants of preferred stock, it has collars that constrain dividend payouts. It also uses credit enhancement via a surety bond.

OPTIONS AND FUTURES

One of the most rapidly evolving areas of corporate finance deals with management of the diverse components of business and financial risk that face the company. Financial engineering, as it is often called, has evolved a diverse set of financial instruments that allow risk to be managed in a multitude of ways. Among the applications covered in this section are:

- Managing the risk of investment strategies: This segment analyzes how futures and options can be used to mitigate the risk of dividend capture and yield curve ride strategies.
- Managing variable borrowing costs: This addresses how the risk of floating rate borrowing can be hedged.
- Hedging price risk: although strictly not part of what is commonly thought of as borrowing and investment policy, this part deals with how commodity price risk can be controlled.

Before delving into the applications, the next section deals with the basic definitions pertinent to the types of derivative securities discussed in this chapter.

Definitions

The types of instruments discussed in this section are often called **derivative securities** to emphasize that they are financial assets that have a price based upon another underlying asset. The underlying asset can be a real asset, such as a commodity or share price, or it can be a more abstract figure, based on a financial asset or index price.

Options
The most basic type of derivative securities are **put** and **call options**. Since they became publicly traded in 1972, they have played a dramatic role in shaping contemporary financial markets. The basic characteristics (described here for the most common case of an option on an underlying stock) are:

- **Exercise price:** This is the price at which the holder of the option can buy (in the case of a **call option**) or sell (in the case of a **put option**) the underlying share. It is also called the **strike price**.
- **Maturity:** This is the data at which the option expires. In the case of a **European option**, the option can only be exercised on this date. An **American option** can be exercised at any date *up to* the expiration date. The majority of traded options are American. Another important

characteristic is the degree of protection against the underlying stock's distribution of dividends. Most options are not dividend protected; an exception is the typical OTC (over-the-counter) option, which is dividend protected and is European.

The theory of option pricing is very well developed. It has proven to be a very reliable pricing mechanism because its foundation is an arbitrage. That is, if the real price deviates from the theoretical price, there is a way to arbitrage away the difference.

An option is **in-the-money** if it has value if it is immediately exercised; otherwise it is said to be **out-of-the-money**. For example, if a call option has three months to maturity and an exercise price of $50 when the underlying stock has a market value of $45, it is out-of-the-money. It would not be worth anything if exercised immediately. However, it would still have value because of the possibility that the underlying stock could exceed $50 by the time the option expires. This points out an important fact: Options on more volatile assets are more valuable. Conversely, a put option with three months to maturity and an exercise price of $50 when the underlying stock has a market value of $45 is in-the-money. It is worth $5 if exercised immediately, since it is the option to sell for $50 when the market price is $45. Another important factor in option pricing is the riskless rate of return.4

Futures

Futures contracts arose from the trading of commodities for future delivery. A highly liquid market for the future delivery of key commodities (such as food products, raw materials, and precious metals) and of financial assets (relating to debt instruments or foreign exchange) has developed. Figure 11-4 shows some of the major futures contracts currently available.

Worldwide, over 200 futures contracts are currently traded. Nearly half of these are financial futures contracts. A **futures contract** essentially is a standardized agreement to buy or sell (on a futures exchange) a specific quantity of a real or financial asset at a predetermined date and price.

It is important to distinguish between futures and **forward contracts**. A forward contract is an agreement to purchase or sell a given quantity of an asset on a future date for a predetermined price. While this is essentially the same result as a futures contract, there are some key differences between the two:

- Futures contracts trade on organized exchanges.
- Futures contracts are based on standardized quantities, delivery dates, and delivery rules.
- Futures contracts use margin accounts to mitigate risk.

Figure 11-4
Selected Financial Futures Contracts

Asset	Contract Size	Exchange
Treasury bond	$100,000	Chicago Board of Trade
90-day T-bill	$1 million	International Monetary Market*
90-day Euro CDs	$1 million	IMM
S&P 500	$500 x index value	IMM
Canadian dollar	CDN$100,000	IMM
Japanese yen	¥12 million	IMM

(*The International Monetary Market (IMM) is a branch of the Chicago Mercantile Exchange.)

Hedging an Equity Investment Strategy

Options and futures can be used in numerous ways to reduce investment risk. As an illustration, consider how a company might hedge the risk of dividend capture. Assume the investor has purchased $1 million of a given utility stock in order to capture its dividend. During the 45-day holding period, the company is exposed to the risk that the stock's price may decline. One of the simplest ways to hedge this risk is through options on the utility (or on a closely correlated security, even an index).

For example, by selling an out-of-the-money call option, the investor gains the call premium, and, if the stock price falls, the company's losses will be offset by the value of the premium (since the call option will be worthless). Similarly, the investor can purchase a put option, which will increase in value as the stock price falls. A third of many possible hedging strategies is to sell a stock index future. Again, the falling stock price will be offset by the increase in the value of the futures position.

In each of these cases, the investor is not fully hedged. In fact, a fully hedged position would not allow the investor to qualify for the dividend received exclusion. In each of the three examples, there is **basis risk**: the movement in the stock is not perfectly correlated with movement in the hedging instrument. In designing a hedging strategy, the investor has to consider this component of risk, as well as the liquidity of the hedging instrument.

Hedging Borrowing Costs

Another important corporate application of options and futures is in hedging borrowing costs. For example, suppose that a company wants to borrow $10 million for 90 days, one month in the future. It is concerned about the future borrowing costs. The most obvious hedging strategy would be to purchase a financial futures contract to offset any potential interest rate rise. Referring to Figure 11-4, two possibilities make sense: the T-bill and the Euro CD contracts. In order to make the hedge as effective as possible, the borrower would choose the futures contract with the least basis risk, which would depend on the how the loan would be priced. For example, if the loan is priced off prime, most short-term interest rate futures are only adequate hedges.

If the chosen contract was the T-bill futures, a reasonable strategy would be to sell 10 contracts (to match the value of the anticipated borrowing). With this position, a rise in interest rates would mean that the higher borrowing costs would be offset by a gain in the value of the futures position. Of course, depending upon the amount of risk the borrower is willing to take, it may choose to purchase fewer than ten contracts to partially hedge its risks.

While the specifics of choosing the precise instrument and hedging strategy can become very arcane, the important fact is that ignoring these hedging strategies can expose a company to excessive risks. Major banks and investment managers can offer companies hedging advice.

Swaps

Another instrument that is very important in hedging risk is the **interest rate swap**. The simplest structure involves a borrower with a fixed rate interest obligation, such as a bond, and another investor with a floating rate obligation, such as commercial paper being rolled over. A swap allows the two parties to exchange interest payments (but not any principal repayments). In essence the swap contract specifies a nominal principal amount and a basis for establishing the fixed and floating rate payments.

Many variants on swaps and options exist and continue to proliferate. For example, a common extension of the above example would involve the two borrowers having their interest obligations denominated in different currencies.

MANAGEMENT REVIEW ITEMS

➡ If your choice of investments has not changed significantly over the past six months, launch a study to evaluate diversification alternatives. For example, you may be able to reconstruct a hypothetical investment portfolio using alternative investments and historical rates (and the help of your major investment dealers or bankers).

➡ List your company's sources of liquidity in the categories shown in Box 11-1. This will provide you with a checklist if financial emergencies arise.

➡ If you have not formalized your investment guidelines, do so by trying to write out your version of the guidelines shown in . Then, get senior management approval, and set annual reviews of the guidelines.

➡ As exceptions to the investment guidelines occur, record them, fully describing the situation and result. If necessary, review the situation a week or two later to gain further perspective. Use these descriptions in your annual review of investment guidelines.

➡ If your investment position changes quickly or if you are notified that it is about to, conduct a formal review of existing investment guidelines and make any necessary adjustments *before* a crisis happens.

➡ Look for regular cash outlays that may be possible candidates for a matching investment strategy. Such items as tax payments, dividend payments, or major capital expenditures are examples.

➡ Look for seasonal swings in your company's business lines to provide excess cash or to require cash. Alert investment dealers or short-term lenders well in advance of your seasonal needs.

➡ Try to avoid seasonal effects in the money markets. For example, avoiding the year-end holiday season is usually wise. Your investment dealers or short-term lenders can often provide useful advice and guidance about the seasonal effects on market liquidity.

➡ If your short-term debt ratings are weakening (which you should be monitoring), explore credit enhancement alternatives with your major banks before your ratings are lowered. In this case, you may have an alternative program you can launch with minimal lead time.

➡ If you have more than $100 million in commercial paper outstanding, investigate a split program. Look for dealers that offer access to different types of investors (ask them to show you their investor profiles).

➡ Always remember to dollar weight your CP rates and days to maturity for analyzing CP performance. Try to look for consistent patterns in best performance by maturity ranges or special transactions.

➡ Use the Fed composite rate as a benchmark (available for a nominal charge from the Federal Reserve Bank of New York). Measure your rates by maturity by day vs. this rate. try to explain any significant differences (e.g., 25 basis point differentials).

➡ Review your commercial paper issuance. If your dealers have consistently had to sell short maturities (less than 10 days), you may wish to substitute a loan participation program for the short maturities and reduce the strain on your commercial paper program.

➡ Calculate all-in costs for various forms of your short-term borrowing (e.g., on a computer spreadsheet). Use the model to develop *margins* between the different forms for easy reference when choosing among the methods.

➡ Managing short-term debt means more than negotiating the best rates. Schedule regular meetings with your investment bankers or major commercial bankers to stay abreast of the latest developments.

➡ Maintain a hypothetical option and futures program to measure the effects of these tools before you try them in a real-time situation. An options dealer should be able to help you do this. An alternative is to try to hedge or protect a small portion of your overall exposure to learn from the experience.

➡ Track CP outstanding, and adjust your backup lines periodically (e.g., semi-annually) based on this experience and your medium-term cash forecast. Use a *cushion* to handle unexpected needs (e.g., an additional $10 million).

CHAPTER 12

GLOBAL TREASURY
MANAGEMENT

This chapter deals with the problems, techniques, and opportunities that are part of global treasury management. Expanding the treasury horizon globally is becoming more common in companies of all sizes. This usually means that a domestic (U.S.) corporate treasury manager will take on similar responsibilities for part or all of the company's foreign treasury activities (e.g., export collections or foreign exchange) or operations (e.g., international holding companies or foreign subsidiaries). While a number of the concerns of domestic treasury manager are shared by the international cash manager and many of the domestic approaches are applicable to international operations, there are a number of other complexities associated with the international setting.

A complete description of international finance would take us beyond the intent of this book, but we will cover the major aspects of global treasury management in this chapter. Some or all of the discussion can be applied to the individual company depending on the extent of the company's foreign sales and operations. To develop the proper perspective for global treasury operations, we will cover:

- An overview of global treasury management
- Fundamentals of foreign exchange
- Foreign banking and payment systems
- International treasury management techniques
- Liquidity management and hedging

AN OVERVIEW OF GLOBAL TREASURY MANAGEMENT

The traditional view of treasury management has been that of managing float, the lag between a buyer's initiation of payment and the seller's receipt of good funds. Total float can be broken down into its component parts — mail float, processing float, and clearing float. In domestic (U.S.) cash management, there are many useful and efficient techniques to control or reduce the overall float by working on its components. Corporate treasury managers have been successful in reducing overall float to an acceptable number of days for the most part.

On the international side, however, much remains to be done. In the international case, total float can often exceed a month. Thus, the incentives and possible gains from international cash management are large, although difficult to realize. Some of the reasons for this lie in the very fundamental differences between United States and international treasury management practices. These include some banking practices (described later in this chapter) that may be unfamiliar to the U. S. treasury manager:

- Value dating
- Overdraft banking
- Interest on credit balances (i.e., corporate checking accounts)
- Restrictions on cross-border funds transfer and information flows

Many aspects of overseas cash management practices and procedures seem strikingly similar to the situation in the United States in the last decade. The lack of a cash management awareness, the strongly decentralized autonomy, the absence of useful bank statistics or service charge comparisons, and the reluctance to report balance or transaction information are all familiar to most experienced treasury managers. Preoccupation with the more peripheral aspects of cash management, such as the short-term liquidity functions, are also typical of past situations in the United States. The existence and automatic use of overdraft checking accounts help foster a laissez-faire attitude among many local cash managers in overseas locations. This is further evidenced by the absence of meaningful analytical activities, ranging from short-term cash scheduling or planning to the effective structuring of a local banking system.

Although many of the U.S. techniques owe their existence and development to the size of the country and the paper-based payment system, the concepts of cash concentration and cash position management are quite applicable overseas. The daily routine must be tailored to the individual country's banking system and available banking services, but the rewards can be substantial if effective procedures are established.

Box 12-1
Differences in Foreign Banking Systems

Value dating

Use of checks and mail

Overdrafts

National banking

Interest on checking accounts

Charges for funds transfers

Paying attention to the levels of and requirements for bank compensation can also prove to be quite beneficial overseas. Particular emphasis on the short-term scheduling of cash flows, just as in the United States, must be an integral part of the cash management activity overseas. This is especially important in instances where the local unit may have short-term excess funds but must invest them for minimum periods, such as one month. In these cases a reliable estimate that is expressed in actual cash flow terms (not in accounting terms) is essential if lost opportunities are to be avoided.

The differences cannot be ignored or downplayed, however. The foreign exchange area alone presents many problems for the multinational cash manager. Its concerns and influences transcend the cash management function, often affecting the accounting and operating areas of the company as well. Governmental controls over funds movements can be troublesome. The controlled practices of overseas banking cartels offer also some stiff challenges.

Foreign Banking Systems

In some respects, banking systems in the developed countries are similar to the U.S. banking system. Corporations can move funds electronically, and the concept of ledger vs. collected balances (often called *cleared* balances overseas) generally holds. On the other hand, there are far more differences in than similarities (see Box 12-1).

Many foreign banking systems incorporate value dating conventions, which defer availability on deposited items or transfers for one to several days (depending on the country and the company's negotiating capabilities). In addition, disbursements are sometimes affected by value dating. In this case checks or other disbursements may be *back* valued by the paying bank one or more business days.

Figure 12-1
Typical Value Dating Arrangements in Days

Receipts

Country	Checks		Notes/Drafts	
	Local	Outside	Local	Outside
Italy	1	2-3	7-13	10-14
United Kingdom	1-3	1-3	N/A	N/A
France	1-2	3-5	2-4	4-5
Brazil	0-1	0-1	7	N/A
Malaysia	1	2	N/A	N/A

Disbursements

Country	Checks
France	1-2
United Kingdom	1-2
Italy	Back valued to check date
Spain	1-2, or back valued to check date
Switzerland	1-2
Belgium	1-2
Brazil	0-1

An extreme case can be found in Italy, where checks can be back valued to the date on the check, obviously making cash position management more difficult.

Value dating conventions should be considered as a form of bank compensation. Banks are compensated for their services by the use of balances created by value dating in addition to any fees charged. The primary implication of value dating is that the transaction cost is not simply the nominal bank charge. The opportunity cost must also be considered. The number of value days may be negotiable, depending on the bank, the country, and/or the customer.

In some countries, only the deferred credit portion may be common. In others, both types are prevalent. Figure 12-1 illustrates typical value dating arrangements for a sample of countries.

Note the wide range of values for the same type of item within a country. Amazingly, these ranges hold even within the same city. This demonstrates a major problem with the value dating concept - its arbitrary and highly negotiable nature. This, in turn, makes it extremely difficult to monitor bank balances at different banks, since negotiated values must be considered for each bank.

Checks are not as predominant in many foreign countries, especially the more developed ones. Electronic transfer and settlement are becoming common means of settling obligations. Retail payments are often made through GIRO systems run by the central government or the postal services.

Within foreign countries (especially the more developed ones), checks may clear very quickly because distances are often much shorter than in the U.S. and there are fewer commercial banks than in the U.S. National branch banking is quite common as well. This helps the clearing process because a smaller number of participants can make the clearing simpler. It is important, therefore, for a U.S. company doing business in a foreign country to use a local clearing bank. In most countries, the banks handle clearing among themselves. Unlike the Federal Reserve in the U.S., foreign central banks are not involved in the clearing process.

In lesser developed countries and other countries with questionable postal systems, the mail is not used for corporate payments because it is not reliable. In these cases, messengers are usually used, although some countries have begun to adopt electronic transfers for corporate payments.

Clearing checks between countries frequently involves significant delays. Checks drawn on foreign banks and deposited in U.S. banks may take 30 days or more to receive available credit. There is no central check clearing agent for inter-country checks. Consequently, banks must clear through correspondent bank networks.

Payment systems and bank services vary greatly from country to country. Unlike the U.S., where regulations forbid interest on demand deposits and make automatic overdraft coverage difficult to administer, most foreign banks are not so constrained. Most foreign countries permit the payment of interest on demand deposits, even if only at a very low rate. Bank compensation, therefore, generally is not in the form of balances, other than those lost through value dating. Service charges are covered either by payment of fees and commissions or by value-dated transactions or by both. Many foreign countries permit overdraft coverage up to a prearranged limit. This is helpful if a back-valued clearing puts the bank account into a deficit position.

Interest on checking accounts and automatic overdrafts mean that positive balances receive interest while negative balances incur interest charges. This ability to earn interest or be charged interest automatically has been cited as a major reason for the lack of strong interest in cash management practices in foreign countries. However, there is a spread between the borrowing rate and the lending rate.

Unlike the U.S., where a flat fee for wire transfers is charged, banks overseas often charge commissions and fees on cross-border transfers as a percent of the face amount of the transfer. This charge is also somewhat negotiable in many countries, so U.S. treasury managers dealing overseas must be aware of the pricing policies and flexibility of foreign banks and should not assume that the banks will charge a flat fixed fee.

International Collections

International collections can be problematic if explicit instructions are not given to foreign customers or sales representatives. Since mail times are substantial and foreign customers often do not have access to U.S. dollar checking accounts, payment by check should be avoided at all costs. Some banks offer courier pickups in major foreign cities, but these services can be quite expensive. Overseas lockboxes are virtually non-existent.

For cross-border collections, it is preferable to instruct customers to use wire transfers. This can be expensive because foreign banks often charge a fee based on the size of the transfer. Therefore, payment terms should explicitly state that the amount due is net of all conversion and transfer charges.Collections within a country can be more difficult as it entails using a local bank and usually a local subsidiary. This means that funds may not be repatriated easily, given local foreign exchange and dividend restrictions.

International Payments

Just like international collections, international payments can be tricky. If the obligation is payable in U.S. dollars, international wire transfer services are readily available. However, for small dollar amounts, this service can be relatively expensive. Some banks offer a foreign draft service for small amounts, and this can be a useful service. The drafts are drawn on the bank and can be negotiated with its overseas branches or correspondent banks. Similarly, many of these banks offer the same kind of service for small amounts of foreign currencies.

Transfer of large amounts of foreign currency entail dealing in the foreign exchange (FX) market and purchasing a spot or forward FX contract. All major banks have active FX trading centers and compete heavily for significant FX business in the major currencies of the world. Note that only the largest multinational banks can provide foreign currencies of smaller countries.

Box 12-2
The International Treasury Management Spectrum

The Major Functions:

Banking System Administration: establishment, review, and control of the overall banking structure or network and the variety of bank products

Information Management: collection and dissemination of different types of treasury-related information throughout the company

Liquidity Management: short-term borrowing and/or investing activities, as well as the establishment or guarantee of credit facilities for foreign subsidiaries

Foreign Exchange: procurement of foreign currencies for international transactions, the monitoring of foreign exchange exposure, and related hedging programs

Influences on the Major Functions:

Business Characteristics: retail vs. manufacturing, sales/market share, need/reliance for bank services, seasonality, exports vs. local sales, net borrowing/invested position of subs, sources of debt/investment, billing/paying currencies, government regulations

Corporate Organization: overseas locations, local vs. central vs. regional responsibilities, accounting factors, routine reporting, credit responsibilities, parent guarantees, inter-subsidiary loans, parent vs. local control over FX, corporate guidelines and policies

Flow of Funds: payables and receivables management, size/frequency of cash flows, internal and cross-border cash flows, cash mobilization, bank compensation, types/frequency of borrowing/investing, funds movement, cash concentration, FX contracts and conversions, foreign currency receipts/disbursements

Standard Treasury Techniques: individual country studies, pooling, bilateral/multilateral netting systems, export collection reviews, international balance reporting, leading and lagging, reinvoicing centers, global credit facilities, exposure management models, hedging

Typical Problems: lack of bank services, local bank control, value dating, lack of information, time delays, misrouted transfers, limited debt/investment alternatives, conflicting organizational autonomies, government controls

The International Treasury Spectrum

As shown in Box 12-2, the scope of international treasury management extends further than its domestic counterpart. The international treasury manager is typically involved in more facets of the financial function than the domestic treasury manager, dealing with different currencies and banking systems as well as overseas personnel accustomed to little oversight or direction from a central point. Of course, the foreign exchange area provides a great deal of complexity to this already difficult function. Each of the functions is heavily affected by the basic influences of treasury management.

Business Characteristics

The size of the business can be a determining factor in deciding on the levels of banking services needed, available forms of credit that banks may offer, or in the attractiveness of short-term investment opportunities. The larger the operation is, relative to local competitors, the greater will be the flexibility in determining billing currencies, payment terms, and collection procedures. This determining influence of the business characteristics of overseas subsidiaries carries over into the foreign exchange area as well.

If the company's overseas subsidiaries are market leaders, they are likely to receive the best forms of short-term financing. If not, their choices may be more limited, especially in lesser developed countries. In addition, if the subsidiary is engaged in a business that is favorably viewed by the local government, then it may be able to obtain cheaper long-term financing or exemptions from governmental financial regulations. This is particularly true in developing countries.

Organization

The organizational structure of overseas subsidiaries can greatly affect the various functions of international treasury management, depending on the degree of decentralization and the relative autonomies of central treasury staff and local financial managers. The organizational structure can affect the banking system administration function to the extent that the subsidiaries determine their local banking arrangements or they are subject to review and/or approval by a central or regional treasury staff.

Just as obvious an influence is the local dispersion of the overseas locations. The more widespread these operations are, the more banking services will be required — not to mention the possible need for cross-border funds transfer services. The structure and relative responsibilities help determine the sources of information and what can or will be reported routinely. Responsibility for credit facilities and the establishment of intersubsidiary loans will be affected by the type of organization and which party (home office or local operation) has the authority to set up such arrangements. This carries over to the foreign exchange area as well with the potential for frequent conflicts as local and centralized approaches to exposure management may differ markedly. One other key organizational influence is the typical background of most overseas treasury management staff members — that is, the accounting area.

Flow of Funds

The third major influence is the nature of the funds flows within and across borders. These require the treasury manager to have a sound grasp of FX principles and the basic vehicles for moving funds within a given country and between countries. A good understanding of local banking practices is also essential. In addition, if there are requirements to move funds frequently, a sophisticated banking network may be required.

The ability to move funds freely among foreign subsidiaries and to and from the parent is an important influence on international treasury management. The more restrictions there are on the foreign subsidiary, the harder it becomes to manage local treasury operations effectively. There are generally tighter restrictions on moving funds in lesser developed countries.

Standard Techniques

The fourth major influence is the availability of international treasury management tools. For the most part, these try to achieve the same goals as domestic cash management tools: the efficient collection, disbursement, and concentration of corporate funds and the corresponding transmission of information on funds flows. The basic techniques include **pooling** (a type of cash concentration), **bilateral** or **multilateral netting** (used to offset cross-border payments within the company), **reinvoicing** (used to control FX exposure and (sometimes) to optimize the overall tax position, and **leading and lagging** (used to shift liquidity among foreign subsidiaries).

Typical Problems

Finally, a very important influence is the lack of credit and non-credit services typically available in the U.S. Practices such as value dating make cash position management as practiced in the U.S. difficult. In addition, there may be very limited opportunities for liquidity management, and, in many cases, the company may be operating under a very different (sometimes hostile) government setting.

Moving funds, whether between corporate entities or to and from customers, can pose problems for the international treasury manager. Transfers can travel by circuitous routes or be misrouted because many foreign banks use correspondent banks to move funds, and these banks may inadvertently lose valuable information that cause the transfers to go astray or, perhaps just as bad, to hit the company's account without any identifying information. Internally, costly foreign exchange transactions may be needlessly undertaken by foreign subsidiaries when a simple netting system would eliminate the need for them.

FUNDAMENTALS OF FOREIGN EXCHANGE (FX)

In 1972, the Smithsonian Agreement attempted to realign world currencies in much the same method as the Bretton Woods system. It only functioned until March 1973, when rates in major currencies began floating against each other. With the floating rate environment, forward markets for most major currencies developed quickly. However, very few countries now allow their currencies to float "freely"; that is, they will intervene in the FX market if they believe that their currency will be weakened too much or will become overvalued.

In addition, 1992 EEC agreements restrict the fluctuations of major European currencies against each other. Therefore, the FX market today is essentially a compromise between fixed and floating rates. Nonetheless, active forward markets and futures contracts do permit corporations to alleviate the potential risk of FX losses by hedging.

Trading Foreign Currencies

Foreign exchange rates are the rates at which one currency is exchanged for another. They fluctuate because of relative supply and demand in the foreign exchange market, changes in interest rates among countries, and intervention from third parties, most commonly the central banks of the more developed countries. There are several avenues open to exchange foreign currency into dollars (see Box 12-3).

A **spot contract** is an "immediate" exchange of bank drafts denominated in different currencies. Settlement in the New York market is one business day for North American currencies and two days for other currencies. Faster settlement is available at higher cost.

Instead of waiting until a future date to determine the spot exchange rate, the company can buy or sell a **forward contract**. The company thereby agrees to deliver or purchase a foreign currency in exchange for U.S. dollars at an agreed rate at a fixed future date. The buyer agrees to receive (buy) a foreign currency in exchange for dollars at a specified rate on a given date. Importers often buy forward contracts when they expect to settle an invoice in a foreign currency and

---

Box 12-3
FX Alternatives

Spot Contracts	Currency Options
Forward Contracts	Currency Swaps
Futures Contracts	Currency Exchange Warrants

---

they want to lock in the exchange rate. The seller agrees to deliver (sell) a foreign currency in exchange for dollars at a specified rate on a given date. Exporters sell forward contracts when they expect to receive a payment in a foreign currency at a later date. Standard forward exchange contracts are available with maturities of 1, 2, 3, 6, and 12 months. For this certainty, the company gives up the opportunities arising from the possibility that rates could become more favorable in the future. The price of the contract depends primarily upon interest rate differentials between the two countries. Corporate contracts are bought or sold primarily through banks. Maturities at odd dates are also possible.

A **futures contract** differs from a forward contract in that it is bought and/or sold at certain exchange clearing houses such as the International Monetary Market (part of the Chicago Mercantile Exchange) and the New York Futures Exchange. These contracts are highly standardized and are only offered for eight major currencies (British Pound, Canadian Dollar, German Deutschemark, Dutch Guilder, French Franc, Japanese Yen, Mexican Peso, and Swiss Franc) in certain large denominations (for example, DM 125,000) and mature at fixed dates throughout the year (generally a specified date in March, June, September and December). Futures contracts can be an alternative to forward contracts as part of a corporate hedging program. They are traded as commodities, and, as such, they do not require an underlying trade transaction. This may be attractive for certain *balance sheet* hedges or to manage a highly changing currency position. Futures are limited by the large denomination sizes, fixed maturity dates, and the fixed number of (hard) currencies for which they are available.

Currency options (both puts and calls) are available for several major currencies (e.g., British pound, Swiss franc, West German mark, Canadian dollar, Japanese yen and French franc). They are traded on the Philadelphia Exchange or the Chicago Board of Options Exchange (one or both). They can be used as part of a corporate hedging program, especially in intermediate-term instances. They can also be used for short-term hedging along with futures.

Currency swaps are essentially spot transactions that are linked to forward contracts. These transactions can involve two or more corporations with a bank usually acting as the intermediary (for a fee). Each party sells cash in its own domestic currency rather than borrow in a foreign currency. Currency swaps are typically used for hedging long-term exposures.

A **currency exchange warrant** is essentially a long-term call option. This hedging tool was introduced to the U.S. market in 1987. As its name suggests, its properties are similar to currency options. As an example, consider the 1987 GECC offering of two million currency exchange warrants. Each warrant allows the holder to sell $50 of yen to GECC at 149.7 yen to the dollar.

FX Exposure

To be competitive, U.S. companies often bill foreign customers in the currency of that country. U.S. companies may also be billed in the currency of the foreign supplier. Risk arises because the company may receive or pay a different amount than it expected by the time the transaction is completed and the exchange of currencies is made because FX rates have changed. The presence of this risk creates foreign exchange *exposure*. Exposure in general refers to the potential loss a company could face from adverse circumstances.

Hence, foreign exchange exposure management seeks to measure the loss that could be suffered if foreign exchange rates were to change adversely and to control or reduce this potential risk to acceptable levels. There are several ways to view exposure: transaction, translation, and economic. Companies must deal with two fundamental types of FX exposure: transaction exposure and translation exposure. They have some choice about dealing with economic exposure.

Transaction Exposure

Transaction exposure is created when a foreign currency must be converted into a domestic or base currency (for U.S. companies, the U.S. dollar). The exposure is created because the value of the foreign currency can change as FX rates change. Thus, if a company does not take some action to fix the value of the foreign currency conversion (e.g., through hedging), it is exposed to a potential loss or gain if the exchange rates change. Transaction gains and/or losses can directly affect the profitability of a sale or purchase as the gains or losses are reflected on the company's profit and loss statement.

Assume a U.S. company operates an import/export business. It carries receivables due from a German company of DM 100,000. It also owes DM60,000 payable to German suppliers. The current exchange rate is 2.5 DM/$. If the DM weakens relative to the dollar (e.g., to 2.67 DM/$) before the accounts are settled, then the company would lose money because instead of receiving $40,000 (DM100,000/2.5) the company would receive only $37,500 (DM 100,000/2.67).

The loss from the receivables is $2,500. However, because the payables partially offset the receivables, the net loss is less. Instead of paying $24,000 (DM 60,000/2.5), the company only has to pay $22,500 (DM 60,000/2.67): a gain of $1,500. The net loss is therefore $1,000. As mentioned above, this type of loss is recorded on the company's income statement.

Translation Exposure

Translation exposure is created when the assets and liabilities of a company denominated in a foreign currency (or more than one) are converted at existing exchange rates to a base currency. This exposure usually exists when a company has overseas subsidiaries and there is the possibility that an exchange rate change will change the company's net worth reported on its balance sheet when the foreign subsidiaries are consolidated with the parent for accounting purposes. The extent of the exposure depends upon which assets and liabilities are translated at the current foreign exchange rate. For reporting purposes, a complex set of accounting rules applies. Since 1981, translation of financial statements is governed by the Financial Accounting Standards Board's Statement Number 52 (FASB 52).

The relationship between this measure of exposure and real economic exposure has been a hotly debated issue. Under FASB 52, translation exposure is defined as the U.S. dollar value of all assets denominated in a foreign currency minus the U.S. dollar value of all liabilities denominated in that foreign currency. Only net worth is not considered exposed. When an accounting statement is prepared, all exposed assets are translated into U.S. dollars at the currently prevailing exchange rates. Gains or losses are posted to special reserve accounts and do not appear on the income statement as they were under the previous regulation, FASB 8.

Transaction exposure and translation exposure rely only on historical costs and current exchange rates. It can be argued that the true measure of exposure is the potential change in market value because of adverse currency movements. Change in market value is tied to expected future cash flows, inflationary expectations, exchange rate expectations, and the company's adaptive capabilities. Hedging this additional **economic exposure** has been recommended as a logical approach to handling foreign exchange risk.

Accounting Policy

Many companies are beginning to recognize their economic exposure to FX rates and are using derivative products in strategic risk management. Unfortunately, the accounting treatment of such hedges may introduce volatility into the income statement for the period between the purchase and maturity of the contract. This does not reflect the underlying objective of managing economic risk.

Deferral accounting, under which any profit on the hedge is amortized over the period for which a risk was anticipated, might be preferable. Current accounting standards, however, allow deferral accounting only for hedges of net investments in foreign entities, company foreign currency commitments, or anticipated foreign currency transactions.

The idea of identifying, quantifying, and hedging economic risk has become more popular with treasury managers as one more way to stabilize earnings and protect the value of the company. Foreign exchange fluctuations are just one aspect of economic risk, and derivative FX instruments are just one tool that can be used to manage it. The challenge remains for strategic planners to expose other such risks, for banks and other financial institutions to respond with appropriate risk management products, and for accountants to combine the two — the risk and the hedge — in reflecting the value of the company accurately through the financial statements.

FOREIGN BANKING AND PAYMENT SYSTEMS

Foreign banking structures and financial practices often present barriers to implementation of techniques that are applicable to the U.S. situation. As mentioned earlier in this chapter, there are many types of problems associated with foreign banking systems, including ineffective or unavailable bank cash management services, the absence of timely bank account information, bank operating problems, value dating conventions, and negotiable bank charges.

Learning about Foreign Banking Systems

Many international treasury managers are often faced with the problem of learning how different banking systems work. One tool that can be used is a *banking systems profile*, which is a standard checklist of items to be covered with local banks or with foreign bankers that visit with U.S. treasury staff. The checklist shown in Figure 12-2 can be used as a rough guide in documenting the possible treasury management alternatives for each country visited. It should not literally be used as a questionnaire; it can be used to summarize notes or impressions from visits. In addition, local treasury representatives can help in completing the details.

Figure 12-2
Banking System Profile

[Check all that are offered, adding explanatory comments as necessary.]

Country:

Bank visited:

Location:

Mechanics of system:

MAJOR METHODS OF PAYING/
RECEIVING FUNDS
Check   [ ]
Paper transfer   [ ]
Electronic Transfer   [ ]
Draft   [ ]
GIRO   [ ]
Other: [ ]

NON-CREDIT SERVICES AVAILABLE
Collecting receivable drafts   [ ]
Check intercepts   [ ]
Concentration/consolidation
 of funds   [ ]
Zero balance accounts   [ ]
Automatic investments   [ ]
Automatic overdraft
coverage   [ ]
Domestic wire transfer   [ ]
International wire transfer   [ ]
Other: [ ]

BANK COMPENSATION
Compensating balances   [ ]
Explicit fees   [ ]
Combination   [ ]
Commissions   [ ]
Other: [ ]

FLOAT & FEES

Quality of postal system (typical mail times):

Value dating for domestic deposits (explain):

Value dating for domestic disbursements (explain):

Value dating for cross-border transactions (explain):
FEES FOR STANDARD SERVICES:

CREDIT FEATURES (show typical rates, costs)
Overdraft facilities   [ ]
Term loans (fixed periods)   [ ]
Committed lines of credit   [ ]
Receivable discounting   [ ]
Promissory note financing   [ ]
Commercial paper   [ ]
Other: [ ]

INVESTMENT ALTERNATIVES (show
         typical rates, costs)
Interest on checking account
balances   [ ]
Call deposits   [ ]
Time deposits
(variable rate/time)   [ ]
Time deposits
(fixed rate/time)   [ ]
Bank CDs   [ ]
Commercial paper   [ ]
Other: [ ]

MISCELLANEOUS
Legal controls (e.g., FX, funds movement):
Any special features (e.g., dual currencies):
Fees for Standard Services:

Payments Mechanisms

Just as in the U.S., international payments can be either paper-based or electronic. While the emphasis in a particular country can be on either, in relatively few countries (Canada and the U.K) do checks play as important a role as in the U.S.

Electronic Payments

In the absence of a system like Fedwire to handle wire transfers between countries centrally, alternative systems have been developed. Historically, banks depended on their international correspondent networks to move funds, using telex (or mail) to transmit the information. A number of major international banks maintain their own telecommunications networks to facilitate international transfers.

Most international wire transfers involve the debiting and crediting of correspondent balances. For example, suppose a company in Mexico wants its Mexican bank to wire funds to a U.S. company that has an account with a U.S. bank. If both banks are correspondents, the Mexican bank can send a cable (or S.W.I.F.T.) message to the U.S. bank to debit the Mexican bank's account and credit the U.S. company's account. If the Mexican bank does not have a correspondent relationship with the U.S. bank, then the transfer is routed through another bank that has a correspondent relationship with both banks or two more banks if the third bank does not have a correspondent relationship with the original two banks. Obviously, this can complicate transfers and possibly introduce transfer errors.

International Payment Networks

S.W.I.F.T. (Society for Worldwide Interbank Financial Telecommunications) is the major international interbank telecommunications network. It transmits international payment instructions as well as other financial messages. The system in 1992 included more than 2200 banks in 55 countries. The primary feature of S.W.I.F.T. is that cable messages between institutions are standardized, and information routing is managed to reduce errors and other costs. Funds transfer instructions can be transmitted through S.W.I.F.T., but settlement has to be made through correspondent networks or networks like CHIPS (Clearing House Interbank Payment System). The vast majority of international transfers involving U.S. dollars clear through the CHIPS system. S.W.I.F.T. provides a standardization of funds transfer instructions and other bank information (such as letters of credit). This permits the execution of international transactions almost instantaneously and at relatively low cost. While S.W.I.F.T. is primarily used for international transfers, it is also important for transfers within countries. This is true in countries like the Philippines that have a poor telecommunications capability. In general, S.W.I.F.T. can offer a relatively inexpensive domestic transfer mechanism in many countries.

CHAPS (Clearing House Automated Payment Service) is the U.K. counterpart of CHIPS. Operated by the clearing and other major international banks in London, it began operation in 1987 and provides similar electronic clearing and transfer services.

Giro Systems

While the preceding systems are used for large value transactions, smaller value and retail transactions are more likely to be made through **giro systems**. Most European countries have a single girobank to operate direct credits and debits. Giro systems have been in use for years. In Europe and elsewhere, giro systems are centralized payment systems with one girobank, generally run by the government, often through the postal service. The giro system operates on the basis of direct debits and credits and is used primarily by consumers for retail payments.

In a giro payment, the seller sends an invoice to the buyer. The invoice includes a giro payment stub (this is called a **giro acceptance** and is usually a computer punch card) encoded with the seller's bank and account number. The buyer signs the stub and takes it to the local post office branch. Sometimes, a value date may be specified. The payor (buyer) transmits the information (usually through the postal service) to the girobank, which debits the buyer's account and credits the seller's account.

Advantages include reduced collection float, low processing costs, and easy concentration of cash. No matter where the buyer is located, the cash is moved quickly into the seller's designated account without a separate concentration transaction, which would be necessary in the U.S. check processing system. Although its primary use is retail, a giro system can be used by corporations for updating customer receivables records faster and more automatically, for small cross-border transfers (if the receiver of funds has a giro account in the sending country), and for local payrolls.

EDIFACT

Financial EDI has also been broadening its horizons. However, the U.S. standard (ANSI X12) is not the one used by major firms and banks overseas. The international standard is one developed by **EDIFACT (EDI for Administration, Commerce, and Transport)**. EDIFACT was created through the United Nations and has received solid support worldwide. U.S. volunteers, who are actively involved with ANSI (American National Standards Institute) efforts, and EDIFACT representatives have formed working groups to cross-map the basic transaction formats between the two standards. This is expected to assist compa-

Figure 12-3
International Check Clearing

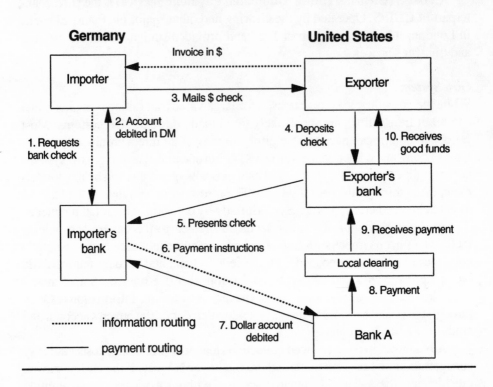

nies involved in international EDI. In the meantime, companies will have to recognize both types of formats.

Paper-Based Transfers

Check payments remain an important international payments mechanism. This is despite the inherent inefficiencies in international check clearing. Figure 12-3 shows the steps involved in a dollar check to be paid to a U.S. company by a foreign customer. Note that for settlement to occur, the check must be issued on a bank located in the country of the payment currency. If the check is drawn on a bank located in a foreign country (in this example, Germany), then extra steps (numbered 5 through 9) are incurred. If the check is drawn on or through a U.S. bank (e.g., the U.S. branch of the German bank), then it is handled just like any other U.S. check and does not present a problem to the U.S. company.

If a U.S. company receives a U.S.-dollar check drawn overseas, it has little choice but to have its depositing bank send it out for collection. Thus delays receipt of payment significantly and incurs substantial collection expenses. Accordingly, U.S. exporters should be sure that their payment terms explicitly state that payment must be in U.S. dollars that are transferred electronically or are payable on or through a U.S. bank.

International Funds Clearing

The basic rule that applies to international movements of funds is that *currencies return to their home countries to clear*. This means that checks drawn in currency A on a bank located in country B will have to clear through country A, the home country of the currency, not the country B, where the drawee bank is located. This includes Eurocurrencies, although there are new, alternative clearing arrangements in London for clearing foreign currencies.

This clearing mechanism causes substantial delays in receiving funds if the drawee bank and currency are not in the same country. As mentioned earlier, a U.S. dollar check drawn on a foreign bank and deposited in a U.S. bank will typically be treated as a collection item; that is, availability will be given only when the U.S. bank can collect the funds. Since such a check must return to the foreign bank and be replaced with an instrument drawn on a U.S. bank, collection may take two to four weeks at a minimum. This contrasts with zero to three business days for domestic checks. In addition, the charges for collecting the item can be quite substantial.

Selling to foreign customers brings potentially greater credit risks. This risk is created because different accounting standards make credit analysis more difficult. In addition, political and economic problems may restrict the flow of funds out of a country. In many countries, communications can be more difficult and expensive, making credit enforcement less effective. Moreover, there are often fewer legal avenues for redress if terms are violated.

Delays in final funds availability to an exporter are controlled by the company (exporter), by the customer, or by the banks used. Company-controlled delays include delays in processing sales orders, shipping the purchase and sending or delivering the invoice. Customers control delays in the payment approval and disbursement processes. Finally, banks control delays in the receipt of payment and the conversion of the payment to good funds to the exporter in a bank account of its choice.

Paper-Based Cash Management Services

Other U.S.-type services may not be as applicable overseas. In many countries where distances are not as great, postal systems are well developed, and banks branch nationally, lockbox services are generally unnecessary. In other countries, such as Latin American nations, relatively few areas have advanced postal services and bank capabilities sufficient to support lockbox services. Some branches of larger U.S. banks offer international lockbox services that collect and clear checks internationally, especially U.S. dollar checks drawn on U.S. banks.

Balance reporting services are not as readily available in some foreign countries as they are in the U.S. It is available through major banks in Europe and in some Latin American and Asian countries. Bank information systems in some countries are not advanced enough to feed balance information into a third-party reporting service on a timely or reliable basis. Moreover, inter-country information services, coupled with global time differences make balance reporting difficult. Banks may simply choose not to offer the service. Nevertheless, some domestic reporting services have enlisted a number of foreign banks. In addition, S.W.I.F.T. provides a balance reporting transaction code, which should help in reporting overseas balances.

Collection Services
A few banks (both from the United States and the United Kingdom) have begun to establish lockbox services comparable to those offered throughout the United States, however, the volume handled is still minuscule. The most commonly cited reason for this lack of development of corporate lockbox services in the overseas banking environment is the efficiency of the local postal services. In addition, the U.S. postal service offers continuous processing of mail, rather than once per day, which is generally the case. This means that there is a substantial advantage to the lockbox bank's capability of multiple mail pickups in a day. In addition, the fragmented nature of U. S. branch banking creates an awkward settling mechanism, which is more inefficient than those in a number of developed countries, such as Canada, the United Kingdom, or West Germany.

International Mail Times
International mail times affect the flow of information internationally. Inter-country mail times are generally significantly longer for corresponding distances than mail times within countries. Mail times within countries vary widely. In some European countries, such as Germany and the United Kingdom, mail times are quite fast and service is reliable. In other countries (especially lesser developed countries), mail service may take weeks. In some countries, companies find it

best not to rely on mail services for financial transactions. Cables, faxes, or couriers are used for messages and cash transfer instructions.

Blocked Funds

A key problems in international treasury management is mobilizing funds in different currencies across borders. In most of the developed countries of North America, Europe, and Asia, this presents no particular problems. However, in an ever-changing range of countries it can prove a significant obstacle.

When considering blocked funds, it is important to note that the concept involves a spectrum of difficulty in moving funds. At one extreme it represents government control over the movement of funds, which may mean that government approval is required for any transfer. At the other extreme, it represents various grades of illiquidity in the market for the currency. One manifestation of the latter is the existence of multiple exchange rates. There is usually an official rate and a black market and other rates tied closer to market forces. In some cases, the official rate has been less than one percent of the market rate. This creates significant problems for corporations attempting to move funds legally.

Companies have a number of options at their disposal in handling this problem:

- Offsetting the blocked funds with expenses in the country: In many cases it is better to incur offsetting expenses in the country rather than trying to repatriate the funds. An example would be the problems in the 1980's in moving funds from the Philippines.

- Cooperation with charitable institutions: One of the most interesting developments in this area has been the interplay between corporations seeking to move money out of a given country and charitable institutions providing it with hard currency funding. A number of companies have cropped up that attempt to match the two sides. For example, if a charitable institution wishes to donate $1 million to a given country and a U.S. company is attempting to move $1 million out of the country. The intermediary may arrange a swap whereby the charitable institution may get 1.5 times the value of their contribution and the U.S. company gets 50 percent of the value of their funds (and the intermediary makes some profit). Governments are more likely to allow this type of transaction because of the participation of a charitable institution.

Dealing with these types of unstable economies and governments provides great challenges to the international treasury manager. Because of this, it is natural that a number of "entrepreneurs" have sprung up to try to take advantage of the situation. One of the most famous situations deals with what has been dubbed the *Nigerian Scam*. For example, a European or North American company receives a letter from (allegedly) an official of the Nigerian government, offering the company some large percentage of a $20 million transfer in exchange for helping move the funds out of Nigeria. The company is asked to provide blank letterhead, invoices, and details of its banking arrangements, which the perpetrator then uses to try to access the company's accounts. It may even try to get the company to pay advance fees or taxes to facilitate this transfer. Some companies have actually been duped out of large amounts of money in this scheme.

INTERNATIONAL TREASURY MANAGEMENT TECHNIQUES

The added complexity of foreign currencies necessitates a thorough understanding of modern treasury techniques, such as:

- Pooling
- Netting systems
- Leading and lagging
- Reinvoicing
- Individual country reviews

Pooling

Pooling is a special procedure offered by banks in a few foreign countries. It is possible where foreign subsidiaries use branches of the same bank for deposits and disbursements. Excess funds in the accounts of cash-rich subsidiaries are offset against deficits of other subsidiaries. Using the same bank branch is usually required to simplify the offset calculation. No funds are actually transferred; only the calculation is made. The main advantage of pooling is to avoid inadvertent interest charges in a multi-subsidiary arrangement.

Netting Systems

Netting systems are used to manage intracompany funds flows. Companies frequently face the problem of transferring cash between subsidiaries. For example, Subsidiary A in one country buys raw materials from Subsidiary B in another country. Then Subsidiary A sells finished product back to Subsidiary B. With each transfer of funds between subsidiaries, there exists exchange rate risk,

Figure 12-4
A Simple Netting System

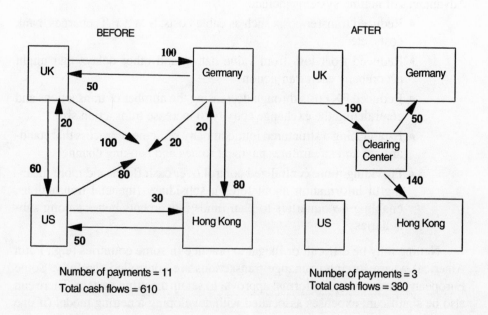

BEFORE

AFTER

Number of payments = 11
Total cash flows = 610

Number of payments = 3
Total cash flows = 380

transaction costs and float loss. To minimize these costs, netting systems have been developed. There are two basic levels: bilateral and multilateral.

In a **bilateral netting system**, purchases between two subsidiaries are netted against each other so that over some period of time (typically one month) only the difference is transferred. For example, during one month Subsidiary A purchases $100,000 worth of goods from Subsidiary B in 10 transactions. During the same month, Subsidiary B purchases $70,000 worth of goods from Subsidiary A in 6 purchases. Instead of 16 transactions, there is only one at the end of the month: Subsidiary A pays $30,000 to Subsidiary B.

The principle is the same for **multilateral netting systems** as for bilateral netting, but more than two subsidiaries are involved. In addition, the foreign subsidiaries and the home office receive or pay only the *net* amount of all their intracompany sales and purchases. A central information gatherer, the **netting center**, usually keeps track of all netting transactions, calculates the net amount for each party in the netting arrangement, and notifies each party of its payment or receipt amounts at the end of the netting period (usually monthly).

Figure 12-4 illustrates a simple multilateral netting system. The netting center often functions as a central purchaser of foreign exchange as well. Advantages of netting systems include:

- Reduced transfer costs such as cable costs, S.W.I.F.T. charges, bank costs, etc.
- Reduced float loss from value dating and other delays that might accompany each transaction
- Reduced FX costs through decreasing the number of transactions and centralizing the exchange activity to increase transaction size
- Establishing a structured intracompany settlement process that standardizes and streamlines payment routes and banking channels
- Providing more centralized control over cash flows and more meaningful information about foreign subsidiary financial transactions, enabling headquarters to plan funds movements better among subsidiaries

Netting may be difficult or illegal to practice in some countries (e.g., Latin America) where foreign exchange transactions are controlled carefully. Some European countries require formal approval to set up a netting system. There can also be significant expenses associated with developing a netting model (if one is used), charges from a netting agent (if one is used), costs of notifying each subsidiary of the monthly netting transactions, funds transfer charges, and FX costs (since some foreign exchange is usually required monthly). Loss of local autonomy may also occur, but this may be intentional. A bank may serve as the netting center for a fee, but most multinational corporations do netting in-house.

Leading and Lagging

Leading and lagging is one of the techniques used by multinational companies to shift liquidity from cash-rich subsidiaries to cash-poor ones. It involves the cash-rich subsidiary paying sooner (leading its payments) while the cash-poor subsidiary extends its payment period (lags its payments). The company's multilateral netting system (if one exists) is the most common means of effecting such transfers.

There are a few limiting factors that must be considered in deciding to use this technique. First of all, the use of this technique may create additional foreign exchange exposures as the acceleration of funds and delay of payments can significantly alter the relative positions of the paying and receiving subsidiaries. Consequently, such effects must be investigated thoroughly prior to initiating the leading/lagging transactions. In addition, governmental exchange controls may prohibit the acceleration of funds as much as is needed. Such controls tend to affect only the longer term leading and lagging decisions. Again, this aspect should be thoroughly investigated, country by country, before deciding to use this technique. Finally, changing payment terms to accommodate the leading and lagging transactions must be carefully reviewed so that terms are consistent with those offered other competitors. In some cases, changing terms may accidentally offer delayed payment terms to competitors. Overall, leading and lagging represents a flexible mechanism for moving funds within the total corporation without tapping external financing sources.

Reinvoicing Centers

Multinational companies may establish **reinvoicing centers** to assist in managing foreign exposure on a centralized basis. Reinvoicing centers include all the features of netting systems as well as other financial benefits. The reinvoicing center functions as an intermediary between the manufacturing entities in the company and the worldwide selling locations. The center purchases raw materials and end products from the appropriate company units and rebills the end products to foreign sales subsidiaries or third-party customers.

The center can be set up independently in a subsidiary or can be run as part of the treasury function. It is usually located in countries with liberal tax laws and FX regulations and a well-developed banking system. Advantages of a reinvoicing center include centralizing FX exposure, removing all such risks from foreign subsidiaries. It also can improve worldwide short-term liquidity management by providing flexibility in inter-subsidiary payments. For instance, this enables leading and lagging arrangements to be implemented easily, improving export trade financing and collections and reducing bank costs and improving FX rates by trading in larger amounts.

Reinvoicing center expenses include the physical location costs as well as those associated with netting centers. Reinvoicing centers are handled in-house by most multinational companies in treasury coordination centers in locations like Belgium. Many companies expand the center to become a finance company that can provide financing for cross-border trade.

Transborder Data Flow

There are two basic types of restrictions on transborder data flows: those affecting access to telecommunications facilities and those that restrict the types of information that can be transmitted. Prior to 1980, most transborder data flow restrictions were based on concerns for the privacy of the information of persons and of legal entities. Countries with these types of restrictions include France, West Germany, Luxembourg, Sweden, and Switzerland. Of particular relevance to the international treasury manager are those countries that restrict access to corporate information. These countries include Austria, Canada, Denmark, Luxembourg, Norway, and South Korea. In addition to these types of restrictions, foreign governments are also legislating the types of hardware, software, and data bases that can be used.

Moving Financial Information Across Borders

Checks drawn on a bank in a foreign country may take a long time to clear. Even wire transfers may be delayed several days to allow for time zone differences and information delays because of the complex network of correspondent banks. It is also common for European banks to practice value dating in which the payor's account may be debited prior to the day the transaction is initiated. This adjustment compensates the bank for its services in addition to any fees it may charge.

Movement of cash across borders may have important tax implications both in the cash-originating country and in the U.S. International tax agreements between countries are extremely complex and vary considerably from nation to nation. In addition, many countries (e.g., Switzerland and Germany) control the flow of financial data both within the country and across its borders.

Transferring funds between banks in different countries may be significantly more expensive than domestic transfers because international transfers typically involve multiple correspondent banks (each of which may charge a fee), may involve an opportunity cost from value dating, and may require more extensive documentation and validation. Unlike the U.S. where banks tend to charge a flat rate for transfers regardless of the amount of the transfer, it is common in foreign banking systems to charge a variable rate depending on the size of the transfer.

Individual Country Reviews

Because conditions are so different in each country, banks and consulting companies are frequently asked to perform country studies for companies that have business in other countries. A typical country study considers such items as a country's banking environment, payment practices, borrowing sources, and taxation policies. For companies that engage in exporting, banks and consulting companies offer export cash management studies. These studies identify and correct sources of delays in receiving payments.

Many international treasury managers have found that developing and using a standard questionnaire for reviewing a foreign subsidiary's operations can be a valuable tool. A sample questionnaire is shown in Figure 12-5. The questionnaire should be customized to fit individual situations. In addition, this checklist can be adapted for use in interviewing foreign bankers. In this manner, a corporate treasury manager can document country banking systems and foreign subsidiary practices. It may be instructive to compare what the banks say is available with what the foreign subsidiary says it is doing.

LIQUIDITY MANAGEMENT AND HEDGING

Liquidity management takes on a much broader perspective in the international setting. The injection of FX considerations increases risk and opportunities. This section introduces some aspects of short-term borrowing and investing, some tools for international collections (documentary collections) and gives a brief example of hedging.

Investing and Borrowing

Short-term investing alternatives may vary by country. In many foreign countries, the commercial banks play the most significant role in providing short-term investment alternatives. In most cases, the funds to be invested can remain in the company's demand deposit (current) account or are transferred to a time deposit account. Funds left in a current account often receive only nominal rates. Better returns are gained by leaving funds on deposit for longer periods. In other countries, funds must be invested for a minimum period of time to gain the best (or any) return. Because this activity is handled within the banks and/or the banking system, there tend to be far fewer banking relationships and wire transfers overseas.

In some of the major foreign money centers, an active money market similar to that in the U.S. does exist. The amounts invested tend to be very large, so only major multinational corporations participate. However, most foreign subsidiaries are satisfied with the return from the banks.

Banks are the primary providers of short-term borrowing alternatives overseas. Just like short-term investments, banks have played a leading role in

Figure 12-5
Foreign Subsidiary Treasury Management Profile

Country: _____

Treasury Contact: _____

Bank Relations

Major banks and services provided (list):_____

Credit facilities available: _____

Compensation methods/agreed-upon charges:_____

Value dates received on deposits (show by bank): _____

Value dates received on disbursements (show by bank): _____

Transactions

Average bank balances (cleared): _____

Average investments: _____

Average short-term borrowings:_____

Methods of collecting (show approximate % of total)

Checks via mail:_____

Checks via messenger: _____

Electronic transfer:_____

Paper transfer: _____

Drafts through own collectors: _____

Drafts through banks:_____

Other: _____

Methods of disbursing (show approximate % of total)

Checks (mailed): _____

Checks picked up: _____

Electronic transfer:_____

Paper transfer: _____

Drafts: _____

Other:_____

Investments (show frequency, average rate, and average amount)

Time deposits (show length):_____

Interest on checking account: _____

Others:_____

(continued on next page)

Figure 12-5 (continued)
Foreign Subsidiary Treasury Management Profile

Credit facilities (show frequency, average rate, and average amount)
Overdrafts: _____

Discounted receivables: _____

Drafts: _____

Other: _____

Foreign Exchange
Banks used (show transaction volume): _____

How rates are obtained: _____

Balance monitoring
How targets are set: _____

Frequency of bank statements: _____

Frequency of receiving bank balances: _____

Show samples of bank statements, balance reports: _____

Describe how value dating is monitored: _____

---

providing short-term borrowing needs for companies overseas. Since overdraft banking facilities, usually in the form of a maximum amount that can be borrowed, are available in most foreign countries (especially in Europe and the Far East), this tends to be the most common type of borrowing. The use of a bank facility in most cases is automatic as overdrafts occur.

Banks also provide other forms of short-term borrowing. One form is a term loan, which is usually a fixed-rate loan for a fixed period of time, such as 30 or 60 days. Banks also provide asset-backed financing, usually in the form of discounted receivables. This is a common form of short-term borrowing in some European and Latin American countries.

Commercial paper markets have begun to spring up in many foreign countries. So far, however, few of the markets have grown to any substantial size. In addition, some of them are not viewed as "true" commercial paper markets (e.g., Italy). Borrowing in foreign currencies fully hedged cannot significantly decrease a company's borrowing costs.

Documentary Collections

Documentary collections and letters of credit are used to reduce the risk in international transactions. In the case of documentary collections, the potential risk is the buyer's inability or unwillingness to honor the draft when it becomes payable. To transfer this risk to the banking system and to obtain a financial guarantee, a company enters into a letter of credit with its bank. The letter of credit specifies that the buyer's bank will honor a draft drawn on the buyer's account if specified documents are received.

Documentary credit is credit tied to a set of documents specifying the conditions of the sale. The obligation is formalized, and often a bank's credit replaces the buyer's credit. Documentary credits are of three basic types:

- **Letter of credit**: This is an agreement with a bank that the specified funds will be available upon meeting certain conditions, such as delivery of goods. In this case, the creditworthiness of the bank is the most relevant consideration to the seller.

- **Trade acceptance**: This is a draft drawn on the buyer by the seller. The buyer "accepts" by signing the draft, which is sent to the bank along with the relevant shipping documents. If the bank has issued an irrevocable letter of credit that guarantees the payment of the draft, it is called a **bankers acceptance**, and the bank stamps "accepted" on the face of the draft.

- **Promissory note**: This is an unconditional, written promise to pay. It is typically used where the dollar value of the item is very high, such as in sales of wholesale jewelry or capital equipment.

An Example
Suppose that a buyer in the U.K. wants to buy $100,000 worth of a product from a U.S. seller. The issuing bank, a British bank, issues the letter of credit (L/C) on the buyer's behalf to cover the amount of the transaction. The buyer is charged a fee for this service. The issuing bank sends the L/C to the advising bank, which is one of its correspondent banks in the seller's country (the U.S.).

The L/C specifies that payment will be made on a specified date (e.g., 90 days from the bill of lading date) subject to delivery of documents. Required documents typically include the invoice, bill of lading, and insurance policy. Once issued, the letter of credit becomes an obligation of the buyer's bank and not the buyer. This substitutes the creditworthiness of the buyer's bank for that of the buyer, providing that the L/C is *irrevocable*.

When a bank draft is drawn on the U.S. bank and payable to the seller at the end of the 90-day period, the seller has two options. One is to receive a discounted payment immediately. The discount is usually determined by the prevailing rates for bankers' acceptances or by negotiation with the bank. The second is to hold the draft for 90 days and receive the full payment.

If the company chooses to receive payment immediately, the bank draft is stamped "accepted" by the bank. The bank can then sell the draft in the acceptance market, hold the acceptance until it receives full payment from the U.K. bank in 90 days or sell the acceptance to the British bank and receive a discounted payment immediately.

Letters of credit generally apply to one transaction but can also be issued for any number of transactions. In the latter case, the bank guarantees that the buyer can purchase on open account, provided the amount outstanding to the seller does not exceed a specified dollar level. Often, it is controlled by limiting the amount that the buyer can purchase on a weekly or monthly basis.

Letters of credit are generally irrevocable, meaning that if all required documentation is presented, the issuing bank must honor all drafts presented by the seller (generally to its bank). Changes must be agreed to by all parties to the transactions. Once ongoing business relationships have been established, however, the seller may require only revocable letters of credit. These are cheaper but do not carry the issuing bank's guarantee. They are used, for example, when joint venture partners trade with each other. Letters of credit may specify payment in either the importer's or the exporter's currency. Thus, only one of the parties bears the exchange rate risk.

Hedging with Options

Assume an American company needs to hedge itself against a strengthening of the dollar against the Japanese yen without disrupting its agreements with suppliers or its physical operations. A purely financial instrument, such as a currency put option, provides this protection. Like an insurance policy with an upfront premium, a put option's advantages "kick in" if the exchange rate, in dollar terms, falls below the strike price. On the other hand, a weakening dollar diminishes the profits of the (unhedged) Japanese competitor without additional cost to the American company. The Japanese company is also free, of course, to use the financial markets to lock in forward exchange rates or otherwise hedge against adverse price fluctuations.

As the holder of a yen put option, the American company profits as the yen falls, sharing in the gains that will accrue to the Japanese company when it repatriates its U.S. earnings. The U. S. manufacturer needs to purchase options in sufficient quantity to offset expected reductions in operating income from increased foreign competition.

MANAGEMENT REVIEW ITEMS

➡ Keep a list of foreign subsidiaries, complete with their bank relationships, value dates, and other relevant data (that you want to monitor). Use this as a handy reference. Send out updates at least annually.

➡ Prepare (or ask for) regular reports from foreign subsidiaries showing local overdraft interest/checking account or other short-term investment rates as well as the *actual* rates for the monthly period (they may not be the same).

➡ Perform an international banking *survey* annually to document bank charges and arrangements. Do not use the words "account analyses" because your foreign subsidiaries probably won't know what you're talking about. Ask for average cleared bank balances.

➡ Make sure your export terms clearly state (in writing and possibly the local language) that payments are to *net of all charges and commissions.* Review your export invoices with credit management annually.

➡ Try to use at least one large multinational bank and one local clearing bank in each foreign country. Large multinational banks, such as Citibank, Bank of America or Chase Manhattan, may have full operating branches in most of the counties where your company is located, so it makes sense to consider using the same U.S. multinational bank wherever you can.

➡ Look for small private banks in many foreign countries that may specialize in your company's lien of business.

➡ Try to convert international lockbox items being mailed to the U.S. to electronic payments, possibly by extending credit terms or offering to help defray the cost of an international wire transfer.

➡ Consider using a foreign draft service, such as those offered by many multinational banks, to make small payments in foreign currencies or U.S. dollars. Many of these services offer useful special features, such local mailing options (overseas) and/or PC origination.

➡ Develop a checklist for ideas to assist your global treasury planning. Box 12-2 can be used as a starting point.

➡ Consider creating a multi-functional task force or working group with representatives from accounting, credit, internal audit, operations, and treasury.

The group can coordinate overseas trips to maximize visits with local subsidiaries, share financial information, establish effective communications, and set major policies (e.g., FX exposure management).

➡ Be sure to buy/sell FX with the trading area or as close to it as you can get. Do not deal with your account officer's group. Keep a list of FX services you use handy as a reference, especially if you're not actively in the market daily.

➡ Remember spot contracts settle in two business days (one for North America). If you want to settle sooner, it will cost extra.

➡ Create a list of FX *sources*, especially for rare currencies that you may not need very often.

➡ Look throughout the company for *natural* hedges, flows of foreign currency that can be used to offset your needs in the same currency. Licensing is a good area to look into.

➡ Remember to consolidate your exposure position by *currency*, not by *country*.

➡ If you are constantly trading forwards in the eight major currencies, consider using futures for a portion of your hedged position.

➡ Remember that currencies return to their home countries to clear.

➡ Always have a "mental" questionnaire, such as the banking system profile (Figure 12-2), along with you on a visit or for a meeting with a multinational banker. Use it to document the foreign banking system specifics you'll need in the future. For overseas visits with foreign subsidiaries, use the treasury management profile (Figure 12-5). Don't use it as a mail questionnaire.

➡ Insist that all export payments be made in U.S. dollars drawn *on* or *through* a U.S. bank. Make sure your invoices state this and that your international credit managers enforce it or charge substantial penalties to violating customers.

➡ Use a multinational bank to facilitate your netting system.

➡ Consider including large, recurring third-party vendors in your netting system, treating them like a foreign subsidiary (after reviewing with tax and credit).

CHAPTER 13

INVENTORY MANAGEMENT

While the management of inventories is one of the most critical areas of working capital management, traditionally, many of the key inventory decisions have been outside the province of finance. These decisions, such as how much of a given good to order or how much of a buffer for uncertainty should be maintained, have typically been made as part of the production or marketing function, with relatively little input from finance.

This has changed in recent years as companies have moved to a more integrated view of the various areas of current asset management. The impetus towards greater integration has allowed and has been spurred by the development of newer approaches to inventory management, such as **just-in-time** methods, which depend heavily upon superior linkages within the company and between the company and its suppliers. In addition to this increased coordination, companies are simultaneously becoming more attuned to the interaction between inventory management and the rest of the company. Companies are beginning to regard investment in inventory in the same manner as they view investment in other assets.

To understand how companies are approaching inventory management, it is necessary to consider the basic types of inventory systems in practice today and how are they implemented. It is also important to review the ways in which companies determine how much of a given item to stock, when inventory should be replenished, and how inventory management performance can be measured.

This chapter discusses inventory management by focusing on:

- Overview of inventory management: develops the basic terminology and introduces the various types of inventory systems
- Cost-benefit analysis: analyzes the formidable problem of placing inventory management into a cost/benefit framework and briefly discusses safety stocks

- Multi-item systems: introduces some of the techniques for managing inventory systems with a diversity of items
- Just-in-time: introduces the key concepts of just-in-time approaches for inventory management
- Managing the overall inventory function: describes procedures for efficiently managing the total inventory function, including implementation, performance evaluation, and electronic data interchange (EDI)

OVERVIEW OF INVENTORY MANAGEMENT

Inventory management, because of the magnitude of its investment and its crucial role in manufacturing efficiency, has been a fundamental concern of companies for many years. Inventory investment represents the second largest category, in terms of aggregate domestic (non-agricultural) balance sheets, behind only fixed assets. In the U.S., aggregate investment in inventories has historically been about 15% of gross national product. Inventory management has undergone major developments in the last few decades.

The first wave of innovation was led by quantitative approaches that emphasized lot sizing (determining order sizes). This was followed by techniques that focused more on order timing, such as materials requirements planning (MRP) and its successors. These techniques, while still being actively used and introduced, have had varying degrees of success. For example, some sources estimate that only 25% of all MRP systems have realized their installation objectives.

The reputed demise of American competitiveness in manufacturing has led to a greater focus on manufacturing and inventory practice. This debate and its attendant admiration for Japanese industry spawned many attempts to adapt Japanese inventory techniques to the western setting. These techniques generally fall under the rubric of "stockless" or just-in-time (JIT) inventory systems, probably overemphasizing their orientation towards minimal inventory levels. This movement has triggered major ancillary shifts in working capital management, probably the most significant being electronic data interchange (EDI). JIT approaches have had a mixed success record outside of Japan.

Factors Influencing Inventory Management

Effective management of inventories is challenging because of the intricacies underlying inventory decisions. These arise from several sources:

- **Uncertainty**: There are many sources of uncertainty in inventory management due to the inability to perfectly anticipate demand and supply. Often this uncertainty is very difficult to forecast.
- **Problems with cost and benefit assessments**: When trying to place inventory management problems in a cost-benefit framework, one is forced to grapple with costs and benefits that are very difficult to assess. In addition, the traditional dichotomy between fixed and variable costs fails to capture some of the potential impact of inventory decisions, such as the gradual reduction in fixed costs attained in some JIT implementations.
- **Variety in product:** Different characteristics of the product (such as perishability, value, demand, and interaction with other items) create important variations in the manner in which the product should be managed.
- **Constraints**: A major factor is the existence of limitations on financing, storage, and supply, which can lead to suboptimal decisions.

Given these factors, it is not surprising that this area has produced an abundance of models and heuristics, ranging from very simple single-item formulations, to highly complex systems integrating production, marketing, finance and other areas of the company.

Types of Inventory

The most basic inventory classification is based on the stages of production:

- **Raw materials inventory**: Factors of production that will be used in a later stage of production or assembly
- **Work-in-progress inventory**: Partially assembled or completed goods
- **Finished goods inventory**: Items ready for distribution or sale

A very important distinction in inventory systems is between items with **independent** versus **dependent** demand. Independent items have demands unrelated to the requirements for other items. A common example is finished goods inventory. In contrast, dependent items derive their demand from the need for other items or finished products. This is the usual case for raw materials and work-in-progress. In the case of independent demand, it is possible to perform a relatively simple analysis of the problem using techniques that are within the scope of this chapter. In contrast, dependent demand items are generally not forecast. Their management is developed within the specific manufacturing

Figure 13-1
Inventory Components

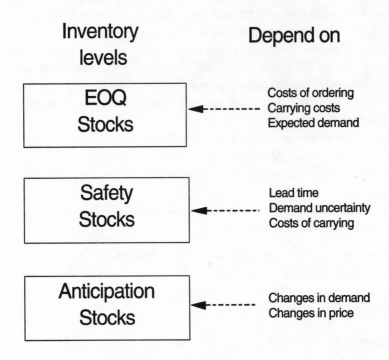

setting, which then involves the entire spectrum of the operations/production management function.

To reduce production- and industry-specific discussion, this chapter will focus on inventories with independent demand. The concepts developed are applicable to dependent demand inventory as well, but concepts dealing with their management go beyond the scope of this book.

In addition to the usual breakdown into raw material, work-in-progress, and finished goods, it is helpful to think of inventory *levels* in terms of three separate components:

- **Economic order quantity (EOQ) inventories**: stocks required to minimize the sum of holding and ordering (or setup) costs
- **Safety stocks**: stocks maintained because of the uncertainty of demand during lead time

- **Anticipation stocks**: items held in inventory in anticipation of price or demand changes.

The company's inventory level is the total of these three classes. This is shown in Figure 13-1, which shows these three components of inventory and the key factors that each depends on.

In addition to these three basic constituents, it is possible to consider other inventory components. Two of the most important are **transportation inventories** (goods in the process of shipment, either from suppliers, between warehouse and/or manufacturing locations, or to customers) and **spare parts inventories** (items maintained as replacement parts). To the extent that these reflect real costs, they must be incorporated into the overall inventory management process. The former are usually handled as part of the purchasing/procurement decision; the latter can usually be handled by the methods treated in this chapter. However, there are often two complications with inventories of spare parts:

- Demand is often tricky to forecast, depending upon the upkeep and usage of other equipment.
- The cost of a stockout can be very high — a stockout of a very inexpensive part can idle a very expensive piece of machinery or stop a production process.

Types of Inventory Systems

The basic inventory systems are either **fixed order** or **fixed period**. The former is also called a **perpetual monitoring system** because inventory levels are examined continuously and an order is triggered whenever the inventory level reaches a predetermined inventory level called the **reorder point**. In contrast, a fixed period system is a **periodic monitoring system**. The inventory system is examined on a regular basis, and an amount sufficient to bring the inventory to the target level is ordered. Hybrids of the two systems can also arise.

Within these classifications, there are a wide variety of inventory management approaches. They are not mutually exclusive as many implementations adopt aspects of more than one approach. The key management techniques are shown in Box 13-1.

The EOQ/ROP or just-in-case approach usually combines a quantitative approach to order size determination (the economic order quantity, EOQ part) and order triggering (the ROP, reorder point part). This approach has been around since the 1930's. It is often an acceptable approach for items with independent demand. As well, it provides a starting point for the development of more elaborate systems or serves as a component of a larger system.

Box 13-1
Key Inventory Management Techniques

EOQ/ROP or just-in-case

Materials requirements planning (MRP)

Materials resource planning (MRPII)

Optimized production technology (OPT)

Just-in-time (JIT)

Materials requirements planning (MRP) was developed in the U.S. in the late 1960's and 1970's to deal with dependent demand items. The key stages in MRP are using the demand for the end product to infer demands for its components, subcomponents, and raw materials and combining this demand with existing inventory balances to establish a net requirement. MRP is an example of a *pull* system. The production of the end products "pulls" the demand for the components.

Materials resource planning (MRPII), an initial refinement of the MRP concept, closed-loop MRP, addresses the problems of production bottlenecks by building feedback into the system. This is done by allowing information on job completions to be included in the scheduling algorithm. This input may trigger a resequencing of jobs. MRPII incorporates closed-loop concepts, but goes further in integrating marketing, finance, and operations.

Optimized production technology (OPT), a proprietary system of Creative Output Inc., is a modification of MRPII, focusing on improving work flow through bottlenecks.

The just-in-time (JIT) concept reflects perhaps more a philosophy than a particular form of inventory management. The key concept in JIT systems is the role of inventory as a mask for inefficient processes.

The different inventory systems will be discussed further in a later section that deals with the implementation aspects. Hybrids of the four systems are common. For instance, MRP systems often use EOQ approaches to determine lot sizes for components. Similarly, JIT can be used in conjunction with MRP. One feature that is common to all of these systems is the cost/benefit framework.

COST-BENEFIT ANALYSIS

Identifying the cost structure in an inventory problem is an essential and often underemphasized aspect of inventory management. The costs are, following the usual economic setting, marginal costs, but the cost data, when available, will normally only be total costs, which are generally aggregated with other cost components. As a minor simplification, the following analysis assumes that it has already been decided to stock the item in question.

Benefits of Carrying Inventory

With inventory systems, it is usually more difficult to quantify the revenue impact than the cost impact, although even the latter can be very elusive. The main motivations for holding inventory are related to service and production requirements. For finished goods, most marketing analyses suggest that product availability is the most important factor in customer satisfaction. With most companies, a predetermined stockout probability (e.g., supply must be on hand 99% of the time an item is requested) or other measure of product availability is a key operating parameter. In addition, the ability to order in larger lot sizes can create economies of scale in pricing, handling, and set-ups.

In manufacturing settings, it is common to concentrate on the role that inventory plays to decouple demand and supply. It makes possible longer production runs and more flexibility in the manufacturing process.

Another benefit of inventory is its contribution to the overall liquidity of the firm. Manipulating inventory levels effectively changes the cash flows of the company; in periods of sufficient liquidity, companies may invest more in inventory in order to increase profitability. Inventory often impacts the company's borrowing. This can occur directly through using inventory financing or less directly through loan agreements that tie borrowing levels of inventory securing the loan.

Inventory Costs

Inventory costs fall into four basic categories (see Box 13-2). **Ordering costs** are also called **procurement** or **replenishment** costs. In a production setting they would correspond to **set-up costs**: the costs associated with delays and costs in resetting machinery to accommodate a different item. They represent the fixed and variable costs resulting from the placement and processing of an order. These include freight, labor, and handling charges. In the theory, these costs are generally assumed to be proportional to the number of orders placed.

Box 13-2
Categories of Inventory Costs

Ordering costs

Carrying costs

Stockout costs

Inventory "policy" costs

The total costs of carrying inventories, particularly opportunity costs of inventory investment, almost always represent the most important component of total costs. **Carrying costs** have several subcomponent costs:

- **Cost of capital**: The opportunity cost of inventory investment or the explicit cost of inventory financing
- **Storage cost**: The cost of the space and equipment required to maintain the item in storage, including leasing costs, property taxes, electricity, etc.
- **Deterioration and obsolescence costs**: The cost of actual physical deterioration or pilferage and any potential obsolescence
- **Insurance costs**
- **Overstocking costs**: The loss due to items remaining after demand has terminated (This occurs most often in settings such as packaging or subassembly where items are made to order for a particular customer. Extreme cases occur in such items as newspapers and periodicals.)
- **Handling costs**

Carrying costs are usually assumed to be proportional to the average inventory level. It is common to split total carrying costs into **financing costs** (the first item) and the remainder, which are called **holding costs**. Adjustments for the riskiness of the item (e.g., because of higher demand uncertainty) can be made by increasing the appropriate cost of capital or by applying a higher obsolescence cost. In either case, the effect is to increase the marginal cost of holding inventory.

The nature of the item being inventoried and the inventory system itself will affect the total carrying cost. However, most observers believe that the majority of companies use a rate that is far too low.

The magnitude of **stockout costs** depends upon the impact of a stockout. The possible actions include:

- **Lost sale**: In this case the demand is permanently lost (e.g., the customer buys at another store).
- **Backorder**: Here the item is backordered, and delivery is delayed until supply is available, usually incurring some penalty cost.
- **Substitution**: This assumes the demand for the item can be satisfied by other items. (This has been refined by certain unscrupulous retailers into the art of the "bait and switch." In this scam, the retailer advertises a desirable item at a very low price; when the customer arrives, he or she is informed that the item is not available and is encouraged to purchase another, more profitable item.)

Stockout costs are most often computed as a loss of good will, typically the profit margin associated with the sale. However, this can be inaccurate in a number of respects. First, it is a confusion of opportunity costs and explicit costs. In addition, it ignores the probability that a customer experiencing a stockout will be less likely to return to that seller in the future. In many models, the cost is usually assumed to be proportional to the number of items short per period.

A related approach to gauging the effect of stockouts is to estimate the percentage of customers that will buy elsewhere if the desired item is not available. Multiplying this figure by the gross margin will give the expected margin loss per unit out of stock. However, this calculation can be subject to wide variation, which clearly calls for differing stockout policies for each item.

A rather different approach, the **perturbed demand method**, does not impose a penalty on the company at the time of a stockout. Instead, it modifies the future distribution of demand. The expected number of stockouts and the customers' responsiveness to these shortages are estimated to come up with the new demand distribution.

Policy costs are often overlooked, but they can greatly affect the overall effectiveness of any inventory system. They include the costs of data gathering (e.g., monitoring inventory levels, obtaining cost data) and operating procedures, human or automated, that depend upon the particular inventory control system used. In certain highly complex (or mismanaged) production settings, these costs can even exceed the total costs of the system being controlled.

Figure 13-2 shows these cost components and where on the income statement they would be reported. This again highlights the fact that marginal costs are very difficult to isolate.

Even with these considerable difficulties, inventory models appear to work reasonably well in practice. A number of elaborate models have been developed. Deriving them is beyond the scope of this book. Interested readers should check the bibliography for additional references.

Figure 13-2
Reporting of Inventory Costs

Cost	Reporting Location (on Income Statement)
Ordering costs	
Preparing purchase orders	Wages
Expediting	Wages
Receiving and inspecting	Wages
Accounting and paying	Wages
Paper costs (forms, postage, ...)	Office supplies
Telephone, fax, telex	General expenses
Equipment costs	Included with interest expense, repairs and maintenance
Carrying costs	
Interest	Interest expense
Insurance	Insurance expense
Warehouse	Rent or mortgage expense
Material handling (manpower and equipment for handling)	Wages and interest
Obsolescence, pilferage, spoilage	Reflected in increased cost of
Record keeping	Wages
Stockout costs	No direct reporting
Policy costs	Wage and salary cost and interest

Source: Royal Bank

Safety Stocks and Reorder Points

Variability in demand should affect inventory decisions. In particular, a company often tries to determine a **safety stock** — a buffer for greater than expected demand. In a fixed-order system, the safety stock is defined to be the difference between the reorder point and the average lead time demand.

There are a number of factors influencing the size of the safety stock. Some of the most important include:

- **Service levels**: By raising the safety stock fewer stockouts will occur.
- **Carrying costs**: Since the safety stock adds to average inventory, the larger the safety stock, the greater the inventory holding costs.

- **Lead time**: The longer the lead time the larger the safety stock required to maintain the same service levels.
- **Demand variability**: The size of the safety stock increases as the ability to forecast demand declines.
- **Order size**: As the number of orders increases, the reorder point will be reached more often, so that a smaller safety stock is needed.

To determine the reorder point under uncertain demand requires a specification of the demand distribution and of the lead time. The basic approaches use past data to determine an empirical distribution or to estimate the parameters of a theoretical distribution, such as the normal.

MULTI-ITEM SYSTEMS

Many empirical inventory models assume that each item is managed without regard to its interaction with other items in the inventory system. There are very few actual circumstances where this is rational. Some of the reasons for this are:

- **Demand interaction**: The effects arising from the relationships between the demands for different items (e.g., substitutability and complementarity of items)
- **Joint replenishment**: Multiple items ordered simultaneously from one supplier
- **Constraints**: Limits on maximum investment or storage (as well as other scenarios where the items must share scarce resources)

Demand Interaction and Joint Replenishment

The most important type of demand interaction is **substitutability**, when the demand for one item can be satisfied by the supply of another item. This can be treated by methods related to the analysis of shortage penalties that adjust the profit consequences of a stockout to account for demand interaction. An item with a high degree of substitutability would be given a lower cost of stockout and lower safety stock than a similar item with no demand interaction.

It is common practice to allow a number of small orders to accumulate before an order is actually placed. This can be because of economies of scale in handling and ordering, minimum order size, or other factors. It is also a natural procedure in a fixed-period system.

ABC Classification

In a multi-item setting, relatively few items will require a high degree of control, so it is important to manage each item with a level of effort that is appropriate to the cost/benefit tradeoff. A standard approach to determining the priorities of items within a system, including an inventory system, is called **ABC classification**. In this approach, items are categorized into three groups:

- **A** items have the highest priority and are the items whose control is the most vital and/or profitable.
- **C** items have the lowest priority.
- **B** items are intermediate between these two.

Classification can be done in many different ways, but a common approach is to rank items in terms of decreasing annual dollar sales. For example, illustrative guidelines might be:

- **A** items represent 20% of all items but 70% of all sales.
- **B** items represent 30% of all items but 20% of sales.
- **C** items represent 50% of items but only 10% of sales.

Of course, these numbers will vary depending on the particular problem. A finer partitioning can be used if required. One of the main reasons for determining this type of a classification is to apply different management policies within the different categories.

The Policy Surface Approach

One important alternative to quantitative models is the **policy surface** (or exchange curve, policy curve, etc.) concept. Rather than explicitly attaching costs, the *attainable surface*, those combinations of shortage probabilities, number of orders, average inventory, and other factors that are attainable by alternative inventory policies, is determined. These criteria create three dimensions for the surface — service levels, workload, and investment — that cannot easily be related in dollar terms. For example, by looking at this type of curve it is possible to see how inventory investment and the number of orders placed interact.

Readers interested in further discussions of the attainable surface approach should consult the references listed in the bibliography.

Box 13-3
Eight Commandments for Effective JIT

1. Short distances between buyer and supplier

2. Dependable quality

3. Small supplier network

4. Dependable transportation

5. Manufacturing flexibility

6. Small lot sizes

7. Effective receiving and materials-handling facilities

8. Strong management commitment

Source: Hoeffer (1982)

JUST-IN-TIME VERSUS JUST-IN-CASE APPROACHES

An important reason for holding inventory is the inability of the company to synchronize delivery with demand. Thus the traditional (western) inventory system is usually the "just-in-case" type. Large safety stocks are maintained to cover the uncertainty of demand because of long and variable lead time or because of lumpiness in the production process. Although much of inventory management revolves around what to do because of this lead time, other approaches work toward eliminating the lead time. The classic example is the JIT system, which surfaces under a variety of names: ZIPS (for zero inventory production, MAN (materials as needed), stockless production, Kanban (for the card delivery system initially used), the Toyota system or the Ohno system (after the JIT pioneer, Taiichi Ohno), and was developed at Toyota Motor Company Ltd. in the 1950's. Although this system is of most relevance for inventory management in a production setting, its overall approach has very general applicability.

As the just-in-time adjective implies, the essence of a JIT system is to coordinate the procurement and production processes so that items are delivered and available precisely when required. Lot sizes may be as low as fractions of a day's usage. It is obvious that a special environment is required for this type of system to work effectively. For example, the vertical integration of Japanese manufacturing is often cited as a major advantage in their JIT implementations.

Hoeffer (1982) offers "eight commandments for effective just-in-time" (see Box 13-3). This type of inventory management has proved highly effective in

Japan and a number of U.S. companies (notably auto makers) have made great strides in adapting it to the U.S. environment. This is requiring radical changes in relationships with suppliers and in materials-handling facilities. But the savings in terms of inventory carrying costs, space utilization, and so on, seem to make this an attractive alternative to existing systems.

MANAGING THE OVERALL INVENTORY FUNCTION

Although inventory decisions must be done on the *micro* level (individual items and individual locations), it is difficult to measure inventory costs (and to some extent, performance), except on the *macro* level. A number of methods have emerged to treat inventory management on a more aggregated level.

Implementation

The general strategy can be viewed as five steps prior to the final implementation:

- **Analysis of the current system**: What are the current performance levels? What are the current system's defects?
- **Establishment of a data base**: What demand and lead time data are available? What are the operating constraints (shelf life, storage space, investment, personnel, etc.)? What cost data are relevant? How are service levels measured?
- **Classification of items**: Can an ABC approach be developed to determine the most important items? What groups of items can be controlled jointly?
- **Determination of control policies**: According to the preceding steps, what are the appropriate forecasting techniques and ordering policies for each (class of) item(s)?
- **Testing**: On a subset of the items, test the chosen operating strategies. Do they perform as predicted? Is this performance adequate? If not, return (contritely) to the previous step.

Illustration: Implementing Inventory Systems
Two examples of large-scale inventory implementations can serve to illustrate these points. The first was developed for a U. S. company with a large inventory of spare parts. Because of the number of items and stocking locations, former inventory policies were simple: Orders were determined as a number of months of supply, and inventory levels were reviewed at most once per week. Cost data

were nonexistent but service levels were considered very important. The system was being reevaluated because of excessively high inventory levels and because of the inability of the system to react to seasonal and fluctuating demands.

After an analysis of the system and establishment of a cost data base, recommendations were made to separate the items into two groups according to their importance: A items (for which detailed cost data would be obtained) and B items (for which only service levels would be considered). These two groups were further subdivided into slow- and fast-moving items. The former were modeled by a Poisson distribution and the latter by a normal distribution. For large values of the mean demand, the Poisson and normal distributions are nearly identical. Thus by using these two distributions there is a degree of consistency. If a reorder point based on either assumption is calculated, the answer is likely to be very similar. EOQ ordering policies were instituted taking shelf life and storage constraints into consideration. The implementation of this system generated a reduction in inventory of 20% with no change in service levels.

The second example is taken from Austin (1977). It describes part of the USAF system for maintaining inventories of weapon spare parts. The existing system had 250,000 items and incurred annual procurement costs of $350-400 million. Demand forecasts were simple time series models. The annual holding charge was calculated as 32% for all items. This was composed of 10% for financing, 1% for storage, and 21% for obsolescence. Safety stock was fixed at one month of demand. The ordering costs were estimated to be $142 for orders of value less than $2500 and $424 for larger orders. Another administrative constraint was that all orders must cover a three-month to a three-year supply.

The preceding system is a natural one for the application of ABC analysis. Austin's group recommended that A items be those where the order quantity was less than a six-month supply. (This turned out to be 4% of all items and 67% of dollar value.) The forecasting methods were also changed. Exponential smoothing worked well, and regression forecasts were developed for the 250 highest dollar demand items. The obsolescence estimates were also modified to range from 0% to 28%. Interestingly enough, this application turned out to have realized savings considerably less than the projected savings. One major reason for this was the enormous difficulty in anticipating spare part demand.

These two examples point out a number of important factors in large scale implementations. First, because of the extreme complexity of running the system, relatively simple procedures must be utilized for the vast majority of the items. The inventory control system should be geared to those type A items whose control will yield the best cost-benefit tradeoff.

Box 13-4
Gross Margin Return on Investment

$$GMROI = \frac{GPM \times Turnover}{(1.00 - GPM)}$$

$$GMROI = \frac{(.25 \times 5)}{(1.00 - .25)} = 1.67$$

Performance Measurement

As noted earlier, measuring the performance of inventory systems is very difficult. In addition, there are major differences between standards for inventory systems relating to production versus finished goods. Despite these difficulties, there are some key measurements, including:

- **Service levels:** This is the major benefit from holding inventories. It is measured in many different ways, including number of shortages and percentage of demand filled from inventory (fill rates).
- **Inventory investment:** The major obstacle to achieving high service levels is the magnitude of the opportunity costs stemming from maintaining large inventories. The usual measure of investment is based on an opportunity cost of capital and inventory turnover.

Other Measures

One interesting measure of inventory performance integrates an item's profitability with its turnover. As developed in Armstrong (1985), the criterion is called the **gross margin return on investment, GMROI**. It is defined by the formula shown in Box 13-4. GPM is the gross profit margin, and turnover corresponds to the usual inventory turnover ratio. For example, if an item has a gross profit margin of 25% and a turnover of five times per year, the GMROI is 1.67. This means that for each dollar invested in this inventory item, the company would earn $1.67 in gross profit.

Emerging Trends: Inventory Management and EDI

The growth of electronic data interchange has been spurred by the development of JIT systems in North America and Europe. JIT has forced a much higher level of integration between manufacturers and their suppliers. This is greatly facilitated by the expansion of computer-to-computer communication.

A very interesting example of the impact that EDI can have on inventory management is occurring at Sears Roebuck and Co. One area of importance is called the Source Availability System (SAS). With SAS, inventory, such as appliances or furniture, that was once maintained by Sears is now maintained at the wholesaler. EDI allows a smooth connection from the store's computer into a data base that accesses information on product availability.

MANAGEMENT REVIEW ITEMS

➡ Keep a record of stockouts by type, frequency, and other relevant parameter. Review your record periodically (e.g., monthly or quarterly, depending on the item or the company) to set inventory policy and to evaluate current inventory management systems.

➡ Try to classify your major inventory systems by type (i.e., EOQ/ROP, MRP, etc., using Box 13-1 as a guide). This will be helpful in assessing their performance and evaluating whether new approaches are appropriate.

➡ Consider forming a multi-functional task force with representation from accounting, marketing, operations, purchasing, systems, and treasury to review inventory management systems regularly and to set optimal inventory management policies.

➡ Develop a working model of costs vs. benefits for the company's carrying inventory and safety stock levels. Use the benefit and cost categories discussed in this chapter as a guide for establishing this model. The model can provide a broader perspective for setting inventory policy.

➡ In establishing inventory costs, always be sure to identify and separate explicit costs from opportunity costs. This should help alleviate typical confusion in establishing inventory costs.

➡ Consider the following items for inventory policy: costs, benefits, safety stock, reorder points, substitutability, JIT applicability, lead times, and ABC classifications.

➡ If you use JIT without EDI, find out why not. The two should go hand in hand. The same rule holds for total quality programs.

CHAPTER 14

MEASURING LIQUIDITY

This chapter deals with the overall analysis of the liquidity of a firm. In this context, liquidity should be interpreted as the financial flexibility the company has. This flexibility has two major aspects:

- **Creditworthiness**: The company that has financial flexibility is able to withstand adverse impacts on its cash flows. It also allows the company to obtain lower borrowing costs and better terms for trade credit.

- **Opportunity:** The more financial flexibility a company has the more it is able to take advantage of short-term opportunities that may present themselves, such as short-lived price reductions.

This chapter develops these issues in the following sections:

- **Analysis of financial statements:** describes the most basic ratios and other measures that are developed from financial statements, as well as their advantages and disadvantages

- **Other liquidity measures:** describes less traditional measures of liquidity

- **The bankruptcy process:** describes the basic procedures and issues in corporate bankruptcy

- **Case studies:** analyzes some of the major recent failures, including R.H. Macy, Olympia and York, and Revco, and some of the lessons that can be learned from each

One logical way to view a company's liquidity is in tiers, as discussed in Chapter 11, showing the six major layers of liquidity (repeated here in Box 14-1, for convenience).

Viewing liquidity in terms of these six layers gives important insight into the evaluation of a company's liquidity. The case studies in a later section will present

---

Box 14-1
Layers of Liquidity

Cash flow, cash balances, and the investment portfolio

Short-term credit

Management of cash flows

Renegotiation of debt contracts

Asset sales

Bankruptcy

---

some practical examples of this structure. Given the importance of short-term borrowing capacity and cash flows, it is important to consider methods that can incorporate this aspect of liquidity. This can be done directly through liquidity measures, like the ones discussed later, or less directly by examining other characteristics of the company that are highly correlated with these measures.

ANALYSIS OF FINANCIAL STATEMENTS

One of the most intensively studied areas in financial analysis is the evaluation of a company's creditworthiness. Its practical applications range from allocating trade credit, to investing in long-term bonds, to overall estimation of company value. While Chapter 7 addresses how these and other financial measurements are used in the credit granting decision, this section describes the type of information that can be garnered from an analysis of financial statements.

For companies that are large enough to have reliable financial reporting, a very common approach to evaluating creditworthiness is analysis of its financial statements. There are three basic types of financial statements:

- **The balance sheet**: This presents a picture of the company's asset and liability structure at a given point in time. Of most interest for the evaluation of liquidity is the **working capital position** — the structure of the company's current assets and liabilities — and the company's **leverage** — the amount of debt in its capital structure.
- **The income statement**: This statement attempts to show where the company generated income and what types of expenses it incurred.

Box 14-2
Parts of the Sources and Uses of Funds Statement

Operating activities: Net income plus sources of cash (such as depreciation and increases in current liabilities, excluding short-term debt) minus uses of cash (such as increases in current assets) equals cash flow from operations.

Investing activities: For example, acquisition of fixed assets

Financing activities: Increases in short- and long-term debt minus dividends and repayment of debt equals net cash flow from financing.

- **The statement of cash flows**: The previous two financial statements are based on an accrual notion of revenues and expenses as opposed to the actual realization of cash. For example, when sales are made on net 30 terms, the revenue is realized immediately in an accrual sense although the actual payment is not received until at least 30 days later. Prior to 1990, companies developed the financial statement called the **sources and uses of funds statement**. Its purpose was to disclose where the company obtained funds in the reporting period and how it had used them. FASB (Financial Accounting Standards Board) 95 redefined this into the statement of cash flows, rather than its previous focus on changes in working capital. Briefly stated, it has three segments (see Box 14-2), which are netted against the changes in cash and cash equivalents to compute the ending period statement of cash and cash equivalents. This statement is very important in measuring liquidity and provides a more useful gauge of cash flow generation than the typical accounting definition — net income plus depreciation.

The analysis of financial statements can be very difficult because of industry differences, size differences, and alternative accounting conventions. In addition, much has been written about the dubious value of these statements. One fact is very important: because of huge variations in companies and reporting procedures, interpretation of financial statements is very much an *art* rather than a precise *science*. One set of data that does provide significant guidance in interpretation is the collection of published standards for the typical financial ratios. There are numerous sources, including:

- Dun & Bradstreet (D&B): This company, the largest gather of business credit data, annually publishes its **Industry Norms and Key Business Ratios,** which presents 14 ratios by quartile and 4-digit standard industrial classification (SIC).
- Robert Morris Associates: Publishes its **Annual Statement Studies,** which provide data similar to D&B for 16 ratios.
- Credit rating agencies: The major credit rating agencies, Standard & Poor's and Moody's, provide various publications that track financial ratios across different industries and credit ratings.

While these standards can help mitigate the enormous differences in ratios across industry and size groupings, they can present a different set of problems. Financial ratio standards developed by rating agencies are developed from companies with publicly traded securities and may have little applicability to the much smaller companies that are typically being analyzed. Conversely, D&B ratios are based on a much broader spectrum of companies (about one million overall) that submit their financial statement voluntarily. This creates a bias: What company would voluntarily submit bad financial statements?

Financial Ratios

Financial ratios are a very fundamental part of liquidity analysis. Figure 14-1 summarizes the definitions of the ratios most relevant for evaluating corporate liquidity.

Some of the major applications of financial statement analysis include:

- **Performance evaluation:** This can represent either an external or an internal perspective. Financial statement analysis forms a quantitative basis for measuring profitability and asset management efficiency.
- **Monitoring**: Financial ratios are important in structuring debt agreements and in monitoring a company's outstanding exposure.
- **Financial projections:** Historical financial statements often form the basis for projecting future financial requirements and other forecasting applications.

Working Capital Ratios

In short-term financial management a great deal of emphasis is placed on the levels of and changes in current assets and liabilities. The two most common measurements are the quick ratio and the current ratio.

The relationship between the levels of current assets and liabilities relative to sales is given by the various **turnover** or **days sales outstanding** (DSOs)

Figure 14-1
Key Financial Ratios

Working Capital Ratios

Liquidity
Current ratio = current assets/current liabilities
Quick ratio (acid test) = (current assets - inventory)/current liabilities

Turnover ratios*
Receivables turnover = credit sales/receivables
Inventory turnover = cost of goods sold/inventory
Cash turnover = sales/cash
Receivables/average daily sales (This ratio is also usable for other current
assets, so that one can have days sales outstanding (DSO) for inventory or cash
as well. Its relationship with the turnover ratios should be clear.)

(*Note the number of possible variations on these definitions. For example, "receivables" could mean (1) an end-of-year figure, (2) an average of end-of-year and start-of-year, or (3) an average over all the 12 months.)

Coverage Ratios

Times interest earned = Earnings before interest and taxes(EBIT)/interest
Fixed charge coverage = (EBIT + lease payments)/(interest + lease payments + after-tax sinking fund payments)
Cash flow coverage = (EBIT + asset sales - capital expenditures + depreciation)/(interest + principal + dividends)

Leverage Ratios

Long-term debt ratio = noncurrent liabilities/total assets
Debt/equity = total liabilities/equity

Profitability Ratios

Return on assets = net income/total assets
Return on equity = (net income - preferred dividends)/common equity

Aggregate Measure

Cash conversion cycle = DSO(AR) + DSO(inventory) - DSO(AP)

ratios. Turnover ratios are generally total sales divided by the amount of the asset. The interpretation of an inventory turnover of 10 would mean that the average inventory item would spend one-tenth of a year in storage. DSO ratios are merely the reciprocal of turnover ratios; an inventory turnover of 10 would correspond to an inventory DSO of 36.5.

Leverage Ratios

One of the most important types of ratios is the one that deals with the amount of financial and operating leverage that a company has. These ratios are also very commonly used in debt contracts and as a basis for credit ratings. **Financial leverage** measures the amount of debt in the company's capital structure. **Operating leverage** measures the extent to which the company's operating costs are fixed. Generally, capital-intensive companies, such as utilities and transportation companies, have high operating leverage. While there are many ways to measure financial leverage, it is very difficult to estimate operating leverage. Companies with high operating leverage usually are less able to take on high financial leverage.

Coverage Ratios

Probably the most meaningful ratios for short-term liquidity analysis are **coverage ratios**. They measure the company's ability to generate cash flows sufficient to meet its fixed obligations. Like most other ratios, there are many variants, but three of the most important are shown in Figure 14-1. The plainest coverage ratio is called **times interest earned**, (TIE), defined by the ratio of earning before interest and taxes to interest payments. Somewhat more complex measure are the **fixed charge coverage (FCC)** ratio and a closely related measure, the **cash flow coverage ratio (CFC)**.

Figure 14-2 shows a sample set of calculations for selected financial ratios.

OTHER LIQUIDITY MEASURES

While traditional financial statement analysis is a primary method of assessing a company's liquidity, there are important alternatives. These deal with different single measures of liquidity or with aggregating individual measurements. This section focuses on two: lambda and net liquid balance.

Figure 14-2
Sample Ratio Calculations

Balance Sheet (in thousands)

Assets		Liabilities	
Cash	300	Accounts payable	1,000
Accounts receivable	1,500	Loans payable	300
Inventory	1,000	Other current liabilities	200
Other current assets	200	Total current liabilities	1,500
Total current assets	3,000	Long-term debt	3,000
Fixed assets	8,000	Capital stock	100
Less acc. depr.	3,000	Paid-in capital	400
Net fixed assets	5,000	Retained earnings	3,000
Total assets	8,000	Total liabilities & equity	8,000

Income Statement (in thousands)

Sales	10,000
Cost of goods sold	6,000
Other expenses	1,000
Depreciation	500
EBIT	2,500
Interest	1,600
Tax	400
Net income	500

$$\text{Current ratio} = \frac{3000}{1500} = 2 \qquad \text{Quick ratio} = \frac{2000}{1500} = 1.33$$

$$\text{Receivables turnover} = \frac{10000}{300} = 6.7 \qquad \text{Inventory turnover} = \frac{6000}{1000} = 6$$

$$\text{Cash turnover} = \frac{10000}{300} = 33.3 \qquad \text{Times interest earned} = \frac{2500}{1600} = 1.56$$

$$\text{Long-term debt} = \frac{3000}{8000} = .375 \qquad \text{Debt/equity} = \frac{4500}{3500} = 1.29$$

$$\text{Return on assets} = \frac{500}{8000} = .063 \qquad \text{Return on equity} = \frac{500}{3500} = .14$$

Lambda

Emery and Cogger (1982, 1984) proposed a novel type of coverage ratio. It tried to correct for a number of flaws in the manner in which traditional ratios were used to measure liquidity. These flaws include the inability of traditional ratios to incorporate the future expectations of cash flows and to consider off-balance sheet sources of borrowing, such as committed lines of credit.

Driving the model is the assumption that a company's cash flow can be statistically characterized by its mean and standard deviation. This cash flow is combined with the company's initial liquid reserve, assumed to consist of cash, marketable securities, and the company's committed lines of credit, to create an anticipated stock of liquidity. This figure is divided by the standard deviation of the anticipated cash flow. Thus, roughly stated, **lambda** represents the anticipated cash reserve in terms of number of standard deviations. Clearly the larger this figure is, the more liquid the company is. Interpreting the standard deviations in terms of the normal distribution, for example, a lambda of *two* would mean that (over the period for which the mean and standard deviation are calculated) the company has a 2.3% probability of exhausting its liquid reserve. One way to define lambda is:

$$\text{Lambda} = \frac{\text{(Initial liquid reserve + total anticipated cash flow)}}{\text{(uncertainty in cash flow)}}$$

The authors show that this measurement can be helpful in predicting bankruptcy. A corporate treasury manager (Beyer) has applied lambda to the calculation of borrowing requirements. Another interesting application is provided in Emery and Lyons (1991), which describes its application in the Amoco Production Company.

Net Liquid Balance

Shulman and Cox (1985) developed a different approach to measuring liquidity. Using a concept of how short-term assets are financed by permanent capital, they developed a simple measure of liquidity, the **net liquid balance**, defined as:

Net liquid balance = Cash + Marketable securities - Notes payable.

In most applications it is divided by total assets to mitigate scale questions. It is very easy to calculate and has performed well in a number of studies of company failure and bond credit ratings. When it is negative, it indicates that the company's

Figure 14-3
Calculating Lambda and Net Liquid Balance

		Operating cash flows	
Year		Company A	Company B
1		30	40
2		20	30
3		10	20
4		60	30
5		30	40
6		40	25
7		20	25
	Average	30	20
	Standard deviation	15.1	7.1
	Cash	30.	20.
	Marketable securities	20.	20.
	Committed credit lines	20.	100.
	Total assets	1000.	1000.
	Notes payable	30.	50.

Lambda

$$\lambda_A = \frac{30 + 30 + 20 + 20}{15.1} = 6.6 \qquad \lambda_B = \frac{30 + 20 + 20 + 100}{7.1} = 23.9$$

Net liquid balance divided by total assets

$$\frac{NLB_A}{total\ assets} = \frac{30 + 20 - 30}{1000} = .02 \qquad \frac{NLB_B}{total\ assets} = \frac{20 + 20 - 50}{1000} = -.01$$

short-term assets are being funded by long-term liabilities, which is a signal of illiquidity.

Sample Calculations

Sample calculations of lambda and net liquid balance are shown in Figure 14-3. In this example, the two measures give different results. Using the net liquid balance, company A appears to be more liquid. However, using lambda, the opposite conclusion is reached. Part of the reason for this is the ability of lambda to consider the companies' volatility of cash flows and differences in their access to credit.

THE BANKRUPTCY PROCESS

One of the dramatic indicators of the business environment is the rate of business and non-business failures. For non-business failures, the figure in 1978 was 172,000, by 1991 the figure had climbed to 872,400. This figure represented an average annual increase of 14%. In only three years (1982 to 1984) did the failure rate decline. Comparable rates have been noted in other countries. For example, in 1992 the failure rate in England and Wales was 1 in 48 firms, an increase of 11% from the previous year.

The Bankruptcy Code

Bankruptcy varies considerably across different countries. In most, a formal filing for bankruptcy is almost always followed by the liquidation of the company. For business failures in the U.S., this is true about two-thirds of the time. The remaining companies that have filed for bankruptcy attempt to reorganize, the rationale being that the companies are worth more as an on-going concern as compared to their value in liquidation.

The basic bankruptcy code was revised in 1978 and updated in August 1983. It remains under fire for several reasons. Perhaps the most important is the degree of uncertainty injected into the procedure by the bargaining process and the highly subjective actions of the courts. These issues are clarified in the case studies presented in the following section.

The current Bankruptcy Code contains the following chapters:
- Chapter 7: Liquidation
- Chapter 9: Debts of a municipality

- Chapter 11: Reorganization
- Chapter 12: Debts of a farmer
- Chapter 13: Debts of an individual (wage-earner plan)

This book will only deal with liquidation (Chapter 7) and reorganization (Chapter 11). With both of these Chapters, the bankruptcy petition can be either **voluntary** or **involuntary**. In the first case, the debtor files the bankruptcy petition. In the latter, a group of creditors (or in certain small cases, a single relatively large creditor) submits the bankruptcy petition to the court, which can elect to dismiss the petition.

In many cases of a company with deteriorating creditworthiness, it often becomes a race between creditors to try to have their obligations repaid while the debtor still has some assets remaining. This led to the institution of a key aspect of the Bankruptcy Code: the **automatic stay** provision. This, more or less, allows for creditors' claims to be settled simultaneously (if not equitably). The automatic stay provision prevents all parties from enforcing any lien or security agreement or continuing any legal action against the debtor. This has allowed some very large companies to buy time and continue operating in the face of huge potential legal liabilities: for example, Texaco, in conjunction with its Pennzoil problems, or Manville Corporation, with respect to its asbestos suits.

In a voluntary filing, the existing management usually retains control of the corporation. There are rare exceptions in case of fraud or severe mismanagement. Management is given a period of 120 days in which it has exclusive right to file a **reorganization plan**, which details how individual classes of creditors will be paid. This plan is usually the outcome of intensive bargaining by and within each of the groups of creditors. In addition, it is routine for bankruptcy judges to allow extensions of this exclusivity period.

In some cases, a Chapter 11 filing becomes liquidation. This is the case when the courts and/or the creditors do not accept the proposed reorganization plan or the company cannot devise a plausible reorganization plan. One such case was Miniscribe, the departed disk drive manufacturer. Miniscribe filed for bankruptcy in January 1990, but because of allegations of massive fraud, the reorganization attempts were abandoned and the company's assets were auctioned off. Some of the accusations included charges that ruined products were counted as inventory and that packaged bricks were shipped to distributors and recorded as sales.

Absolute Priority Rules

One of the basic tenets of debt contracting is the **relative priority** of creditors to a company. Corporate debt is usually labelled as senior or subordinated, corre-

---

Box 14-3
Relative Priority (After Secured Creditors)

1. Administrative expenses

2. Wages, salaries, and commissions

3. Contributions to employee benefits

4. Claims for taxes

5. Unfunded pension fund liabilities

6. Unsecured creditors

7. Preferred stockholders (up to par value of the stock)

8. Common stockholders

---

sponding to its priority in the event of bankruptcy. Under the current bankruptcy law, secured creditors receive their collateral (or equivalent value) to the extent to which the collateral exists. If the collateral's worth exceeds the value of the claim, during the bankruptcy proceedings, the creditor may receive interest on its claim. This does not occur if the claim is undercollateralized. After secured creditors, the order of priority (approximately) is shown in Box 14-3.

While this is the theoretical picture, in reality the bargaining process that follows the bankruptcy filing distorts this structure. The analysis of these deviations from absolute priority has been considerable. Weiss (1991) shows that in his sample of 37 exchange-listed companies that filed for bankruptcy between 1980 and 1986, in only eight cases did absolute priority hold. In the majority of cases, (26, or 70%), there was a violation of priority between unsecured creditors and equity holders. In each of these cases, equity holders received something while unsecured creditors did not receive the full value of their claims. In three cases, there was even a violation of priority for secured creditors. In each of these cases, they did not receive full compensation and unsecured creditors received from 20% to 87% of the value of their claims. In one case, Stevcoknit, secured creditors received from 37% to 77% of the value of their claims; unsecured creditors received 33%; and equity holders received 12%.

These deviations have caused considerable discussion about the fairness of the current Chapter 11 procedures. Several authors have suggested that a more equitable arrangement would be to liquidate the company as soon as it enters bankruptcy. Recent research shows that these violations appear to be implicit in the pricing of risky debt.

Preferences and Fraudulent Conveyance

Once an entity has filed for bankruptcy the bankruptcy court has the right to void certain types of transactions if it believes that the transaction has resulted in a certain creditor being given better treatment than other creditors of the same type. For example, if a given trade creditor receives full payment while other trade creditors receive none, the court may call this payment a **preference** and require the company to repay the funds. A more complex problem arose during the protracted LTV bankruptcy proceedings in 1990, when it was ruled that bondholders that had participated in bond swaps prior to the filing were not entitled to have their claims valued at the face value of the original bonds.

A **fraudulent conveyance** is a transfer of assets with the intent of damaging the position of unsecured creditors. In these cases, the bankruptcy courts can set aside the security interests of secured lenders, and collateral can be subordinated to the unsecured lenders. An interesting question recently raised has been whether or not some LBOs are a fraudulent conveyance.

Pre-packaged Bankruptcies

Because of the inordinate delays that are part of many major bankruptcies, the **pre-packaged bankruptcy** has become an important part of bankruptcy strategy. In this maneuver, the debtor negotiates with its creditors and obtains a reorganization plan *before* filing for bankruptcy. In effect, using the bankruptcy court only to control the organization of settlements. The idea would be that this greatly decreases the time a company spends in bankruptcy. It also has the advantage that if the plan is approved by the court (and by at least half of the bondholders holding a total of at least two-thirds of the debt), its terms can be "crammed down" on the dissenting minority. This is partially to avoid a small group of dissenting creditors from extorting a better settlement than more senior creditors can obtain. A number of major Wall Street firms have (or had) funds that engaged in this type of blocking. There are numerous firms that engage in trading in the debt and equity of highly distressed and bankrupt companies — engaging in a sort of "financial necrophilia."

One of the most publicized prepackaged bankruptcies was the October 1990 plan by Southland Corporation. This convenience store operator was taken private in 1987 for $4.9 billion. Again, the debt burden proved too much, and numerous attempts to restructure its debt failed. Under the reorganization plan, the equity holders were to receive about 13 cents on the dollar and retain about 5% of the equity. As is usual in bankruptcies, the different classes of bondholders did not receive equal treatment. In 1991, Southland did emerge successfully from a brief stay in Chapter 11.

Proposed Changes in Bankruptcy Law

There is an ongoing debate about how best to correct the perceived flaws in the existing bankruptcy law. One of the most interesting approaches has been described by Bradley and Rosenzweig (1992), which suggests auctioning off the assets of companies filing for bankruptcy since the bankruptcy process is inefficient and creditors bear these costs. In addition, the value of the company deteriorates further when incompetent management remains in control of the bankrupt company.

Performance of Companies After Bankruptcy

One of the interesting empirical and practical questions is whether the outcome of Chapter 11 filings can be predicted from publicly available data at the time of filing. Here the evidence indicates that this prediction is very difficult.

Further evidence has been assembled on the performance of companies "successfully" reorganizing under Chapter 11. In general, even the few companies that re-emerge after reorganization perform poorly (estimated by the government at 10%). Multiple bankruptcy filings are also frequent. For example, Braniff Airlines (at last count) had filed three times.

CASE STUDIES

This section describes some of the most interesting case studies of company failure, including:
- R.H. Macy
- Olympia & York
- Revco

R.H. Macy

One of the most interesting recent illustrations of company failure was the bankruptcy filing of R.H. Macy & Company on January 27, 1992. It has a number of very important lessons for financial liquidity. Macy was the progeny of the leveraged buyout (LBO) binge of the 1980's, and its problems began shortly after the 1986 $3.5 billion LBO left the company with a extremely heavy debt service load. Even with this debt level, it proceeded to spend $1.1 billion to acquire I. Magnin and Bullock's. The inflexibility caused by this debt service left Macy unable to respond to the deteriorating fortunes of retailing in the late 1980's.

When the recession struck in 1990, Macy was unable to meet its debt obligations and began an extensive series of renegotiations with its banks on its credit lines. The revision in December raised the floor on its cleanup provision from $2 million to $150 million for 30 consecutive days and $75 million for seven consecutive days. It also needed to issue letters of credit to placate its suppliers, which had threatened to stop shipping goods for the Christmas season. In mid-January, Macy announced that it would be delaying payments to its suppliers by two weeks in order to meet the clean-up provisions of its bank debt agreement. This led S&P to downgrade Macy's junk debt, which had lost 5% of its value in the previous week.

The final stroke came when Prudential, which held 12% mortgages on 70 of the company's stores, refused to cut the interest rate. This led to the withdrawal of Laurence Tisch's refinancing bid.

The basic Macy's capital structure is presented in Figure 14-4. While much of Macy's problems can be attributed to a sluggish economy and an enormous debt burden, there were other factors. A number of sources indicated that one key to its demise was its reliance on advertising to cure all problems. Another was the use of price reductions to try to spur sales. While this had an immediate benefit, it created an expectation of lower prices in consumers, who were then reluctant to purchase at the regular price. The bankruptcy proceedings have thus far held no major surprises. The Federal judge, considered to be one of the most pro-debtor, on May 19, 1992, extended Macy's exclusive right to file a reorganization plan to February 26, 1993. Closures and sales of some of the less profitable stores have been announced.

Olympia & York

On May 15, 1992, Olympia & York (O&Y) the world's largest real estate development company filed for bankruptcy in Toronto. Simultaneously, several U.S. entities under O&Y's control filed for Chapter 11 in New York. This was the largest bankruptcy ever filed in Canadian courts. O&Y at the time of filing was estimated to have a total of 16.4 billion ($US) in debt. Of this figure, $12 billion was bank debt, generally secured by the diverse real estate holdings of the company. The Reichmann family of Toronto, which controlled O&Y, had made their huge fortune by being contrarian (e.g., building the World Financial Center in Battery Park at a time when New York real estate prices were gloomy). The

Figure 14-4
R.H. Macy Capital Structure

(Pro forma as of 2/1/92; millions omitted)

	Amount	Rate (%)
Secured Debt:		
Bank revolver	230	9.25%
Six-year term loan	170	9.00
Purchase note*	400	12.855
Mortgage Debt:		
Prudential	800	13.00%
Swiss Bank Corp.	561	11.00
Special RE Cap. Corp.**	180	10.00
Warehouse	53.2	11.00
Mortgage notes	74.9	9.19
Other	1.9	11.00
Capital leases	26.7	12.00
Total Secured Debt	2,498	11.525
Unsecured Debt:		
14.5 Senior Subordinated '98	379	14.50%
14.5 Sub. debenture '01	383.4	14.5
Junior Sub. debenture 0/16.5	503.9	16.5
Total Debt	3,764	12.79
Equity		
Preferred stock	16.4	
Common stock	1.8	

From these data, the total weighted average cost of capital is 12.8%.

*Remaining from acquisition of I. Magnin and Bullocks from Federated.
**This entity, secured by ten stores, was formed to issue commercial paper.

Source: Lehman Brothers High Yield Research

failure came at a time of internationally depressed real estate markets, and it was on the heels of the dismal performance of its huge Canary (in a coal mine) Wharf project in London. On May 27, the Canary Wharf project was also placed into bankruptcy.

The case is interesting (and will continue to be interesting as it unfolds) for a number of reasons:

- **Asset sales**: Just prior to the bankruptcy filing, O&Y attempted to sell off assets (including its holdings in the railroad company, Santa Fe Pacific Corporation, estimated to be worth about $426 million but encumbered by a $275 million bank loan, and some of its office buildings) in order to meet principal and interest payments. Another major planned divestiture was its holding in Home Oil Company.

- **Debt renegotiation**: Since its default on a series of bonds, O&Y attempted to renegotiate the debt with the bond trustee, Royal Trust Company. This discussion very quickly spread, and O&Y began negotiating with its 91 major credit banks for various types of debt relief. In April, O&Y attempted to get its banks to infuse additional capital to avoid bankruptcy, and just prior to filing, it offered bondholders equity for debt on most of its $12 billion in debt. As O&Y officials phrased it, somewhat optimistically, O&Y was "... inviting its lenders to join hands as partners in the business."

- **Short-term borrowing**: O&Y's cash flow problems were greatly exacerbated after the February 1992 collapse of its $675 million commercial paper program. This began on February 13, when Dominion Bond Rating Agency downgraded O&Y's debt issues.

- **Financial disclosure**: Though wide recognition of O&Y's problems only came after its commercial paper problems, it had experienced trouble meeting other financial obligations as early as the previous summer. For example, in August 1991, the O&Y Credit Corporation had stopped paying interest on a $500 million loan from a consortium of Japanese banks. However, the diverse and international nature of its holdings often made it very difficult for debtors to gauge the overall health of the enterprise.

- **Security**: One of the complexities of real estate lending is the structure of the borrowing corporation. Most deals are done as separate developments and lenders often have difficulty resorting to the parent in case of nonpayment. Furthermore, many mortgages are done on a **non-recourse** basis, meaning that the debt is secured only by the given property and not other assets of the debtor. Some banks, including Citibank of Canada, also allowed O&Y to pledge collateral used to secure Citibank loans to other projects.

- **Impact on banks**: By the time of filing, most banks had already taken loan loss provisions in anticipation of it. The hardest hit were the major Canadian banks. In particular, the Hongkong and Shanghai Banking Corporation and the Canadian Imperial Bank of Commerce held about $750 million in O&Y debt.

- **Government reactions:** It is interesting to note that, despite the huge impact of the bankruptcy in Canada and the U.K., both governments steadfastly refused to assist in any deal to bail out O&Y. In the U.S., one of the major impacts of a filing would have been the relief from property tax payments, which were estimated to be over $150 million in New York City.

- **Growing internationalization**: As the world's economy grows more closely linked the effect of international diversification, such as that exhibited by O&Y, grows less effective. Although its real estate holdings were spread across Canada, the U.S., and the U.K., 1992 saw these markets simultaneously in the doldrums.

- **Differences in bankruptcy law:** In the case of the Canary Wharf project, as is typical in U.K. filings, administrators are elected to run the company and to create a reorganization plan, if appropriate. In contrast, in the U.S., except in cases of proven fraud or gross incompetence, the existing management is left to run the company while it is in Chapter 11 and is given (initially) sole right to develop the reorganization plan. U.S. bankruptcy law is considered far more debtor friendly than any other country's. Also, in Canadian bankruptcies, creditors can challenge the automatic stay provision, which cannot be done in the U.S.

Revco

Another interesting bankruptcy case is Revco, which in December 1986 went private through an LBO. A scant 19 months later, it collapsed, leaving observers to speculate whether the buyers paid too high a price, whether the company was too highly leveraged, or whether it was just not very profitable.

In 1986 Revco was the largest owner of retail drug stores, operating more than 2,000. Its post-LBO capital structure featured the usual debt structure with a sliver of equity:

- Bank term loan: 37.3% (of total)

Figure 14-5
Revco Key Events

1984	Jan.	Stock reaches historical high of $37.50
	April	A subsidiary's vitamin product blamed for the 38 infant deaths
		Stock falls by 25% to $24
	May	Revco purchases Odd Lot Trading for $113 million in Revco stock to try to squelch a possible takeover by Odd Lot's sole owners, Bernard Marden and Isaac Perlmutter, who subsequently form a dissident coalition
1985	Feb.	Marden and Perlmutter are fired
	June	EBIT drops by 44% to $113 million
		LBO discussions begin
1986	Dec.	LBO consummated
1987	March	New CEO changes Revco's pricing strategy and greatly expands product offerings
		EBITD (earnings before interest, taxes and depreciation.) is $167.8 million (47% short of projections)
	Sept.	Because of changes in management, banks require that the board and management inject a further $3.8 million in equity
	Dec.	Poor holiday season, partly due to shortages of basic items and slow sales of higher ticket items
1988	April	Revco fails to make $46 million interest payment; debtholders annoyed
		Asset sales languishing
	May	EBITD $96 million
		Drexel hired
		Private debt workouts fail
		Large debtholder demands full payment of principal and interest
	July	Revco files for Chapter 11
1992	June	Revco emerges from Chapter 11

- Junk bonds: 32.9%
- Preferred stock: 16.1%
- Pre-existing debt: 11.5%
- Common stock: 2.2%

The basic time frame for the events leading up to its bankruptcy filing are shown in Figure 14-5.

These stages again represent the strata of liquidity presented earlier. Revco attempted debt renegotiation and asset sales before it was forced to file for bankruptcy. It also pointed out one important fact: Chapter 11 proceedings are more difficult and protracted for retailers because of the generally large number of trade creditors that must agree to the reorganization plan. Bruner and Eades (1992) use simulation to study whether or not the LBO left Revco with a high probability of failure. Using a wide variety of company-specific and industry data, they estimated that Revco had a probability of between 5% and 30% of meeting its financial obligations in the three years following the LBO.

Revco emerged from four years of bankruptcy on June 1, 1992. The company appears to have reasonable prospects, showing increased sales and recording a profit of $16.2 million in the quarter ending February 8, 1992. Despite this, three days after emerging from bankruptcy, the board of directors fired Boake Sells, who had been chairman and chief executive through the years in Chapter 11.

MANAGEMENT REVIEW ITEMS

➡ Keep a list of all your sources of short-term credit and financing options available. Annotate each source with your rationale for when to use each one. This will be handy in cases of emergencies or queries from senior management. Get help in building your rationales from your investment bankers, commercial bankers, and other financial managers.

➡ Track key ratios for your company (by major business line if appropriate) and review them quarterly (or more frequently if appropriate). In addition, track the same ratios for three comparative groups: your direct competitors, a select group of companies that are rated one level *above* your company, and a select group of companies that are rated one level *below* your company. Typical ratios to track should include current ratio, current asset turnovers, times interest earned, cash flow coverage, debt to equity, return on assets, and return on equity.

➡ Use your ratio tracking to prepare regular reports to senior management and to prepare for meetings with public debt rating agencies and other interested third parties (e.g., your banks). Ratios can be computed and tracked using a simple computer spreadsheet model.

➡ Even if you don't want to compute a lambda ratio for your company, comparing your anticipated cash reserves (liquid reserves plus anticipated net cash flow) over time has the benefit of assessing the general liquidity of your company and should suggest appropriate actions for you to take.

➡ Calculate net liquid balance measures and monitor them over time. Look at the trend, and, especially if the measure turns negative, try to explain any major shifts.

➡ Don't expect your current banks to be supportive or to offer much assistance (or probably even be friendly) if your company files for Chapter 11 bankruptcy protection. The experience of other companies, however, does suggest that other, non-current banks will be willing to step in and offer cash management services after the filing.

BIBLIOGRAPHY

Aggarwal, R. and J. Baker, "SWIFT as an International Funds Transfer Mechanism," in *Advances in Working Capital Management*, Vol. 2, eds. Y. Kim and V. Srinivasan, JAI Press, Greenwich, 1991.

Altman, E.I., "Commercial Bank Lending: Process, Credit Scoring, and Costs of Errors in Lending," *Journal of Financial and Quantitative Analysis*, November 1980.

Altman, E.I., "Evaluating the Chapter 11 Bankruptcy-Reorganization Process," *NYU Salomon Center Working Paper*, 1992.

Armstrong, D., "Sharpening Inventory Management," *Harvard Business Review*, November-December 1985.

Austin, L., "Project EOQ: A Success Story in Implementing Academic Research," *Interfaces*, Volume 7, No. 4, August 1977.

Beyer, W., "Liquidity Measurement in Corporate Forecasting," *Journal of Cash Management*, November/December 1988.

Bort, R., "Implementing financial EDI: the last link in the chain," *Journal of Cash Management*, November-December 1990.

Bradley, M. and M. Rosenzweig, "The Untenable Case for Chapter 11," *Yale Law Journal*, March 1992.

Bruner, R. and K. Eades, "The Crash of the Revco Leveraged Buyout: The Hypothesis of Inadequate Capital," *Financial Management*, Spring, 1992.

Cole, R., *Consumer and Commercial Credit Management*, 8th edition, Irwin, Homewood, IL, 1988.

Dolan, J., *The Law of Letters of Credit*, 2nd edition, Warren, Gorham and Lamont, Boston, 1991.

Emery, G., "Measuring Short-Term Liquidity," *Journal of Cash Management*, July-August 1984.

Emery, G., and K. Cogger, "The Measurement of Liquidity," *Journal of Accounting Research*, 20, 1982.

Emery, G. and R. Lyons, "The Lambda Index: Beyond the Current Ratio," *Business Credit*, November-December 1991.

Farragher, E., "Factoring Accounts Receivable," *Journal of Cash Management*, March-April 1986.

Hale, Roger, H., *Credit Analysis: A Complete Guide*, John Wiley & Sons, New York, 1983.

Hoeffer, E., "GM Tries Just-in-Time American Style," *Purchasing*, August 19, 1982.

Journal of Cash Management, "Commercial banking: 1991," July-August 1991.

Kallberg, J. G. and K. L. Parkinson, *Current Asset Management: Cash, Credit and Inventory*, John Wiley & Sons, New York, 1984.

Mavrovitis, B.P., *The Entrepreneur's Guide ... Cashflow, Credit and Collection*, Probus, Chicago, 1990.

Nelson L., *Credit Manual of Commercial Laws*, NACM, Columbia, 1990.

Parkinson, K. L., *Managing Bank Relations*, Treasury Information Services, Teaneck, N.J., 1991.

Perry, E., *Practical Export Trade Finance*, Irwin, Homewood IL, 1989.

Rapin, P. and R. Martino, "Getting More Aggressive in Trading Commercial Paper," *Journal of Cash Management*, March-April, 1987.

Ruzek, R. P. and K. L. Parkinson, *How to Prepare an RFP for Bank Services*, Treasury Information Services, Teaneck, N.J., 1992.

Samson, S., "Credit Analysis," in *Handbook of Modern Finance*, 2nd edition, D. Logue editor, Warren, Gorham and Lamont, Boston, 1990.

Saunders, A., *Modern Banking*, Irwin, Homewood, IL, 1992.

Shulman, J. and R. Cox, "An Integrative Approach to Working Capital Management," *Journal of Cash Management*, November-December 1985.

Stigum, M., *The Money Market*, 3rd edition, Dow Jones-Irwin, Homewood, Illinois, 1990.

Stone, B., *One To Get Ready: How To Prepare Your Company For EDI*, CoreStates Banks, Philadelphia, 1988.

Tucker, D., "The Conflicting Roles of the Federal Reserve as Regulator and Services Provider in the U.S. Payment System," in *The U.S. Payment System: Efficiency, Risk and the Role of the Federal Reserve*, D. Humphrey, editor, Kluwer, Boston, MA, 1990.

Weiss, L., "The Bankruptcy Code and Violations of Absolute Priority," *Journal of Applied Corporate Finance*, Fall 1991.

INDEX

V

W

Y

Z

Thank you for choosing Business One Irwin for your business information needs. If you are part of a corporation, professional association, or government agency, consider our newest option—Business One Irwin Custom Publishing. This service will help you: create customized books, manuals, and other materials from your organization's resources; select chapters of our books; or both.

Business One Irwin books are also excellent resources for training/educational programs, premiums, and incentives. For information on volume discounts or Custom Publishing, call 1-800-448-3343, ext. 2715.

Other books of interest to you from Business One Irwin . . .

- **Corporate Valuation**
  Tools for Effective Appraisal and Decision-Making
  Bradford Cornell
  Bridging the gap between finance theory and appraisal practice, this guide is intended to give all those who make operating decisions an intuitive understanding of the factors most likely to affect firm value *as well as* a working knowledge of the actual appraisal process.
  ISBN: 1-55623-730-8

- **Valuing a Business**
  The Analysis and Appraisal of Closely Held Companies
  Second Edition
  Shannon P. Pratt
  More than 20,000 copies sold in the first edition! It's the most comprehensive treatise available on business valuation! Step-by-step ways to compile the information you need for a final appraisal report.
  ISBN: 1-55623-127-X

- **Valuing Small Businesses and Professional Practices**
  Second Edition
  Shannon Pratt
  Updated with the latest changes in the field, this classic reference continues to serve as the ultimate guide for every professional and small business owner involved with business valuation.
  ISBN: 1-55623-551-8

- **Workouts and Turnarounds**
  The Handbook of Restructuring and Investing in Distressed Companies
  Edited by Dominic DiNapoli, Sanford C. Sigoloff, and Robert F. Cushman
  Nationally recognized professionals who put together profitable turnarounds show you how to pick the right strategy, determine the tactics that work best, and choose the right people to drive the turnaround.
  ISBN: 1-55623-335-3